D0382309

Theory U

Theory U

Leading From the Future as it Emerges

THE SOCIAL TECHNOLOGY
OF PRESENCING

C. OTTO SCHARMER

CAMBRIDGE, MASSACHUSETTS

2007

Published by SoL (The Society for Organizational Learning, Inc.)

25 First Street, Suite 414

Cambridge, MA 02141 USA

1-617-300-9500

publisher@solonline.org

SoL is a nonprofit global membership organization that connects researchers, organizations, and consultants to create and implement knowledge for fundamental learning and change. A portion of the net proceeds from SoL publishing sales are reinvested in basic research, leading-edge applied learning projects, and building a global network of learning communities. For information on membership, professional development opportunities, events, and other publications—including the e-journal *Reflections*—please visit www.solonline.org.

Library of Congress Control Number: 2007923064

ISBN 10: 0-9742390-5-4

ISBN 13: 978-0-9742390-5-7

Dedicated to
Katrin Käufer

Man knows himself only to the extent that he knows the world;
he becomes aware of himself only within the world,
and aware of the world only within himself.
Every object, well contemplated, opens up a new organ of
perception within us.

– Johann Wolfgang v. Goethe

Contents

Part II   Entering the U Field

Part III   Presencing: A Social Technology for Leading Profound Innovation and Change

Foreword

PETER M. SENGE

A longtime mentor of mine once said that the greatest of all human inventions is the creative process, how we bring forth new realities. Understanding the creative process is the foundation of genuine mastery in all fields. This knowledge is deeply embedded in the creative arts and, though rarely spoken of, defines those moments "where there is magic in the air" in theater, music, dance, and sports. It pervades the mysterious state of surrender whereby, in Michelangelo's words, the sculptor "releases the hand from the marble that holds it prisoner" or, in Picasso's statement, "the mind finds its way to the crystallization of its dream." It plays no lesser role in science; as the economist W. Brian Arthur states: "all great discoveries come from a deep inner journey." Against this backdrop of deeply shared but largely esoteric knowledge, Otto Scharmer suggests that the key to addressing the multiple unfolding crises of our time—and the future course of human development—lies in learning how to access this source of mastery collectively.

Two predominant strategies characterize reactions to the unfolding environmental and social breakdowns evident in climate change, political paralysis and corruption, spreading poverty, and the failures of mainstream institutions of education, health care, government, and business: "muddling through" and "fighting back." Muddling through is the strategy that characterizes most of us in the rich northern countries. It embraces a combination of working to preserve the status quo combined with an almost hypnotic fascination with wondrous new technologies that, so the belief goes, will solve our problems. Fighting back, as is evident in the vocal protests of millions of people around the world opposed to the "Washington consensus" view of globalization, combines a longing for an earlier social and moral order with anger at having lost control over our future.

But beyond surface differences, the two strategies and their adherents are not as dissimilar as they may first appear. Many—perhaps most—of the "muddlers" share a pervasive uneasiness. This is evident in anxiety about the future, growing dissatisfaction with and distrust of virtually all social institutions, and withdrawal from public discourse and civic engagement. Even those who say little about it sense that deep imbalances exist in the global industrialization process and that these threaten to worsen. But there is little hope that anything can be done about them; hence we "carry on carrying on." Perhaps the ultimate irony is that even the most ardent technological optimists feel deep down that the course of technology development shapes itself and that there is little that can be done about it. Likewise, many of those fighting back share similar fatalistic feelings of trying to stop immutable forces, as evidenced by the anger and violence of their actions. As a dear friend and recognized leader in the environmental movement recently confided, "I am becoming convinced that many of the most aggressive environmentalists believe that the human species is deeply flawed and does not deserve to survive." Last, both strategies are anchored in the past: advocates of the status quo future basically extrapolate what they regard as positive trends from the past; opponents fight these trends.

Otto Scharmer's Theory U embodies a third view, one that I believe is growing around the world. This view holds that the future will, inevitably, be very different from the past, simply because the predominant trends that have shaped global industrial development cannot continue. We cannot continue to concentrate wealth in a world of growing interdependence. We cannot continue to expand the "take, make, waste" industrial model in a world where there is, increasingly, no "away" to throw our waste and toxins to. We cannot continue to put more and more carbon into the atmosphere, when carbon dioxide concentration is already 30 percent higher than at any time in the past 450,000 years and carbon dioxide emissions are already at three to five times the rate at which the substance is being removed from the atmosphere. Second, this view holds that we are not powerless to alter the dominant trends of the industrial age. These trends are based not on the laws of physics but on human habits, albeit habits on a large scale. These habitual ways of thinking and acting become embedded over time in social structures we enact, but alternative social structures can also be created. Achieving the changes needed means nothing less than "creating the world anew," based on a radically different view, as you will see below, of our collective capacity to, as Martin Buber put it, "Listen to the course of being in the world . . . and bring it to reality as it desires."

As a friend and partner of Otto Scharmer for more than ten years now in developing this work, I have been waiting for this book, as have many of our colleagues. Without question, we regard Otto as the premier theorist of the "U methodology." Moreover, his extensive practical experience, especially in long-term systemic change projects, gives him a unique depth of understanding of the challenges and possibilities of applying the methodology.

Those of us involved with this work also have come to appreciate that understanding and gaining proficiency as a practitioner with the U methodology take time. I think this learning starts with thinking seriously about a few basic ideas, and I think the book will help a great deal with this.

First, in every setting, from working teams to organizations to larger social systems, there is much more going on than meets the eye. Many of us have known firsthand the excitement and energy of a team that is deeply engaged in its work, where there are trust, openness, and a pervasive sense of possibility. Conversely, we also have seen the opposite, where fear and distrust pervade and where each statement has thick political overtones of defending one's position or attacking others'. Scharmer calls this the "social field" and has, to my mind, unique insights into how it arises and can evolve.

Sadly, mostly it does not evolve. The social field of most families, teams, organizations, and societies remains largely unchanged because our level of attention renders it invisible. We do not attend to the subtle forces shaping what happens because we are too busy reacting to these forces. We see problems, then "download" our established mental models to both define the problems and come up with solutions. For example, when we listen, we usually hear very little other than what we have heard before. "There she goes again," calls out the voice in our heads. From that point onward, we selectively hear only what we recognize, interpret what we hear based on our past views and feelings, and draw conclusions much like those we have drawn before. So long as this level of listening prevails, actions tend to preserve the status quo, even though the actors may sincerely espouse an intention to change. Change efforts that arise from this level of attention usually focus on making changes in "them" or in "the system" or on "implementing" a predetermined "change process," or in fixing some other externalized object—rarely on how "I" and "we" must change in order to allow the larger system to change.

When the "structure of attention" moves deeper, so too does the ensuing change process. Here Scharmer identifies three levels of deeper awareness and the related dynamics of change. "Seeing our seeing," so to speak, requires the intelligences of the *open mind*, the *open heart*, and the *open will*.

The first opening arises when people truly start to recognize their own taken-for-granted assumptions and start to hear and see things that were not evident before. This is the beginning of all real learning and a key, for example, for a business attempting to decipher significant changes in its environment.

Still, recognizing something new does not necessarily lead to acting differently. For that to happen, we need a deeper level of attention, one that allows people to step outside their traditional experience and truly *feel* beyond the mind. For example, countless businesses have been unable to change in response to changes in their environments even though they recognize those changes intellectually. Why? As Arie de Geus, author and former planning coordinator at Royal Dutch Shell, says, "the signals of a new reality simply could not penetrate the corporate immune system." Conversely, when people living inside a shifting reality begin to "see" what was previously unseen *and* see *their own part* in maintaining the old and inhibiting or denying the new, the dam starts to break. This can happen in a company or a country. For example, in my experience, this deeper seeing began to occur widely in South Africa in the mid- to late 1980s and is happening in many parts of the world today. This requires people from many different parts of a society, including many within the power establishment, to "wake up" to the threats they face if the future continues the trends of the past. In South Africa, enough people started to see that the country simply had no future if the apartheid system stayed in place and that they were part of that system.

When this sort of waking up starts to happen, it is crucial that people also "see" that the future could be different, lest they either be paralyzed by the new awareness or react in ways that still preserve the essence of the old system. By this "seeing into the future," I do not mean they are convinced intellectually that something can change. We all know what it means to nod our heads and then go right back to doing what we have always done. Rather, a third level of "seeing" can unfold that unlocks our deepest levels of commitment. This *open will* is the most difficult of the three shifts to explain in abstract terms, but it can be powerful and self-evident in concrete terms. For South Africans twenty years ago, I believe it unfolded in whites' and blacks' discovering their love for their country—not for their government or established systems, but for *their country itself.* I heard this expressed first in many conversations with white South Africans, who, to my surprise, declared that they were "Africans," that they felt deeply connected to the land, and the place, and the people of the country. This deep connection to place existed for most black South Africans as well, despite their oppression. I truly believe that the new South Africa was forged through this common connection, this deep sense that it was an almost sacred duty to create a country that could survive and thrive in the future—and only together could this be done.

The open will often manifests in the sense that "This is something that I (or we) must do, even though the 'how' may be far from clear." I have often heard people say, 'This is something I cannot not do.'" As our colleague Joseph Jaworski says, "We surrender" into this sort of commitment. This is similar to what others have termed "recognizing a calling," although many times I have heard people speak of this without the parallel understanding of the open mind and the open heart. When responding to a "calling" is not coupled with the continual opening of the mind and heart, commitment easily becomes fanatical obsession and the creative process becomes a distorted exercise in willpower. A key feature of Theory U is the connection of all three openings—mind, heart and will—as an inseparable whole.

When all three levels of opening occur, there is a profound shift in the nature of learning. Virtually all well-known theories of learning focus on learning from the past: how we can learn from what has already happened. Though this type of learning is always important, it is not enough when we are moving into a future that differs profoundly from the past. Then a second, much less well recognized, type of learning must come into play. This is what Scharmer calls "learning from the future as it emerges." Learning from the future is vital to innovation. Learning from the future involves intuition. It involves embracing high levels of ambiguity, uncertainty, and willingness to fail. It involves opening ourselves to the unthinkable and sometimes attempting to do the impossible. But the fears and risks are balanced by feeling ourselves part of something important that is emerging that will truly make a difference.

Finally, the theory and methodology of the U have a great deal to say about the nature of leadership, especially leadership in times of great turbulence and systemic change. This leadership comes from all levels, not only from "the top," because significant innovation is about *doing* things differently, not just *talking* about new ideas. This leadership arises from people and groups who are capable of letting go of established ideas, practices, and even identities. Most of all, this leadership comes as people start to connect deeply with who they really are and their part in both creating what is and realizing a future that embodies what they care most deeply about.

Though these ideas are critical elements of Theory U, what is especially important is that they are not just theory. They have arisen from extensive practical experience with the U methodology. Woven throughout the following chapters are stories about and reflections on long-term change initiatives in business, health care, and education. For example, the largest systemic change project I have yet seen, the Sustainable Food Laboratory, today involves more than fifty businesses and nongovernmental and governmental organizations working together to address the forces driving global food systems in a "race to the bottom" and to create prototypes of alternative, sustainable food systems. You'll also find here other examples that cover health care, education, and business innovation. While practical know-how in implementing Theory U is still in its infancy, these projects demonstrate clearly that these principles can be translated into practice and that, when this is done, they reveal immense capacities for changing social systems that previously appeared to many to be unchangeable.

There are many encouraging systemic change initiatives in the world today. Yet what is largely missing is a way to develop the capacity to develop collective wisdom across diverse settings and involving diverse organizations and actors, especially in the context of confronting multisector, multistakeholder challenges. What do you do when confronting such a problem? Theory U suggests that the basic procedure to shift social fields is the same across all levels, from teams to organizations to larger social systems, even to global systems—laid out in a summary of 24 principles and practices in the last chapter of this book. I see these not so much as the "final word" but as an extraordinary protocol to engage many of us who are active in forging a social technology for real leadership.

Finally, a word to the reader. This is an unusual book because it lays out theory and method in equal proportions. Although many academic books expound theories, they usually represent their authors' thinking but not their lived experience. On the other hand, most management books are full of purported practical ideas but very light on where these ideas come from—the presumption apparently being that most practical people are too busy fixing problems to have much interest in serious thinking. In the pages that follow, Otto Scharmer shares his autobiography with us. And his blind spots. He encourages us to look at the problems we each face, and learn to recognize that they arise from systematic blind spots in our thinking and ways of doing things. When that is the case, new tools and techniques applied from within the same mental models and ways of operating are not likely to produce much real change. As he illustrates, we all need alternative ways forward, and the U model is one.

Integrating theory and method places real demands on the reader, and this undoubtedly is why such books are rare. They require us to be both open to a challenging intellectual journey and to be willing to form our critical understanding based on testing the ideas in practice. Too many books continue the "downloading" of unexamined assumptions and beliefs, even while challenging us intellectually with new ideas. The question is always one of practice—of doing, not just thinking. So consider yourself warned. To truly benefit from this book on Theory U, you must be prepared to undertake *your own journey* of sensing, presencing, and realizing.

In this sense, this is a book for those whom my MIT colleague, Donald Schön, called "reflective practitioners," managers, principals, team leaders, government officials, and community organizers who are far too committed to practical results and dissatisfied with their current capabilities to rest on past habits; pragmatic, engaged people who are open to challenging their own assumptions and listening to their deepest inner voice. For it is only through this listening that we will unlock our collective capacity to create the world anew.

Acknowledgments

D ad, will you ever be finished with that book?" I completed the first draft of *Theory U* when our nine-year-old daughter, Hannah Magdalena, was born. She and her younger brother, Johan Caspar, have lived with it all their lives. In the meantime, they have both produced numerous handwritten "books," graciously reminding me of my own uncompleted project. Now that it's completed, my first and foremost thanks go to Katrin and our children, Hannah and Johan Caspar, who, all three, have never given up on me over the past ten years.

I want to express my deepest appreciation to a unique circle of colleagues and friends with whom I have had the privilege to work over the past couple of years and who helped me to become aware of and clarify the various key elements of the theory that is outlined throughout this book. This circle includes:

Joseph Jaworski, who coined the notion and practice of sensing and who taught me many things on the journey, including what it takes as an individual to connect and operate from source;

Peter Senge, who inspired my thinking about a deeper view on social systems, namely, that the real issue of systems change is the split between matter and mind that we collectively enact in the various social systems. Peter encouraged me to stick to the term "presencing," even though I got a lot of negative feedback when I first started using it. In my joint work with Joseph and Peter, we refined and sharpened many of the initial core ideas that underlie the U process, as we documented in our book *Presence: An Exploration of Profound Change in People, Organizations, and Society*, which we co-authored with Betty Sue Flowers. Peter's work brought me to the United States, and his partnership and friendship have been crucial to the work that led to this book;

Ikujiro Nonaka, who has inspired my thinking by his work on *ba*, the Japanese word for "place," which represents the quality of a social field in which the split between matter and mind on a collective level does not apply, and his continued integration of deep philosophical and management thought (as exemplified in his concepts of tacit knowledge and phronesis). Jiro has supported my work through personal encouragement and friendship over many years;

Edgar Schein, who, with his living, teaching, and embodying of his Process Consultation philosophy, has not only provided the backbone for all of my consulting work but also, particularly through his principles of process consultation, has created a real parent discipline for the U process of presencing that continues to inspire and influence my work;

Katrin Käufer, who has been a major thinking partner in the process of articulating Theory U and has greatly contributed to clarifying the core concepts that underlie this work. Among others, she made me aware of the fire story and how it exemplifies the two types of learning. Katrin has also provided much of the leadership in various research projects that now have led to the formation of the Presencing Institute, which we have founded to function as a vehicle for investigating and developing the foundations of presencing and leading profound change;

Ursula Versteegen, who has been my close colleague in various significant projects of presencing-based systems transformation and leadership capacity building programs and who co-developed with me the practice of deep-listening and dialogue interviews;

Judith Flick and Martin Kalungu-Banda, who are my colleagues in using the U process approach in a multistakeholder project on beating HIV/AIDS in Zambia and to whom I owe much of my understanding of profound multistakeholder innovation under the conditions of pandemic challenges, systemic breakdowns, and social disintegration;

Dayna Cunningham, who leads and co-creates with me and others the global ELIAS project and who has helped me understand and refine the use of the U process in the context of marginality and massive structural and cultural violence;

Beth Jandernoa and the Circle of Seven, who are described in Chapters 10 and 11 in detail and to whom I owe a lot of my understanding on the collective dimension of operating from source—presencing—and what practices it takes to cultivate the collective holding space. They practice this discipline faithfully, and I am grateful that they have held me and this writing project over the past two years;

Charles and Elizabeth Handy, who always encouraged me to keep going and who suggested I use the term "blind spot" as a key phrase as well as an anchor concept of the book;

Ken Wilber, who made me aware of the distinction between *states* of consciousness and developmental *stages* and who suggested that the different levels of the U coincide with different states of consciousness that he has found across all cultures and wisdom traditions;

Nicanor Perlas, to whom I owe the concept of threefold and trisector collaboration among the three sectors of business, government, and civil society;

Ekkehard Kappler, to whom I owe nearly all my insights and practices about the university of the future and who pioneered the concept of higher education as the "praxis of freedom" in which studying does not mean "to fill a barrel" but "to light a flame";

Arthur Zajonc, to whom I owe the deepening of my understanding of the Goetheanic method of science and how it evolved in the work of Rudolf Steiner and Francisco Varela;

Francisco Varela, to whom I owe the three folds of the core process of becoming aware: suspension, redirection, and letting go (which mark the left-hand side of the U);

Eleanor Rosch, to whom I owe the concept of primary knowing (as the type of knowledge that arises from the bottom of the U) and the idea that "science needs to be performed with the mind of wisdom";

Johan Galtung, whose concept of trilateral science (integrating data, theory, and values) has inspired my path to action research and whose global analysis of direct, cultural, and structural violence has shaped my thinking about global social issues today;

Bill Torbert, who clarified for me the concept of developmental thinking in organizations and leadership as well as his approach of action inquiry by integrating first-, second-, and third-person knowledge;

Seija Kulkki, to whom I owe the encouragement to blend my European and my American intellectual roots, that is, to combine the practical action research work (that I only learned when I came to the East Coast in the U.S.) with the deep epistemological inquiry into the first foundations of science and philosophy (that reflects the European intellectual roots in the tradition of phenomenology and Goetheanic science);

Brian Arthur, who helped me articulate the three-step version of the U: observe, observe, observe; retreat and reflect: allow the inner knowing to emerge; act in an instant;

Master Nan Huai-Chin, to whom I owe the seven meditative stages of leadership as a Confucian-Buddhist-Daoist articulation of the U;

Fritjof Capra, to whom I owe many great insights on the evolution of systems theory and systems thinking throughout the twentieth century in our time;

Bill Isaacs, with whom I worked during the 1990s in the MIT Dialogue Project and whose own work inspired my thinking and development of the four-quadrant model that is represented in Part III of the book and that was later reframed according to the four different levels of the U (Chapter 17);

Sara Niese, Ralf Schneider, Ikujiro Nonaka, and Arndt Zeitz, who helped refine the concepts and methods at issue here in ways that have made them accessible to top management audiences at DaimlerChrysler, Fujitsu, and PricewaterhouseCoopers throughout the past five years;

Adam Kahane, who helped me refine many of the practical applications of the U approach to change and who suggested referring to the deep state of presencing as "regenerating";

Steven Piersanti, who suggested the title of the book: *Theory U*;

Tom Callanan and the Fetzer Institute for funding the meetings that led to founding the Presencing Institute;

Michael Jung, whose dream helped me launch the Global Dialogue Interview Project about eleven years ago; it created the real foundation for the whole line of research that is documented throughout this book—so without Michael, probably none of this would have happened;

and last, but not least, my parents and the farm community at Hof Dannwisch in Germany to whom I owe the basic inspiration of this book: the relationship between the field of the earth and the living social field.

I also wish to express my appreciation to the 150 interviewees of the Global Dialogue Interview Project who met with me and, on occasion, with Joseph Jaworski, in order to dialogue about the deepest question that underlies their work. Much inspiration grew out of these conversations, and they greatly influenced and shaped the line of inquiry that is presented throughout this book.

I also greatly appreciate all my colleagues and friends who commented on the earlier drafts of the manuscript. While I assume full responsibility for mistakes that still may be found, many ideas and improvements must be credited to the valuable comments I received from the reviewers of the draft. They include (in addition to the individuals mentioned above): Arawana Hayashi, David Rome, Hinrich Mercker, Joel Yanowitz, John Heller, Margaret O'Bryon, Michael Milad, Ricardo Young, Sheryl Erickson, Tracy Huston, Tobias Scheytt, Claudia Mesiter-Scheytt, Andre Glavas, Claus Jakobs, and Walther Dreher.

I have been blessed to work with great editors who helped me with this manuscript: Nina Kruschwitz, who worked on an early draft; Janet Mowery, who edited the second iteration; and Karen Speerstra, who shaped the final draft and helped me incorporate the feedback from the readers listed above.

My special thanks go also to Sherry Immediato, Nina Kruschwitz, and Arthur Klebanoff for leading, managing, and advising the design and production of this book through SoL Press.

My final thanks go to my colleague Janice Spadafore, who orchestrates and steers the whole project ecology that has been emerging around the Presencing Institute, and whose organizing genius has worked as a hidden factor that enabled the completion of this book.

Thank you all!

Cambridge, Massachusetts, March, 2007

Introduction

We live in an era of intense conflict and massive institutional failures, a time of painful endings and of hopeful beginnings. It is a time that feels as if something profound is shifting and dying while something else, as the playwright and Czech president, Václav Havel, put it, wants to be born: "I think there are good reasons for suggesting that the modern age has ended. Today, many things indicate that we are going through a transitional period, when it seems that something is on the way out and something else is painfully being born. It is as if something were crumbling, decaying, and exhausting itself—while something else, still indistinct, were rising from the rubble."[1]

Facing the Crisis and Call of Our Time

Because our thin crust of order and stability could blow up at any time, now is the moment to pause and become aware of what's rising from the rubble.

1

The crisis of our time isn't just a crisis of a single leader, organization, country, or conflict. The crisis of our time reveals the dying of an old social structure and way of thinking, an old way of institutionalizing and enacting collective social forms.

Frontline practitioners—managers, teachers, nurses, physicians, laborers, mayors, entrepreneurs, farmers, and business and government leaders—share a sense of the current reality. They can feel the heat of an ever-increasing workload and pressure to do even more. Many describe this as running on a treadmill or spinning in a hamster wheel.

Recently I participated in a leadership workshop with one hundred leaders of a well known U.S. Fortune 500 company. The speaker before me had a great opening. He reminded us that only twenty years ago we were having serious discussions about what we should do with all of the *extra free time* that we would soon gain through the use of new communication technologies. Laughter erupted around the room. Painful laughter—for the reality that has come to pass is very different.

As we perceive our own rising pressures and diminishing freedoms, we cross the street to meet the other side of the same system in which several billions of people are born and raised in conditions that will never, ever give them a chance to participate in our global socioeconomic system in a meaningful and fair way. One of the primary issues is and remains that our current global system works for only a relatively small, elite minority of us, while in many parts of the world it doesn't work at all for the vast majority of the population. We all know the basic facts and figures that prove this point:

- We have created a thriving global economy that yet leaves 850 million people suffering from hunger and 3 billion people living in poverty (on less than two dollars per day). The poor of the world—about 80 percent of mankind—live on 15 percent of the world's total GNP.[2]
- We invest significant resources on our agriculture and food systems only to create nonsustainable mass production of low-quality junk food that pollutes both our bodies and our environment, resulting in topsoil

degradation of a territory as large as India (the equivalent of 21 percent of the present arable land in the world).[3]

- We spend enormous resources on health care systems that merely tinker with symptoms and are unable to address the root causes of health and sickness in our society. Our health outcomes aren't any better than those in many societies that spend far less.
- We also pour considerable amounts of money into our educational systems, but we haven't been able to create schools and institutions of higher education that develop people's innate capacity to sense and shape their future, which I view as the single most important core capability for this century's knowledge and co-creation economy.
- In spite of alarming scientific and experiential evidence for an accelerating climate change, we, as a global system, continue to operate the old way—as if nothing much has happened.
- More than half of the world's children today suffer conditions of deprivation such as poverty, war, and HIV/AIDS.[4] As a result, 40,000 children die of preventable diseases *every day.*

Across the board, we collectively create outcomes (and side effects) that nobody wants. Yet the key decision makers do not feel capable of redirecting this course of events in any significant way. They feel just as trapped as the rest of us in what often seems to be a race to the bottom. The same problem affects our massive institutional failure: we haven't learned to mold, bend, and transform our centuries-old collective patterns of thinking, conversing, and institutionalizing to fit the realities of today.

The social structures that we see decaying and crumbling—locally, regionally, and globally—are built on two different sources: premodern *traditional* and *modern* industrial structures or forms of thinking and operating. Both of them have been successful in the past. But in our current age, each disintegrates and crumbles.

The rise of fundamentalist movements in both Western and non-Western countries is a symptom of this disintegration and deeper transformation process. Fundamentalists say: "Look, this modern Western materialism doesn't work. It takes away our dignity, our livelihood, and our soul. So let's go back to the old order."

This reaction is understandable, as it relates to two key defining characteristics of today's social decay that the peace researcher Johan Galtung calls *anomie*, the loss of norms and values, and *atomie*, the breakdown of social structures.[5] The resulting loss of culture and structure leads to eruptions of violence, hate, terrorism, and civil war, along with partly self-inflicted natural catastrophes in both the southern and northern hemispheres. It is, as Václav Havel put it, as if something is decaying and exhausting itself.

What, then, is *arising* from the rubble? How can we cope with these shifts? What I see rising is a new form of presence and power that starts to grow spontaneously from and through small groups and networks of people. It's a different quality of connection, a different way of being present with one another and with what wants to emerge. When groups begin to operate from a real future possibility, they start to tap into a different social field from the one they normally experience. It manifests through a shift in the quality of thinking, conversing, and collective action. When that shift happens, people can connect with a deeper source of creativity and knowing and move beyond the patterns of the past. They step into their real power, the power of their authentic self. I call this change a shift in the *social field* because that term designates the totality and type of connections through which the participants of a given system relate, converse, think, and act.

When a group succeeds in operating in this zone once, it is easier to do so a second time. It is as if an unseen, but permanent, communal connection or bond has been created. It tends to stay on even when new members are added to the group. The following chapters explain what happens when such shifts occur and how change then manifests in significantly different ways.

The shift of a social field is more than a memorable moment. When it happens, it tends to result in outcomes that include a heightened level of individual energy and awareness, a sustained deepening of one's authenticity and personal presence, and a clarified sense of direction, as well as significant professional and personal accomplishments.

As the debate on the crisis and call of our time begins to unfold, proponents of three distinct positions can be heard:

1. Retromovement activists: "Let's return to the order of the past." Some retromovements have a fundamentalist bent, but not all of them. Often, this position comes with the revival of an old form of religion and faith-based spirituality.
2. Defenders of the status quo: "Just keep going. Focus on doing more of the same by muddling through. Same old same old." This position is grounded in the mainstream of contemporary scientific materialism.
3. Advocates of individual and collective transformational change: "Isn't there a way to break the patterns of the past and tune into our highest future possibility—and to begin to operate from that place?"

I personally believe that the current global situation yearns for a shift of the third kind, which in many ways is already in the making. We need to let go of the old body of institutionalized collective behavior in order to meet and connect with the presence of our highest future possibility.

The purpose of this book, and of the research and actions that have led to it, is to delineate a social technology of transformational change that will allow leaders in all segments of our society, including in our individual lives, to meet their existing challenges. In order to rise to the occasion, leaders often have to learn how to operate from the highest possible future, rather than being stuck in the patterns of our past experiences. Incidentally, when I use the word "leader," I refer to all people who engage in creating change or shaping their future, regardless of their formal positions in institutional structures. This book is written for leaders and change activists in corporations, governments, not-for-profit organizations, and communities. I have been often struck by how creators and master practitioners operate from a deeper process, one I call the "U Process." This process pulls us into an emerging possibility and allows us to operate *from* that altered state rather than simply reflecting on and reacting to past experiences. But in order to do that, we have to become aware of a profound blind spot in leadership and in everyday life.

The Blind Spot

The blind spot is the place within or around us where our attention and intention originates. It's the place from where we operate when we do something. The reason it's *blind*, is that it is an invisible dimension of our social field, of our everyday experience in social interactions.

This invisible dimension of the social field concerns the sources from which a given social field arises and manifests. It can be likened to how we look at the work of an artist. At least three perspectives are possible:

- We can focus on the *thing* that results from the creative process; say, a painting.
- We can focus on the *process* of painting.
- Or we can observe the artist as she stands in front of a *blank canvas*.

In other words, we can look at the work of art *after* it has been created (the thing), *during* its creation (the process), or *before* creation begins (the blank canvas or source dimension).

If we apply this artist analogy to leadership, we can look at the leader's work from three different angles. First, we can look at what leaders do. Tons of books have been written from that point of view. Second, we can look at the *how*, the processes leaders use. That's the perspective we've used in management and leadership research over the past fifteen or twenty years. We

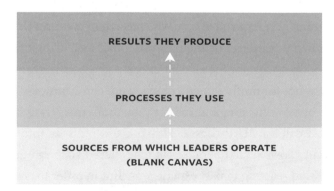

FIGURE 1.1 THREE PERSPECTIVES ON A LEADER'S WORK

have analyzed all aspects and functional areas of managers' and leaders' work from the process point of view. Numerous useful insights have resulted from that line of work. Yet we have never systematically looked at the leaders' work from the third, or blank-canvas, perspective. The question we have left unasked is: "What sources are leaders actually operating from?"

I first began noticing this blind spot when talking with the late CEO of Hanover Insurance, Bill O'Brien. He told me that his greatest insight after years of conducting organizational learning projects and facilitating corporate change is that the success of an intervention depends on the *interior condition* of the intervener.

That observation struck a chord. Bill helped me understand that what counts is not only *what* leaders do and *how* they do it but their "interior condition," the inner place from which they operate or the *source* from which all of their actions originate.

The blind spot at issue here is a fundamental factor in leadership and the social sciences. It also affects our everyday social experience. In the process of conducting our daily business and social lives, we are usually well aware of what we do and *what* others do; we also have some understanding of *how* we do things, the processes we and others use when we act. Yet if we were to ask the question "From what source does our action come?" most of us would be unable to provide an answer. We can't see the *source* from which we operate; we aren't aware of the place from which our attention and intention originate.

Having spent the last ten years of my professional career in the field of organizational learning, my most important insight has been that there are *two different sources* of learning: learning from the experiences of the *past* and learning from the *future* as it emerges. The first type of learning, learning from the past, is well known and well developed. It underlies all our major learning methodologies, best practices and approaches to organizational learning.[6] By contrast, the second type of learning, learning from the future as it emerges, is still by and large unknown.

A number of people to whom I proposed the idea of a second source of learning considered it wrongheaded. The *only* way to learn, they argued, is from the past. "Otto, learning from the future is not possible. Don't waste your time!" But in working with leadership teams across many sectors and industries, I realized that leaders cannot meet their existing challenges by operating only on the basis of past experience, for various reasons. Sometimes the experiences of the past aren't very helpful in dealing with the current issues. Sometimes you work with teams in which the experiences of the past are actually the biggest problem with and obstacle to coming up with a creative response to the challenge at hand.

When I started realizing that the most impressive leaders and master practitioners seem to operate from a different core process, one that pulls them into future possibilities, I asked myself: How can we learn to better sense and connect with a future possibility that is seeking to emerge?[7]

I began to call this operating from the future as it emerges "presencing."[8] Presencing is a blending of the words "presence" and "sensing." It means to sense, tune in, and act from one's highest future potential—the future that depends on us to bring it into being.

This book describes the process and the result of a ten-year journey that was made possible only through the support and collaboration of a unique constellation of inspirational colleagues and friends.[9] The question that underlies that journey is "How can we act from the future that is seeking to emerge, and how can we access, activate, and enact the deeper layers of the social field?"

Entering the Field

A field, as every farmer knows, is a complex living system—just as the earth is a living organism.

I grew up on a farm near Hamburg, Germany. One of the first things my father, one of the pioneers of biodynamic farming in Europe, taught me was that the living quality of the soil is the most important thing in organic agriculture. Each field, he explained to me, has two aspects: the visible, what we see above the surface, and the invisible, or what is below the surface. The quality of the yield—the visible result—is a function of the quality of the soil, of those elements of the field that are mostly invisible to the eye.

My thinking about social fields starts exactly at that point: that [social] fields are the *grounding condition*, the living soil, from which grows that which only later becomes visible to the eye. And just as every good farmer focuses attention on sustaining and enhancing the quality of the soil, every good organizational leader focuses attention on sustaining and enhancing the quality of the social field—the "farm" in which every responsible leader works day in and day out.

Every Sunday my parents took me and my brothers and our sister on a *Feldgang*—a field walk—across all the fields on our farm. Once in a while my father would stop and pick up a clump of soil from a furrow so that we could investigate and learn to see its different types and structures. The quality of the soil, he explained, depended on a whole host of living entities—millions of organisms living in every cubic centimeter of soil—whose work is necessary for the earth to breathe and to evolve as a living system.

This book invites you to take a field walk across the social landscape of our contemporary global society. And just as we did during the *Feldgang*, once in a while we will stop at a furrow and pick up a little piece of data we want to investigate in order to better understand the subtle territory of social fields. As McKinsey & Company's Jonathan Day once noted about his experience helping global corporations through the process of transformational change, "What's most important is invisible to the eye."[10]

But how can we begin to see, more consciously and clearly, this hidden territory?

The Archimedean Point

What is the strategic leverage point for intentionally *shifting* the structure of a social field? What could function as the *Archimedean point*—the enabling condition—that will allow the global social field to evolve and shift?

For my father, the answer was quite clear. Where do you put your "lever"? On the soil. You concentrate on constantly improving the quality of your top-soil. Every day. The fertile topsoil is a very thin layer of a living substance that evolves through the intertwined connection of two worlds: the visible realm above the surface and the invisible realm below. The words "culture" and "cultivation" both originate from the concept of this very activity. Farmers cultivate the topsoil by *deepening* the connection between both worlds—that is, by plowing, harrowing, and so forth.

So where is the leverage point in the case of a *social* field? At precisely the same place: the interface and connection between the visible and invisible dimensions of the social field. An organization's fertile "topsoil" exists where these two worlds meet, connect, and intertwine.

What, then, in the case of social fields, is the visible matter? It's what we *do, say* and *see.* It's the social action that could be captured and recorded with a camera. And what is the invisible realm? It's the *interior condition* from which the participants of a situation operate. It's the originating *source* of all we do, say, and see. According to Bill O'Brien, that's what matters most if you want to be an effective leader; that is, if you want to shape a future that is different from the past. It's the blind spot, or the place from which our attention and intention is happening.

In Part I of this book, "Bumping Into Our Blind Spot," I will argue that across all levels, systems, and sectors we face basically the same problem: the challenges we face require us to become aware and change *the inner place* from which we operate. As a consequence, we need to learn to attend to both dimensions simultaneously: *what* we say, see, and do (our visible realm) and the *inner place* from which we operate (our invisible realm, in which our sources of attention and intention reside and from which they operate). I call the intermediate sphere that links both dimensions the *field structure of attention*. It's the functional equivalent of the topsoil in agriculture; it links both dimensions of the field.

Collectively seeing our field structure of attention—that is, collectively becoming aware of our inner places from which we operate in real time—may well be the single most important leverage point for shifting the social field in this century and beyond, for it represents the *only* part of our common consciousness that we can control completely. Each of us creates the structure of attention ourselves, so we can't blame a lack of it on someone else. Hence, when we can see this place, we can begin to use it as the lever for practical change. It enables us to act differently. To the degree that we see our attention and its source, we can change the system. But to do so, we have to shift the inner place from which we operate.

Shifting the Structure of Our Attention

The essence of leadership is to shift the inner place from which we operate both individually and collectively.

The soil in my father's fields ranges from shallow to deep. Likewise, in our social fields, there are fundamentally different layers (field structures) of attention, also varying from shallow to deep. The field structure of attention concerns the relationship between observer and observed. It concerns the quality of how we attend to the world. That quality differs depending on the *place* or position from which our attention originates relative to the organizational boundary of the observer and the observed. In my research that led to this book, I found that there are four different places or positions that each gives rise to a different quality or field structure of attention.

They are: (1) *I-in-me*: what I perceive based on my habitual ways of seeing and thinking, (2) *I-in-it*: what I perceive with my senses and mind wide open, (3) *I-in-you*: what I tune in to and sense from within with my heart wide open, and (4) *I-in-now*: what I understand from the source or the bottom of my being, that is, from attending with my open will. The four field structures differ in the *place* from which attention (and intention) originates: habits, open mind, open heart, and open will, respectively. Every action by a person, a leader, a group, an organization, or a community can be enacted in these four different ways.

To clarify this distinction, let's take the example of listening. In my years of working with groups and organizations, I have identified four basic types of listening:

"Yeah, I know that already." The first type of listening is *downloading*: listening by reconfirming habitual judgments. When you are in a situation where everything that happens confirms what you already know, you are listening by downloading.

"Ooh, look at that!" The second type of listening is *object-focused* or *factual* listening: listening by paying attention to facts and to novel or disconfirming data. In this type of attending, you focus on what differs from what you already know. Your listening has to switch from attending to your inner voice of judgment to attending to the data right in front of you. You begin to focus on information that differs from what you already know.   Object-focused or factual listening is the basic mode of good science. You ask questions, and you carefully observe the responses that nature (data) gives you.

"Oh, yes, I know how you feel." The third, yet deeper level of listening is *empathic listening*. When we are engaged in real dialogue, we can, when paying attention, become aware of a profound shift in the place from which our listening originates. As long as we operate from the first two types of listening, our listening originates from within the boundaries of our own mental-cognitive organization. But when we listen empathically, our perception shifts. We move from staring at the objective world of things, figures, and facts into the story of a living being, a living system, and self. To do so, we have to activate and tune a special instrument: the open heart, that is, the empathic capacity to connect directly with another person or living system. If that happens, we feel a profound switch; we forget about our own agenda and begin to see how the world unfolds through someone else's eyes. When operating in this mode, we usually feel what another person wants to say before the words take form. And then we may recognize whether a person chooses the right word or the wrong one to express something. That judgment is possible only when we have a *direct sense* of what someone wants to say *before* we analyze what she actually says. Empathic listening is a skill that can be cultivated and developed, just like any other human relations skill. It's a skill that requires us to activate a different source of intelligence: the intelligence of the heart.

"I can't express what I experience in words. My whole being has slowed down. I feel more quiet and present and more my real self. I am connected to something larger than myself." This is the fourth level of listening. It moves

beyond the current field and connects to a still deeper realm of emergence. I call this level of listening _generative listening_, or listening from the emerging field of the future. This level of listening requires us to access our open heart and open will—our capacity to connect to the highest future possibility that wants to emerge. On this level our work focuses on getting our (old) self out of the way in order to open a space, a clearing, that allows for a different sense of presence to manifest. We no longer look for something outside. We no longer empathize with someone in front of us. We are in an altered state—maybe "communion" or "grace" is the word that comes closest to the texture of this experience that refuses to be dragged onto the surface of words.

You'll notice that this fourth level of listening differs in texture and outcomes from the others. You know that you have been operating on the fourth level when, at the end of the conversation, you realize that you are no longer the same person you were when you started the conversation. You have gone through a subtle but profound change. You have connected to a deeper source—to the source of who you really are and to a sense of why you are here—a connection that links you with a profound field of coming into being, with your emerging authentic Self.

Theory U: Leading from the Highest Future Possibility

Each of us uses, in any action we take, one of these four different ways of paying attention. We access one of these layers of consciousness whether we act alone or in a large group. I suggest we call these ways of acting our _field structures of attention_. The same activities can result in radically different outcomes _depending on the structure of attention from which a particular activity is performed_. Put differently, "_I attend_ [this way]—_therefore it emerges_ [that way]." This is the hidden dimension of our common social process, not easily or readily understood, and it may be the most underutilized lever for profound change today. Therefore, I have devised Theory U to help us better understand these _sources_ from which all social action constantly comes into being.

Theory U addresses the core question that underlies this book: What is required in order to learn and act from the future as it emerges? In Chapter 2, we will follow this key question in order to learn to deepen our leading, learning, and acting from Levels 1 and 2 (reacting and quick fixes) to Levels 3 and 4 (profound renewal and change).

The turbulent challenges of our time force all institutions and communities to renew and reinvent themselves. To do that, we must ask: Who are we? What are we here for? What do we want to create together? The answers to these questions differ according to the structure of attention (and consciousness) that we use to respond to them. They can be given from a purely materialistic-deterministic point of view (when operating on Levels 1 and 2), or they can be given from a more holistic perspective that also includes the more subtle mental and intentional spiritual sources of social reality creation (Levels 3 and 4).

A New Science

This book is intended to do more than just illuminate a blind spot of leadership. Rather, it seeks to uncover a hidden dimension in the social process that each of us encounters in our everyday life, moment to moment. To do this, we need to advance our current form of science. As the psychologist Eleanor Rosch from the University of California at Berkeley likes to put it, "Science needs to be performed with the mind of wisdom." Science as we know it today may still be in its very infancy.

In 1609 Galileo Galilei devised a telescope that allowed him to observe the moons of Jupiter. His observations suggested strong evidence in support of the heretic Copernican view of the heliocentric universe. Sixty-six years prior, Nicolaus Copernicus had published a treatise that put forth his revolutionary idea that the sun was at the center of the universe, and not—according to the view by Ptolemy—the earth. In the half century since its publication, however, Copernicus' theory had been met with skepticism, particularly by the Catholic Church. When Galilei looked through his telescope, he knew that Copernicus was right. But when he put forth his views, first in private conversations and later in writing, like Copernicus, he met his strongest opposition from the Catholic Church, which claimed his view was heresy and summoned an inquisition. In his attempts to defend his view, Galilei urged his Catholic counterparts to take a look through the telescope and convince themselves of the evidence with their own eyes. But although some in the Catholic leadership supported Galileo's position, the main Church leaders refused to take that daunting look. They didn't dare to go beyond the dogma of Scripture. Although the Church succeeded in intimidating the seventy-year-old Galileo during the inquisition trial (forcing him to renounce his views), the real victory was his, and today he is considered the father of modern experimental physics. Galileo Galilei helped pioneer modern science by not backing off, by looking through the telescope, and by letting the data that emerged from his observations teach him what was true and what was not.

And now, four hundred years later, we may again be writing another breakthrough story. Galileo transformed science by encouraging us to use our eyes, our senses, to gather external data. Now we are asked to broaden and deepen that method by gathering a much more subtle set of data and experiences from within. To do that, we have to invent another type of telescope: not one that helps us to observe only what is far out—the moons of Jupiter—but one that enables us to observe the observer's blind spot by bending the beam of observation back upon its source: the *self* that is performing the scientific activity. The instruments that we need to utilize in order to bend the beam of observation back upon its source include not only an *open mind*, the normal mode of inquiry and investigation, but also an open *heart* and *open will*. These more subtle aspects of observation and knowing will be discussed in more detail below.

This transformation of science is no less revolutionary than Galileo Galilei's. And the resistance from the incumbent knowledge holders will be no less fierce than the one that Galilei met in the Catholic Church. Yet, when looking at the global challenges of our time, we can recognize the call of our time to come up with a new synthesis among science, social change, and the evolution of self (or consciousness). While it has been a common practice for social scientists and management scholars to borrow their methods and paradigms from natural sciences such as physics, I think it is now time for social scientists to step out of the shadow and to establish an advanced social sciences methodology that integrates science (third-person view), social transformation (second-person view) and the evolution of self (first-person view) into a coherent framework of consciousness-based action research.

Such a framework is already emerging from two major turns in the field of social sciences over the period of the last half century. The first one is usually referred to as the "action turn" and was pioneered by Kurt Lewin and his followers in a variety of approaches to action science throughout the second half of the twentieth century.[11] The second one followed in the late twentieth and early twenty-first centuries and is often called the "reflective turn"; however, it would probably be better referred to as a *self-reflective* turn toward patterns of attention and consciousness. This new synthesis in the making links all three of these angles: science (let the data speak), action research (you can't understand a system unless you change it), and the evolution of consciousness and self (illuminating the blind spot).

Twenty-three hundred years ago Aristotle, arguably the greatest pioneer and innovator of Western inquiry and thought, wrote in Book VI of his *Nicomachean Ethics* that there are five different ways, faculties, or capacities in the human soul to grasp the truth. Only one of them is science (*episteme*).[12] Science (*episteme*), according to Aristotle, is limited to the things that cannot be otherwise than they are (in other words, things that are determined by necessity). By contrast, the other four ways and capacities of grasping the truth apply to all the other contexts of reality and life. They are: art or producing (*techne*), practical wisdom (*phronesis*), theoretical wisdom (*sophia*), and intuition or the capacity to grasp first principles or sources (*nous*).

So far the primary focus of our modern sciences has been, by and large, limited to *episteme*. But now we need to broaden our view of science to include the other capacities to grasp the truth, including applied technologies (*techne*), practical wisdom (*phronesis*), theoretical wisdom (*sophia*), and the capacity to intuit the sources of awareness and intention (*nous*).

Our Field Journey: This Book

Organization

After Part I, "Bumping into Our Blind Spot," we move on to Part II, "Entering the U Field," followed by Part III, "Presencing: A Social Technology for Leading Profound Innovation and Change."

The first part of this field walk deals with different aspects of the blind spot. I argue that the central issue of our time deals with hitting our blind spot—the inner place from which we operate—across all system levels. On all these levels we are confronted with the same issue: we cannot meet the challenges at hand if we do not change our interior condition and illuminate our blind spot—the source of our attention and action.

In Part II we will explore the *core process* of illuminating the blind spot—how is it possible to do this? The third part of our field walk focuses on summarizing this core process in terms of an *evolutionary grammar* that is then spelled out in two forms: as a new social field theory (Theory U) and as a new social technology (24 Principles and Practices of Presencing). The book concludes with an Epilogue, "Birthing a Global Action University." In it are ideas about and a broad plan for a global action university that puts the above principles into practice by integrating science, consciousness, and profound social change.

The following twenty-one chapters integrate the insights from dialogue interviews with 150 eminent thinkers and practitioners in strategy, knowledge, innovation, and leadership around the world. You should know that this book is also based on my own life story—recognizably that of a white male European now living in the United States—together with my research at MIT and the results of numerous reflection workshops among colleagues and co-researchers. In addition, I have based Theory U on the results of consulting and "action research" projects with leaders of grassroots movements and global companies and NGOs, among them Fujitsu, DaimlerChrysler, GlaxoSmithKline, Hewlett-Packard, Federal Express, McKinsey & Company, Nissan, Oxfam, PricewaterhouseCoopers, and Shell Oil.

I have always found major sources of inspiration in working with close colleagues from the field of the creative arts, for example, with Arawana Hayashi, who developed the embodied presence practices and who leads a project in which we work on co-creating a new art form called Social Presencing Theater.[13] I also chose to include a number of illustrations throughout the book based on my own hand-drawn figures, along with many more professionally rendered figures, which illustrate and bring alive some of the concepts much better than words can. It is my hope that by including them, some of the more challenging ideas of this book will be made a bit more accessible.

Purpose

This book sets out to do three things. It provides a social grammar of the social field that illuminates the blind spot (Chapters 15, 20). Second, it exemplifies this grammar by revealing four fundamental metaprocesses that underlie the collective process of social reality creation, moment to moment. They are: thinking, conversing, structuring, and globally connecting (global governance) (Chapters 16–19). And last, it outlines a social technology of freedom that puts this approach onto its feet and into practice through a set of principles and practices of presencing (Chapter 21).

The set of 24 principles works as a matrix and constitutes a whole. That said, they can also be presented as five movements that follow the path of the U (see Figure 1.2). These five movements are:

- *Co-initiating: listen to what life calls you to do,* connect with people and contexts related to that call, and convene constellations of core players that co-inspire common intention.
- *Co-sensing*: go to the places of most potential; observe, observe, observe; listen with your mind and heart wide open.
- *Co-presencing*: go to the place of individual and collective stillness, open up to the deeper source of knowing, and *connect to the future that wants to emerge through you.*
- *Co-creating*: build landing strips of the future by prototyping living microcosms in order *to explore the future by doing.*

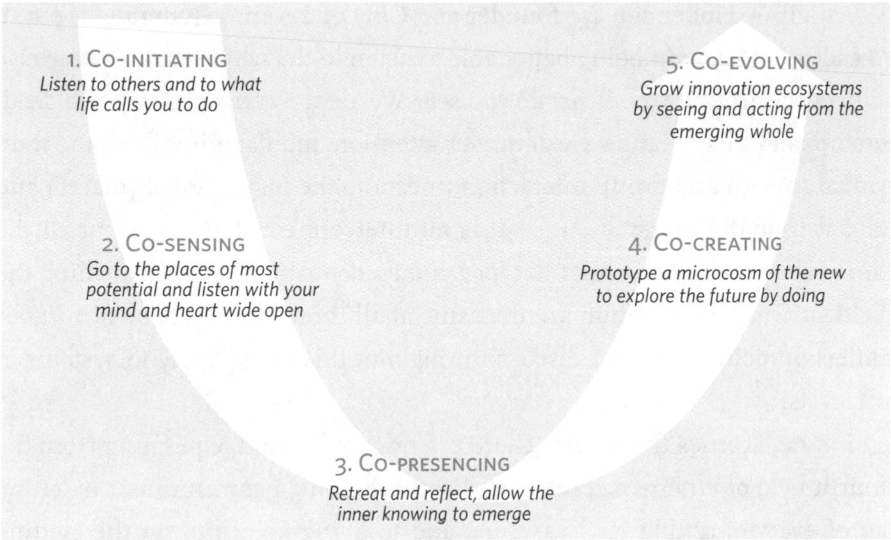

1. CO-INITIATING
*Listen to others and to what
life calls you to do*

5. CO-EVOLVING
*Grow innovation ecosystems
by seeing and acting from the
emerging whole*

2. CO-SENSING
*Go to the places of most
potential and listen with your
mind and heart wide open*

4. CO-CREATING
*Prototype a microcosm of the new
to explore the future by doing*

3. CO-PRESENCING
*Retreat and reflect, allow the
inner knowing to emerge*

FIGURE 1.2 FIVE MOVEMENTS OF THE U PROCESS

- *Co-evolving*: co-develop a larger innovation ecosystem and hold the space that connects people across boundaries through *seeing and acting from the whole.*

Method

Our field walk incorporates three methods: phenomenology, dialogue, and collaborative action research. All three address the same key issue: the intertwined constitution of knowledge, reality, and self. And all of them follow the dictum of Kurt Lewin, the founder of action research, who observed, "You cannot understand a system unless you change it." But each method has a different emphasis: phenomenology focuses on the first-person point of view (individual consciousness); dialogue on the second-person point of view (fields of conversation); and action research on the third-person point of view (enactment of institutional patterns and structures).

You will notice that I don't refer in this book primarily to individual leaders but to our distributed or collective leadership. *All* people effect change, regardless of their formal positions or titles. *Leadership in this century means shifting the structure of collective attention—our listening—at all levels.*

As Jeffrey Hollender, the founder and CEO of Seventh Generation, put it, "Leadership is about being better able to listen to the whole than anyone else can." Look around you. What do you see? We are now engaged in global leadership, and this means we extend our attention and listening from the individual (micro) and group interaction (meso) to the institutional (macro) and global (mundo) systems levels. It is all interconnected and present all the time. The good news is that the *hidden inflection points* for transforming the field structure of attention are the same at all these levels. These turning or inflection points, which I discuss throughout this book, apply to systems at all levels.

But here comes the caveat: There is a price to be paid. Operating from the fourth field of emergence requires a commitment: a commitment to letting go of everything that isn't essential and to living according to the "letting go/letting come" principle that Goethe described as the essence of the human journey: "And if you don't know this dying and birth, you are merely a dreary guest on earth."[14]

The real battle in the world today is not among civilizations or cultures but among the different evolutionary futures that are possible for us and our species right now. What is at stake is nothing less than the choice of who we are, who we want to be, and where we want to take the world we live in. The real question, then, is "What are we here for?"

Our old leadership is crumbling similar to the way the Berlin Wall crumbled in 1989. What's necessary today is not only a new approach to leadership. We need to go beyond the concept of leadership. We must discover a more profound and practical integration of the head, heart, and hand—of the intelligences of the open mind, open heart, and open will—at both an individual and a collective level.

I invite you to join me on this journey of discovery.

PART I

Bumping into Our Blind Spot

We all recognize social acts when we see them: people talking, laughing, crying, clashing, playing, dancing, praying. But where do our actions come from? From what place deep within (or around) us do our actions originate? To answer this question, it is helpful to look at the creative work of an artist in three ways. First, we can look at the result of her work, the *thing*, the finished painting. Or we can observe her while she is painting: we can watch the *process* of her colorful brush-strokes creating the work of art. Or we can observe her standing *in front of the empty canvas*. It is this third perspective that creates the guiding questions of this book: What happens in front of the completely white canvas? What prompts the artist to make that first stroke?

THIS BOOK IS written for leaders, the individuals or groups who initiate innovation or change—The "artists." All leaders and innovators, whether in business, communities, government, or nonprofit organizations, do what artists do: they create something new and bring it into the world. The open question is: Where do their actions come from? We can observe *what* leaders do. We also can observe *how* they do it, what strategies and processes they deploy. But we can't see the inner place, the *source* from which people act when, for example, they operate at their highest possible level or, alternatively, when they act without engagement or commitment.

That brings us to the territory of what I call our "blind spot." The blind spot concerns that part of our seeing that we usually don't see. It's the inner place or source from which a person or a social system operates. That blind spot is present every day in all systems. But it is hidden. It is our task, as leaders, and as creators, to notice how the blind spot shows up. For instance, Francisco J. Varela, a professor of cognitive science and epistemology in Paris, told me that "the blind spot of contemporary science is experience." This blind spot shows up in many different ways. We will learn about them as we continue this "field walk," this "learning journey," together.

The following seven chapters offer seven perspectives from which we can explore the different ways the blind spot shows up in society, in science, and in systems thinking as a defining feature of our time. Blind spots appear in individuals, groups, institutions, societies, and systems, and they reveal themselves in our theories and concepts in the form of deep epistemological and ontological assumptions.

I invite you to explore, with me, several different areas of the blind spot. We start from the view of the self and move through the team, the organization, society, the social sciences, and, finally, philosophy.

Facing the Fire

When I left my German farmhouse that morning for school, I had no idea it was the last time I would see my home, a large 350-year-old farmhouse thirty miles north of Hamburg. It was just another ordinary day at school until about one o'clock, when the teacher called me out of class. "You should go home now, Otto." I noticed that her eyes were slightly red. She did not tell me why I needed to hurry home, but I was concerned enough to try to call home from the train station. There was no ring. The line was obviously dead. I had no idea what might have happened, but by then I knew it probably wasn't good. After the usual one-hour train ride I ran to the entrance of the station and jumped into a cab. Something told me I didn't have time to wait for my usual bus. Long before we arrived, I saw huge gray and black clouds of smoke billowing up into the air. My heart was pounding as the cab approached our long driveway. I recognized hundreds of our neighbors, area firefighters and policemen along with people I'd never seen before. I jumped from the cab and ran down through the crowd, the last half mile of our chestnut-lined driveway. When I reached the courtyard, I could not believe my eyes. The world I had lived in all my life was gone. Vanished. All up in smoke.

There was nothing—absolutely nothing—left except the raging flames. As the reality of the fire in front of my eyes began to sink in, I felt as if somebody had ripped away the ground from under my feet. The place of my birth, childhood, and youth was gone. I just stood there, taking in the heat of the fire and feeling time slowing down. As my gaze sank deeper and deeper into the flames, the flames also seemed to sink into me. Suddenly I realized how attached I had been to all the things destroyed by the fire. Everything I thought I was had dissolved into nothing. Everything? No, perhaps not everything, for I felt that a tiny element of my self still existed. Somebody was still there, watching all this. Who?

At that moment I realized there was a whole other dimension of my self that I hadn't previously been aware of, a dimension that related not to my past—the world that had just dissolved in front of my eyes—but to my future, a world that I could bring into reality with my life. At that moment time slowed down to stillness and I felt drawn in a direction above my physical body and began watching the scene from that unknown place. I felt my mind quieting and expanding in a moment of unparalleled clarity of awareness. I realized that I was not the person I had thought I was. My real self was not attached to all the material possessions smoldering inside the ruins. I suddenly knew that I, my true Self, was still alive! It was this "I" that was the *seer*. And this seer was more alive, more awake, more acutely present than the "I" I had known before. I was no longer weighted down by all the material possessions the fire had just consumed. With everything gone, I was lighter and free, released to encounter the other part of my self, the part that drew me into the future—into *my* future—into a world waiting for me, that I might bring into reality with my forward journey.

The next day my eighty-seven-year old grandfather arrived for what would be his last visit to the farm. He had lived in that house all his life, beginning in 1890. Because of medical treatments, he had been away the week before the fire, and when he arrived at the courtyard the day after the fire, he summoned his last energy, got out of the car, and went straight to where my father was working on the cleanup. He did not even once turn his head to the smoking ruins. Without seeming to notice the small fires still burning around the property, he went up to my father, took his hand, and said, *"Kopf hoch, mein Junge, blick nach vorn!"* "Keep your head up, my boy, look forward!" Then he turned, walked directly back to the waiting car, and left. A few days later he died quietly.

Only years later did I realize that my experience in front of the fire was the beginning of a journey. My journey began with the recognition that I am not just one self but two selves. One self is connected to the past, and the second self connects to who I could become in the future. In front of the fire I experienced how these two selves started to connect to each other. Today, twenty-years later and several thousand miles away in Boston, Massachusetts, the question "Who is my true self?" still lingers. I still ask, how does this self relate to that *other stream of time*—the one that seemed to draw me from the future that is wanting to emerge—rather than extending and reenacting the patterns of my past? And how does this self that connects to the future connect to my work? I believe these questions eventually prompted me to leave Germany for the United States in 1994 to continue my research at what was then the MIT Organizational Learning Center. And these same questions motivated the writing of the following chapters of this book.

CHAPTER 2

The Journey to "U"

Theory U • Interview with Brian Arthur at Xerox PARC •
Francisco Varela on the Blind Spot in Cognition Sciences •
The Inner Territory of Leadership

Theory U: Beginnings

As just discussed, the blind spot concerns the structure and source of our attention. I first began noticing this blind spot in organizations when I spoke with Bill O'Brien, the former CEO of Hanover Insurance. He told me that his greatest insight after years of conducting organizational learning projects and facilitating corporate change was that "the success of an intervention depends on the interior condition of the intervener." That struck a chord! So it's not only *what* leaders do and *how* they do it but their "interior condition," that is, the inner place from which they operate—the source and quality of their attention. So what this suggests is that the same person in the same situation doing the same thing can effect a totally different outcome depending on the inner place from where that action is coming.

When I realized that, I asked myself: What do we know about that inner place? We know everything about the *what* and the *how*, the actions and the processes that leaders and managers use. But what do we know about that inner place? Nothing! I wasn't even sure whether there were only one or many of these inner places. Do we have two? Ten? We don't know because it's in our blind spot. Yet, what I have heard time and time gain from very experienced leaders and creative people is that it is exactly that kind of blind spot that matters most. It is that blind spot that sets apart master practitioners and leaders from average performers. Which is why Aristotle 2300 years ago made a distinction between the normal scientific "what" knowledge (*episteme*) and the practical and technical "how" knowledge (*phronesis, techne*) on the one hand and the inner primary knowing of first principles and sources of awareness (*nous*) and wisdom (*sophia*), on the other.[1]

Shortly after I came to MIT in 1994, I watched a live broadcast on organizational learning. In response to a question from the audience, Rick Ross, co-author of *The Fifth Discipline Fieldbook*, went to the whiteboard and drew the following figure:

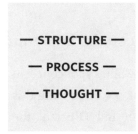

FIGURE 2.1 LEVELS OF ORGANIZATIONAL CHANGE

Seeing that simple drawing made me realize that organizational change happens on different layers. In a flash I began mentally seeing these layers. Diagramming them helped because the changes from structure to process to thoughts present more and more subtle shifts. When I completed the drawing in my mind, I had added two more levels—above structure and below thought—as well as a horizontal dimension of change as we move from perceiving something to actually acting on it. This is how it began to look:

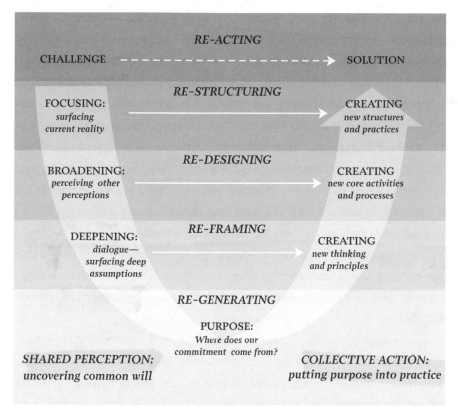

Figure 2.2 Five Levels of Change

I began calling the state at the bottom of the U "Presencing." We will learn much more about this in Part III, but for now, we can call it "seeing from our deepest source." That is, sensing and operating from one's highest future potential. It is the state each of us can experience when we open not just our minds but our hearts and our wills—our impetus to act—in order to deal with what is emerging all around us as new realities.

Whenever I used this framework in presentations and in my work with groups, organizations, or communities, I noticed how deeply it resonated with experienced practitioners. As they worked with this U image, people began to understand its two key dimensions. One is the distinction between *perception* and *action* that defines the horizontal axis, as we work from deeply connecting and sensing toward enacting and realizing. The vertical axis then shows us the different levels of change from the shallowest response: from "Re-acting" down through the deepest, "Re-generating."[2]

Most change and learning methods are based on the Kolb Learning Cycle, which suggests a version of the following sequence: observe, reflect, plan, act. By grounding the learning process this way, the learning cycles are based on learning from the experiences of the past.[3] The distinction of Harvard and MIT's Chris Argyris and Don Schön between single-loop and double-loop learning refers to learning from experiences of the past.[4] Single-loop learning is reflected in the levels of reacting and restructuring, while reframing is an example of double-loop learning (which includes a reflection of one's deep assumptions and governing variables). However, the deepest level of the U graphic—referred to as regenerating—goes beyond double-loop learning. It accesses a different stream of time—the future that wants to emerge—and is what in this book I will refer to as presencing or "the U process."

The concept of the U, of course, didn't spring from nothing. It emerged from many years of change work in a variety of contexts and movements and some study, that are documented in two of my earlier books.[5] Important sources that informed my early thinking about social development and change include a global learning journey across all the major global cultural spheres to study the dynamics of peace and conflict. This led me to India to study Gandhi's approach of nonviolent conflict transformation, and to China, Vietnam, and Japan to study Buddhism, Confucianism, and Daoism as different approaches to development and life. I also had the fortune to work with unique academic teachers, Ekkehard Kappler and Johan Galtung, who taught me that critical thinking and science can function as a powerful force for social transformation and change. Other sources that influenced my thinking include the work of the avant-garde artist Joseph Beuys, and the writings of Henry David Thoreau, Martin Buber, Friedrich Nietzsche, Edmund Husserl, Martin Heidegger, Jürgen Habermas, as well as some of the old masters like Hegel, Fichte, Aristotle, and Plato. Among the philosophical sources, perhaps most influential was the work of the educator and social innovator Rudolf Steiner, whose synthesis of science, philosophy, consciousness and social innovation continues to inspire my work and whose methodological grounding in Goethe's phenomenological view of science has left signicant imprints on Theory U.

The key insight that I got from reading Steiner's foundational book, *The Philosophy of Freedom*, is the same insight that I walked away with from completing my first research project at MIT with Edgar Schein. In that project we looked at all the different theories of change that researchers at MIT's Sloan School of Management had come up with. When trying to summarize and conclude our findings from all these different theories and frameworks, Ed reflected on our result, a pretty complex integration of frameworks of various sorts, and said, "Perhaps we have to go back to data and to start all over again. Maybe we have to take our own experience in dealing with change more seriously." To paraphrase Steiner, we have to investigate our own experience and our own *thought process* in a clearer, more transparent and rigorous way. In other words, trust your senses, trust your observations, trust your own perception as the fundamental starting point of any investigation—but then *follow that train* of your observation all the way back to its source, exactly the same way that Husserl and Varela advocated in their work on the phenomenological method. Steiner's *The Philosophy of Freedom* focuses on individual consciousness. In *Theory U*, we will explore the field structures of collective attention.[6]

Interview with Brian Arthur at Xerox PARC

In 1999, I started a project with Joseph Jaworski, author of *Synchronicity: The Inner Path of Leadership*. Our task was to create a learning environment to help a group of line leaders in an organization formed by the recent merger of Shell Oil and Texaco learn faster and develop the capacity to innovate in the changing business environment.

To do so, we interviewed practitioners and thought leaders on innovation, including W. Brian Arthur, the founding head of the Economics Program at the Santa Fe Institute. He is best known for his pathbreaking contributions to understanding high-tech markets. As Joseph and I walked up to the Xerox

PARC building in Palo Alto, California, I couldn't help but think about all the revolutions that had begun in this very spot. Ever since the 1970s the original Xerox PARC team has been considered probably the most productive research and development team ever. It invented the Macintosh-type interface found on almost every desktop on Earth; it also invented the mouse, as well as numerous core ideas and technologies used by many successful companies today, including Apple Computer and Adobe Systems. The irony is that all these inventions and breakthrough ideas did not help the parent company, Xerox, which did not capitalize on these breakthrough ideas. Instead, these ideas were taken and developed further by people and organizations who were not distracted by the running of a once-successful copy machine company.

Arthur met us, and we immediately started talking about the changing economic foundations of today's business world. "You know," Arthur said, "the real power comes from recognizing patterns that are forming and fitting with them." He went on to discuss two different levels of cognition. "Most tend to be the standard cognitive kind that you can work with in your conscious mind. But there is a deeper level. Instead of an understanding, I would call this deeper level a 'knowing.'"

"Suppose," he said, "that I was parachuted into some situation in Silicon Valley—not a real problem, just a complicated, dynamic situation that I'm trying to figure out. I would observe and observe and observe and then simply retreat. If I were lucky, I would be able to get in touch with some deep inner place and allow knowing to emerge." He continued, "You wait and wait and let your experience well up into something appropriate. In a sense, there is no decision making. What to do becomes obvious. You can't rush it. Much of it depends on where you're coming from and who you are as a person. This has a lot of implications for management. I am basically saying that *what counts is where you're coming from inside yourself.*"[7]

What Joseph and I heard that day resonated deeply with what we had heard from other leading practitioners we had worked with across many sectors and industries. Leaders need to deal with their blind spot and shift the inner place from which they operate.

Arthur asked us to imagine what would happen if Apple Computer, for instance, decided to hire a CEO from, say Pepsi-Cola? That leader would bring one sort of cognition: cost down, quality up, whatever the mantra is. And it wouldn't work. But now imagine a Steve Jobs coming in—someone who can distance himself from the problem and think differently. "When he came back to Apple, the Internet was just beginning. No one knew what that might mean. Now look at him: he turned Apple around." Top-notch scientists do the same thing, Arthur continued. "Good, but not quite first-rate scientists are able to take existing frameworks and overlay them onto some situation. The first-rate ones just sit back and allow the appropriate structure to form. My observation is that they have no more intelligence than the good scientists do, but they have this other ability and that makes all the difference."

This "other way of knowing" shows up in Chinese and Japanese artists as well. Arthur said, "They'll sit on a ledge with lanterns for a whole week, just looking, and then suddenly they'll say, 'Ooohh' and paint something very quickly."

On the return trip we realized that the conversation with Arthur had furnished two principal insights. First, that there is a distinction between types of cognition: normal (downloading mental frames) versus a deeper level of knowing. And second, that in order to activate the deeper level of knowing, one has to go through a three-step process similar to Arthur's parachute example: observe deeply, connect to what wants to emerge, and then act on

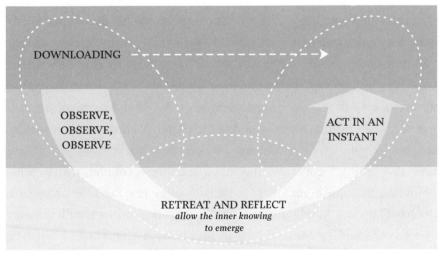

FIGURE 2.3 THREE MOVEMENTS OF THE U

it instantly. It was obvious to connect this conversation with my earlier work on the U. So I drew a U figure on a piece of paper and mapped the key points of the conversation with Brian Arthur onto it and showed it to Joseph.

We realized we were onto something very significant. What followed was an intense period of spelling out, crystallizing, and refining the framework. My joint work with Joseph on these issues has taught me much about operating from one's deeper source of knowing. His life story, which he shares in his book *Synchronicity*, is itself a great illustration of how an individual can tap into this deeper source of creativity. The next question that came to mind was: What would it take for a group, an organization, or an institution to operate on a similar level? Finding the answer became our quest.[8]

Francisco Varela on the Blind Spot in Cognition Sciences

After that trip, I shared the drawing of Brian Arthur's three movements through the U with many people. When they followed the pattern of "observe, retreat and reflect, then act in an instant," many said, "I know this. I have seen this in highly creative people. I have seen this in highly creative moments of my own life." But then when I asked them, "Okay, and what do work and life actually look like in your current context and organization?" they usually responded, "Not like this, it's different. It's more like this downloading thing." What remained puzzling was that most people know this deeper place of creativity, yet in our everyday work and life, particularly in the context of larger institutions, we seem unable to access it. We remain locked in the old patterns of downloading. Why? I believe we have trouble navigating this deeper territory because we lack a higher-resolution map. We need more than just those three steps. We need a map that shows the archetypal folds and thresholds in between, as well as the stumbling blocks where the process of "observe, observe" is hitting the wall. What would that higher-resolution map look like?

Holding that question, I left for Paris to interview the famous cognitive scientist Francisco Varela. At the time I was working on a parallel research project sponsored by Michael Jung of McKinsey & Company. When I first met Varela in 1996, he told me about the blind spot of cognition research.

"There is an irreducible core to the quality of experience that needs to be explored with a method. In other words, the problem is not that we don't know enough about the brain or about biology. *The problem is that we don't know enough about experience.* . . . We have had a blind spot in the West for that kind of methodical approach. Everybody thinks they know about experience. I claim we don't."

Little did I know as I sat in his office in January 2000, it would be our last meeting. One of the most outstanding and promising cognitive scientists of our time, he passed away in 2001. In the course of our conversation, he explained that his current work entailed a triangulation of approaches to the how: psychological introspection, phenomenology, and contemplative practices. "What is common in all of them? What is it that all human beings have?" Varela mused. ". . . So that Germans in the 1880s could do their creative kind of introspection or the inheritors of the Buddha Shakyamuni in the fifth or fourth centuries before Christ could create the techniques of *samatha* or that somebody like Husserl could create a whole new school of thinking about phenomenology? What is common to these three practices of pragmatics about human experience?"

"The key is how will you become aware?" For three years Varela had been working on a book called *On Becoming Aware*.[9] In it he posed the question "Can this core process be cultivated as an ability?" "By looking at these three traditions as practices, you first have to distinguish for lack of a better term, the purely first-person point of view and what one does as an individual at the interface between the first and second person. When it comes to the first person what seems to happen is better seen in terms of three gestures of becoming aware. They are: suspension, redirection, letting-go."

The Three Gestures On the Left-Hand Side of the U

This is something everyone knows instinctively, he said, "But just as a runner must train to become a marathoner, understanding and mastering this process requires study and coaching." We walked together through the three gestures. Varela explained. "By *suspension* I mean the suspension of habitual patterns. In Buddhist meditation, you put your butt on the cushion and move one level above your habitual engagement and see from a more aerial perspective." We went on to discuss how many people sitting in meditation claim that nothing happens. Why? "Because the whole point is that after suspension you have to tolerate that nothing is happening. Suspension is a very funny procedure. Staying with that is the key."

Then he explained his second and third gestures: *redirection* and *letting go*. Redirection is about redirecting your attention from the "exterior" to the "interior" by turning the attention toward the source of the mental process rather than the object. Letting go has to be done with a light touch, he cautioned. As he wrote with his co-authors Natalie Depraz and Pierre Vermersch, it means "to accept our experience."[10]

What strikes me about Varela's description is that the three gestures or turning points in transforming one's quality of attention match my own experiences in groups. Varela was talking about the deep folds in the structure of our attention that begin to unfold as we progress through the cycle of becoming aware: suspending habitual judgment; redirecting attention from perceived objects to the process of collectively co-creating them; and finally, changing the quality of our attention by letting go of old identities and intentions and allowing something new to come in *some emerging future identity and purpose*.

When I walked out of Varela's office, I knew I had been handed a gift. Now all I had to do was figure out how to unpack it. As have other facilitators, I had seen these "folds" many times in team processes and workshops as I tried to usher a group through turning points so they could access some deeper place of creativity. First, you help the group *suspend* judgments in order to see the objective reality they are up against, including the basic figures and facts. Second, you help them *redirect* their attention from the object to the process in order to help them view the system from a perspective that allows them to see how their own actions contribute to the problem at hand. It is at that point when people begin to see themselves as part of the issue, they begin to see how they collectively create a pattern that at first seemed to

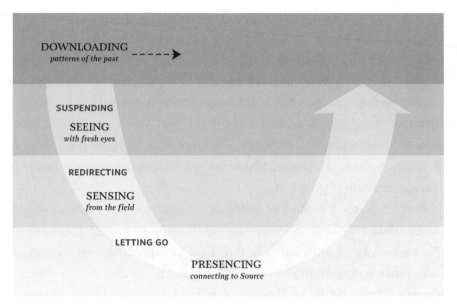

FIGURE 2.4 THE OPENING PROCESS OF THE U

be caused by purely exterior forces. And then, if you are lucky, you can bring them to a *deeper place of stillness* where they let go of the old and start to connect with their higher-order intentions. I could see in an instant how these folds could be mapped onto the U (Figure 2.4).

But I still had more questions. If Varela's core process of *becoming aware* illustrates the journey down one side of the U, what about the other part of this journey? What is moving up the right-hand side? It seemed to me that most researchers, educators, and cultivators of cognition and mindfulness were occupied primarily with the "opening process"—the left-hand side of the U—and paid little or no attention to the drama of collective creation that happens when we enter the right-hand side of the U. As every practitioner, innovator, and leader knows, there is a whole other dimension to the collective creativity process that happens on the right-hand side of the U and that deals with intentionally bringing the new into reality. How does something new manifest? How does the new come into being?

The Inner Territory of Leadership

Mapping the Right-Hand Side of the U

Going down the U moves us through the cognitive spaces of downloading, seeing, sensing, and presencing. But to successfully enter these deeper cognitive spaces, we have to cross the thresholds that Varela was talking about: *suspension*, *redirection*, and *letting go*. I realized that going up the U may be the same journey, except that you cross the thresholds coming from the opposite direction (Figure 2.5).

Accordingly, the threshold of *letting go* (on your way down) turns into the threshold of *letting come* (on your way up), leading you to the space of crystallizing vision and intention. The threshold of *redirecting* from the exterior to the inner way of seeing (on your way down) turns into the threshold of redirecting from the inner vision to the exterior action in order to *enact* a rapid-cycle prototype (on your way up). And finally, the threshold of *suspending* habits and routines (on your way down) turns into the threshold of institutionalizing by *embodying* the new in actions, infrastructures, and practices (on your way up). So in each of these cases the same threshold is crossed, but from the other side.

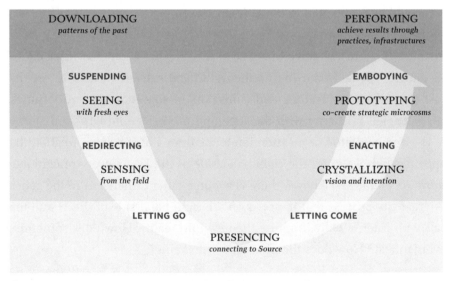

FIGURE 2.5 THE COMPLETE U: SIX INFLECTION POINTS

I have seen groups moving across these thresholds various times. When such a process of profound innovation and change happens, you can watch a group going through some version of the following subtle shifts of the social field (see Figure 2.5):

- *Downloading:* reenacting patterns of the past—viewing the world through one's habits of thought
- *Seeing:* suspending judgment and seeing reality with fresh eyes—the observed system is separate from those who observe
- *Sensing:* connecting to the field and attending to the situation from the whole—the boundary between observer and observed collapses, the system begins to see itself
- *Presencing:* connecting to the deepest source, from which the field of the future begins to arise—viewing from source
- *Crystallizing* vision and intention—envisioning the new from the future that wants to emerge
- *Prototyping* living microcosms in order to explore the future by doing—enacting the new through "being in dialogue with the universe"
- *Performing and embodying* the new in practices and infrastructures—embedding the new in the context of the larger co-evolving ecosystems

If we look at the whole set of these seven cognitive spaces, we can think of it in terms of a house with seven distinct rooms or spaces. Each room represents one of the seven spaces of attention (see Figure 2.5). The problem with most organizations and institutions today is that they use only a few of these rooms—usually the spaces at the upper half of Figure 2.5—while the other ones are rarely used or seldom leveraged. Part II of this book, "Entering the U Field" shows us in much more detail what each of these "rooms" represents and how we can enjoy and leverage being in them and grow from that experience.

The rest of my journey toward uncovering Theory U can be best summarized in terms of five key insights or propositions that are introduced here and will be discussed in more detail throughout the remainder of the book.

1. We Need a New Social Technology That Is Based on Tuning Three Instruments

While participating in numerous profound innovation and change projects and initiatives, I realized that while most experienced leaders actually do know these deeper levels of the U from their own experience, most organizations, institutions, and larger systems are firmly stuck in Levels 1 or 2. Why? I believe it is because we lack a new social leadership technology. Without a new leadership technology, leaders don't really shift fields but end up with more of the same. We call these attempts "restructuring," "redesigning," or "re-engineering" and more often than not they serve only to deepen our frustration and cynicism.

What I am suggesting as an alternative is to develop a new type of social technology that is based on three instruments that each of us already has—an open mind, an open heart, and an open will—and to cultivate these capacities not only on an individual level but also on a collective level.

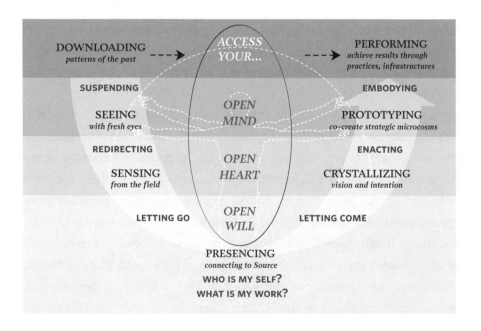

FIGURE 2.6 THREE INSTRUMENTS: OPEN MIND, OPEN HEART, OPEN WILL

The first instrument, or capacity, the *open mind*, is based on our ability to access our intellectual, or IQ, type of intelligence. This allows us to see with fresh eyes, to deal with the objective figures and facts around us. As the saying goes: the mind works like a parachute: it only functions when it is open.

The second capacity, the *open heart*, relates to our ability to access our emotional intelligence, or EQ; that is, our capacity to empathize with others, to tune in to different contexts, and to put ourselves into someone else's shoes.

The third capacity, the *open will*, relates to our ability to access our authentic purpose and self. This type of intelligence is also sometimes referred to as intention or as SQ (spiritual intelligence). It deals with the fundamental happening of the letting go and letting come.

We can tune each of these three instruments on an individual (subjective) as well as on a collective (intersubjective) level.

2. The Most Important Leadership Tool Is Your Self

The second insight deals with the evolving nature of every human being and the recognition that we are not "one" but "two." One self is the person or community we have become as a result of a journey that took place in the past. The other self is the person or community we can become as we journey into the future. It is our highest future possibility. People sometimes refer to the first self using a lowercase "s" and to the second self with a capital "S."

When these two "selves" talk to each other, you experience the essence of presencing.

How does this happen? Later we will take this up in more detail, but for now let's describe it this way. At the bottom of the U is a fundamental threshold one must pass. We might call it going through the eye of the needle. If the process of going through falls short, all our change efforts will remain somewhat superficial. They won't touch our essential core, our best future Self. We must learn to drop our ego and our habitual "self" in order for the Self to emerge.

When our "self" and our "Self" begin to communicate, we establish a subtle but very real link to our highest future possibility that can then begin to help and guide us in situations in which the past can't offer us useful advice (Figure 2.7).

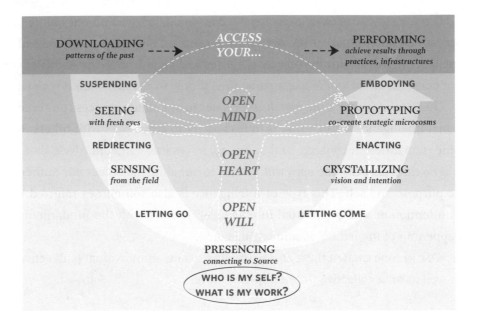

FIGURE 2.7 THE MOST IMPORTANT TOOL: YOUR SELF

Thus, the most important tool in such a new leadership technology is the leader's self—your Self.

3. THE LEADER'S INTERIOR WORK DEALS WITH MEETING AND MASTERING THREE ENEMIES

The third insight deals with this puzzle: Why is the journey to the deeper levels of the U always the road less traveled? Because it requires difficult inner work. To go "through the eye of the needle" requires that we face and deal with at least three inner voices of resistance, three enemies that can block the entrance to one of the deeper territories. The first enemy blocks the gate to the open mind. Michael Ray calls this enemy the Voice of Judgment (VOJ). Unless we succeed in shutting down our Voice of Judgment, we will be unable to make progress in accessing our real creativity and presence.

The second enemy blocks the gate to the open heart. Let us call this the Voice of Cynicism (VOC)—that is, all types of emotional acts of distancing.

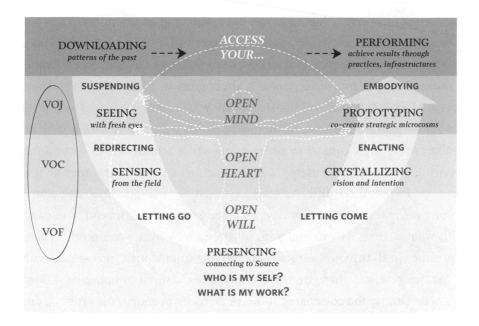

FIGURE 2.8 FACING THREE ENEMIES: VOJ, VOC, VOF

What is at stake when we begin to access the open heart? We must first put ourselves into a position of vulnerability, which distancing usually prevents. I am not saying you should never follow your VOC. I *am* saying that if you want to get to the bottom of the U—to your authentic Self—then your VOC is dysfunctional because it blocks your progress on that journey.

The third enemy blocks the gate to the open will. This is the Voice of Fear (VOF). It seeks to prevent us from letting go of what we have and who we are. It can show up as fear of losing economic security. Or fear of being ostracized. Or fear of being ridiculed. And fear of death. And yet meeting and dealing with that voice of fear is the very essence of leadership: to facilitate the letting go of the old "self" and letting come the new "Self." Then we can step into another world that only begins to take shape once we overcome the fear of stepping into the unknown.

4. THE U IS A LIVING FIELD THEORY—NOT A LINEAR MECHANICAL PROCESS. The fourth insight concerns an observation that puzzled me when I noticed

that some of the early adopters of the U process applied the principles of this theory in a rather mechanical, linear manner. What this brings to mind is that the essence of Theory U is just the opposite: it works as a matrix, that is, it works as an integral whole, not as a linear process. When you watch Bruce Lee, or Muhammad Ali, or Michael Jordan, you'll notice that their actions do not follow a linear process. Rather, they dance with the situation they are dealing with—they constantly observe and sense (connect), allow the inner knowing or intuition to emerge, and then act in an instant. And they do it all the time. It's not three different stages enacted sequentially. You can't plan to do one each week, with a few days of break in between. Instead, you dance with what surrounds you and with what emerges from within *all the time*. You dance to all three movements of the U simultaneously, not sequentially.

Yet, for practical purposes there is also a real benefit to breaking it down this way: During the co-sensing movement, focus primarily on sensing; during the co-presencing movement, focus on inner knowing; during the co-creation movement, focus on enacting. But keep in mind that all the other movements and capacities are always present. You could think of the U as a holographic theory: each component reflects the whole, yet in a very specific and particular way.

In order to enhance their resonance with the deeper fields of emergence, organizations need to establish three different kinds of infrastructures and places:

- Places and infrastructures that facilitate a shared seeing and sense-making of what is actually going on in the larger surrounding ecosystem (co-sensing)
- Places and cocoons of deep reflection and silence that facilitate deep listening and connection to the source of authentic presence and creativity, both individually and collectively (co-presencing)
- Places and infrastructures for hands-on prototyping of new forms of operating in order to explore the future by doing (co-creating)

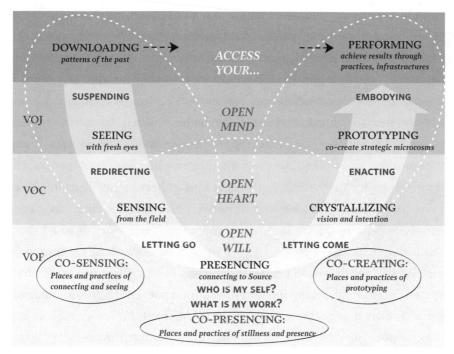

FIGURE 2.9 CREATING THREE INFRASTRUCTURES

5. The Rise of the Social Space of Emergence and Creation (Cycle of Presencing) Is Connected to the Dying and Transformation of Social Space of Destruction (Cycle of Absencing)

Our final insight concerns the observation of the massive rise of destruction, violence, and fundamentalism at the same time that we also see an opening to the deeper layers of the social field. That double movement, the opening to the deeper levels of emergence, on the one hand, and the enhanced power of the forces of destruction, on the other, is a defining feature of our time. This proposition tries to shed some light on how these two forces—those of presencing and absencing—relate to each other. It suggests that both are aspects of a single evolutionary movement. Often we see how people in the face of the utmost destruction have the ability to wake up to a higher level of awareness and consciousness. Throughout this book I will share several of these stories, including the story of my colleague Adam Kahane with a group in Guatemala and the story of the women of the Rosenstrasse in Berlin in

1943. These and other stories illustrate that all of us around the world participate in two different social types of connection, two different bodies of the
social field. One of them is governed by the dynamics of antiemergence and
destruction; it's the collective social body that is about to die. The other is
governed by the dynamics of emergence and collective creativity; it's the
emerging new social body that is about to be born. What happens in numerous social situations of violence and connection today is that we are torn
between these two worlds. We can switch from one space (the space of collective creativity) to the other (the space of collective destruction) in an
instant and almost any time and anywhere, and our noticing this switch
depends on how awake we are to one another.

In the remaining chapters of Part I we will go on a learning journey in
which we will see that in all these system levels basically the same thing happens: we increasingly bump into our own blind spot. That is, time and again,
we are thrown into empty-canvas situations that require us to look at ourselves, at our collective patterns of behavior; to reinvent ourselves, who we
are, and where we want to go as an institution, as an individual, and as a
community.

In Part II we will uncover the core process of illuminating this blind spot.
And in Part III we will investigate in much more detail how this profound
transformation of the global field is playing out across all systems levels from
the individual (micro) to groups (meso), institutions (macro), and the world
(mundo).

As you go through the journey of this book—if you choose to do so—you
will notice that at times I share with you some frameworks that at first may
seem a little complex (for example, Table 20.1). But what you will also notice
is that all these frameworks and distinctions are derived from the examples
and stories discussed throughout the book. When you look at them all
together, you may realize that what you see is something that could be called
the footprints of our collective evolutionary process. It's the evolutionary
grammar that we enact collectively across all systems levels. Every day. It's
our own story. So seeing, recognizing, and attending to these patterns is not

just a theoretical exercise—it gives us a whole different way to act as change agents who can collectively bring forth a world that is profoundly different from that of the past.

How to do this, how to begin to operate from the future as it emerges, is the question that underlies and organizes this book. With this question in mind, let us now turn our attention to how a team learns.

CHAPTER 3

Fourfold Learning and Change

Levels of Learning and Change • Thought Leader Interview Project
• The Split Between Matter and Mind • Two Sources and Types of
Learning • Organizational Learning's Blind Spot

Levels of Learning and Change

In Chapter 1, "Facing the Fire," I recounted how, as a young boy in
Germany, I was literally shaken into a new level of experience or being
by our family farm's fire. In retrospect, I see that experience as a gift life
handed me: the gift of experiencing a profound shift in my attention field, in
the way I attend to the world. That's the easy part.

The difficult part is to perform this shift in the context of groups and
organizations. How can we as a group shift our attention field so that we connect to our best future potential instead of continuing to operate from the
experiences of our past? And how can we perform this shift of attention without having our family farm burning down every day? That is exactly the challenge that brought me to the MIT Organizational Learning Center in the
mid-1990s.

When I arrived in Boston in the fall of 1994, I had just completed my
Ph.D. in economics and management. My thesis, "Reflective Modernization

of Capitalism: A Revolution from Within," argued that in order to cope with the challenges of our time, societies need to develop the capacity to learn across institutional boundaries.

In all of the key areas of society, we collectively produce results that few people (if anyone) want: schools that prevent our children from unfolding their capacity for deeper learning; health care systems that fight symptoms rather than address the root causes of health problems; industrial production systems that are out of sync with the principles and laws of our planetary ecosystem; an approach to world politics that focuses on issues such as terrorism by reacting to the symptoms rather than addressing the systemic causes. In each example the fundamental problem is the same: How can we approach problems in ways that don't repeat the (failing) patterns of the past? One of my first insights after arriving at that MIT Organizational Learning Center was this: there are several different dimensions for how to approach change, some more visible than others. The most common one and the most visible: a crisis or a need for change occurs and we "react."

Four levels of responding to change are pictured in Figure 3.1. Level 1 is

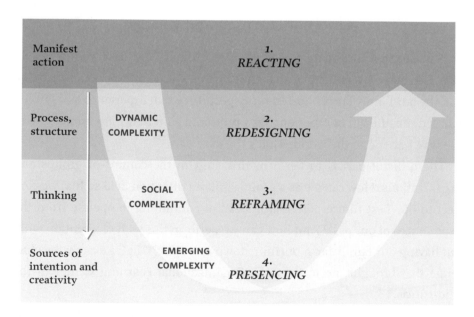

FIGURE 3.1 FOUR LEVELS OF LEARNING AND CHANGE

reacting, to respond by operating on existing habits and routines. Level 2 is redesigning: changing the underlying structure and process. Level 3 is reframing: changing the underlying pattern of thought. Most time and resources in our current organizations and institutions are spent on Levels 1 and 2, reacting to issues and reorganizing structure and process. While in some cases this type of reaction is perfectly appropriate, in others it is not. According to some studies, about 70 percent of business reengineering projects undertaken during the 1990s failed.[1] Why? Because reengineering usually operates at the first two levels only. The people involved do not deeply rethink or "reframe" the problem.

By contrast, organizational learning methods approach the task of managing change by addressing not only the first two levels but also the third, the level of rethinking and reframing one's fundamental assumptions about the situation at issue. Harvard and MIT researchers Chris Argyris and Donald Schön suggest a terminology where we can refer to Level 2 as single-loop learning and to Level 3 as double-loop learning. Single-loop learning means that we reflect on our actions. Double-loop goes one step further and includes a reflection on the deep, taken-for-granted assumptions.

Until now, organizational learning has been concerned primarily with how to build, nurture, and sustain the learning process based on single- and double-loop learning, on learning from past experience. There are many fine examples, good research, and great books that demonstrate how to put these learning cycles into practice.[2] Today, we know a lot about what it takes to build environments that sustain and foster processes of learning that correspond with Levels 2 and 3 of Figure 3.1.

However, in working with companies in various cultures and sectors, I found that leadership teams are wrestling with challenges that cannot be adequately addressed by reflecting only on the past (Level 3). Companies are struggling to succeed in an unprecedentedly turbulent, complex, and rapidly changing global context. Their executives realize that simply reflecting on what has happened in the past will not be adequate to help them figure out what to do next. By watching leadership teams analyze and address such challenges, we began to recognize a fourth level of learning and knowing:

learning from the future as it emerges (see Figure 3.1). I have named this discipline "presencing" because it involves a particular way of being aware of and experiencing the present moment. Presencing denotes the ability of individuals and collective entities to link directly with their highest future potential. When they are able to do this, they begin to operate from a more generative and more authentic presence in the moment—in the now.

Thought Leader Interview Project: What Is the Source of Our Collective Action?

When I first met Michael Jung in 1994, he was the head of McKinsey & Co.'s office in Vienna and of a worldwide research initiative on leadership. In Munich, we began an intriguing conversation about leading and organizing. At the end of that conversation, Jung asked whether I would be interested in conducting a global interview project with the world's leading thinkers on the topic of leadership, organization, and strategy. "All of the interviews will be made public. You can use them for your postdoc research, and I can use them in my work at McKinsey. Furthermore, anyone else who's interested can download them from a Web site. It is our hope that people will use them to stimulate their own thinking and creativity."

Of course I was interested, so after returning to Boston I asked several people for their input and help, and within a few days we had developed a list of people we considered to be among the most interesting and innovative thought leaders, including academics, entrepreneurs, businesspeople, inventors, scientists, educators, artists, and others.[3]

One of the first interviews I conducted was with Peter Senge, who was then head of the Center for Organizational Learning at MIT. Senge's book *The Fifth Discipline* was one of the main reasons I had wanted to join the Center. I started the interview the same way I often did, by asking "What underlying question does your work address?"

Senge said that his deepest interest concerned the conscious evolution of human systems. He then told me about his recent encounter with Karl-Henrik Robèrt, a Swedish physician and founder of the worldwide environmental organization The Natural Step. "Something in his story really struck me," Senge explained. "And I realized there is a direct parallel to my own experience. Robert's been doing research on cancer for most of his professional career and has dealt with hundreds of families facing the cancer of a parent, a child, or a spouse. He said, 'What's always amazed me are human beings' incredible reserves of strength. You know what a strong force denial is, but you tell people incredibly difficult things—[such as] your three-year-old has cancer—and stand amazed at how weak those forces are compared to people's capacity to face the truth and work together as families, as loved ones facing the most horrible situations you can imagine.'"

Senge said he too had come to recognize the great power of facing reality from years of leading a well-known personal growth course called "Leadership and Mastery." One overarching question, he told me, governs his work: "How does one help people collectively tap into the real reserves that exist for profound change, for facing things which seem insoluble, impossible to alter?" He continued: "Many people would say that human beings are basically self-centered and fundamentally materialistic, and that's why society is the way it is. *That's just the way things are.*

"But, of course," he continued, "the *way things are* is just a mental model, and in the right setting, people confront that and they experience real generosity. So how do you begin to release that kind of energy collectively?"

As Peter continued to tell his story, I listened and started to feel time slowing down. I began to attend from a deeper level.

"I had an interesting conversation a year ago with Master Nan, the Chinese Zen master who lives in Hong Kong," Peter said. "In China he's a very revered figure. He's considered an extraordinary scholar because of his integration of Buddhism, Taoism, and Confucianism. I asked him, 'Do you think that the industrial age will create such environmental problems that we will destroy ourselves and that we must find a way to understand these problems and change industrial institutions?'"

Master Nan paused and shook his head in response. "He didn't completely agree with that. It wasn't the way he saw it. He saw it at a deeper level, and he said, 'There's only one issue in the world. It's the reintegration of matter and mind.' That's exactly what he said to me, *the reintegration of matter and mind.*"

Those words hit on something that resonated deeply with my own question: What does the split between matter and mind mean to our social world as a whole, to the social body that we collectively enact? I was reminded of my parents' work. The visible result of farming, the harvest, depends on the invisible quality of the field itself. So I wondered: What if the quality of the visible social worlds is a function of this invisible field that resides in our blind spot of perception? The quality of this invisible field—our blind spot—defines the quality of our visible social action. Master Nan said our primary issue is the reintegration of matter and mind. That implies that if we want to increase the quality of our action as a group or a team, we need to pay attention to the invisible dimension of its source: the place from where we operate.

The Split Between Matter and Mind

I asked Senge how he saw the separation of mind and matter relating to our world of groups and organizations. "We basically create organizations which are like matter in the sense that they obtain an apparently independent existence outside ourselves," he replied, "and then we become prisoners of those organizations."

Organizations work the way human beings create them. They maintain that it is "the system" that causes their problems. It's always something external, some *thing* that imposes itself on them. So the reality might actually be: "Thought creates organizations, and then organizations hold human beings prisoner," or, as the quantum physicist, David Bohm, used to say, "Thought creates the world and then says 'I didn't do it!'"

"To me," continued Senge, "here's the essence of what systems thinking is about: People begin to consciously discover and account for how their own patterns of thought and interaction manifest on a large scale and create the very forces by which the organization then 'is doing it to me.' And then they *complete that feedback loop.* The most profound experiences I've ever seen in consulting have always been when people suddenly say things like, 'Holy cow! Look what we are doing to ourselves!' . . . or 'Given the way we operate, no wonder we can't win!' And what is always significant to me, in those moments, is the *we*. Not 'you,' not 'them,' but we. . . . A true systems philosophy closes the feedback loop between the human being, their experience of reality, and their sense of participation in that whole cycle of awareness and enactment."

I had read a lot about organizational learning and systems thinking, but it had never occurred to me this clearly and simply. The essence of systems thinking is to help people close the feedback loop between the enactment of systems on a behavioral level and its invisible source of awareness and thought. To that comment Senge responded quietly, "Yes, I don't think I've ever thought about it quite this way anytime before."

I left that conversation feeling as if I had somehow encountered an essential aspect of my own question. I couldn't verbalize the question, but I could *feel* it. It was physical—a distinct bodily sensation that lasted for a week or two.[4] When it faded away, I started to think about it in terms of seeing the deeper aspects of social reality, the deeper conditions from which social action arises moment by moment. I realized that that deeper territory—the sources or the deeper field conditions from which we operate—is what we so often miss. It may be the most important blind spot in contemporary social systems theory.

Two Sources and Types of Learning

When I first arrived at MIT, I was a rather conventional white male European academic: strong on intellectual reflection, weak on practical experience and useful knowledge. What attracted me to MIT was the opportunity to learn the craft of advanced action research from some of its outstanding representatives, such as Edgar Schein, the co-founder of process consultation and organizational psychology. According to the founder of action research, Kurt Lewin (1890–1947), who was born in Germany and emigrated to the United States when Hitler came to power, the starting point for action research is the knowledge that in order to really understand the social process, researchers must not just study but also work and participate in practical and real settings. But how does one know whether a particular piece of "knowledge" is true? When does an action researcher *know* he knows? When I posed this question to Ed Schein, he replied, "When my knowledge is helpful to the various practitioners in the field—that is the moment when I know that I know."[5]

This idea continues to be a guiding principle for my own research. In numerous action research projects I have worked to help leadership teams go through deep processes of change. While I have gained some firsthand knowledge about the world of companies and the issues their leaders face, I have also gone down a path that took me far from established institutions and into the world of grassroots activists, entrepreneurs, and revolutionary innovators.

What I learned in these different worlds of inquiry and action can be summed up in a single sentence: *There are two sources of learning: the past and the emerging future.*

How to learn from the past is well known: its sequence is action-observation-reflection-design-action.[6] But how can one learn from the future? That is the subject and goal of this book.[7]

Organizational Learning's Blind Spot

Teams and organizational units that try to follow this new trail of learning often give up in frustration. They realize that it is not possible to effect deep change of the type discussed above by applying the conventional methods of learning and change that they have used before. Learning from the past doesn't work. It's not as simple as saying, "Let's just add 'learning from the emerging future' as the final step of this process." It doesn't work that way. We need to do on a collective level what happened to me when I was standing in front of the burning farmhouse. We have to drop all our old tools and attend to the situation with fresh eyes.[8] We have to abandon our conventional ways of reacting and operating. We have to deepen our attention to and wonder about the world. We have to bend our habituated beam of attending to the world and redirect it onto its source—the blind spot from which we operate moment by moment. We have to connect to this source in order to tune in to the future that is seeking to emerge.

It is a quest. But we have what I have come to call the subtle, invisible dimension—the underlying source to help us. The deep structures of the social field determine the quality of our actions just as the field of the farmer determines the quality of the yield. We can shift the quality of this underlying field in such a way that it opens our horizon to higher future possibilities. It is then when we begin to accomplish profound social renewal and change.

Organizational Complexity

Dynamic Complexity • Social Complexity • Emerging Complexity
• The Manager's Job • From Product to Process to Source •
Leading with a Blank Canvas • The Co-Evolving Context of
Organizations • The Institutional Blind Spot

Dynamic Complexity

L eaders in all organizations and institutions face new levels of complexity and change. I decided to take a closer look at where that complexity originates. Inspired by the work of Senge and Roth and their distinction between dynamic and behavior complexity, I found three different types of complexity that impact the challenges that leaders have to deal with: dynamic, social, and emerging complexity.

Of the three, dynamic complexity is more often used and most often easily recognized. Dynamic complexity means that there is a systematic distance or delay between cause and effect in space or time. Take, for example, the dynamic complexities of global warming. Our emissions of carbon dioxide (CO_2)—one *cause*—will have a long-term impact on the future of our planet. The greenhouse *effects* that we observe today are caused mainly by emissions from (and up to) the 1970s. If my organization decides to reduce its emissions of CO_2, we will reduce our impact on the global climate. But what if

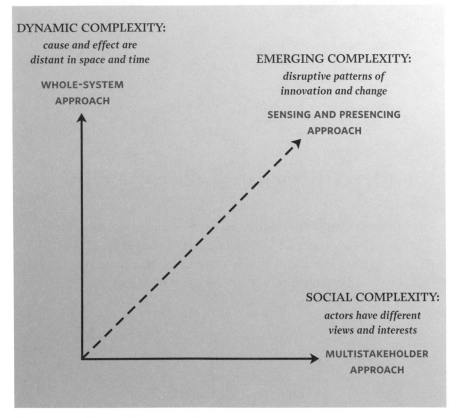

FIGURE 4.1 THREE TYPES OF COMPLEXITY

our products are a part of a larger product that increases the emission of CO_2? Or what about emissions produced by the transportation of our goods? The longer and more complex this chain of cause and effect, the higher the dynamic complexity of the problem. If the dynamic complexity is low, it can be dealt with piece by piece. If the dynamic complexity is high, a "whole-systems" approach that pays sufficient attention to cross-system interdependencies is the appropriate approach. The managerial implications of dynamic complexity are straightforward: the greater the dynamic complexity, the higher the interdependence among the subcomponents of a system, and, therefore, using a whole-systems approach to problem solving becomes even more important.

Social Complexity

Once the dynamic complexity of an issue is addressed, the more likely it is that a second type of complexity will move to the foreground: social complexity. Social complexity is a product of diverse interests and worldviews among stakeholders. For example, the Kyoto protocols on climate change and the reduction of CO_2 emissions have been agreed upon and supported by most international experts. However, these protocols are of limited use because three of the most polluting countries—the United States, India, and Brazil—have not signed the treaty. This issue clearly illustrates diverse interests, worldviews and values. The lower the social complexity, the more we can rely on experts to guide decision and policy making.[1] The greater the social complexity, the more important it is that a multistakeholder approach to real problem solving that includes all of the relevant stakeholders' voices be employed.

Emerging Complexity

Emerging complexity is characterized by disruptive change. Challenges of this type can usually be recognized by these three characteristics:

1. The solution to the problem is unknown.
2. The problem statement itself is still unfolding.
3. Who the key stakeholders are is not clear.

When the future cannot be predicted by the trends and trajectories of the past, we must deal with situations as they evolve. The greater the emerging complexity, the less we can rely on past experiences. We need a new approach—one that builds on sensing, presencing, and prototyping emerging opportunities. These three will be described more fully in Chapters 10, 11, and 13. But for now, we should describe *sensing* as the view from "within"—a perception that begins to take shape when we begin to feel and sense the whole field. It is usually accompanied by increased energy and a shift to a "deeper place." *Presencing*, as we have already briefly touched upon, is the state we experience when we have opened our minds, our hearts and our intentions or wills and can, as a result, view things from the source. It allows us to connect and move with emerging new realities and rapid change that cannot be addressed by reflecting on past experiences. Prototyping follows the crystallizing stage, or the stage when we actually develop a sense of the future that wants to emerge. *Prototyping* means to explore the future by doing, and builds on a practical integration of the head, heart, and hand. It very quickly creates practical results that can then generate feedback and suggestions for improvement by all key stakeholders of the system at issue. The rise of generative complexity in many important leadership challenges is due to the increasingly turbulent environment in which business, civic, and public-sector organizations operate. That change in context is the principle driver of the need to learn and lead from the right side of the "U": from the emerging future.

The Manager's Job

When it comes right down to it, the only "job" we have as managers is to mobilize action and produce results. To do this, we must integrate goals, strategies, personalities, and processes. Over the past several decades, we have seen two major shifts in how we approach our work. First, we have shifted from an emphasis on the *what* to the *how*.

Second, we have shifted the *how* to the *where*; from process (how) to the inner place from which managers and systems operate and act (who).

I first noticed this shift of focus in 1996, when I asked Richard LeVitt of Hewlett-Packard in Palo Alto, then the company-wide director of quality, about HP's quality concerns. "First, we used to focus mainly on product outcomes and concrete results like product reliability." LeVitt paused. "Though these are still important, we realized we could achieve more by shifting our focus upstream and thinking about the processes that produce these results. This stage of managing quality was the heart of the TQM [total quality management] movement in the eighties. But once we got the processes right, we asked—what next? What will be the next basis for competitive advantage?"

LeVitt went on to describe what he saw as the next performance threshold: "For us, one critical new focus area has been how managers can improve their quality of thought and their *deep perception of customers* and the experiences customers should have with us."

From Product to Process to Source

HP's shift from *product* to *process* and from process to *source* can be observed in all of the functional areas of management.

Figure 4.2 depicts twelve different management areas. The upper half features the more tangible functions (manufacturing, HR, R&D, finance, accounting, strategy, marketing, and sales) and the lower half the less tangible functions (quality, knowledge, leadership, change, and communication).

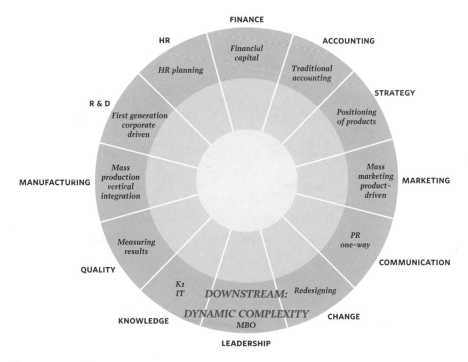

FIGURE 4.2 TWELVE MANAGEMENT FUNCTIONS: DOWNSTREAM VIEW

Over the past couple of decades, similar developmental shifts and story lines have unfolded in all functional areas: we notice a shift of focus from *product* to *process* and from process to *source* in all of the functional areas of management.

The First Shift: Moving from a Focus on Tangible Results to a Focus on Process (Downstream to Midstream)

In the initial stage, the focus is on the downstream functions such as measuring the results of product reliability, as depicted in the outer ring in Figure 4.2. One key characteristic of this stage is *functional differentiation* which means that the management tasks are split up into a set of subtasks— finance, strategy, human resources, manufacturing, and so on. A second characteristic of this phase is what I call a downstream focus. Each separate managerial area puts its main focus on functional performance metrics such as costs, parts delivered on time, product reliability, and so forth. The various management areas are integrated through the mechanism of hierarchy.

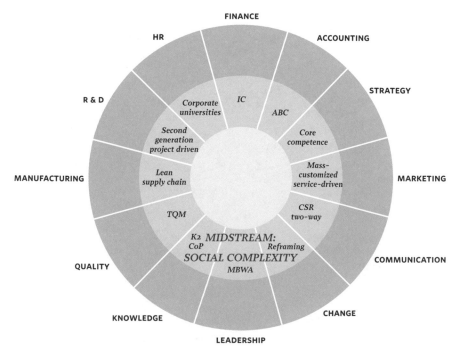

FIGURE 4.3 TWELVE MANAGEMENT FUNCTIONS: MIDSTREAM VIEW

During the 1980s and 1990s, the mainstream focus of management shift-ed toward processes. This change, depicted in Figure 4.3, shows movement from the outer circle toward the middle circle, that is, to a more process-based view. Examples are process-based philosophies such as total quality management (TQM), knowledge management processes, organizational learning, lean production, and activity-based costing (ABC). In all these examples, the focus is on how to improve the *process*; in other words, how to approach, organize, and optimize certain activities and managerial tasks. For example, in the case of organizational learning, the experiential learning cycle functions as a basic framework for designing learning infrastructures that support organizational learning processes. Another aspect of this shift-ing of managerial attention is the issue of cross-functional integration. In order to integrate and coordinate work across functional and organizational boundaries, people need to learn how to handle social complexity in the con-text of increasingly interdependent ways of organizing and performing. The leaders of each subtask or function have their own interests, networks, and goals, so they need different management skills in order to handle the social complexity of cross-functional integration in the core processes of value creation.

The Second Shift: Moving from a Focus on Process to a Focus on Source (Midstream to Upstream)

The third stage, which started during the 1990s and continues today, shifts the focus from process to sources of innovation and change (see Figure 4.4). As Richard LeVitt put it, once you have your processes right, what is your next leverage point to enhance the stream of value creation? The third stage, represented by the center of the management wheel, deals with the issue of emerging complexity and is characterized by a collapse of boundaries between functions. Each function may enter through a different door, but they all arrive at essentially the same place. As Michael Jung put it, "Everybody is climbing the same mountain, but each views it from a differ-ent angle and believes that it is an entirely different mountain." In spite of all the different labels, names, and discourses, in the center of the wheel all

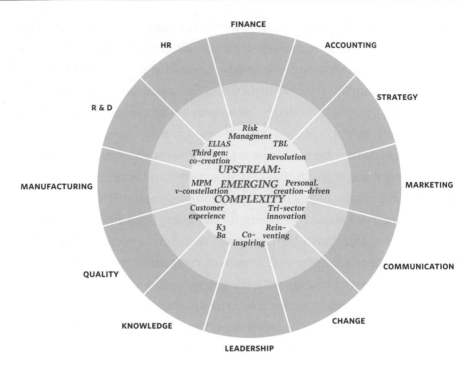

FIGURE 4.4 TWELVE MANAGEMENT FUNCTIONS: UPSTREAM VIEW

twelve functions deal with the same fundamental realities: how to access and sustain the source for resilience, profound innovation, renewal and change—that is, how to deal effectively with emerging complexity.[2]

The wheel of management depicts an organic breathing process. The completeness of that breathing determines the health and wholeness of an organizational field. Breathing in moves attention from execution toward the sources of attention and intention, while whatever emerges from the center is breathed out and enacted in the downstream areas of managing and organizing. The point is not to argue for an upstream point of view of leadership at the expense of processes, capabilities (midstream), and execution (downstream), but to conceive of the whole field of leading and organizing as a single living entity, one that is grounded in and constantly renewed from the source of attention and intention at the center. In this view the whole of an organization or field is dependent on and emerges only from the relationship of all its parts. The center does not exist without the periphery, and vice versa.

Underlying the wheel of management are two axes: the more tangible functions are on the upper half; the exterior-oriented functions are on the right side of the wheel and the interior-oriented functions show up on the left. Good management has to do with balancing and integrating all twelve aspects—a job that, as Henry Mintzberg once pointed out, researchers usually tend to leave to practitioners.

The nature of successful managing and organizing has to do with seeing, appreciating, and integrating a diverse range of perspectives.

For example, in strategy, this development is evident in the shift from *core competence* to *sources of industry revolution*. First there were the conventional approaches to strategizing that revolved around positioning in terms of product–market combinations.[3] Such approaches dealt with well-defined products in well-defined markets. Then, in 1990, along came a *Harvard Business Review* (HBR) article by Gary Hamel and C. K. Prahalad entitled "The Core Competence of the Organization," which shifted the focus of attention from downstream to midstream, from product to core competence.[4] Real strategy work, the authors argued, must revolve around the clarification of core competencies that generate the downstream product–market combinations.

When I first met and interviewed Gary Hamel in 1996, I was surprised to learn that he hadn't given a single speech on core competencies for the previous five years. He was already working on the next shift of focus, which he subsequently articulated in his 1996 HBR article "Strategy as Revolution" and his 2002 book *Leading the Revolution*. His main point in these publications was that reinventing industries requires a capacity different from that required to sustain existing core competencies. Future business success requires the capacity to sense *tomorrow's* core competencies and opportunities.

While the mainstream approach of the 1990s tapped into then-current best practices, Hamel thought that, in the upstream approach to strategy, the source of knowing comes from tapping the resources of dormant innovations and ideas that reside on the periphery of a company, thereby extending the scope of strategizing beyond organizational boundaries by involving customers, partners, and frontline employees.

In their book *Competition for the Future*, Hamel and Prahalad compare this upstream shift of focus to pregnancy. "Like competition for the future, pregnancy has three stages—conception, gestation, and delivery," they wrote. "It is the last stage of competition that is the focus of strategy textbooks and strategic planning exercises. Typically, the assumption is that the product or service concept is well established, the dimensions of competition are well defined, and the boundaries of the industry have stabilized. But focusing on the last stage of market-based competition, without a deep understanding of pre-market competition, is like trying to make sense of the process of childbirth without any insight into conception and gestation."[5]

The question for managers to ask themselves at this point, they argue, is "Which stage receives the bulk of our time and attention: conception, gestation, or labor and delivery? Our experience suggests that most managers spend a disproportionate amount of time in the delivery room, waiting for the miracle of birth . . . But as we all know, the miracle of birth is most unlikely unless there's been some activity nine months previously."

Our current decade brought a shift of context for managing innovation from high growth to massive market turbulence and resulted in a higher emphasis on capabilities such as resilience and deep values such as ethical integrity.[6]

The rise and fall of Enron, a company featured frequently in Hamel's *Leading the Revolution*, has been a wake-up call for many. Enron has proved that revolutionary strategy and innovation are not values in themselves but must be embedded and grounded in a shared sense and real connection with the larger social context or whole. That connection to the larger social context can function as a strategic entry point for rethinking and reinventing one's strategy towards serving the needs of the 3 billion people that live on less than $2 a day, as C.K. Prahalad argues in his 2005 book *The Fortune at the Bottom of the Pyramid: Eradicating Poverty Through Profits* (2005). What it takes to radically rethink one's approach to strategy based on serving the needs of the people whose needs in the current system are unmet, is a capacity to operate from the blank canvas. As depicted in Figure 4.4's core or inner circle, managers and leaders today stand more and more in front of challenges that require them to operate from the blank canvas, to sense and actualize emerging opportunities as they arise.

Let us now look at two other examples.

Example 1: Knowledge Management

Like any artistic creation, each stage of management requires a different type of knowledge. For instance, when managers measure the outcomes of the production process, they usually operate with explicit knowledge. Explicit knowledge is knowledge that can be expressed in spreadsheets and e-mails. In the first stage of knowledge management, people relied on IT to manage knowledge systems and databanks. After several years (and several billion dollars) it has become obvious that IT is but one part of a larger puzzle. Many say, the easy part. Managers soon realized the challenge lies in moving beyond information management to knowledge management.

In the second stage of knowledge management, people focused on process improvements, such as TQM; here we find embodied or tacit knowledge; this is knowledge that is simply "known" and carried out in everyday actions.

However, when managers move into the upstream realm of innovation, as they do in the third phase of knowledge management, they find, like an artist standing in front of a blank canvas or like Michelangelo carving David, they have to first *see it*.

In Figure 4.5, above the arch, we have explicit knowledge, corresponding with the outer ring in the management wheel (Figure 4.2); below the wave lies our tacitly embodied knowledge, corresponding to the middle ring in the management wheel (Figure 4.3) and our self-transcending knowledge, corresponding to the inner hub of the management wheel (Figure 4.4).

Johnson & Johnson's Michael Burtha portrays the movement of knowledge management from explicit to tacit when explaining that the real challenge lies in creating spaces for peers to share complex knowledge across units, functions, and organizations that will enable high-performance teams to operate effectively. From this perspective, knowledge is not a *thing* but *something living*, situated and embedded in work practices.[7] Knowledge without context is not knowledge; it's just information.[8] Real knowledge, argue

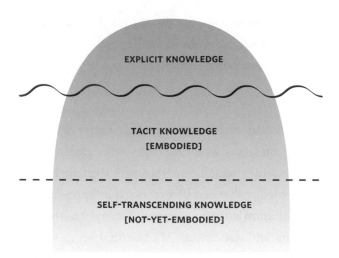

FIGURE 4.5 THREE FORMS OF KNOWLEDGE

Ikujiro Nonaka and Hirotaka Takeuchi in their groundbreaking book, *The Knowledge-Creating Company,* is a "situational living process that evolves in a spiraling movement between explicit and tacit dimensions of knowledge held by individuals, teams, and the organization."[9]

This new definition of knowledge as a living process was embraced in the 1990s. The late 1990s and early 2000s saw a further shift, one that deals with the conditions and sources of profound innovation and change. We now wish to learn how to respond to turbulence and disruptive change with resilience and flexibility, how to sense and seize emerging future opportunities, how to tune in to the sources of "not-yet-embodied" knowledge.[10] This most recent stage is reflected in Nonaka's concept of *phronesis,* practical wisdom, and *ba,* the Japanese word for "place," which refers to the physical, social, and mental context of knowledge creation. *Ba* is "context in motion," according to Nonaka. I call it "not-yet-embodied" or "self-transcending" knowledge.[11]

Many people agree with Nonaka's assessment that knowledge cannot be managed. Why? Because it's a living process, not a dead body. Instead of managing or controlling knowledge, Nonaka says, we need to create the conditions that will allow all three aspects of knowledge management to emerge: IT systems, a knowledge creation process, and places that are conducive to this kind of work.

Example 2: Manufacturing

Tom Johnson, the co-author of *Relevance Lost: The Rise and Fall of Management Accounting and Profit Beyond Measure,* told me in an interview the following story of how car manufacturing moved from mass to lean production. He used this example of what is probably the world's most famous auto factory, located near Detroit.

"Coming out of World War II, Ford and Toyota looked at Henry Ford's River Rouge plant. The plant was built during World War I and ran in the 1920s building the Model Ts. That was the classic model of mass production, and every automaker knew it by heart. It was a useful model if you were going to mass-produce one car, one color, one way.

"Following the war, the big question then was how to a make a variety of cars without building a separate plant for each variety. Ford Motor Company came up with a solution by building something to massive scale and then

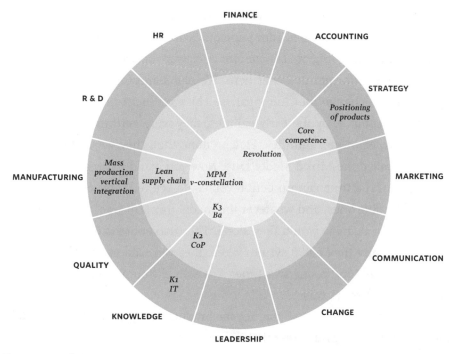

Figure 4.6 Shifts of Focus from Downstream to upstream

running it at the highest possible throughput rate you could. Always keeping it up and running meant your cost would be as low as possible. . . .

"The problem was, you couldn't produce variety in a continuous line flow like Henry Ford was running, because to make two different varieties along the same line means you've got to stop and change over somehow, somewhere. Their solution was to *decouple* the line. Break up the continuous flow that Ford had, and put your paint shop in one place, your stamping plant in another place, do your welding or your riveting somewhere else. . . .

"So economies-of-scale thinking grew at the heart of Ford's, and GM's, and other American manufacturing thinking in all those years."

By contrast, the development of the next manufacturing stage, later referred to as "lean production," began as a *different way of seeing reality*—in fact, in a different way of looking at Henry Ford's River Rouge plant. When the Toyota engineers looked at the River Rouge plant, according to Johnson, they concluded that its costs were low because of the *continuous flow*. They went back to Japan, and since they didn't have any factories left after the war, they decided they'd do it all in one plant in one continuous flow.

"By the 1970s," continued Tom Johnson, "when we first started to become aware of what was going on, changeover rates were down to minute fractions of what we took for granted over here. We had stamping presses that took eight hours to change, but the Japanese changed them in twenty or thirty minutes. Eventually, by the early eighties, they were getting it down in the range of six, eight, ten minutes. Having done that, they were able to build what they called the Mixed Model Line. Now you could have a continuously flowing line, and for a certain period you could see red ones come through, followed by blue ones, and whatever the model mix that was required by the customers for that day would flow along. They had enormous variety at very low cost because they had a system where they were able to build one order at a time, to fill one order at a time. A wholly different conception of the world is lying behind this."

The stunning success of the Toyota production system became widely known through an MIT study that described the process principles behind this way of manufacturing as lean production.[12] It uses less capital and labor while reengineering the manufacturing process as a synchronized single flow.[13]

In the time it took the Western auto industry to move from mass production (stage one) to lean production (stage two), Toyota had already started moving toward a stage-three production system. The downside of the lean production approach was a lack of synergy and integration across projects and platforms. By contrast, the new system, which MIT's Michael A. Cusumano and Kentaro Nobeoka call "multiproject management," simultaneously links and coordinates engineering efforts in different projects and platforms. According to Toyota sources, the new system helped reduce development costs on the average project by 30 percent and the number of testing prototypes by 40 percent. It relies on huge increases in component sharing and intensive communication and coordination between engineering and testing functions, creating communication infrastructures that facilitate simultaneous innovations across projects and platforms.

Manufacturing has shifted from vertical integration (stage one) to more horizontally integrated supply chain management (stage two) and web-shaped "value constellations" that focus on innovating and optimizing the whole system (stage three).[14] Whereas supply chains presuppose a linear stream of value creation that follows the flow of material from suppliers to customers, web-shaped value constellations conceive of customers not only as end-of-the-pipe recipients of products but as active co-creators of the economic value rendered by a web-shaped network of collaboration.

For example, when Mercedes-Benz customers fetch their new cars in Germany, they do not simply pick up a new vehicle. They can get an inside view of the factory, which allows to become real witnesses to and participants of the manufacturing process that created their car.

Leading with a Blank Canvas

While management is about "getting things done," leadership is about creating and cultivating the larger context—the fertile common ground and soil—in which things can happen.[15]

First, business leaders embraced a directive approach: command-and-control. They set clear agendas and objectives designed to mobilize and guide an entire company. While no one would say this type of leadership is obsolete, it has become increasingly clear that something more is needed in order to succeed in our complex, dynamic and unstable work environments. How can you "command" and "control" when the most important goals, objectives, issues, and opportunities are not known up front but tend to emerge over time?

In response, organizations moved to more local adaptation, participation, learning and process styles of leadership. Tom Peters and Robert Waterman popularized principles of "management by walking around."[16] Leaders in this second phase had to learn to balance setting goals and direction with enhancing the degree of participation of people throughout the entire organization.

We now find ourselves in a third phase, which is concerned with creating the conditions that inspire people and collective entities to operate from a "different place"—from that inner circle of our management wheel (see Figure 4.4). As Saatchi & Saatchi's Kevin Roberts put it, "We've already moved from management to leadership—and we're about to go beyond leadership to inspiration. In the 21st century, organizations have to achieve peak performance by creating conditions that allow them to unleash the power of their people—not leading them, not by managing them, but by co-inspiring them."[17]

For high performance organizations to evolve, leaders have to extend their focus of attention from processes to using the "blank canvas" dimensions of leadership. They must help people access their sources of inspiration, intuition, and imagination. Just like the artist standing in front of the blank canvas, leaders in current business environments must develop a capacity to shift their organization so that its members can sense and articulate emerging futures, both individually and collectively. I once asked one of the most successful leaders of the telecom industry what she considered to be the essence of her leadership work. She responded, "I am facilitating the opening process so my team can sense and seize emerging opportunities as they arise from the fast paced business environment we are operating in."

But, you might say, that canvas is so *incomplete*! It is, and that is precisely its genius. I first became aware of this incompleteness when I joined the MIT Organizational Learning Center in Cambridge. I was sitting in the midst of a large audience listening to Peter Senge speak. I noticed that the people sitting around me were engaged differently—more fully—by his presentation than by others I had witnessed. Rather than delivering a set piece, with foregone assumptions, bullet points, and PowerPoint summaries, he seemed to be doing not only less but also something quite different. His presentation seemed to grow organically, as if he were just talking to us. He created a real-time connection, making us feel as if we were participating in the presentation as it unfolded. It seemed to be more of a story than the type of academic presentation I was familiar with. The European intellectual in me had some misgivings, but I realized that while it may not work for everyone, Senge had opened a space for a different type of "seeing"—for a different "music" to be heard.

I sat there thinking that Senge's presentation was more like a modern painting than classical art. We weren't presented with a completed picture. It was more like a Mark Rothko, with simple blue that covers a canvas. Or like John Cage's composition "4'33" Tacet for Large Orchestra," with its four and a half minutes of silence. What is the impact, I wondered, of silence on listeners? Of a completely blue canvas on a viewer?

I now realize that Senge was not really doing less but rather making a presentation from a *different place*. It's a place from which he can access and operate in front of a blank canvas, and he invites the audience to become co-creators with him. They bring their own meanings, experiences and beliefs to interpreting what they see or hear. The real skillfulness of leading in front of a blank canvas, then, is based as much on the art of *not doing* things as it is on *doing* things. It demands the courage to say less in order to create a gateway by bending the collective beam of attention back toward its source.

What would it take for teams and organizations to operate from that different place? Is there a communal space they can access? And what kind of collective leadership could activate that kind of white-canvas space?

The Co-Evolving Context of Organizations

Jim Collins decided to study high-performing companies. He and his team selected eleven companies from more than 1,400 that had been listed in the Fortune 500 for thirty years, from 1965 to 1995. Each of the eleven companies had had mediocre results for fifteen of those years and then had gone through a transition. From that point on, they outperformed the market by at least three to one. Furthermore, they sustained that level of performance for at least fifteen years. When compared with like-industry companies of about the same size, Collins identified one single key factor: leadership. But leadership that paradoxically blended personal humility and professional will. Characteristics of what Collins terms "level 5 leadership" include seeing reality or "being brutally realistic in determining what the company can be best at in the world." They must also have egoless selves by "channeling their ego needs away from themselves toward building a great company—often by sacrificing their own gain for the gain of the company." And, finally, they must be willing to assume responsibility for poor results while at the same time giving credit for successes to others.[18]

Performing with humility or a selfless self seems to be a precondition for the collective field to advance to a higher level. Since the dot-com bubble burst, CEOs with swollen egos, together with their companies, have crumbled like the Berlin Wall. Everyone seems to agree that a different, more responsible leadership is needed now, not just in the business sector but also in the public (and civic) one. We know of individuals, teams, and even organizations who, for a certain period of time, have operated with a higher quality of "primary knowing," as UC Berkeley's Eleanor Rosch calls it. But we still know very little about how to enable larger cross-institutional systems to operate from this place, let alone sustain it over time.

The shift of focus in how managers approach their work mirrors a larger shift in our economy. We have moved from a product-driven economy to a service-driven economy and are now shifting to an experience-, knowledge- and innovation-driven economy.

Table 4.1 The Changing Economic Context

	Goods	Services	Innovation
Focus of value creation	Make standardized products	Deliver customized services	Stage and co-create personalized experiences
Customer as	Target for mass marketing	Target for mass customization	Partner for co-creation
Economics	Economies of scale	Economies of scope	Economies of presencing
Organizational model	Functional, single sphere: mass production	Divisional, two spheres: production; customer interface	Networked, three spheres: production; customer interface; innovation
Locus of entrepreneurial impulse	Center of one's own organization (product focus)	Periphery of one's own organization (customer focus)	Surrounding sphere of one's own organization (co-creation focus)
Relationship logic with customers	Product-driven (push)	Service driven (pull)	Co-creation driven (presence)
Primary class	Working class	Service class	Creative class
Managerial mind-set	The world is as it is (self = onlooker)	The world evolves as people interact (self = participant)	The world arises as we choose to attend (self = source of co-creation)

As you can see in this table, most organizations today are not one but three. And each of their three spheres functions according to a different set of principles. In production, the primary principle is economies of scale; in customer interface, it is economies of scope; and for those who innovate, it is the economies of presencing, that is, the capacity to sense and shape emerging future possibilities. To see these patterns accurately, one must look beyond a single organization and begin to view larger economic contexts in which companies co-evolve. Each column of this table traces one dimension of this larger contextual shift, but it leaves some footprints we can track, in order to determine where the larger context is heading.

As the focus of value creation has shifted from making standardized products to delivering customized services and creating personalized experiences, the firm's relationship to the customer has evolved from push (product driven) to pull (service driven) to co-creating (presencing.) Unfortunately, I have witnessed many organizations struggling with trying to fit their work from one sphere (for example, push marketing) into another (experience-driven co-creation) only to find out that it doesn't work.

Each relational mode—push, pull or presence—requires a different managerial mind-set and relationship competence, as each mode is based on a different worldview. For instance, push-oriented relationships are based on a traditional worldview that assumes things are only outside of us. That they are separate from us and not influenced by our thoughts or our behaviors. By contrast, in a customer-driven, pull-through organization, the worldview is still an external one. It is all about the customer, multi-stakeholder dialogues, and social complexity.

As companies evolve into this next stage, they begin to see the increased need to develop their presence-based relational skills. In order to deal with disruptive stakeholder situations, managers must be able to tap into their inner sources of creativity and operate from the "bull's-eye" of the management wheel—not just individually but as part of a larger organizational field. They must learn to function within emerging complexity.

The Institutional Blind Spot

Organizations are often blind to emerging complexity, characterized by unexpected opportunities and disruptive change. Together, we, the global community of management practitioners, consultants, and researchers, are struggling to discover a reliable response to this challenge. We have learned how to deal with dynamic and social complexity, with interdependency issues and conflicting stakeholder views. But we don't yet have a reliable problem-solving methodology for dealing with emerging complex challenges. We may recognize all three types of complexity in today's institutions, but we continue to deal with them inappropriately.

Formerly, centralized and vertically integrated institutions responded first by decentralizing and reorganizing in smaller, more focused, and more flexible units that, then, realigned horizontally according to different streams of value creation. But decentralization leads to the next challenge: how to reintegrate the whole. What methods will work to align the different parts of an organizational whole when the nature of that whole keeps changing? What do you do when you realize that you have outsourced core competencies that are vital to the future of your organization?

Institutions around the world and across all sectors are struggling to find solutions to these challenges. Some focus on recentralizing functions, some bet on more networked integration, and some put their chips on the traditional matrix type of organizational structure. But the underlying issue is not organizational structure. Rather, the question is: How may we best differentiate and reintegrate the three spheres of value creation in the context of the larger ecosystem? This ecosystem incorporates not only the economies of scale and scope but also those of presencing.

Organizations that wish to succeed must develop and apply all the different sets of relational principles (push, pull, and presence) that apply to each sphere.

Institutional blind spots encompass both leadership and structure. We must face the sobering fact that we, as leaders and managers, do not have a methodology for approaching the key challenges that surface in emerging complexity. We just do not know what it takes to lead effectively from "in front of the blank canvas" when the ground under our feet erodes and pulls away.

From a structural point of view, the blind spot concerns the fact that most of the key issues of institutional development cannot be solved at the level of the organization. Today's organizations are often too big to deal with the small problems that are better solved locally, and too small to adequately address the big problems that must be considered in the context of the larger ecosystem of value creation.

What's missing? The "cross-institutional places" in which we could enable productive conversations among all key stakeholders, including supply-chain members, customers, the community, investors, innovators, and the stakeholders that are marginalized or voiceless in the current system. That's the institutional blind spot today. We must find room for all the key players in any given ecosystem if we are to gather and co-create our futures. It is time for us, as I describe throughout our field walk, to begin to lead from the emerging future.

CHAPTER 5

Shifts in Society

The Genesis of a New World • The Rise of a Global Economy •
The Rise of a Network Society • The Rise of a Cultural-Spiritual
Shift • Three Movements, One Stream • Arenas of our Social
World • Society's Blind Spot

The Genesis of a New World

At the end of Chapter 4, we came to the conclusion that because our institutional blind spots permeate both our institutional leadership and structure, we are met with a challenge: How can we produce productive conversations among all key stakeholders? How might we gather together the key players in order to co-create our future? To better understand how we might do that, we first turn our attention to some major shifts in society—major enough to be called the genesis of a new world.

When the Berlin Wall collapsed in 1989, followed by a ripple of disintegrating socialist systems in Central and Eastern Europe as well as the Soviet Union, many people felt the world was entering a new era. Nobody expressed this sense of anticipation more eloquently than the playwright and Czech President Václav Havel, who said in a speech in Philadelphia, "It is as if something were crumbling, decaying and exhausting itself—while something else, still indistinct, were rising from the rubble."[1]

Our task is to notice what's rising from the rubble. We are in the midst of three axial shifts that are redefining the coordinates of our global system. They are:

- The rise of the global economy: a technological-economic shift
- The rise of the network society: a relational shift
- The rise of a new consciousness: a cultural-spiritual shift

These shifts have created many good things, but also three types of poverty that define our age: economic poverty (three billion people living on less than two dollars a day), sociocultural poverty (a loss of inner values in a culture of materialism), and a spiritual poverty (a loss of connection to the collective body of humankind).[2] The deepening of these three poverties results in a backlash from three fundamentalisms that characterize our age: cultural-religious fundamentalisms, which are blind to the beliefs and values of those who are different; economic fundamentalisms, which are blind to the social, ecological, and cultural side effects of our global economy; and geopolitical fundamentalisms, which are blind to the multipolar and multicultural reality of today's global community.

The sociologist Manuel Castells of the University of California at Berkeley, in his book *End of Millennium*, argues that our current situation was formed from three independent processes in the late 1960s and early 1970s: the information technology revolution; the structural crisis and restructuring of socialism (perestroika) and capitalism (Reaganism, Thatcherism); and the blooming of cultural social movements such as libertarianism, human rights, feminism, and environmentalism.[3] What arose from this, according to Castells, is a new informational global economy, the network society, and a new culture of "real virtuality." For a new society to emerge, it will come from new relationships of production, power, and experience.[4]

The Rise of a Global Economy

A *world economy* is an economy in which "capital accumulation proceeds throughout the world." By contrast, a *global economy* is an economy with the capacity to work as a single unit "in real time on a planetary order." While a world economy has existed in the West since the sixteenth century, only in the late twentieth and early twenty-first centuries has the world economy become truly global on the basis of new infrastructures provided by information and communication technologies.[5] Three driving forces continue to reshape today's global economy: the globalization of capital; net-shaped, globally extended enterprises; and technology.

The Globalization of Capital

Since the collapse of the socialist economies in 1989–90, for the first time the whole planet is organized around a largely common set of economic institutions and rules.

Even though there are significant differences among the U.S., Japanese, and European economies, they share some of the same socioeconomic transformations:

- Downsizing of government
- Dismantling of the social contract between capital and labor
- Deregulation and privatization of state-owned industries (particularly in the telecommunications sector)
- Liberalization of financial markets
- Restructuring of corporations from relatively stable, domestically oriented and vertically integrated entities to dynamic, globally extended powerhouses that collaborate, dissolve, and reconfigure continuously according to the horizontal flows of value creation

Global financial markets and their networks of management are now the nerve centers of capitalism.[6] Because the flow of goods and services tends to produce random patterns of informational turbulence, we have seen severe crises and crashes in recent years: in Mexico (1994), the Asian Pacific (1997), Russia (1998), Brazil (1999), and Argentina (2002). These financial market crashes threw more than 40 percent of the world's population into deep recession.[7] As Castells summarizes it, "Money has become almost entirely independent of production and services by escaping into the virtual reality of electronic networks. At its core, capital is global. As a rule, labor is local."[8]

Net-Shaped, Globally Extended Enterprises

As industries have morphed into more open, fluid, and net-shaped constellations, the internal structure of companies has often done so, too. When I interviewed the strategy guru Gary Hamel, he emphasized that radical innovation requires the full diversity of the intellectual "gene pool." I asked him, "Where in the context of a larger company is there less diversity and more investment in the status quo?" Without a moment's hesitation, he replied, "At the top!" Teams at the top are least likely to come up with something really new. Yet executives generally have a monopoly on strategy making. Therefore Hamel focuses on seeding a team for innovation by selecting people who are young, located far from corporate headquarters, and recently hired.[9]

As organizations and strategists began looking outward rather than inward, the locus of innovation shifted as well. Traditional R&D groups focused on funding research staff in centralized corporate settings. New patterns, however, replicate Hamel's. They show movement from the center to the periphery. In the 1990s and early 2000s, the greater Boston area became a biotech research hub outside of corporate headquarters.

As a result, a dynamic innovation ecosystem was created by loosely connecting university institutes, research entities, and corporate R&D departments.[10]

Technology as the Driving Force of Innovation

The innovations that gave rise to the information and communication technologies (ICT) revolution were seeded twenty years earlier with the invention of the microchip, the development of the personal computer, and innovations in telecommunications infrastructures. In less than three decades the World Wide Web grew from a small network serving a dozen research institutions into an interconnected system linking millions (soon to be billions) of users, computers, and networks around the world. The revolution continues into biotechnology.

The challenge is to sense the next wave of (discontinuous) change and then to make it happen. The economist Brian Arthur calls this sensing capability "precognition." It is similar to presencing—and tuning in to the future that is about to emerge.[11]

Another issue concerns the ethical dimension of emerging technologies. The integration of robotics, genetic engineering, and nanotechnology confronts mankind with a future in which *Matrix*-type machines will control the evolution of the human species and in which the future won't need us any longer.[12] Is that *Matrix* type of future the inevitable trajectory we are on, or are we going to consciously choose a different collective evolutionary path?

The author Daniel Pinchbeck discusses the speed at which our technology moves this way: "The Stone Age lasted many thousands of years, the Bronze Age lasted a few thousand years, the Industrial Age took three hundred years, the Chemical Age or Plastic Age began a little more than a century ago, the Information Age began thirty years ago, the Biotechnology Age geared up in the last decade. By this calculus, it is conceivable that the Nanotechnology Age could last all of eight minutes. At that point, human intelligence might have complete control of the planetary environment, on a cellular and molecular level. This could lead to utopian creativity or dystopian insanity—perhaps both would arrive at the same moment."[13] But the choice is ours.

The Rise of a Network Society

Globalization of Governance

For the first time in history, the world economy is governed largely by the same set of institutions, including the United Nations, the World Bank, the International Monetary Fund, and the World Trade Organization. Each has its critics. Take the World Trade Organization, established in 1994, for instance. The WTO's Agreement on Trade-Related Aspects of Intellectual Property Rights criminalizes some traditional practices of seed saving and seed sharing by farmers in India and other countries. According to Vandana Shiva, a world-renowned environmental thinker and activist, "The

Agreement on agriculture legalizes dumping of genetically engineered foods on countries and criminalizes actions to protect the biological and cultural diversity on which diverse food systems are based." The key issue with today's globalization, says Shiva, is that the "resources move from the poor to the rich and pollution moves from the rich to the poor."[14] There is indeed tension between supranational institutions on the one hand and national sovereignty on the other.

Furthermore, the mechanisms that exist to provide valuable feedback to institutions of global governance are partial, distorted, or missing. The criticism of the World Bank and the IMF centers on the social, cultural, and ecological side effects of their structural adjustment programs (SAPs), first developed in the 1970s and since then implemented more than five hundred times.[15] These programs often result in a social and environmental race to the bottom rather than producing the intended prosperity for all.

In his book *Confessions of an Economic Hit Man*, John Perkins tells of his life as an insider in the global economic institutions. He describes how, time and time again, he intentionally participated in delivering inflated economic growth forecasts for various developing countries, which then, funded through the World Bank, got talked into oversized energy infrastructure investments. These investments benefited U.S. companies such as Halliburton but for the country at issue resulted in significant long-term debts and dependencies on the global North.[16]

While one part of the global South is moving into even deeper dependency, another group of countries has emerged as a set of dynamically evolving economies that are pushing the center of gravity of the global economic system from the North and the West toward the East and the South. The prime examples of these rapidly growing economic powerhouses are the five countries of the BRICS group: Brazil, Russia, India, China, and South Aftrica. The BRICS group is changing the global geometry of power from a primarily mono-centric system (with the OECD and particularly the United States in the center) to a more multipolar and multiregional world. Each country in the group functions as a driving force and anchor in the development of its region: South America (Brazil), the former Soviet Union (Russis), South Asia

(India), East Asia (China), and Africa (South Africa). Vis-à-vis these newly emerging countries, the countries of the triad European Union, United States, and Japan are also sometimes referred to as newly declining countries (NDCs), because their relative power and share of the whole keep going down.

The Network Society

In the network society, argues Castells, political institutions are bargaining agencies rather than sites of power. Power, however, does not disappear. It resides in the networked relationships and cultural codes through which people and institutions communicate. The global city is less a place than "a process by which centers of production and consumption of advanced services . . . are connected in a global network, while simultaneously downplaying the linkages with their hinterlands, on the basis of information flows."[17]

This brings us to the darker side of the network society—those who are not equipped with the right kinds of knowledge, skills, and networks are socially excluded and polarized. The loss of lifetime employment and social security and the weakened bargaining power of many workers have led to a higher incidence of family disruption. Castells calls these personal crises, loss of assets, and loss of credit the "black holes of informational capitalism." It is difficult to escape from these spiraling vortexes.

Perpetual Individualization

Robert Putnam, the author of *Bowling Alone*, uses the decline of bowling leagues as a metaphor for the steady drop in our civic engagement. He claims that by every conceivable measure, social capital has eroded steadily— and sometimes dramatically—over the past two generations. Living without social capital is not easy. Social capital, he says, is a strong predictor of life satisfaction. How can we replenish our lost social capital? And will our perpetual individualization continue to drive human history?

Today we are confronted with more choices about how to live our lives and develop our careers than ever before. Again and again, we are thrown into situations where we have to reinvent our professional, personal, and relation-ship lives—redefining who we are and where we want to go.[18]

The Rise of a Cultural-Spiritual Shift

There is a new revolution afoot. I call it the *revolution from within*. This sub-tle shift in personal and public perception may well have a profound signifi-cance in the twenty-first century for both individuals and businesses. Several forces seem to be driving this global shift: the birth of civil society as a global force, the rise of the creative class, and the emergence of a new spirituality.

The Birth of Civil Society as a Global Force

While Putnam was collecting his evidence about the decline of civic engagement in America, almost unnoticed—and exactly in the blind spot of his data gathering—civil society and millions of fast-growing non-governmental organizations (NGOs) emerged as a major force in the world. NGOs such as the Red Cross have existed for more than a hundred years, but in the past couple of decades their number has exploded. They've grown not only in number but also in their prominence, and abil-ity to precipitate change, according to the Worldwatch Institute. "They have cajoled, forced, joined in with, or forged ahead of governments and corporations on an array of actions as disparate as the decommissioning of nuclear reactors, brokering cease-fires in civil wars, and publicizing the human rights abuses of repressive regimes."[19] NGOs and civil society, using the Gandhi-inspired strategy of nonviolence, emerged as major actors and driving forces in the four pivotal historic events that shaped the last four decades of the twentieth century:

- The rise of the civil rights movement in the 1960s
- The rise of the environmental movement in the 1970s
- The rise of the peace and human rights movement and the collapse of the Cold War system and of communism in Eastern Europe in the 1980s
- The dismantling of apartheid in South Africa in the 1990s

Each of these four major events marked the spirit of that decade. In each, the underlying driving forces were the same: the power of civil society combined with a disciplined strategy of nonviolent transformation.

The globalization of governance was first created through the UN organizations at the end of World War II. The globalization of business and companies emerged only in the last couple decades of the twentieth century. It is just since the 1990s that NGOs and civil society have emerged as global actors.[20]

The Rise of the Creative Class

Another driving force of the revolution from within is described by Richard Florida of Carnegie Mellon University as "the rise of the creative class." It has created much of today's economic development. Some 38 million Americans, or 30 percent of all employed people, belong to this new class, whose core includes people in science, engineering, architecture, design, education, arts, music, and entertainment together with professionals in business, finance, law, health care, and other related fields. What do all these people have in common? Florida says it's a shared creative ethos that values creativity, individuality, difference, and merit. The key difference between people in the creative class and other classes lies primarily in what they are paid to do. Those in the working class and the service class are paid primarily to execute according to plan, while those in the creative class are paid to create and have considerably more autonomy and flexibility than other people.[21] What led him to these conclusions?

In 1998, while he was studying the locations of high-tech industry clusters, Florida met with a doctoral student who had been looking into the location patterns of gay people. When they put their studies together, they matched. "Though most experts continued to point to technology as the driving force for broad social change, I became convinced that the truly fundamental changes of our time had to do with subtler alterations in the way we live and work." Florida saw a common thread: the role of creativity as the fundamental source of economic growth and the rise of the creative class.[22]

What we are learning through studies like Florida's is that creativity can't be bought, sold, or turned on or off at will. But geographic patterns do emerge. Companies, particularly in the area of high tech, gravitate to the same areas and clusters where the people of the creative class settle. Because creativity requires an environment that nurtures its sources and many forms, people who rely on their creative capacities gravitate to areas that provide that stimulus and context. Florida believes that all attempts to rebuild the old forms of social capital are doomed to fail: "They fly in the face of today's economic realities."[23] This may explain why Novartis, the global pharmaceutical company, is following other European pharmaceuticals and moving its main R&D operations from Europe to the medical high-tech belt between Boston, New York, and Washington, D.C.

Just as competition in the creative economy changes, so do the fundamental social forms. The decline in the strength of our ties to people and institutions is a product of the increasing number of ties we have. We see more people in one day than many of our parents or grandparents saw in a month. As a result, we have to build and rebuild our own identities. We exist in a constant creation and re-creation of the self, often in ways that reflect our creativity.

The Emergence of a New Spirituality

Spirituality can be defined as the source of our creativity. It is distinct from religion, for it concerns experience and not belief systems. According to *Business Week*, a journal not known for its coverage of spirituality, a spiritual revival is sweeping across corporate America "as executives of all stripes incorporate mysticism into their management, importing into office corridors the lessons usually doled out in churches, temples and mosques." But spiritual events aren't happening only in exclusive executive circles. A case in point: "For the past six years 300 Xerox Corp. employees—from senior managers to clerks—have participated in 'vision quests' as part of the struggling copier company's $400 million project to revolutionize product development."[24]

Once, on a spiritual retreat in northern New Mexico, a dozen Xerox engineers saw a lone, fading Xerox paper carton bobbing in a swamp of old motor oil at the bottom of a pit. They vowed then and there to build a machine that would never end up polluting another dump. The eventual result: the design and production of the 265DC, a 97 percent recyclable machine. Those engineers went beyond their blind spot.

A McKinsey & Company study found that employee programs that include a spiritual component have led to significant productivity improvements and reductions in the turnover rate. "We have seen," reports a senior partner at McKinsey, "that change processes which include the dimension of personal mastery can lead to overcoming significant performance thresholds . . . not only for individuals, but for the team as a whole."[25] At the same time, such a finding, of course, also creates a problem: Will we now begin to misuse spirituality for the sake of increasing profit margins?

But the emergence of spirituality is not confined to the world of business. The sociologist Robert Wuthnow of Princeton University reports that 40 percent of all Americans claim to be currently involved in a small group that meets regularly and provides support or cares for its participants. Roughly half of these groups are church-related. It's a "quiet revolution" in American society that is redefining community in a more fluid way.[26]

This "quiet revolution" shows a ballooning interest in topics such as personal mastery, dialogue, and flow. The power of attention and the experience of flow, as described by Mihaly Csikszentmihalyi,[27] have long been cultivated in the practice of dialogue. At its essence, dialogue involves a collective shift of attention from politeness to conflict, from conflict to inquiry, and from inquiry to generative flow.[28] My colleague Bill Isaacs, the founder of the MIT Dialogue Project, has used dialogue as a change method in a steel mill, in a local health care system, and as a way to build leadership capacity in multinational companies.[29]

Is the rise of spirituality just an epiphenomenon of the baby-boom generation's growing more reflective, or is it related to a cultural shift in society at large? When I met with Francisco Varela, at one point he reached for an issue of the *Journal of Consciousness Studies*. It dealt with methods of accessing first-person experience—including meditation. "This would have been unthinkable three or four years ago," he said. And I concur. But now meditation practices are widely accepted, not only in my leadership seminars but in many other unlikely places. The sociologist Paul Ray's study of more than 100,000 people in the United States points to a profound shift in our culture. He divided society into moderns, traditionals, and cultural creatives. While the "creatives" represent only 26 percent of the population, it is the fastest-growing segment. Across Europe, cultural creatives account for 30 to 35 percent of the population. Characteristic of this group is their values of simplicity, sustainability, spirituality, and social consciousness.[30]

Yet, recent survey data have shown that the value shift toward the cultural creatives is countered by a backlash into a narrow, self-centered, reactive view, particularly (but not only) in the United States. According to a survey of 1,500 Americans by the market research firm Environics, the number of Americans who agree with the statement "To preserve people's jobs in this country, we must accept higher levels of pollution in the future," increased from 17 percent in 1996 to 26 percent in 2000. The number of Americans who agreed that "Most of the people actively involved in environmental groups are extremists, not reasonable people," leapt from 32 percent in 1996 to 41 percent in 2000.[31]

Three Movements, One Stream

When I met Fritjof Capra at a study group on systems thinking in the social sciences, we discussed countercultural movements and he said he thought they should always incorporate three aspects: the ecological, the social, and the spiritual. "The issue is that these movements tend to dissociate what in reality belongs together. When I realized that the New Age movement did not truly embrace the ecological, social, and political aspects of transformational change, I decided to dissociate myself from it." This made perfect sense to me. A couple of months later I happened to be in Oxford, England, in a dialogue workshop with leaders from various cultures and sectors. The gathering was framed as an inquiry into the emerging patterns of our time, particularly the widespread spiritual renewal evident to many of the participants from corporations, government, and NGOs. In sharing why we were there, I found myself talking about my own involvement with the three movements Capra had talked about.

I was sixteen years old, I told them, when I first "woke up" and started to think about political issues. Together with about 100,000 people from all over Germany, I went to the atomic power plant construction site at Brokdorf, one of the most famous European battlefields of the antinuclear movement of the 1970s. Brokdorf is a small village in northern Germany, close to my family's farm near Hamburg. We were protesting against the unhealthy alliance of the atomic industry and big state-owned electrical utility monopolies that sucked up tens of billions of dollars of taxpayers' money to subsidize a technology that carried more risks than opportunities in the eyes of the majority of the population. In retrospect we know that the massive subsidies and focus on the nuclear technology contributed to the fact that Germany missed the train on a much more important technological revolution: the ICT revolution, which began to take shape in the Silicon Valley area in California and the Route 128 area in Massachusetts at just about the same time.

The march in Brokdorf was not legal and the site was guarded by a massive police force, but things went peacefully until it was almost over. We had just started retreating from the main site to walk back to our buses and cars located a couple of miles away, when suddenly we heard a deep, rhythmic drumming and loud shouting. We turned to see hundreds, perhaps a thousand, heavily armed police drumming their batons on their battle shields and running toward us with a deep rumbling cry of attack. Everybody knew what to do next: run. They chased us over the fields like chickens. As the distance between us and the police closed, I first heard and then saw a swarm of helicopters approaching. They flew so low that people to my right and left were pushed down by the wind pressure. Without stopping, I looked back to see what had happened to them. Each was surrounded by baton-swinging cops.

Half an hour later, those of us who had escaped were walking quickly and quietly, tightly bunched together, on a broad highway back to our buses and cars. A deep red setting sun bathed the whole scene in cinematic light. When the sun had set, just before we reached our vehicles, the police attacked again, erupting from the woods to our left—out of total darkness—batons in hand and voices raised. As they approached us, something strange happened: everyone stopped walking and stood in absolute silence, body by body, as if the whole of us were one big collective form. Nobody ran. Everything stopped for a moment of total silence. Then the next moment they reached us. They began beating the people within reach of their batons. Still the crowd did not move. Their truncheons cut into our collective body like a knife through butter. After a little while they realized that no one was fighting back. The collective body remained still. Surprised by that, they stopped and soon retreated from their attack.

When I returned that night, my physical body was unharmed. But I came home a different person. Our collective body—the living body I became "one with" during that event—had been attacked and wounded, that is: *opened*. I felt that I had seen the enemy—an oppressive system that used physical force to push the agenda of a small special interest group against the vast majority of people in our country.

I knew then that my future work would involve transforming *that* system.

In 1983 I moved to West Berlin to study at the Free University. The Cold War still divided Berlin, yet powerful grassroots human rights and peace movements grew and flourished. I was surrounded by people who felt a sense of what was possible for themselves and society and who chose to live from that deeper sense of possibility and awareness. Whenever you crossed into Central Europe in those days, you could feel instantly connected to circles and networks of people whose openness to an emerging future was palpable.

Later, I sometimes wondered where all those people had gone. Then, during the mid-1990s, while I was attending the first semi-annual meeting of the MIT Learning Center, a nationwide gathering of advanced organizational learning practitioners, it hit me: all those people I missed from my Berlin days were now wearing business suits and operating in networks like this one at the Learning Center. The bond that connected us wasn't primarily an environmental or social agenda but a consciousness-raising and institutional change agenda. These people were interested in enhancing their access to sources of creativity, both individually and collectively. I had "come home" to a circle of people I had never met or even heard of before. The telling of this story in Oxford helped me clarify why single-issue movements hold so little appeal. Like Capra, I want to associate with people who work to reintegrate all three roots: the ecological, the social, and the spiritual. And like him, I am interested in doing this based on a new blending between science and consciousness, by going not backward into the past but forward.

Three Clashes and Root Questions

The three revolutions described above are patterns of a larger transformation process. Something is coming to an end. But what is the new structure that is currently arising from the rubble? We don't know. What we do know is that each of the three revolutionary shifts comes with a major backlash. The cultural-spiritual shift comes with a rise of cultural fundamentalism, leading to a clash of premodern, modern, and postmodern cultures. The shift toward a global economy comes with the shadow of an economic apartheid that excludes billions of people from having their basic needs met. The rise of the network society and of global multilateral institutions comes with a backlash of empire building that backfires and prevents new multilateral regimes like the Kyoto Protocol on climate change from working effectively.

At the root of these three conflicts—the socioeconomic, the geopolitical, and the cultural—we as a global society are confronted with three root questions. I find these root questions alive in the hearts and minds of people across various cultures and civilizations. They are:

1. How can we create a more equitable global economy that would serve the needs of all, including today's have-nots and the future generations?
2. How can we deepen democracy and evolve our political institutions so that all people can increasingly directly participate in the decision-making processes that shape their context and future?
3. How can we renew our culture so that every human being is considered a carrier of a sacred project—the journey of becoming one's authentic self?

In order even to ask these questions, we enter a common force field that drives the rise of civil society today. This common field incorporates:

- A deeply felt social sense that all of humankind is connected through a tacit, invisible bond or field
- A deeply felt democratic sense that eventually all legitimacy flows from structures that enable inclusive participation
- A deeply felt cultural-spiritual sense that we are on a journey of becoming who we really are—both individually and collectively

The common ground of these felt senses is a view of the human being as a being of freedom—as a being that is defined by the capacity to make the choice between acting in habitual ways and connecting with one's deepest source of creativity, ethical action, and freedom.

Arenas of Our Social World

The clashes and backlash that the transformation described above generates play out in three arenas of social life. They are (1) objective structures and systems, (2) enacted structures and processes, and (3) deep sources of enactment.

The First Arena: Objective Structures and Systems

The main focus of the founding fathers of sociology, Auguste Comte, Émile Durkheim, and Max Weber, centered around the first arena. They conceived of the social world as something that can be studied and described in terms of unchangeable laws, across space, time, and consciousness.[33] Comte, who coined the term "sociology," lived in the early nineteenth century and believed that history evolved in a linear sequence of successive stages from theology to metaphysics to positivism. Like Comte and the Catholic counter-revolutionaries, Émile Durkheim, who lived from 1858 to 1917, disliked social disorder. He studied the forces and structures that are external to and coercive of the individual. Max Weber, who died in 1920, emphasized rationalization as the foundation of a more or less linear development. He saw people trapped in an "iron cage" in which material goods have "increasing and finally unavoidable power over people."[33]

The Second Arena: Enacted Structures and Systems

The Chilean biologist Humberto Maturana noted that "all things said are said by *somebody*," so we can also say that all systems and structures are enacted "by somebody." Max Weber's social iron cage exists only insofar as people *enact* it in their everyday behavior and practice. Anthony Giddens claims that agency and structure must be seen as two sides of the same coin. Structure is reproduced in and through a succession of situated practices that in turn are organized by it. Jürgen Habermas, arguably the most important living philosopher and sociologist, sees society as the "systems-world" and the "life-world." Our relationship between the two, he says, is like colonization. "The imperatives of decoupled subsystems penetrate into the life-world—just as the colonists did into a tribe—and enforce their assimilation."[34] But both of these perspectives fall short of taking us to a deeper ontological point of view—the one Master Nan had in mind.

The Third Arena: Deep Sources of Enactment

None of our sociological scholars fully considered what Bill O'Brien called "the interior condition of the intervener." But we are at a stage now where we can begin to understand that our awareness and our consciousness determine the qualities of our actions and results. Habermas's notion of the Husserlian concept of life-world comes closest, but in Habermas's writings they capture only the rational dimension of discourse, not the deeper aesthetic-spiritual aspects of generative dialogue and flow.[35] In order to transcend these views, we may have to "go back to the data and to start all over again," as Ed Schein, the grand old man of organizational culture and change at MIT, put it. While the standard social science method tends to be based on observational data, Kurt Lewin and his successors, action science scholars such as Chris Argyris, Ed Schein, Peter Senge, and Bill Torbert, claimed that we have to use more than just third-person views. We need, as Bill Torbert has said, to access third-, second- and first-person knowledge. That is, we should incorporate observational, conversational, and first-person experiential data. But, of course, questions continue to pop up: How do you know that you know? What criteria help you to validate your knowledge?

> "I know that I know when my knowledge is actionable—that is, when I can produce it." (Chris Argyris)
>
> "I know that I know when my knowledge is helpful to the various clients and practitioners in the field." (Ed Schein)
>
> "I know that I know when I develop the capacity to create the results I really care about—when what you know allows you to create." (Peter Senge)

Each of these arenas stages a set of clashing forces. The left-hand column lists three arenas where social reality comes into existence. Each arena offers a distinct perspective on those three core issue areas Capra described: ecological, social-economic, and cultural-spiritual. Each issue has its own community of scholars and practitioners.

The first view or arena is governed by the philosophical metacategory of *objectivity*. This is the world of quasi-objective facts and things. Accordingly, the issues in this arena include *the social divide*: the gap and clashes between the haves and the have-nots (social justice); *the ecological divide*: the gap and clashes between civilization and nature (environmental protection); and *the cultural divide*: the gap and clashes between Western and non-Western civilizations (geo-politics).[36]

The second arena, *intersubjectivity*, is where the life-world is situated in a web of collectively evolving relationships. Here the same core issues are viewed through a different lens. From this perspective the social divide shows up as a clash between systemic imperatives and social living worlds (as discussed at length by Habermas).[37] The ecological divide shows up as a collision between linear industrial system designs and new, more ecologically intelligent design and systems ("cradle-to-cradle design").[38]

The cultural divide shows up as a gap between the worldview of Western

TABLE 5.1 ISSUE MATRIX

Arenas of Clashing Forces	CORE DIVIDES		
	Social-economic Issues	*Ecological Issues*	*Cultural-spiritual Issues*
Arena I: Systems **A 19th-century view: Primacy of objectivity**	Gap and clash between haves and have-nots (social justice)	Gap and clash between civilization and nature (environmental protection)	Gap and clash between cultures or civilizations (development)
Arena II: Agency **A 20th-century view: Primacy of intersubjectivity**	Clash of- systemic imperatives vs. life-world (critical theory)	Clash of old industrial designs versus eco- systemic design (cradle to cradle)	Clash of materialism versus antimaterialism (value shift)
Arena III: Sources **A 21st-century view: Primacy of transsubjectivity**	Separation of self from the other ° I-Thou (dialogue)	Separation of self from the senses ° awakening through our senses (sensing)	Separation of self from Self ° self-Self = connecting the current with the best future Self (presencing)

materialism, on the one hand, and various forms of antimaterialism, on the other. We often see both an overlay of Western materialism and consumerism across cultures and civilizations (the colonization of culture) and simultaneously the growing public resentment of such Western materialism. That cultural clash, however, also plays out within Western societies. For example, the strategic value method-based research from Ted Nordhaus and Michael Shellenberger gives an excellent example of tracking this cultural clash as a conflict between more traditional, more material and more post-material sets of needs and value orientations that shape the political discourse and create conflict within the United States and other Western societies.[39]

The third arena is governed by *transsubjectivity*. This is the most upstream perspective. It's the world of "living presence," as Husserl put it. This arena shows a new battlefield, where the most significant battle of our time is currently being fought: the arena of Self.

What is new here is how all of this is interlinked and grounded in the emerging arena of *sources* and *self*. If what you see in Table 5.1 were a tree, the first two arenas would be the leaves, branches, and trunk, but the third arena would be the root system—that part of the living system that is invisible to the eye.

At this deeper level, the root of the social divide is not outside but within. It is the self. To be more precise: it is the separation between *self* and *other*, which materializes in social conflicts (meso level, or midlevel), and in the social divide (macro level). As long as we aren't ready to face and confront this inner abyss, we are probably still stuck in premodern patterns, which will do nothing really useful to facilitate crossing the current abyss.

At the root of the ecological divide is the separation between the *senses* and the *self*. Here we enter the aesthetic dimension of ecological crises. The term "aesthetics" comes from the Greek word, *aistesis*, "sensual sensing"; it means activating all our senses. Unless we rediscover our senses as gateways to the living field around us, we will never resolve the environmental crisis. Just as the social divide reflects the loss of the other on an interpersonal level, the ecological crisis reflects the loss of the senses as gateways into the living field of nature. People often fill the void left by the loss of the senses with consumption—which in turn deepens the exterior manifestation of the ecological crisis.

Finally, investigating the spiritual question at this deeper level leads to perhaps the most significant clash: the clash between the *self* and the *Self*. It is the clash between one's old self, the person one has always been, and one's emerging higher self, the self that embodies one's highest future possibility—the Self that I first encountered when watching the fire that destroyed my family's home. On one side of that clash are all of one's accumulated accomplishments and ego forces, good and bad. On the other side is a source of possibility that, in order to come into presence, to be activated, requires one to *let go* of the old and open up to the now. The living connection between these two selves—self and Self—in the now is what I refer to as presencing.

Institutions rarely cross the boundaries of this issue matrix divide. Each field has professional graduate programs, training courses, research programs, funding mechanisms, international gatherings of experts, journals, and communities of practice. What's missing is the discourse in between. What's needed is for pioneering intellectuals to focus on all nine boxes at once. Some have begun doing this.

Manuel Castells's work, for instance, presents an integrative view of society involving the domains of production, power, and experience, although his work is stronger in the first two arenas, than in the third. His work describes the world that has taken shape over the past thirty years.

As we've already mentioned, Fritjof Capra integrates the biological, cognitive, and social dimensions of life. "Living systems," he says, "are self-generating networks that are organizationally closed within boundaries but open to continual flows of energy and matter."[40] Starting as a physicist, he applied the findings of twentieth-century systems science not only to biological life and cognition but also to social life. He described six life-sustaining principles of ecology that also pertain to economic systems and business ecologies:

- *Networks:* living systems communicate with one another and share resources across boundaries.
- *Cycles:* ecosystems generate no waste; matter cycles continually through the web of life.
- *Solar energy:* through photosynthesis, solar energy drives the ecological cycles.
- *Partnership:* life took over the planet not by combat but by cooperation.
- *Diversity:* ecosystems achieve stability through diversity—the more diverse, the more resilient.
- *Dynamic balance:* an ecosystem is an ever-fluctuating network: all variables fluctuate around their optimal values; no single variable is maximized.

He pointed out, however, that the crucial difference between the ecological networks of nature and the corporate networks of human society is this: in an ecosystem no being is excluded from the network. By contrast, many segments of our population are excluded from corporate networks. While his work offers a brilliant analysis of the networked nature of our current system, it offers less about what individuals acting alone or collectively can do to *shape* the new world or drill down into the third level of social reality.

The philosopher Ken Wilber's integral approach is probably the most comprehensive integrative framework developed to date. His "all-quadrants, all-levels" (AQAL) approach embraces the significant truths of premodernity, modernity, and postmodernity and integrates them in a synthesizing holistic framework. His framework is based on two sets of distinctions. The first one, built on Jürgen Habermas and Karl Popper's work, differentiates between three (or four) dimensions of the world: the It-world (objectivity); the We-world (intersubjectivity); the I-world (subjectivity); and a collective version of the It-world that Wilber calls "interobjectivity."

The second set of distinctions differentiates among the developmental stages of the self, which Wilber found to be the same in wisdom traditions across cultures and ages. Different traditions may use different terms, but the levels themselves are universal. One popular example of a developmental view that Wilber cites in his recent writings is exemplified in the influential work of Don Beck and Christopher Cowan, who distinguish among levels of consciousness in the preconventional, conventional, and postconventional stages of development and self.[41]

Wilber's "all-quadrants, all-levels" approach integrates all three dimensions of the world (I, We, It) and all nine developmental levels of consciousness. Wilber's integral view creates a framework and synthesis of diverse perspectives and intellectual traditions not described by any earlier philosopher. One of his major contributions is that his framework makes it legitimate to include the transpersonal or spiritual dimension in scientific, academic, and educational discourse. His definition of an integral approach—all quadrants, all levels—opens the door to a more comprehensive discourse that includes the more subtle aspects of reality that otherwise tend to be marginalized or left out. Wilber's integral framework continues to evolve and now includes "all quadrants, all levels, all lines, all states, all types."

Reading his work gives us a bird's-eye view of the "battlefield" of human and social development.[42]

A follow-on question that relates to this perspective is: What would a mapping of the battlefield look like if it were mapped from the perspective of the evolving self in the midst of battle on that field? We will return to this question later on this journey.

Society's Blind Spot

In November 1999, I was invited to join Master Nan and some of his students for dinner. Master Nan has written more than thirty books and is a revered teacher in China, but few have been translated or made available outside China. We discussed the rise of spiritual awareness and how it relates to the global issues of our time. "What has been lacking in the twentieth century is a central cultural thought that would unify all these things—economy, technology, ecology, society, matter, mind, and spirituality," he said. This decline in integrative awareness and thinking, we concluded, has been replaced by a focus on business and making money as the default common aim. Through his translator, Master Nan said, "It will definitely go this way—in a spiritual direction. But this route will be a different spiritual route from that of the past, either in the East or West. It will be a new spiritual path. It will be a combination of natural science and philosophy."

"The way I understand it," I responded to Master Nan, "is that the blind spot concerns our inability to see the process of the coming into being of social reality. We perceive our reality as a thing, as something that is separate from and outside us—something that happens to us. We don't see the process through which we bring forth social reality in the first place. And then I understood you to say that in order to illuminate this blind spot, you have to practice seven meditational stages of leadership that you talk about in your new book. Is that right?" Master Nan replied, "This understanding is right."

Our blind spot, from a person or people point of view, keeps us from seeing that we do indeed have greatly enhanced direct access to the deeper sources of creativity and commitment, both as individuals and as communities. It is one of our most hopeful sources of confidence because we can access a deeper presence, power, and purpose from within. From a structural point of view, the societal blind spot deals with the lack of these cross-sector action groups that intentionally operate from a future that wants to emerge. Instead, we see only special interest groups and three types of fundamentalism, each trying to solve our current mess in a single-minded way. This blind spot also keeps us from viewing the issue matrix as a whole. Castells, Capra, and Wilber have all been pioneers in moving toward integrating it, each from a different vantage point. But none fully meets Argyris's criterion for action research: that real knowledge enables you to create the reality it talks about. To discover this type of knowledge, we must trust our own senses, experiences, and insights—without having a clue as to where that journey will lead next.

Philosophical Grounding

Our Field Walk • Ontological and Epistemological Grounding

Our Field Walk

L et's pause for a moment to reflect on where our field walk or learning journey has taken us up to this point. First, we investigated how the blind spot shows up on the level of individual experience—as in my story about the fire. It was then that my own journey began, as I felt my old world going up in flames and the ground pulled out from under me. At that point I connected to that *other part of my self* that I didn't even know existed.

We spent a fair amount of time becoming acquainted with the U and started to identify with its parts. Then we investigated how the blind spot pops up in the experience of teams and how they learn. Teams face new challenges that cannot be addressed by relying on learning from the past. So we have to let go of the past, let it "go up in flames" and open up to the future that wants to emerge through us. This we call Level 4 leading and learning.

Next we investigated how the blind spot takes shape in the context of institutional experience. Leaders face new types of challenges that cannot be successfully addressed by conventional problem-solving methodologies. In order to deal with emerging complexity, we have to learn to drop our old tools in order to attend to and operate from the perspective of the blank canvas—that is, the source where organizational value is created.

Following that, we looked at ways the blind spot shows up in society, in the guise of the third revolution. That revolution, a beginning shift in consciousness, could help us to reframe the core societal issues more from a root or source perspective rather than just looking at the visible part of the "tree."

And finally, we took our field walk into social sciences, where the source of the blind spot concerns the inability to catch the process of social reality creation in flight. At each stage, we realize that we are thrown into situations calling for new attention and awareness. What does all this mean for us as "action scientists"?

Ontological and Epistemological Grounding

In 2000, I had another occasion to have a further in-depth conversation with Fritjof Capra. He and I walked together in a wooded area near the University of California, Berkeley, one September afternoon, discussing the new book he was writing. In it, he planned to apply his idea about systems theory and systems thinking to the world of social relationships.[1] I asked, "What do you consider to be the most important developments in systems theory and systems thinking over the course of the past century?"

He responded by saying he thought they all boiled down to two key developments: first, the welcoming by modern systems thinkers of the phenomenon of emergence, and second, the acceptance of the idea of embeddedness—that all systems and knowledge are situated in context.

On the flight back to Boston, I drew this little table that captured the two dimensions we had just talked about.

In the upper left-hand corner we have the old mainstream systems theory (S1), grounded in linear systems and explicit knowledge (K1). From that corner, we can progress in two directions: from S1 (linear systems) to S2 (nonlinear systems) accounting for the phenomenon of *emergence*; and from K1

TABLE 6.1: TWENTIETH-CENTURY SYSTEMS THEORY: EPISTEMOLOGICAL AND ONTOLOGICAL GROUNDING

	K1 *Explicit Knowledge:* **Independent of Context**	K2 *Tacit Embodied Knowledge:* **Situated in Context**	K3 *Self-transcending "Primary Knowing":* **Not Yet Embodied**
S1 Linear systems **Simple systems**	**"Old mainstream":** Conventional systems theory	**Situated action:** All knowing happens in a *context*.	
S2 Nonlinear, dynamic systems **Autopoietic systems**	**Nonlinear, dynamic systems theory:** Accounts for the phenomenon of *emergence*.	**"New mainstream":** Accounts for both emergence and being situated in context.	Blind spot: sources of knowing
S3 Sources of deep emergence **Self-transcending systems**	Blind spot: sources of emergence		

(explicit knowledge) to K2 (tacit knowledge), accounting for the fact that all knowledge is situated and *embedded* in context.

Etienne Wenger's and Jean Lave's concepts of situated learning and communities of practice, along with John Brown, Alan Collins, and Paul Duguid's concept of situated cognition[2] are examples of how the main focus of social systems theory has moved from (S1, K1) to (S2, K2). Like Capra's dimensions, these frameworks account for both phenomena: emergence and embeddedness.

In analyzing this table further, it became clear to me that my own investigation had drawn me closer to the interface between the light gray shaded and dark gray shaded squares. It is here that we face and encounter the extreme boundaries of human existence. Here we enter the uncharted territory that evolves at the edges of human consciousness. And it is here where we find ourselves grounded in the deeper philosophical assumptions about being (ontology) and knowing (epistemology).

Nietzsche once said that the highest goal would be *to view science from the viewpoint of the artist and art from the viewpoint of life*. To view science from the viewpoint of the artist means to apply scientific investigation not only to the object in front of us but also to the creative process and the scientist/artist who is performing that activity. Or in the words of Aristotle, science not only as *episteme* but also as applied art (*techne*) and practical wisdom (*phronesis*). To view art from the viewpoint of life means to perform the scientific activity in order to serve a deeper intention, to serve the larger evolutionary whole. That is, in the words of Aristotle, a scientific activity that would advance the frontiers of science toward including both wisdom (*sophia*) and the awareness or intuition of first principles and the sources of intention (*nous*).

Other philosophers who pushed my thinking deeper in those directions were Edmund Husserl and Martin Heidegger. By reading the work of Husserl, I came to better understand the epistemological boundary from the normal state of K1 awareness, which he called "natural attitude," to a K2 awareness, which he called "phenomenological attitude." By contrast, the work of Heidegger can be read as pushing the ontological boundary from a depiction of the world as an abstract set of things to a concrete *being in the world* that always happens from the background of a concrete context. Reality as viewed by Heidegger is not a "thing." Rather, it is a process of *coming into being*—a process of emerging from concealment into the open clearing of being. It represents a shift in perspective from S1 to S2.

Reading the late Husserl and Heidegger leaves one with a much more meditative sentiment along with the feeling that both were struggling with yet another boundary shift that would eventually turn the philosophical investigation to the source level on both dimensions: the epistemological (K3) and the ontological (S3). The epistemological question is: Where do our attention and knowing originate? This is Husserl's struggle with the issue of a transcendental self. And the ontological question is: What is the source of our collectively enacted social structures and processes? In other words, who is becoming present and acting through us when we engage in deep social or collective processes?

Yet Husserl and Heidegger both leave the impression that perhaps the most important aspect of their work is yet to be done—that is, to push the boundary of the philosophical investigation from the "what" (K1, S1) and "process" (K2, S2) levels to the "source" on both dimensions, epistemology and ontology (K3, S3). This is the work that these giants left for our generation and our century. *We* are to extend the philosophical and the scientific investigation from the upper left four boxes (representing the discourse of the twentieth century in philosophy and systems thinking) to the whole matrix of nine fields.

The implication for such an extension of the philosophical investigation in the twenty-first century is that philosophers and systems thinkers must leave their reading rooms and immerse themselves in the real world in order to actively participate in its unfolding. Such an action-science philosophy would engage in a different kind of knowing—the knowing of the heart. As the Japanese philosopher Kitaro Nishida has put it: "Knowledge and love are the same mental activity; to know a thing we must love it, to love a thing we must know it." Love, he continues, "is the power by which we grasp ultimate reality. Love is the deepest knowledge of things."[3]

When we learn to access that deepest part of the U, we begin to realize that love takes no position, as the author David Hawkins says. Love is global, he believes, and it rises above separation. "Love is unconditional, unchanging and permanent. It doesn't fluctuate—its source isn't dependent on external factors. Loving is a state of being. . . . Love isn't intellectual and doesn't proceed from the mind. Love emanates from the heart. It has the capacity to lift others and accomplish great feats because of its purity of motive."[4]

Our field walk is now about to take us for a close-up look at how we can lift ourselves and others across the threshold that has been at issue up to this point. We will review the threshold and the blind spot that we investigated so far and get poised for diving deeply into the bottom of the U and surfacing up the other side.

On the Threshold

Crossing the Threshold • The Signature of Our Time

At the beginning of our journey, we posed the question: Where does our action come from? To answer that question, we took a walk through the social field. We found that there is an invisible shift going on in the world. It's as if we were standing on a threshold, about to cross through a new doorway into rooms we could never before access. But something is keeping us from moving into these rooms and seeing the world from them. That hidden barrier is our blind spot, as well as our teacher. You will remember that we tracked the emergence of that blind spot across systems at all levels:

- At the individual level, we met the blind spot metaphorically described as flames, capable of destroying my old identity and clearing a space in which to encounter previously unknown aspects of my self.
- At the group level, we faced the blind spot as a team; our old approaches to learning—learning from the past—aren't getting us anywhere, and

thus we raise the questions: What would it take to connect to the subtle fields of future possibility? How can we learn from the future as it emerges?

- At the organizational level, we saw the blind spot as a new type of leadership challenge. Leaders face pressing issues that are high in emerging complexity and cannot be solved by using conventional problem-solving techniques. We raised the questions: How can we operate effectively in a blank-canvas situation, in which the world we are used to is crumbling? How do we reinvent our institutions as the ground under our feet is pulled away?

- At the societal level, we encountered the blind spot in the guise of three simultaneous global revolutions that are culminating at the beginning of this century: the rise of the global economy, the emergence of the networked society, and the development of new forms of individual and collective consciousness. As these revolutions transform the geometry of power across systems and cultures, we witness the crumbling and accelerating breakdowns and failure of the old institutional systems and structures, calling for radical new approaches to how to address the pressing issues and fundamental challenges of our time.

- In the social sciences, the blind spot shifted our focus from objective structures to the process view of enacted systems, and from there to the *sources* from which social reality formation originates. While the mainstream of nineteenth- and twentieth-century social sciences has been guided by the primacy of the meta-category of objectivity and intersubjectivity, the social sciences that are needed in this century and that might be helpful in dealing with the most pressing issues of our time have to include a third metacategory: the metacategory of transsubjectivity, which differentiates among structures of individual and collective attention as a defining feature of any social field.

- At the meta level of systems theory, we saw how the blind spot in systems thinking and philosophy shifts from entities to processes and from processes to incipient sources of emergence and knowing—that is, to the ontological and epistemological grounding of the situation we are operating in (our sources for both action and thought).

On each level we encountered the same fundamental shift of attention, a shift that extends the depths of reality perception to include the formerly invisible condition of the blank canvas—that is, the *source* of attention, intention and collective action. As the challenges at work, at home, and in our communities increasingly force us to deal with the manifestations of the blind spot in one way or another, we confront and encounter a fundamental threshold. We face that threshold as individuals, teams, organizations, and global social systems. In order to enter deeper territory and cross the threshold, we must confront the source level of the situation we are dealing with— we must learn to face our Self.

Crossing the Threshold

The word *threshold* comes from the age-old process of threshing—beating the husks away from the grain. So threshold literally means "sitting on the gold." Goethe's fairy tale of "The Green Snake and the Beautiful Lily" comes to mind here, when we think of thresholds and gold. In that story, we meet a green snake, beautifully illuminated by the gold she has swallowed. As the story goes, she finds four kings in a subterranean temple. One of the kings questions her about her ability to come to where they were. "How did you get here?" he asks her, and she replies, "Out of the clefts where gold dwells." Then the question is posed: "What is more glorious than gold?" and the answer is "Light." Then they ask her, "What is more quickening than light?" and she answers, "Conversation."

We can cross the threshold when we begin to function as a vehicle for something even more precious than gold or light. What we soon discover is that this threshold challenge is consistent across all systems. When we realize that our habitual way of seeing and acting is not getting us anywhere, we have to redirect and bend our beam of our (individual or collective) attention and redirect the edges of perception back upon its source, back upon the one who is performing the activity. When this shift happens, we begin to attend to the situation from a different place. The field structure of attention describes the realm between the visible world (what we see) as it meets the invisible world (the source or place from which we perceive it). When we change the way we attend, a different world is going to come forth.

When the fire burned my home to ashes, my field structure of attention changed from seeing the world through my habits of sitting in the class during the first part of the day (1), to suddenly seeing *it*: the smoke and the fire far off through a taxi window (2), to seeing the fire and the current self: experiencing a collapse of the boundary between observer and observed by standing in front of the fire and feeling the flames sinking into my mind and realizing that everything I thought I was, was gone (3). When time slowed down, I was at that threshold, about to cross over into "gold." A door was about to open between my old self and my emerging future self—that was my threshold moment. In that moment I began to cross it (4).

Threshold situations at the collective level display the same characteristics. They confront us with experiences that require us to bend, redirect, and transform our collective field of attention. When the Berlin Wall crumbled in 1989 and the World Trade Center towers collapsed twelve years later, we were confronted with two situations that invited us to deepen our perceptions and to open the boundary between the observer and the observed. In those fractured moments, some of us began to see how what is "out there" relates to our actions and identities "in here." Of course, not everyone crossed this threshold. For many, the collapse of the twin towers in New York City triggered nothing but the oldest and most tired habits of reaction: "An evil empire struck us from outside, so we must strike back in kind." The result of responding in that way (Level 1) to such a situation is predictable: it will create and magnify the problem that it claims to solve. Any Level 1 response is structurally blind to how one's own actions co-create the system (world) one lives in. A military superpower may be able to get away with such a low-level response for a few years, but sooner or later it will inevitably fail.

Unlike forceful nations, companies or NGOs in highly dynamic environments have to be much more responsive to the changes around them, to the "golden" opportunities that life is presenting to them. Like the green snake, they already glow. That is, they also have to learn how to harness the gold that their interaction with local contexts has offered to them. Some of them are agile enough to quickly reconfigure, reinvent, and realign themselves as needed. "Golden" organizations function as a bridge between two worlds, linking the current operational environment with the sensing and seizing of emerging opportunities. Crossing that bridge is the hallmark of organizational excellence and the key to high performance in rapidly changing environments. Being stuck on one side (current reality) or the other (emerging future) usually means mediocre organizational quality in stable environments—or going out of business really quickly in the case of fast changing environments.

The Signature of Our Time

Our professional and personal experiences require us to reach that lower subterranean level Goethe wrote: about the deep underground cavern where the green snake met the kings. It is the same level that we earlier referred to as the root system of the tree—that part of the field that usually remains invisible to the eye. We must confront these deeper levels of social reality creation by being willing to step over the thresholds of our time. So how do we know whether we are getting there?

Those thresholds or doorways usually begin to appear when our conventional ways of operating no longer work, when we hit a wall. We have to drop our old tools and redirect and bend the beam of our attention to the field unfolding around and within us. It's like a crack in our reality: suddenly that crack is right there, right in your face. Then you have the choice: brush over it, or stop. If you stop: drop your tools, attend to the crack that is opening up in front of you, tune in to that crack, redirect your attention into it. And then, go with the flow. The capacity to see the crack—to stop and then to tune right in to it—is a key discipline of our time. It's a discipline without which we cannot deliver high performance when it matters. It's a discipline that needs attention and cultivation just as the soil of any farm needs attention and cultivation. It's the discipline of tuning in to the U.

While the methods and tools farmers use to cultivate and improve the quality of their fields are well known, we often lack a similar body of methods and tools for cultivating the inner conditions of the social field in order to become more skillful at seeing, stopping, and tuning in to the crack. Part II, "Entering the U Field," will help us access those tools.

Look around. Something is happening. We might call it the signature of our time written large. It is inviting us to look beyond our blind spots and to open our eyes to the images that are beginning to take shape on our blank canvases. The challenges we face right now are pressuring us to look differently, to sharpen and deepen our attention. We need to cultivate the collective capacity to shift the inner place from where we operate.

I believe that all systems and all levels use the same fundamental shifting procedure or process. Whether you are a great leader, educator, artist, athlete, physician, writer, or coach, whether you work alone or belong to a team or organization, you cross the threshold by transforming the structure of your attention, by seeing and tuning in to the crack.

The Indo-European root of the word "lead" and "leadership," *leith*, means "to go forth," "to cross the threshold," or "to die."[1] Sometimes letting go feels like dying. But what we've learned about the deeper process of the U is that something has to change—a threshold must be crossed—before something new can come. The journey ahead of us entails uncovering and deciphering the principles and practices of that fundamental process so they can serve as a language that will help to illuminate the invisible leadership realm of the blind spot.

PART II

Entering the U Field

I n the Introduction, we discussed how my family went on a *Feldgang*, a field walk, every Sunday. It was the opportunity for my parents to connect with and investigate the current state of the fields across the farm. We stopped every now and then, bent over, looked more closely, and picked up bits with our hands. This book is our *Feldgang*—our chance to look at our blind spots with greater precision and clarity. One conclusion of the first part of the book is that in order to deal with the challenges of our time, we need to learn to shift the way we attend, the *field structure of our attention*. The way we pay attention—the place from which we operate—is the blind spot on all levels of the society.

IN PART II, we focus on the core process that allows us to shift the *field structure of attention*. That core process will help us to discern the different folds, turns, and territories of the blind spot. The body of knowledge resulting from this investigation is the basis of Theory U.

Theory U, at its core, makes a distinction between different levels of emergence, meaning different qualities of how action comes into the world. Theory U is grounded in the observation that any social entity or living system can operate from more than one inner place. The challenge lies in our *not seeing* and not activating the other places.

By mapping the topography of the blind spot, Theory U offers a language and a road map for crossing the threshold to authentic renewal and change. To accomplish this, we have to shift the place from which we and our systems operate. This is an enormous task, but it is, I believe, what leadership in our time is all about.

CHAPTER 8

Downloading

Patterns of the Past • The Field Structure of Downloading •
GlobalHealthCompany • Four Barriers to Organizational
Learning and Change

Patterns of the Past

Whᵃt we do is often based on habitual patterns of action and thought. A familiar stimulus triggers a familiar response. Moving toward a future possibility requires us to become aware of—and abandon—the dominant mode of downloading that causes us to continuously reproduce the patterns of the past.

When the Berlin Wall collapsed in the fall of 1989—followed by a ripple of collapsing socialist systems throughout Central and Eastern Europe, and the Soviet Union shortly thereafter—Western governments were quick to announce that this event had come out of the blue and that nobody could have anticipated such a geopolitical shift. Was that true?

Just two weeks earlier, I had been with an international student group on a study trip around the world, including through Central and Eastern Europe and the Soviet Union. During that trip, we talked with representatives of the official system as well as grassroots activists in civil rights movements. In many of these conversations, especially with the activists in Central Europe, we sensed that they anticipated a profound change. It was in the air. A pattern of the past was about to shift dramatically.

During our stay in East Berlin, a week prior to the collapse, the peace researcher Johan Galtung offered a public wager in his speeches that the Berlin Wall would collapse by the end of 1989. I vividly remember that no expert or analyst, on either side, had ever predicted anything like it before. I heard his statement with ambivalence. On the one hand, what Galtung predicted fully resonated with what we had seen in Eastern Europe. But then my mind reverted to old habits of thinking: Hasn't this system existed for half a century? And haven't these same problems, issues, and civic countermovements always existed? Budapest 1956, Prague 1968. People had tried to bring socialist regimes to their knees, but their efforts had amounted to nothing. Red Army tanks just kept rolling over people. The bottom line remained the same: the old system prevailed.

So there I was, twenty-seven years old and exposed to fresh evidence that the Eastern European socialist system was about to collapse. Yet in my mind I was *unable to recognize* what I had seen with my own eyes. I thought that Galtung's prediction was maybe a little off or far-fetched.

It was not. He was dead on. Having seen the Berlin Wall collapse on schedule (according to his prediction), I had to ask myself what had kept me from accepting the "truth" I had seen with my own eyes? Why did Galtung, who was exposed to the same data as we all had been during the trip, emerge with a clear conclusion, while I developed a murky "on the one hand, on the other" view?

The primary difference between me, the student, and Galtung, the master researcher, wasn't the amount of knowledge accumulated but a different way of seeing. He had a more disciplined way of *paying attention* to the world. He was able to *suspend* his habitual judgment and pay undistorted attention to the reality in front of him.

The Field Structure of Downloading

When we truly pay attention, we stop our habitual mode of downloading and open up to the reality in front of us. As long as our mental mechanism's

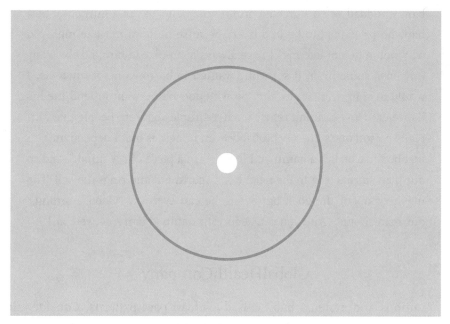

FIGURE 8.1 THE FIELD STRUCTURE OF DOWNLOADING

attention is guided by habitual patterns, the source of our attention originates from the center of our own organization. Figure 8.1 shows the mechanical structure of this field by depicting the *source* of attention and action (represented by the white dot) in the center of the *boundaries of its own organization* (represented by the blue circle).

Meetings and habitual conversations in organizations, for example, are often based on downloading past patterns. We collectively reproduce existing patterns of behavior and thought. When operating from the place of downloading—that is, from within the closed boundaries of our own organization—we are captured in our old world like a prisoner in a cell: there is no way out. We see only the mental constructs that we project onto the world.

The philosopher Paul Watzlawick gives a wonderful example of this type of operating:

> A man wants to hang a picture. He has a nail, but no hammer. The neighbor has one so our man decides to borrow it. But then a doubt occurs to him. "What if the neighbor won't let me have it? Yesterday he

barely nodded when I greeted him. Perhaps he was in a hurry. But perhaps he pretended to be in a hurry because he does not like me. And why would he not like me? I have always been nice to him; he obviously imagines something. If someone wanted to borrow one of my tools, *I* would of course give it to him. So why doesn't he want to lend me his hammer? How can one refuse such a simple request? People like him really poison one's life. He probably even imagines that I depend on him just because he has a hammer. I'll give him a piece of my mind." And so our man storms over to the neighbor's apartment and rings the bell. The neighbor opens the door, but before he can even say "Good morning," our man shouts. "And you can keep your damned hammer, you oaf!"[1]

GlobalHealthCompany

Institutions and systems habitually download past patterns. Consider the example of the GlobalHealthCompany (a fictitious name), one of the biggest and most successful companies in its industry.[2] A European branch of this company experienced a major breakdown after introducing a new product in the 1990s. The company hired a huge sales force to launch the product, only to find that the more effort it put into selling the product, the less successful it was. Eventually, a television program aired a report on the side effects of the product. The program investigators asked to speak with the managers, but the company declined. A year later, one customer who had been using the product died.

In retrospect, it seemed obvious that there had been warning signs about both the side effects and the fact that this product needed a specialized marketing approach. The question is: Why did the managers fail to see and recognize these early-warning signals?

The Manufacturing of a Corporate Virus

The answer to this question is deeply connected to both the culture and the history of the company. In *Organizational Culture and Leadership* (1992) Schein describes two principles that are essential to understanding what the company did wrong.[3] First, the role of the founder is always critical to under-standing an organizational culture. And second, today's organizational cultures are based on assumptions that are related to practices that have been successful in the past. Because all companies in existence today have, in one way or another, succeeded in the past, the current culture is always based on assumptions that have a long record of success. Here is how these two principles show up in the case of the GlobalHealthCompany.

Four CEOs

CEO I: 1960s

"The first general manager of GlobalHealthCompany came to us in the 1960s," says one of the senior managers who was with the company then. "His first job was to sell. He had very fixed ideas about the company. He ruled in a very authoritarian way. He built up a sales force, but he always maintained that our country was a special place—you could not sell the same way here in this country."

Some of that same dogmatism could be seen in the person of the path-breaking research figure at the headquarters as well. Says an employee of GlobalHealthCompany, "He would forbid anyone to talk to regulatory authorities about such side effects, because if there were a problem, it *could not* be from the product itself."

CEO II: 1980s

In the 1980s, a second CEO replaced the founding CEO. He moved the headquarters to a large city. "He was a ruinous leader," recalls another GlobalHealthCompany manager. "He sacked people outright if they did not agree with him. You were sacked if you said something about the company that you should not say—your job was to protect the company." He was aloof, and people rarely saw him in the organization. For all the first CEO's authoritarianism, you could say what you thought, even if you disagreed with him. Says the manager, "He might throw a tantrum, but you could speak out."

CEO III: EARLY 1990S

The second CEO lasted for three years and was followed by the third CEO in the early 1990s. He also was very authoritarian, like CEO I and CEO II, but he brought a different style. "He would go around and talk to people, and this went down very well, especially in contrast with his direct predecessor. He was autocratic, but people took it better because he knew them."

A senior R&D manager from GlobalHealthCompany recalls, "Then he got ambitious. He increased the number of people in the organization, especially the sales force, by a huge amount in preparation for the launch of the new product. He had good intentions, but he was taking over a difficult situation."

She continued, "Soon, he began to lose touch with the organization as it grew. Also, he was very dependent on only a few people to give him information about what was going on. The former research director, on whom he was quite dependent, required, like the corporate research director, only good news about the compounds.

"One of the disadvantages of the era of [CEO III] was that it was very marketing oriented. The head of marketing simply looked at sales calls. He believed that making more calls would increase sales, despite the high price and the documented side effects of the product. . . .

"He fought to keep the high price and he would not allow the reps to talk across the three lines, and the medical department was not allowed to talk to the marketing department.

"When the product's side effects became impossible to ignore, he [CEO III] did not want to talk to anyone outside the company who was critical of GlobalHealthCompany's actions. Now we realized that we must go out to our customers as partners, and deal with issues such as the side effects. But CEO III essentially said: 'Shhhhh! not so loud! Be quiet. Don't give so much information to customers, to newspapers.'"

CEO IV: MID-1990S

The senior manager recounts, "Right from the beginning, CEO IV took a lot of trouble to explain to everyone what he was trying to do. For the first time, we were introduced to an open policy, not closed meetings. And closed meetings went on all the time before."

Over the previous years, the example from management had resulted in similar behavior throughout the organization: building up a culture of not sharing information, holding meetings behind closed doors, and so forth. A manager recalls, "Knowledge was power, and people pretty much looked after themselves, covering themselves. There was almost a code of secrecy in the company."

Accordingly, the new and open style of CEO IV was greeted with skepticism. "People were not prepared to talk to each other, to share negative information. They still felt they could be sacked."

One of the actions that CEO IV took was to bring in a global consulting company to "reengineer" the organization. The outcome of the task forces that worked with the consultants was not surprising. The major issues the company had to work on were communication, customer satisfaction—working better with customers, the authorities, the public, all external constituencies. But then, instead of implementing the proposed changes, the reengineering effort was terminated in preparation for a major merger. This, of course, was exactly the result that many people had expected and predicted from early on: that all the talk about change would eventually result in nothing except more talk—no implementation. Another manager recounts, "There have been too many bad experiences in this organization with managers saying one thing and doing another, or not following through. We've had reengineering, process improvement, team projects. We have had lots of analyses but no implementation. In many projects, people worked hard, sometimes for a year or more, but there were no results."

The repetition of this pattern over time translated into cynicism. "People have to see results. But if management does not change, you can't expect people to change. We have lots of meetings and we work to produce results. They might as well be thrown in the wastebasket, because no one will implement them."

Summing up, another senior R&D manager said, "People have no trust in management, and the company is considered from the outside to be large and anonymous." She continued, "[GlobalHealthCompany] suffers from a virus—which is, sad to say, a legacy of its history. Even new people 'catch' the virus. They get infected very quickly, and that's a shame. Management needs to recognize that this is still a very bad situation."[4]

Four Barriers to Organizational Learning and Change

The case of GlobalHealthCompany illustrates the key issues that prevent a successful organization from moving past downloading and therefore running into trouble. The executive behavior that at first may be functional in a specific business context quickly develops a life of its own and turns into a habit throughout the organization. This creates increasingly dysfunctional behaviors that keep being reproduced and downloaded, just like a virus in an organism. Executive behavior that at first happened to be useful is downloaded and disseminated throughout the organizational culture, where it infects the members of the organization with learning disabilities that prevent them from seeing and dealing with the realities the organization is up against. Four learning barriers keep the virus alive and keep the system locked into the mode of downloading:

1. Not recognizing what you see (decoupling perception and thought)
2. Not saying what you think (decoupling thinking and talking)
3. Not doing what you say (decoupling talking and "walking")
4. Not seeing what you do (decoupling perception and action)

Barrier 1: Not recognizing what you see

The behavior of the first CEO eventually resulted in learning disability. "He had very fixed ideas about the company. He ruled in a very authoritarian way." Like most founders and pioneers, CEO I trusted his own ideas (what he believed) more than he trusted the data that the world presented to him (what he saw). All pioneers act on the primacy of their vision over current reality. However, if this type of behavior is not transformed over time, any chance for success is blocked by repeatedly downloading behavioral patterns.

This very quickly becomes an obstacle to moving the company forward. Hence, the legacy of Barrier 1 behavior is an inability to recognize what you see. In the case of GlobalHealth, its executives didn't see the side effects of the drug.

Barrier 2: Not saying what you think

CEO II's behavior caused the second learning disability: not saying what you think. "He sacked people outright if they did not agree with him. You were sacked if you said something about the company that you should not say." This kind of executive behavior forced people to develop the second component of the corporate virus. In order to survive under this executive, other managers, too, had to learn *not to say what they thought.* Anyone who violated this rule got fired, i.e., erased from the "gene pool" of that corporate culture. The only behavior that ensured survival and was passed on was keeping quiet about what you thought; that is, engaging only in conversations that reproduced the company line. This element of the corporate virus prevented the company from learning from its own experience and not repeating the same mistakes.

Barrier 3: Not doing what you say

CEO IV tried to change the culture that was based on the first two virus components but failed when he didn't do what he said he would do. A lot of talk about reengineering and change was not translated into action. Those who acted on the assumption that leaders do what they say found themselves wasting their energy and thrown into deep frustration. On the other hand, those who saw that all the talk about change was just that—talk—were better off because they did not invest their time in grand projects that eventually went nowhere.

Barrier 4: Not seeing what you do

The fourth component is not seeing what you do. That is, all of the executives had blind spots about that fact that their behavior had led to the creation of the four learning disabilities.

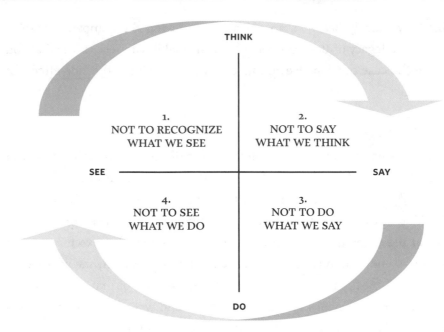

FIGURE 8.2 FOUR BARRIERS TO LEARNING AND CHANGE

The story of GlobalHealthCompany illustrates how deeply the institutional mechanism of downloading is embedded in organizational culture and what a powerful force it is for reproducing the patterns of the past. It is a force that individuals often view as impossible to change.

The first step in the U process is to learn the skill of "stopping downloading." This applies to all areas: individuals, groups, organizations and even societies. Stopping downloading is the precondition for entering the U process. Only when the downloading ends can we wake up and see the reality, which brings us to the next cognitive space of the U: seeing.

Seeing

How We See • The Shift from Downloading to Seeing •
Seeing in Action • Field Notes

How We See: The View from Outside

W hen we stop the habit of downloading, we move into the state of see-ing. Our perception becomes more acute, and we become aware of the reality we are up against. If we operate from this cognitive space, we perceive from the periphery of the organization, at the boundary between observer and observed. Take, for instance, what happened when Goethe tried to see Newton's "phenomenon of colors," as the physicist Arthur Zajonc recounts in *Catching the Light*.[1] It was January 1790, and Goethe was being pressured to return a box of optical equipment he'd been keeping in his closet. In the box was a prism. A servant stood waiting to retrieve the box as Goethe hastily pulled out the prism in a last attempt to see the rainbow that Newton had seen. Instead, he saw something very different in the January light. Arthur Zajonc explains that Goethe "looked at the white walls of the room expecting them [according to the Newtonian theory] to be dressed in the colors of the rainbow. Instead he saw only white!" In that moment, he knew Newton was wrong.

Surprised, Goethe turned again to the window, whose dark cross frame stood out sharply against the light gray January sky behind it. There, at the edge of the frame and sky, where light and darkness met, he saw bright colors.

The Shift from Downloading to Seeing

At the moment when Goethe lifted the prism and looked, the place from which his attention operated (the white dot in Figure 9.1) shifted from the center of his organization—that is, inside his world of habits and routines—to the periphery, that is, right at the edge of his organizational boundary (the blue circle). From there he was looking out of the window of his organization onto the world that presented itself in front of him.

When I went to school on the morning of April 11, 1978, I followed a host of daily routines: riding the train, walking through the park between the train station and the school, reading the weekly *Der Spiegel* during class instead of paying attention to the usually much less interesting class conversation, and

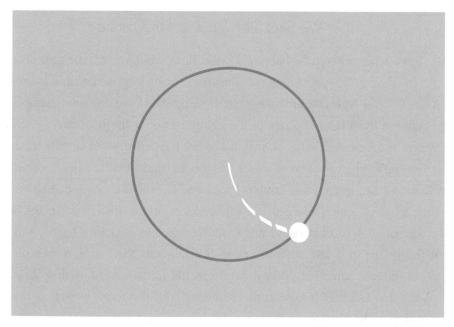

FIGURE 9.1 THE FIELD STRUCTURE OF SEEING

so on. But these actions, based on downloading routines, started to change when I began paying attention to two observations I couldn't make sense of: the red eyes of the teacher when she talked to me and the dead phone line when I tried to call home. As I was sitting in the taxi, my field structure of attention shifted completely: suddenly I saw what was going on—the sky was darkened by black clouds rising from the place where the farm used to be. I, the observer, was still sitting in the taxi, but the membrane—the front window—was transparent and allowed me to recognize what was happening outside (observer is separate from observed).

The shift from downloading to seeing is simple—although not always painless. Sometimes it happens without visible activity on the side of the observer, as in the case of the fire. All I did was be a witness to it. Sometimes it requires much more discipline on the part of the observer, as it did with Goethe's prism. Goethe was said to be an extraordinary master of observation who, throughout his life, cultivated his capacity of perception.

Three distinct principles can help us move from downloading to actually seeing. They are: (1) clarify question and intent, (2) move into the contexts that matter, and (3) suspend judgment and connect to wonder.

Clarify Question and Intent

While traveling and working with the peace researcher Johan Galtung, I noticed that when taking questions after giving a talk, he would often scribble something on his notepad before responding. When I asked him what he wrote, he said that whenever he was asked an interesting new question he would first write it down—not his response but the question—because otherwise he might forget this important input. Good questions, he said, are raw materials for making good science.

When working with senior designers from IDEO, sometimes called the world's most influential design company, I was amazed to see how much time the designers spent up front, before beginning a project. "The quality of the creative design process," explained one IDEO leader to me, "is a function of the quality of the problem statement that defines your starting point." I used to think that to be creative meant you were open to all possibilities all the time. Not so. Just as scientists clarify and crystallize a research question before beginning an experiment, so too must designers clarify their task. Only much later did I learn that having a clear research question or problem statement up front does not mean you can afford to be blind to emergence. You can still be attentive to what is emerging slightly off tangent, but you must do so in a fully conscious way.

Move into the Contexts That Matter

The context can be thought of as a living lab, the place where the activity of observation is performed. Christopher Alexander, the mathematician-architect believes that the ultimate object of design is form and pattern. He explains, "The form is that part of the world which we decide to shape, while leaving the rest of the world where it is. The context is that part of the world which puts demands on this form . . . the form is the solution to the problem; the context defines the problem."[2] In Goethe's case, he created a context that allowed him to observe what he was interested in (seeing the colors through the prism). In the case of management and social sciences, this laboratory is often situated in a living social context, such as Eastern Europe when Galtung and our student group were visiting. However, in both cases the observers moved into a context that allowed them to study and observe the phenomenon up close.

Over the past two decades or so, many companies and organizations have been getting smarter about moving into the context of customers, partners, and suppliers. What started as talking *about* customers and then shifted to talking *with* customers now appears to be shifting toward accessing the experience of customers in order to learn about their untapped capabilities and unmet needs. However, it is one thing to talk about customer experience and another to actually access it.

To illustrate the primacy of moving into context for developing the capacity to see, Francisco Varela shared with me the story of a cruel experiment with kittens. It takes newborn kittens a couple of days to open their eyes. In this experiment the newborn cats were bundled in pairs of two, with one on the back of the other. In each pair only the lower kitten was able to move. The upper kitten (the one on the other's back) experienced the same spatial move-ments—but without performing the legwork, which was left to the lower cat. The result of this experiment was that the lower cat learned to see quite nor-mally, while the upper cat did not—it remained blind or its capacity to see developed in very insufficient ways. The experiment showed (and Varela's point was) that perception isn't passive. Perception is an activity that the body enacts.

We, as the "upper cat" in knowledge management and strategy work, hire experts and consultants to tell us how the world works instead of figuring it out ourselves. We outsource the legwork. For simple problems, this may be an appropriate approach. But the greater the complexity of a situation, the more important it is *not to outsource*: one must stay in touch with the issue as it evolves. Without a direct link to the context of a situation, like the upper cats, we cannot learn to see.

Suspend Judgment and Connect to Wonder

Charles Darwin, the father of modern evolutionary theory, was known to keep a notebook with him to capture observations and data that contradicted his theories and expectations. He was well aware that the human mind tends to quickly forget what does not fit into familiar frameworks. Like Goethe, who suspended his judgment about colors in light, Darwin also knew that today's disconfirming data are the raw material of tomorrow's theory innova-tions, so he wrote things down before his mind conveniently forgot what it didn't know how to catalog.

Where, in our major institutions today, do we have mechanisms that help to perform the suspension of judgment? What comes to mind are a few examples such as "brainstorming" and "deferring judgment." But by and large our conversations and interactions within and across institutions are structured so that we are encouraged to voice opinions and to articulate judg-ment rather than suspend it.

But it is only in the suspension of judgment that we can open ourselves up to wonder. Wonder is about noticing that there is a world beyond our pat-terns of downloading. Wonder can be thought of as the *seed* from which the

U process grows. Without the capacity for wonder, we will most likely remain stuck in the prison of our mental constructs.

Wonder is one of the greatest gifts that children bring into our lives, for children embody wonder in the purest sense. But to develop this capacity more fully, children need to have it reinforced in their environment. Growing up in a social context that doesn't include wonder is like a plant trying to grow without water.

I have found that the more profound a person's knowledge, the greater the likelihood that this person has cultivated a capacity for wonder. And the narrower, shallower, and more limited a person's knowledge, the less likely it is that this person will have cultivated a capacity for wonder.

A few months after interviewing Brian Arthur, I met with one of his colleagues at Xerox PARC, Jack Whalen. Whalen is a highly respected expert on knowledge communities and ethnographic observation. Captivated, I listened as he told me how he had developed an ethnographic method for observing and analyzing people's work *practices*. At the end, I asked him, "If you apply your methodology to yourself, what are your own most critical work practices? What work practices do *you* use that allow you to perform your kind of work?"

He reflected for a moment and then said, "Building relationships with people and cultivating a deep interest in other scientific disciplines." He paused. "And wonderment. Essentially what I do is to develop a discipline of endless wonderment. Oh, look, look at this world!"[3]

While the capacity for seeing is difficult for individuals to develop, it is even more challenging in the collective context of organizations. Yet it is a critical function of leading change. Some say it is *the* critical function.

Most efforts to bring about change do not fail because of a lack of good intentions or noble aspirations, but because their leaders fail to fully *see* the reality they face—and act. I first learned this from Ed Schein in his course on managing change at MIT. But I only came to appreciate it fully when I witnessed it myself.

In his classes Schein always emphasized that the most important principle of managing change is to "always deal with reality"; that is, start by seeing what is actually going on. Our challenge is to find a way to cultivate and enhance the collective capacity of seeing.

Dialogue as Seeing Together

David Bohm and Bill Isaacs define dialogue as the art of thinking together. Giving this definition a little spin, I suggest defining dialogue as the art of *seeing together*. This variation seems minute, but it has very concrete methodological implications.

Why do I insist on the primacy of perception? Throughout my life I have never come across a situation that was too much for a person to face (although such situations certainly exist). Whenever I saw breakdowns happen—both inside and outside of organizations—they always resulted from denial; that is, from *not* seeing, from *not* facing.

On the other hand, I have been amazed that regardless of how difficult a situation may seem, at the moment you choose to actually look at the situation, to look straight into its ugly face, new powers to deal with it are given to you. And the interesting thing is that those powers always match the challenge that you are presented with. Remember the physician who expressed amazement that the forces of denial were so weak in comparison with people's capacity to face the most horrible situations imaginable? Compare this with the sad story of GlobalHealthCompany. The issue there was not that the various CEOs lacked aspirations or vision. They all had lots of vision, core values, and purpose statements. No shortage there. But the issue was something else. The issue was that all four CEOs increasingly lost touch with reality—they lost touch with what really was going on. They failed to see reality. And then the more they applied pressure—using the mind-set of "driving change"—the more the system pushed back. People resist change only if they are asked to make difficult changes and sacrifices without being able to see the bigger picture and understanding the context that makes change necessary. This led some of the salespeople in GlobalHealthCompany to say, "We're supposed to generate sales like adults, but in terms of what's going on in the organization, we're being treated like children."

Seeing reality together may sound easy, but it is extremely challenging to do properly. Many leaders, like those four CEOs, are unable to see the reality that faces them.

Contrary to wide belief, I do not think that a leader's primary job is to create a vision, goals, and direction. Too often this limited view turns into a liability and prevents organizations from being in touch with what's really going on while their leaders go about broadcasting what they think the next change program should be about.

The primary job of leadership, I have come to believe through my work with Schein, is to enhance the individual and systemic capacity to see, to deeply attend to the reality that people face and enact. Thus the leader's real work is to help people discover the power of seeing and seeing together.

Seeing In Action: The Patient-Physician Dialogue Forum

In 1998 my colleague Dr. Ursula Versteegen and I started a new project with a regional network of physicians in Germany.[4] At that time Ursula was the chief knowledge officer of a Munich-based health care start-up, and she and I had been working with this regional health care network for more than two years. As the network was entering a new phase of negotiations with insurance companies, we met with the core group of physicians in the network initiative to prepare for a meeting of the entire network that was scheduled for the following week. Representatives of the insurance providers were about to announce whether they would fund the emergency care project proposed by the physician network.

The physicians, whose network depends on insurance companies to administer and control health care budgets, expected the insurance companies to back out of the plan, and they began complaining that they depended too much on "these bureaucrats." You could feel the energy in the room go down. People started eyeing their watches. But when it was almost over, the evening took a surprising turn—all because of George.

When we first entered the room that evening, I was walking in with somebody whom I hadn't met before. We said hello, and I asked where he was coming from. His name was George, he said, and he had just returned from India, where he had been leading a project that had created a mobile hospital to serve a local slum area. "Wow," I said, "that sounds interesting," and thought that I'd love to hear more. Once the meeting started, I forgot about our brief exchange until just before the meeting was over, when our eyes met and we knew we were having the same thought: "What the heck is going on here? Why is everybody's energy level so low?" I took a chance and asked him whether he would mind telling us about his India project. It didn't have any obvious link to our discussion, but I had a hunch that it could provide a different perspective. As he began to speak, you could literally see the field around this man charging up. Ten minutes into his story, the whole crowd was part of the energy radiating through him. Leaving the meeting on schedule was no longer an option.

"I was on holiday to India. By chance, I met a physician who ran a nearby rural hospital. He told me about the medical conditions in the slum of a town with six million people. He showed me around, and when I saw the conditions in the slum I intuitively felt that there must be a way to make a difference. A vision began to form: we could create a local-global project for providing basic medical care to that community. So I started to work on a plan and dedicated all my energy to putting this vision into reality. It has been a long journey. Several times it looked as if we would fail. But every time I saw the problems grow, I ended up responding by heightening my level of focus and energy. I simply couldn't give up. I *couldn't not* do it.

"I nearly gave up at one point, though. I had convinced my best colleagues from all over the world to spend their vacation time on this project, and they had agreed to work in India without pay. We had medical equipment ready, all the donations in place, and I got a call saying 'We're sorry, but we have to cancel the aircraft that we promised you.' Dejected, I left for Frankfurt, and en route I struck up a conversation with a man to whom I told this story. Within days, I got a call from his office. He was the CEO of Lufthansa. 'We would like to help.' They delivered our equipment and twenty-seven physicians to Hyderabad, India, almost free of charge. For twelve hours a day, we examined and treated patients—about a hundred a day. We worked in

schools and in tents. Within ten days, we provided medical support for fifteen thousand people.

"Today more than a thousand volunteers are engaged with Humedica, the
organization that we co-founded with our colleagues in India. Eight hundred
of them are doctors, nurses and emergency assistants. But without that miracle help regarding the air transportation on our first mission, nothing of
that would exist today. If we had not had a success at that first time, there
would be no Humedica doctor team now."[5]

It was then that Ursula spoke up: "Thank you, George. Your story makes
me wonder whether our physicians' network project presents problems too
big to solve—or too small to be inspiring."

So we asked ourselves, "Where is the real need in this system—the local
equivalent of the Indian slum George had just told us about? What is the
higher purpose that could *mobilize people's best energy* and commitment?"

What surfaced were comments like this: "You know, everybody talks about
health care reforms and patient-centered health care, but it's rare that people
talk with the *patients* about their experiences." So we began asking questions
such as: How do patients experience their patient-physician relationship?
How do they experience health? What is health, as defined by the patients?
Where do their illnesses come from? What are the deep sources of people's
health and illness?

These questions probed deeply into the first-person dimension, into the
actual *experience* of the current health system from the perspective of the
patients. Up to that point, this had been a significant blind spot in current
outcome-based medicine research.

We quickly developed a plan to conduct dialogue interviews with 100
patients in order to learn how they experienced health and sickness in their
lives, and with their 35 physicians. Three students who had been invited as
guest participants at this meeting offered to undertake the interviews as part
of their thesis project.[6] The next morning we gave the students some feedback on their initial interactions with the physicians the day before. Then we
continued with a half-day training session on how to conduct dialogue and
deep-listening interviews (see Figure 9.2).[7]

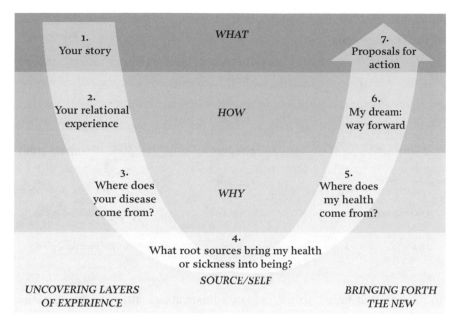

FIGURE 9.2 LANDSCAPE OF LISTENING

Shortly after that, the students began their study by shadowing some of the physicians for two weeks in order to get a sense for the larger field that they were about to enter. Only then, having experienced the routine of day and night emergency calls themselves, did they begin to conduct the 135 interviews.

Three months later, on a chilly Saturday in February 1999, we invited all of the interviewed patients and physicians for a daylong feedback session in the elementary school of a nearby town. Of the 135 interviewees, nearly 90 showed up. After the preliminary welcoming remarks, we presented our findings in the form of an iceberg-shaped figure that depicted four different layers of the patient-physician relationship, each of which related to a level of understanding about health and the mind/body connection (see Figure 9.3).

Level 1: Broken Parts

On the first level, health issues are simply perceived as broken parts that need to be fixed quickly. One patient said, "I go to the doctor with a problem and expect him to solve it. My role is that I need help. The role of my doctor

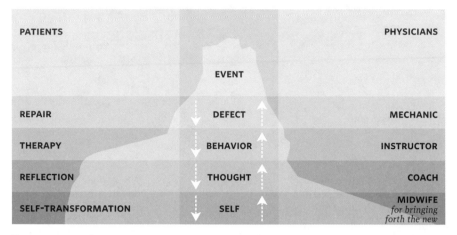

PATIENTS		PHYSICIANS
	EVENT	
REPAIR	DEFECT	MECHANIC
THERAPY	BEHAVIOR	INSTRUCTOR
REFLECTION	THOUGHT	COACH
SELF-TRANSFORMATION	SELF	MIDWIFE *for bringing forth the new*

FIGURE 9.3 FOUR LEVELS OF THE PATIENT-PHYSICIAN RELATIONSHIP

is to provide that help." In the case of a heart attack, for example, a patient would expect a doctor to provide emergency treatment.

Level 2: Behavior

Almost every health issue a person deals with is caused by a behavior. A heart attack might be caused by stress and overwork; and so forth. In this regard, one patient questioned her experience and relationship with the physician: "Does it always have to be a pharmaceutical treatment? I say no, not for me. I want to be told: 'It's your attitude, you must change your behavior. You must do more for yourself.'" On this level, the role of the doctor can be that of an instructor: giving the right instructions to the patient to change his or her behavior.

Level 3: Thought

Addressing health issues on the level of behavior sometimes works—but sometimes we have to take our approach to a deeper level. Behavior originates from people's assumptions and habits of thought—what matters most from our point of view. A heart attack may follow from certain assumptions about work and family that lead to putting one's career first, leaving no time for family and friends, the people one is working so hard for. As one patient told us, "One becomes sick in order to think." When you say you don't have the time, time will be forced on you through illness. I am quite certain about this. What are my future plans? When you don't care about those and you don't consider life to be a gift, you become sick. Boom. Forced to think. Many people tell me, "I didn't realize how life was or how important it is that I am alive. You take it for granted." For people operating on this level, the role of the doctor is that of a coach who helps his patient to reflect on his life and patterns of thought.

Level 4: Self-Transforming Presence

Finally, there is a fourth level that is even deeper than the other three. Here, issues of health are seen as the raw material for a journey of personal development and inner cultivation. They invite us to access the full potential of one's inner sources of creativity, to embark on a journey to who one really is. "I am somebody who never got sick," a woman told us. "And then all of a sudden I had cancer. I used to be the entertainer everywhere. I worked hard, I was a member of various committees, and I just ignored the fact that I was sick. It was a fight. I didn't want it to be in me. I told myself: just ignore it. I went back to work full-time, with the result that two years later I had a breakdown. I was forced to stop working. Afterward, after surgery, I went to therapy and I learned to talk about my disease, just as I am doing with you now. You know, I only learned at the age of fifty-eight to say 'no.' Before, I was always ready to go. I always functioned. I didn't even realize that I had lost my identity on the way down. And now I am not concerned about my future anymore. Today's important to me. *Now.*"

On this, the fourth level of the patient-physician relationship, the role of the physician is that of a midwife of the new. After the presentation, we asked participants whether they felt these four levels adequately represented their experience. They discussed the question first in small groups and then in the large group and agreed that this was at least a useful way of putting it. Then, just before taking the morning break, we asked the participants to vote. Each participant voted with two dots placed on a large chart: a blue one to mark where they believed the current health care system operated, and a white dot to mark the level of their desired future health care system.

Field Notes: Developing the Collective Capacity to See

In looking at the Patient-Physician Dialogue Forum, we can see how the following four principles created what we called a Patient Landscape of Listening.

1. *Crystallize intention.* When the core team had almost finished setting up the room for the forum the night before, we gathered in a small circle, all of us standing, for a very short intention-building session. Each of us would say in a single sentence what we considered to be the ultimate purpose of the event the next day. Once every individual had articulated that purpose, we closed with a brief moment of silence and got back to work.

2. *Move into context.* We connected with each and every participant through the interviews before the session. In these deep-listening interviews people told the story of their life's journey—that is, they shared the context they were coming from.

3. *Suspend judgment and connect to wonder.* One of the most effective mechanisms for suspending judgment and connecting to wonder is to draw people into one another's first-person stories. The first step of this happened in the one-on-one interviews.[8] The second step happened during the presentation, when we quoted the patients themselves. There is nothing as simple and powerful as using people's own words to articulate essential aspects of the collective experience.

4. *Dialogue: enter the space of seeing together.* The process of seeing together evolved through three different activities. First, people listened to the concept of the four relational levels and the examples that brought these levels alive. Second, they related to their own and other people's experience (in small-group discussions). Third, they came to a collective assessment through voting. Which brings us to the continuation of the story: sensing.

CHAPTER 10

Sensing

The Patient-Physician Dialogue Forum • The Field Structure of
Sensing • Principles • Sensing in Action • Two Types of
Wholeness • Epistemological Reversal • Field Notes

When moving from seeing to sensing, perception begins to happen *from the whole field*. Peter Senge believes that this turn is at the heart of systems thinking. It's about closing the feedback loop between people's experience of reality ("what the system is doing to us") and their sense of participation in the whole cycle of experience. When that happens, he said, people say something like "Holy cow! Look what we're doing to ourselves!"

The Patient-Physician Dialogue Forum

It was time to review the voting. This (Figure 10.1) is what people saw.

As you recall from the previous chapter, we asked the forum participants to vote. Each participant could place two dots onto the iceberg: a blue one to mark where they believed the current health care system operated and a white one to mark the level of their desired future health care system.

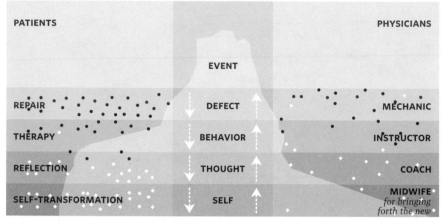

FIGURE 10.1 ICEBERG MODEL OF PATIENT-PHYSICIAN RELATIONSHIPS

More than 95 percent of the participants—both physicians and patients—put their dark dots on Level 1 or 2; that means that more than 95 percent of them experienced the focus of the current health care system as mechanical reengineering. And about 95 percent of the participants put their white dots on Levels 3 and 4, expressing their wish that the main focus of the system were on Levels 3 and 4, dealing with health issues through development, self-transformation, and inner growth.

"You all seem to agree," I began, "that the current system operates on Levels 1 and 2, while at the same time you also agree that the future system should shift to operate from Levels 3 and 4. So, given the fact that you are the patients and the physicians of this system and this is something you all agree on, what keeps you from operating that way? Because, after all, *you are* the system. The system is not "them" in Berlin, it's not "them" in Brussels. The system is right here in this room. The system is created through the relationship among you—nowhere else."

You could have heard a pin drop. Then, after the silence, a different kind of conversation emerged. People were more reflective and began asking thoughtful questions of others and of themselves. Something had shifted. Before the break, the conversation had been more like an exchange of statements between patients and physicians. But now people were relating direct-ly to one another and reflecting more deeply. "Why," some of the participants asked, "do we collectively produce results that nobody wants?"

After the physicians openly told of the hardships, pressures and frustra-tions they experienced, one man stood and introduced himself as the mayor of the town. "What we see in our health care system is the same as in poli-tics and government. We always operate on Levels 1 and 2. All we do is react to issues and crises, just as we've always done it in the past. But if we oper-ated from those deeper two levels, maybe we could make something differ-ent happen." A brief silence followed after the mayor sat down. Then a woman at the other end of the room stood up. "I am a teacher, and I teach in a school nearby, and you know what?" She paused and looked at the mayor and the whole group. "We are facing exactly the same problem. All we do in our schools is to operate on these first two levels." She pointed to the wall with the white and black dots and continued, "We organize our school around mechanical methods of learning. We focus on memorizing the past, on testing old bodies of knowledge, instead of teaching kids how to access their intellectual curiosity and their capabilities for creativity and imagina-tion. We are reacting to crises all the time. And we never succeed in moving our learning environments toward there [pointing to Levels 3 and 4 of the iceberg chart], where our kids could learn how to shape their future."

Then the man next to me stood up and said, "I am a farmer, and we are wrestling with exactly the same issue. All we do in conventional agriculture today is tinker with the mechanical issues on Levels 1 and 2. We use chemi-cal fertilizers, pesticides, and all kinds of stuff that we drum into the earth just as you drum a dead body of knowledge into the head of your students. The whole industrial way of doing agriculture is focused on fighting symp-toms and issues with the mechanical solutions of the past. We fail to con-ceive of our farms and our whole earth as a living organism—as our collec-tive and communal holding space."

Each person spoke from a much more authentic place, from the true "I" and with deep sincerity. Then one woman leaned forward and, looking at the physician, whom she had just listened to deeply, said in a gentle voice, "I feel very concerned about you. I don't want our system to kill you and our best physicians. Is there something that we could do to help you?" Silence followed.

The Field Structure of Sensing

Everyone who participated in the conversation that morning felt the presence of a deeper connection. It was no longer like most other conversations. Instead of expressing opinions and making statements, people started to ask genuine questions. People were not just talking together—they were thinking together. Time seemed to slow down; the space around us seemed to thicken and open up. People talked more slowly, punctuated by silence. The structure of how people related to one another had changed. Something had moved them beyond the usual state where people argue as separate individuals, as captives inside their own brains.

When this happens, the place from which our perception arises (white dot, Figure 10.2) moves from inside individual heads (looking *at* the field) to

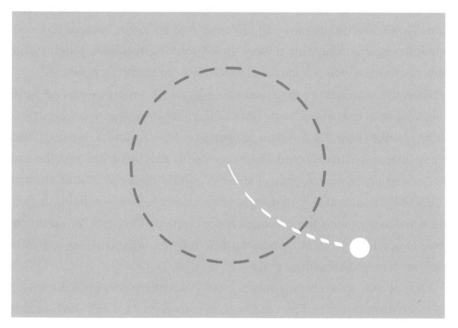

FIGURE 10.2 THE FIELD STRUCTURE OF SENSING

outside the organizational boundaries of the observer (blue circle, Figure 10.2), that is, the <u>perception begins to happen *from* the field.</u>

When this shift happens, the boundary between observer and observed collapses and the observer begins to see the system from a profoundly different view: a view that includes himself as part of the system that is being observed. <u>The system is no longer something that's out there ("what *they* are doing to us"), it's also something in here ("look what *we* are doing to us").</u>

When a group starts to operate from such a place, its participants also begin to see their relationship to the system and how they collectively enact it.

Principles

Four main principles come into play when entering the collective field of sensing: charging the container, deep diving, redirecting attention, and opening the heart.

Charging the Container

Weaving the collective body of co-sensing happens in places. In the case of the Patient-Physician Dialogue Forum, this place was intentionally created by designing the:

- Physical space: Throwing out all "stuff," emptying the place except for the walls; bringing in simple and minimal elements of design such as light and *Steelen*, a set of large pillars of cardboard on which we posted photographs and displays depicting the story of the ANR (Artzt-Notruf, or emergency call) initiative.[1]
- Time space: creating an energetic timeline in which the preparation and the agenda facilitated a natural flow through the U throughout the day (morning: moving down the left arm of the U—co-sensing; afternoon: moving up the right arm of the U—co-creating).
- Relational space: establishing (1) a <u>personal relationship with each of the participants prior to the meeting, (2) clear roles</u> (such as greeters at the door of the meeting place), (3) <u>process</u> (managing the details, such as

delivering a great presentation or reading the interview quotes), and (4) infrastructures (beverages, food, and so forth).

- Intentional space: clarity and quality of purpose within the full core group: Why are we doing all of this? What future possibility do we want to serve? What are we trying to create?[2]

Deep Diving

The gateway into the field of sensing and co-sensing is total immersion in the particulars of the field—in the living presence of the phenomenon. It is becoming *one* with the phenomenon you study. It is *not* studying your customer. It is *not* creating dialogue with your customer. It is *becoming, being* your patient or customer. It is living in the full *experience* of that world—and becoming one with it.[3]

In the Dialogue Forum, we did that by reading verbatim first-person accounts aloud, presenting key quotes from interviews, and then asking people to share their own stories in response to these trigger quotes.

As a facilitator in charge of moving a whole group through this collective field shift, part of your strategy should be to keep people from entering a debating/downloading behavior and mind-set; you intervene at the moment when people start issuing their usual debate-style statements. And you try to move people toward focused and nonjudgmental observation that will allow them to open up and connect with other viewpoints. The gateway to the deeper territories is immersion and direct, *sensual* encounter with the particulars of a living field.

Redirecting Attention

As you move through examples and manifestations of a living field—such as the different experiences of patients and physicians—you try to redirect people's attention from the "object" (the individual stories) to the formative field, or "source." In other words, you invite people to enter the place from which those examples emanate. In practical terms, you try to move into the field of each example that you study, you stay with it, and, as you do this, you *hold* the earlier examples in your mind. You do that with one example after another. You listen deeply to one view after another. As your listening deepens, you also begin to pay attention to the space in between the different views. You stay with it, and then, when you are just about to follow the next examples, suddenly a shift takes place that allows you to see the collective pattern that gives rise to all of the specific examples in front of you—you see the formative forces that is connecting them.

One simple test will help you judge whether you have successfully redirected your attention: the picture of the whole you see should include yourself—the observer—as part of the system you are trying to fix. When I said, "*You are* the system—but why do you collectively enact results that nobody wants?" people began to shift. Participants began actually to see themselves as part of the picture. The breakthrough happened when the mayor, the teacher, and the farmer stood up and said that they faced exactly the same issues as the patients and physicians.

The UC Berkeley cognitive psychologist Eleanor Rosch describes this shift as moving from seeing the system "out there" to seeing the system *from* the field. I asked Rosch what she meant by the term "field." "In a field," explained Rosch, "intention, body, and mind become integrated together. You start to be aware of perception happening *from the whole field*, not from within a separate perceiver. The notion of field was the closest I could come to this sense of integration in our current sciences."[4]

Opening the Heart

Then I asked Rosch, "So what is the nature of this whole field, and how do you connect or relate to it, or nurture it?" She looked at me, paused, and said, "Through the heart. *The heart in any contemplative tradition is not a sentimentality or an emotionality but a deep yogic centerpoint.*"

Opening the heart means accessing and activating the deeper levels of our emotional perception. Listening with the heart literally means using the heart and our capacity for appreciation and love as an organ of perception. At this point, we can actually see with the heart.

Almost always, when such a deeper field shift happens, we observe a little previous incident that creates the crack or opening for such a deeper shift.

That little spark is often connected with a moment of deep silence and/or a question that comes straight from the heart. It happened when the patient said to the physician in the example of the patient-physician network, "I feel very concerned about you. I don't want our system to kill you and our best physicians. Is there something that we could do to help you?"

The Grail Question

To better understand this particular turn and opening, let me tell you a story that I first read when I was a young kid. The story begins with a boy living in the twelfth century.[5] He was the son of a woman named Heart Sorrow. Her husband and two older sons had met their deaths as brave knights, so she decided to raise him in a distant place in order to prevent him from becoming a knight and meeting the same fate. His name was Parsifal. Parsifal means "innocent fool," but he doesn't learn his name and real identity until later in his life, when he was able to open his heart.

One spring day, young Parsifal rode out to throw his javelins—something he did very well—when suddenly, from out of nowhere, five magnificent knights in full armor rode by on their huge war horses. "They must be gods—or angels!" he thought. He nearly fainted when they actually stopped to talk to him. He asked them question after question about who they were and what they did with their lances and shields, and then raced home to tell his mother. I've met the most wonderful knights! And I'm going to join them." This was her worst nightmare, but since he couldn't be dissuaded, she said, "All right. Go. But promise me three things: go to church every day, be respectful of all fair maidens, and don't ask questions."

Parsifal began his life's adventure by traveling to King Arthur's court, for he had heard that the king could make a boy a knight. On the way, he passed a magnificent warrior, clothed completely in scarlet. Unknown to Parsifal, this Red Knight had been terrorizing King Arthur and his court, and none could better him. The innocent fool went right up to him and said, "I plan to take your armor, your weapons and your horse, once I've been made a knight." The Red Knight wryly replied, "Okay. That sounds like a good idea. Hurry back after you become a knight and have a try."

Nearly everyone in Arthur's court scoffed when the bumpkin Parsifal arrived and announced, "Make me a knight!" A young woman who hadn't smiled for six years approached Parsifal, looked him in the eyes, smiled, and reassured him, "You will be the best and bravest of all knights." Parsifal left the court ready to challenge the Red Knight.

When they met again, the Red Knight said, "Oh, it's the innocent fool come back." Parsifal sent his javelin right through the knight's head, killing him. Then Parsifal put the Red Knight's armor on, over his rough country clothing, mounted the Red Knight's horse, and rode off.

He had many adventures after that, including a stay at a nobleman's castle, who taught him the skills of knighthood . . . and to speak less.

Parsifal traveled on until he came to the castle of Anfortas, the Fisher King, the keeper of the Holy Grail. The wounded king was carried on a pallet into the great banquet hall. He was in such pain caused by a spear to his groin that he could barely lie still. The room glistened with expectation. A court jester had prophesied that he would be cured only when a true innocent came to the court. Moreover, this innocent had to ask the question "What ails you?" Everyone was waiting for Parsifal. But did he ask the question? No. He wanted to cry out, "What ails you, Uncle?" but he had been cautioned and taught not to ask so many questions. So the Fisher King was carried off to bed and Parsifal went to sleep, thinking that he'd be sure to ask the king what ailed him in the morning.

But, alas, in the morning the castle was empty. He had missed his chance. Dejected, he and his horse rode off across the drawbridge; it closed behind him, and the castle disappeared.

Parsifal then set off at a gallop in a vain search for the inhabitants of the castle. At one point he came upon a maiden sitting under a tree who asked him his name, and for the first time in his life he uttered his name: "Parsifal." She was holding the dead body of her lover. "Where have you been?" she asked him. When he told her that he hadn't asked the question at the Grail Castle and, as a result, he had brought misery to many, she informed him that his mother, too, was now dead—of a broken heart.

Saddened at that news, he left her after promising to avenge the death of her lover. The story continues. Parsifal searched in vain for many years, until eventually, after a long road of trials and tests, he did find his way back to the Grail Castle, where he managed to bring his full presence to the situation. He asked the Grail Question, "What ails you?," and restored the health of the king as well as the kingdom.

Parsifal's challenge was to act from the authentic presence of his open heart, rather than following what "good education" and social norms expected him to do. When the woman at the Dialogue Forum expressed concern for the doctor, she asked the Grail Question: "Physician, what ails *you*?" That question transformed the usual conversational pattern between doctor and patient. The power of such a heart question lies in its authenticity. It operates from the opening of a "crack" in the situational script, from the present moment, the now.

Sensing in Action

The Circle of Seven

I first came across the Circle of Seven when co-facilitating a workshop with Beth Jandernoa. Of all the facilitators I know, she is probably the best at standing in front of a group and, while seeming to do nothing, in an instant can establish a heart-to-heart connection with the whole room. For normal folks like me, it takes hard work and at least two or three days to arrive at such a relationship. But Beth simply gets up, looks at the audience, smiles with her eyes and her heart, and within a few moments everybody is drawn in.

I once asked her point-blank, "How do you do this?"

"It's really very simple," she responded. "Before I go up front, my practice for over thirty years is of opening my heart and consciously sending unconditional love to everyone in the room. It's creating a field or surround of love. What has helped me to deepen my capacity to be present is meeting with a circle of women called the Circle of Seven over many years."

Circle of Seven, who is that? I wondered. "It's a circle of good friends; we meet three or four times a year for three days to support and hold one another in our journeys. We started as six women, meeting first in Santa Fe in 1995." She told me the others were Anne Dosher, Barbara Coffman-Cecil, Glennifer Gillespie, Leslie Lanes, and Serena Newby.

That was the first time I had heard of such a circle. Since then, I've heard many other stories about similar groups that meet on a regular basis in order to just listen to each other and to collectively support each of their friends as their lives unfold. What I find remarkable about the members of these groups is that they appear to have a tangible impact on one anothers' lives even between their physical meetings. Beth, for example, uses her experience with the circle as a conscious gateway for opening her deeper capacities of relationship, allowing her to act with much more presence and effectiveness in both her professional and her personal life.

So I became interested in learning more about her circle's story. I asked Beth if I might join them so I could interview the whole group. They graciously agreed, and on September 15, 2003, I flew out to Ashland, Oregon, and spent the next two and a half days with them.

I learned that their initial plan had been to develop a program for women who were going through changes in their professional and personal lives. After their first meeting, however, they gave up their noble purpose of helping others. No matter how hard they tried to create an event for other leaders, they kept being redirected to their own lives. Though each was dedicated to serving others, they realized that their own healing needs at that time overshadowed what they sought to do for others. They decided to find out what it would be like to unfold the next phase of their lives from deep within themselves and the field of their circle.

Later, the Circle of Seven did create programs for emerging leaders, allowing them to share the benefits of their experience. This also coincided with a maturing of their professional lives. Satisfaction for them had ceased to lie in the heroics of changing organizations; they found it more fulfilling to pass on the sensitivities and orientation toward leadership they had learned in their work to the next generation of women who carried a dream for a healthy and integrated world.

Charging the Container by Diving into Experience

The first ten or fifteen minutes of my interview with the circle illustrate the principles discussed above. I started by asking, "When you begin the circle work, what do you do first?"[6]

"We always rediscover together how to begin," responded Barbara. "It's not as though we do exactly the same thing every time. Having said that, our first concern is to create a charged container in which we can work." "For example, look at what we did at the beginning of this interview," Glennifer explained. "We lit a candle, rang a Tibetan bowl, and went into silence together." During the silence, they may be doing different things internally, she further explained. Some listen to what's inside; some listen to the silence. "Our practice is meant to drop us more fully into the field together. Then we move into a deep check-in, giving each other all the time we need to fully bring what each of us is working with in our lives. This charges our space more and more." Listening to these opening remarks, I realized that what they described as "charging the container" is quite different from how people normally start a meeting. Usually meetings start with a "head" presentation or by following a set agenda. By contrast, this group started with a "heart" element of shared experience.

Opening the Wisdom Intelligence of the Heart

"One of our circle practices consists of inventing processes on the spot that seem to address whatever an individual might be wrestling with or how this fits with what is going on in the larger world," began Beth. "A particular process we invented for me was to have people play different parts of me so that I could keep stepping back to discover a part of myself I was not familiar with. During that session, I discovered what I would call my inner wisdom figure.

"It felt so present, so real, as though it were in a cave inside me, as if there were a special place inside me from which insight and understanding came. It was opened in the circle gathering, and I stood in that place and came from that place myself. . . . Because of the collective, I was able to discover a place in myself that, ever since, is the place I go to when I'm looking for wisdom.

"Since this process, I find that I make wiser choices. I have a larger perspective. For me, that's a story of a powerful thing that's come out of our work and continued in my life and lives with me all the time."

I mentioned to Beth that when she talked about that other place, her hands were pointing to her heart. And when she talked about her "self" she also pointed to the same place. "Can you describe some elements of that experience?" I asked. "How do you know whether you're operating from a normal identity or from this deeper authentic place? How does it feel different?"

"Well, I slow down a lot when I'm in the place of deeper knowing," she responded. "I try to be aware of my bodily sensations. My breathing is slower; the world seems to slow down, and so do I. The sensation is in my heart region. It feels like a deep, open, dark, yet illuminated place. It also feels strong, yet fluid, and different from the normal place from which I operate."

Holding the Container

Just as the story of Parsifal's Holy Grail and its circle of knights symbolizes collective and feminine presence, the Circle of Seven also functions as a gateway into the deeper sources of creativity and journey for each of its members. In order to collectively create this holding space, the members of the Circle of Seven consciously design and shape the space (physical environment), the time (three to four times a year), and the relational and intentional space.

Beth continued, "One commitment we've had is to keep the field clear in all our one-on-one relationships when we're not together. We work at it. I assume it's like being in a marriage. If you're really doing the relationship well, you work at it. Very few collectives commit to that.

"It's not that we're so interested in the personality level in the end. My perception is that working the personality level is a prerequisite. . . . But there's commitment at another level that's a big enabler for the collective field.

"If nobody gets in the way with their own agendas, then we see more possibilities. Once we get over the threshold, there's a certain richness—a collective listening capacity that is humbling. It's unimposing.

"It becomes obvious that the reason you *do something*, as opposed to just *talking about it*, is that doing it brings the energy of the situation into the room, as opposed to having an intellectual conversation about it. So it's a way of making everything real time. That's why we do it."

I left that interview feeling very grateful for having been invited into their "sacred" circle space. I realized that what I had witnessed was just a snapshot in time and that these women, by their careful attention, were continuously creating and evolving their practice field. They explained to me that they constantly find new ideas and let go of ways that once worked but are no longer accurate or useful to a new time and space.

Facilitating the Turning Points

In April 2001, a group of high-potential leaders of a global IT corporation gathered for a three-day workshop in San Francisco. It was a situation every facilitator knows well. On the first day, people complained about how difficult the culture was and how it stifled innovation and learning. On day two the group collectively changed direction: the participants, all of whom already held management positions in their company, began to see how they *themselves* enacted the features of the culture that until then they had seen as being imposed on them by "the system."

"We do to others exactly what we complain about others doing to us," said one of the East Asian participants, "so we'd better change ourselves instead of whining about the pathologies of the system." As a facilitator, I know that if we do not get to this self-reflective turn by late in the first day or early in the second, I have not really earned my fee. Facilitating this kind of turn is not an esoteric discipline—it is a bread-and-butter issue for lots of people in the field of management, consulting, and leadership.

The tools that facilitated the turn in this case included much of what the Circle of Seven has learned together: develop emotional time lines (diving into experience); practicing deep listening and dialogue (redirecting attention from me to the other); understanding the systemic patterns that the team collectively enacts; and telling stories in small groups about team experiences and personal turning points in order to open up to deeper levels of knowing (opening the heart).

The Process of Sensing

A similar thread runs through all stories of deep gathering.

They begin with people *diving into* concrete experience: listening to key quotes from the patients' interviews, listening to the silence that opens the circle gathering, and listening to the corporate employees' organizational and individual histories.

They continue with people redirecting their attention from operating inside their own heads to happening *from the whole field*: It happened in the silence of the health care forum when the picture of the white dots and the dark dots began sinking in, when people started to see themselves collectively enacting the system. It happens in the Circle of Seven when they create a field of connection that shows up in the form of an energetic knowing. In the case of the leadership workshop, it happened when people started to see themselves as co-creating the system that earlier they had been complaining about.

And they deepen this shift by acting from an inner *knowing of the heart*.

Two Types of Wholeness

Recently, these subtle shifts of seeing and sensing have attracted some interest among scientists who, in the light of twentieth-century physics, are wrestling with the phenomenon of wholeness. One of the best articulations of this emerging new view of science is Henri Bortoft's *The Wholeness of Nature*. Drawing on diverse sources such as Goethe's work on science and twentieth-century hermeneutics, phenomenology, and quantum theory, Bortoft suggests a postpositivistic way of doing science in which the observer actively and knowingly lives and participates in the phenomenon and its coming into being.

When I met him in London in July 1999, Bortoft began by telling me how the quantum physicist David Bohm, who was one of his teachers and advisers, had advised Bortoft to study Nils Bohr very carefully. Bortoft was very interested in the notion of wholeness, a term that Bohr had introduced in quantum physics. Bohr saw the whole more as a limit to our thinking. But Bohm thought differently, Bortoft explained. "Bohm thought that you can understand wholeness. He used the hologram as a model. I found that very illuminating. It shows that the whole is present in its parts."

Bortoft distinguishes between two types of wholeness: the *counterfeit whole* and the *authentic whole*. Both notions of wholeness are based, he said, on different faculties of cognition. The counterfeit whole is based on the intellectual mind that is abstracting from the concrete sensual perception. When operating in that mode, the mind is "moving away from the concrete part" to get an overview. The result is an abstract and nondynamic notion of the whole.

By contrast, continued Bortoft, the authentic whole is based on a different cognitive capacity, the "intuitive mind"; that is, it is based on opening some higher qualities of perception. The intuitive mind, he continued, operates by "moving right into the concrete parts" in order to encounter the whole—that is, by diving into the concrete experience of the particulars.

When Bortoft came across Goethe's work in his studies, he was struck by Goethe's notion of a different kind of seeing, "a seeing that strives from the whole to the parts." That, explained Bortoft, "was very close to Bohm's hologram."

Bortoft claims that we cannot know the whole in the same way that we know a thing, because the whole is not a thing. The challenge is to encounter the whole as it comes into presence in the parts. Says Bortoft, "The way to the whole is into and through the parts. It is not to be encountered by stepping back to take an overview, for it is not over and above the parts, as if it were some superior all-encompassing entity. The whole is to be encountered by stepping right into the parts. This is how we enter into the nesting of the whole and thus move into the whole as we pass through the parts."

I asked Bortoft, "What does it take to develop that capacity of seeing?" He explained to me the Goethean notion of exact sensorial imagination. This term captures Goethe's articulation of the principle of *diving in*.

"You have to cultivate a quality of perception that is striving out from the whole to the part" said Bortoft, paraphrasing Goethe. "It takes time. You have to slow down. You see and you follow every detail in imagination. You create the image of what you see in your mind, and you do that as precisely as possible. For example, you look at a leaf, and you create the shape of the leaf as precisely as possible in your mind. You are moving the shape of the leaf around in your mind, and you follow every detail. The phenomenon becomes an image in your mind. You have to be active with your mind."

He added, "There is a huge resistance in ourselves against doing that. Most of us are way too busy downloading most of the time. If you want to do this, you have to slow down. "You do this with one leaf, with another leaf, and so on, and suddenly there is a movement, a dynamic movement, as you begin to see not the individual leaf but the dynamic movement. The plant is the dynamic movement. *That* is the reality."

He continued, "This imagination becomes an organ of perception. You can develop it. I get the sense that when you do it, you are moving in another space, an imaginary realm. It is a movement. And it seems more alive and real than the outer world. It is more real because *you* are doing it. *You* are active. Goethe had an enormous ability in that regard. The same is true for Picasso. The way he painted. When you look at his pictures, you see the metamorphoses."

Bortoft's description embodies all three principles of sensing that we earlier identified: first, diving into the sensory experience; second, redirecting your attention; and third, activating the deeper capacities of cognition.

Epistemological Reversal

Conventional science considers theory the container and facts the content. Goethe and Bortoft, on the other hand, consider sensory facts to be the container.[7] Bortoft explained, "This transformation from an analytical to a holistic mode of consciousness brings with it a reversal between the container and the content. In the case of positivism, the theory is considered to be only the container for the facts. Now, if the theory, in Goethe's sense, is the real content of the phenomenon, then it can be said that in the moment of intuitive insight we are *seeing inside the phenomenon*.[8]

"The unfolding of nature in itself is an epistemological reversal," he continued. "The plant is a dynamic movement. You see its leaves as traces that embody and manifest certain imprints of this movement. That becomes so strong when you see it. That is the intuitive seeing from inside of the phenomenon. The dynamic movement is the reality."

I told Bortoft that his distinctions resonated deeply with experiences that my colleagues and I had had in the field of leading profound organizational change. I explained that another aspect of that other way of seeing concerned the opening of the heart, the inversion of one's emotions and feelings into senses for a deeper and much more profound relationship to the world. "This is exactly the core theme I have been recently working on," he replied. We both regretted we didn't have more time to explore this phenomenon of seeing and thinking with the heart.

Field Notes: Moving out of the Prison

When we get a glimpse of the sensing experience—the view from within—we realize that our normal way of operating—the view from outside—offers us, as Plato eloquently put it, nothing but a shadow (or secondary) reality, rather than the primary reality. For that reason the image of being imprisoned inside a cave is not totally inappropriate.[9] As long as we are merely downloading, we are fully imprisoned. All we see are shadows on the wall, shadows produced by passing figures in our own mind.

As we have discussed, when we switch from the state of downloading (viewing from projecting past patterns) to seeing (viewing from outside), we turn our head and realize that the shadows on the wall are actually our own projections and that reality is outside the cave. At this stage, three principles come into play: turning around (moving into context), realizing that there is something different than what we project (suspension and wonder), and wondering what the reality outside looks like (questioning).

At the moment we switch from the state of seeing (viewing from outside) to sensing (viewing from within), we emerge from the boundaries of the cave to the world outside. Again three principles come into play while going through this transition. First, we have to immerse ourselves in the concrete particulars (dive in). We cannot leave the cave by continuing to habitually download *abstract* thought. We cannot leave the cave on someone else's back (like Varela's upper cat, which remains blind). The only way out is to activate our own senses. Second, we *redirect* our attention and begin to grasp reality by sensing inside the formative field. And third, as we deepen this movement, we deploy a different cognitive capacity: a knowing that emerges from the intelligence of the heart. We grasp reality not only from the perspective of the individual observer but also from the perspective of life and its source, the sun. The result is *seeing with the heart*.

Unless we make the effort to move, to use our senses to relate to the world outside our current boundaries, we will stay blind and remain stuck in our cave.

Goethe put it this way: "Man knows himself only to the extent that he knows the world; he becomes aware of himself only within the world, and aware of the world only within himself. *Every object, well contemplated, opens up a new organ within us.*"10

Most cross-institutional change processes fail because they miss the starting point: co-sensing across boundaries. We need infrastructures to facilitate this process on a sustained level across systems. And because they don't yet exist, organized interest groups go out and maximize their special interests against the whole, instead of engaging practitioners in the larger system in a process of sensing and innovating together. As long as we continue to organize our society on the backs of others, like Varela's upper cat, we will continue to get unsatisfactory results. Just as you can't expect the blind upper cat to operate in a dynamic environment, you cannot expect an unseeing society or social system to adapt and operate successfully in increasingly turbulent times.

CHAPTER II

Presencing

Seeing from the Source • Two Root Questions of Creativity •
The Field Structure of Presencing • Two Types of Knowledge and
Knowing • Moments of Truth, Beauty, and Goodness •
Principles of Presencing • Field Notes

Seeing from the Source

Presencing, the blending of *sensing* and *presence*, means to connect with the Source of the highest future possibility and to bring it into the now. When moving into the state of presencing, perception begins to happen from a future possibility that depends on us to come into reality. In that state we step into our real being, who we really are, our authentic self. Presencing is a movement where we approach our self *from the emerging future.*[1]

In many ways, presencing resembles sensing. Both involve shifting the place of perception from the interior to the exterior of one's (physical) organization. The key difference is that sensing shifts the place of perception to the current whole while presencing shifts the place of perception to the *source* of an emerging future whole—to a future possibility that is seeking to emerge.

As I watched my family's farmhouse burn, I began to feel that everything I thought I was, was gone—*that* was an example of sensing. When the boundary between the fire and me collapsed and I became aware that I wasn't separate from the fire and that the house that went up in flames wasn't separate from me—*that* was also sensing. In sensing, my perception originated in the current field: the burning fire right in front of me. But the next moment, when I felt elevated to another sphere of clarity and awareness and experienced a pull toward the source of silence and Self—*that* was a foreshadowing of presencing.

Two Root Questions of Creativity

The territory at the bottom of the U is about connecting with the source of inner knowing that Brian Arthur talked about. A deep threshold there needs to be crossed in order to connect to one's real source of presence, creativity, and power.

To find out more about that source, Joseph Jaworski and I interviewed Michael Ray, who had developed a Stanford Business School course on creativity in business. Over the years people had told me that taking his course had changed their lives. So I was interested in finding out how this man, according to *Fast Company* the "most creative man of Silicon Valley," helped practitioners connect to their sources of creativity.[2]

"How do you do this? What is the essential activity that actually helps people become more creative?" Ray responded, "I create learning environments in all my courses that allow people to address and work on the two root questions of creativity." He paused and then continued: "Who is my Self? and What is my Work?" The "capital-S Self." By this, Ray said, he means one's highest self, the self that transcends pettiness and signifies our "best future possibility." Similarly, "capital-W Work" is not one's current job but one's purpose, what you are here on earth to do.

"Know thyself" echoes my conversation with Master Nan, who told me that in order to be a good leader, you must know yourself. "Know thyself" appears throughout all great wisdom traditions. I remember it being a principal teaching when I studied the teachings of Gandhi in India. "You must be the change you seek to create." It also was attributed to Apollo and inscribed at the entrance of the ancient Greek temple in Delphi. And Goethe knew that the essence of nature cannot be found without turning your attention back upon yourself, that you can learn who you are only by immersing yourself in the world. Today the self is at the core of what we study, not only in philosophy but also in physics, sociology, and management.

The Field Structure of Presencing

Presencing happens when our perception begins to connect to the source of our emerging future. The boundaries between three types of presence collapse: the presence of the past (current field), the presence of the future (the emerging field of the future), and the presence of one's authentic Self. When this co-presence, or merging of the three types of presence, begins to resonate, we experience a profound shift, a change of the place from which we operate. When I stood in front of the fire, I experienced the presence of my authentic Self and felt connected both to the journey that had brought me there (the presence of the past) and to what I felt emerging from the future (the presence of the future).

One day I was hiking in the Alps, in Val Fex, a small valley near the border between Switzerland and Italy, right next to Sils Maria, where the philosopher Friedrich Nietzsche used to write. This area is a special place in Europe because it is the watershed for three major rivers: the Rhine, flowing to the northwest; the Inn, flowing to the northeast; and the Po, flowing to the south. I decided to follow the Inn to its source. As I hiked upstream, I realized that I had never in my life followed a stream all the way to its source. In fact, I had never seen what the source of a major river really looks like.

The stream grew narrower and narrower until it was simply a trickle, and I found myself standing near a pond in the wide bowl of a valley, encircled by glacier-covered mountaintops. I just stood there and listened. With surprise, I realized that I was at the center of countless waterfalls streaming off the mountains. They were making the most beautiful symphony one can imagine. Stunned, I realized that there was no such thing as a single point of origin. I watched the source all around and above me, streaming off the circle of glaciated mountaintops and then converging in the small pond. Was the pond the source? Was it the circle of waterfalls? Or was it the glaciers on the mountaintops? Or the whole planetary cycle of nature: rain, rivers flowing to the ocean, and evaporation?

Metaphorically speaking, presencing is the capacity that allows us to operate from this extended notion of the source, to function as a watershed by sensing what wants to come forth and then allowing it to come into being. In other words, by bringing the water from the surrounding waterfalls to a single point, the pond fills and spills into the river, bringing it into being.

Presencing enhances sensing, just as sensing enhances seeing. Sensing extends seeing by moving our locus of attention "inside" a phenomenon. Presencing enlarges the activity of sensing by using our Self. The root of the word presencing is *es*, which means "to be," that is, "I am." *Essence, yes, presence*, and *present* (gift) all share this same Indo-European root. An Old Indian derivative of this same root from India is *sat*, which means both "truth" and "goodness." This term became a major force in the twentieth century, when Mahatma Gandhi used it to convey his key notion of *satyagraha* (his strategy of truth and nonviolence). An Old German derivative from the same root, *sun*, means "those who are surrounding us" or "the beings who surround us."[3]

In Figure 11.1, the place from which we operate moves not only from the center (downloading) to the periphery (seeing) and from there to beyond the boundary of our own organization (sensing), but progressing on to the surrounding sphere, that is, to "the beings who surround us."

To learn more about this way of operating, I went to Berkeley, California, to meet with Eleanor Rosch, whom I introduced to you in Chapter 10. She is one of the eminent cognitive psychologists of our time and a professor in UC Berkeley's Department of Psychology.

I first encountered her work when reading *The Embodied Mind*, a book she co-authored with Francisco Varela and Evan Thompson. We met after the Berkeley Knowledge Forum, a conference on knowledge management hosted by Ikujiro Nonaka at the Haas School of Business. Rosch had just made a stunning presentation in which she introduced the notion of "primary knowing."

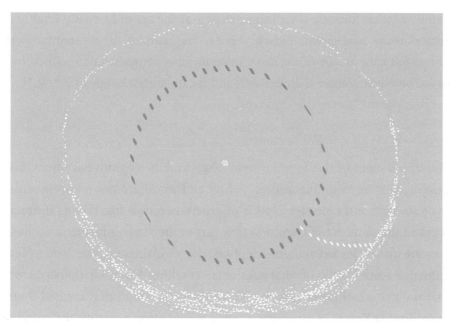

FIGURE II.I THE FIELD STRUCTURE OF PRESENCING

Two Types of Knowledge and Knowing

In her presentation she drew a distinction between two types of knowledge: conventional analytical knowledge and "primary knowing," or wisdom awareness. The analytical picture offered by the cognitive sciences, Rosch argues, is based on conventional analytical knowledge—that is the field structure of attention described above as "seeing." In this state the world is thought of as a set of separate objects and states of affairs, and the human mind as a machine that isolates, stores, and retrieves knowledge as an indirect representation of the world and oneself.

By contrast, primary knowing characterizes a sensing and presencing type of cognition in which one "is said to know by means of interconnected wholes (rather than isolated contingent parts) and timeless, direct presentation (rather than through stored re-presentations). Such knowing is "open," rather than determinate; and a sense of unconditional value, rather than

conditional usefulness, is an inherent part of the act of knowing itself. . . .
Action from awareness," Rosch argues, "is claimed to be spontaneous,
rather than the result of decision making; it is compassionate, since it is
based on wholes larger than the self; and it can be shockingly effective."[4]

Mind and World Are Not Separate

The implications of this view for psychology and the cognitive sciences, says
Rosch, are sweeping. She argues, "Mind and world are not separate. Since
the subjective and objective aspects of experience arise together as different
poles of the same act of cognition (are part of the same informational field)
they are already joined at their inception." Rosch claims that we need a "fundamental reorientation of what science is," recalling Albert Einstein's dictum
that problems can never be solved with the same mind that created them.
According to Rosch, "Our sciences need to be performed with the mind of
wisdom." It was clear to me that Rosch is developing a language around the
subtle experiences that most of us have but barely notice.

As we walked back to her office, she said, "Just saying that mind and world
are not separate is only part of it. All the lists of attributes that I outlined . . .
actually all go together as one thing. That one thing is what some Tibetan
Buddhism calls the natural state and what Taoism calls the Source. It's what
is at the heart of the heart of the heart. There is this awareness and this little
spark that is positive—and completely independent of all of the things that
we think are so important. This is the way things happen, and in the light of
that, action becomes action *from* that. And lacking that, or being ignorant of
it, we just make terrible messes—as individuals, as nations, and as cultures."

The Field Knows Itself and Leads to Action

Back in her office, she continued, "Think of everything that is happening
as moment-by-moment presentations from this deep heart source that
has a knowing dimension to it. Tibetan Buddhism talks about emptiness,
luminosity, and the knowing capacity as inseparable. That knowing capacity

actually is the field knowing itself, in a sense, or this larger context knowing itself."

"So your own activity is to help this process, the field knowing itself?" I asked.

"If you follow your nature far enough as it moves," she continued, "if you follow so far that you really let go, then you find that you're actually the original being, the original way of being. The original way of being knows things and does things in its own way. When that happens, or when you get even a glimpse of it, you realize that we don't actually act as fragmented selves the way we think we do. Nothing you do can produce this realization, this original way of being. It's a matter of tuning in to it and its way of acting. It actually has a great intention to be itself, so to speak, and it will do so if you just let it."

Rosch talked about the same turning points I had frequently observed in workshops and that Varela also talked about: *redirection* (tuning in) and *letting go*. For example, when in the Patient-Physician Dialogue Forum the participants looked at the wall with the white and dark dots, letting the picture sink into their minds, they weren't taking in any additional data. What was shifting in that moment was the place from which they were gazing at the picture in front of them. Before that, they had operated from their conventional interior selves, or what Rosch calls "the individual locked inside his skin looking out through his eyes." After the shift, the forum participants began to operate from a different place, a self that is partly inside and partly outside their own skin and bodily organization.

When you operate from the self-transcending, enhanced sense of self—from a place that is *both inside and outside* the observer's organization—you see your self as part of the system and you start to see the process of people enacting that system. You feel as if you are not just observing the system from a single point (the "balcony perspective") but from multiple points simultaneously, from the surrounding field or sphere. This is what Bortoft called "striving from the whole to the part" and what Rosch refers to as "the field knowing itself," a field that, if you succeed in tuning in to it, actually "has a great intention to be itself."

Moments of Truth, Beauty, and Goodness

How does this all work? Well, let's now look at a couple of examples. The first example comes from Erik Lemcke, a sculptor and management consultant from Denmark.

My Hands Know

"After having worked with a particular sculpture for some time," he told me about his work, "there comes a certain moment when things are changing. When this moment of change comes, it is no longer me, alone, who is creating. I feel connected to something far deeper and my hands are co-creating with this power. At the same time, I feel that I am being filled with love and care as my perception is widening. I sense things in another way. It is a love for the world and for what is coming. I then intuitively know what I must do. My hands know if I must add or remove something. My hands know how the form should manifest. In one way, it is easy to create with this guidance. In those moments I have a strong feeling of gratitude and humility."

Erik's examples beautifully demonstrate that the essence of presencing and the essence of the deepest creative processes are one at the same.

The second example comes from an interview with Steven, a young, high-potential leader in one of the largest global car companies. He had just been given a critical task upon which much of the economic future of that company would hinge: to integrate key technical components across all platforms of the company, which operates across all cultures and continents. It's the kind of assignment that would cause most people to say: that's really key to the future of the company—yet, given all the turf issues, its very unlikely to happen. Here are Steven's own words:

DIARY ENTRY: I'M FALLING APART
New budgets, new thinking, new way of working: all by the following week. Not possible, of course.

Starting line-up: A handful of department heads who come from the model groups, and who now, instead of going into breadth within the model, each have to go into depth in one specific area for all of them. One of them says: "This is the last job I would have picked out." The old organization, in its death throes, wasn't even twitching. But every time you face it you can feel the resistance against you.

Just the spatial concentration alone, the structure of departments with people who don't know each other. After three days everything needed to be ready. There was no chance to settle into things...from one day to another, no steps, no strategy, no relationships. Many, many people have to be moved in order to get just 260 of them into halfway close proximity to each other...

Here comes my emotional memory: A real crossroad for me was speaking on the third day in front of 260 people. This was after we had more or less hauled together the department heads for a couple of hours, to tell them both what we knew and mostly what we didn't know. I worked all night long on my PowerPoint presentation: Center re-start. Opening balance. Strain on liquidity with cutback targets. Everything clear. No problem. You don't even feel yourself at all. Your intellect tells you what to do.

Inside I felt horrible: I need my emotions, my highs and my lows. With these I can make it through life, this is my directional and orientation system. My skin is porous, not armored like that of some of my colleagues, but I also have no inability to make decisions as some others do. My skin is an instrument that I can make thicker or thinner, depending on the situation. In the evening I look back on the day: How was it today, where did I want to go, where did I arrive? On this night the bow is drawn to the breaking point. The personal encounter is very important to me. The things that have been with me in my life from the beginning: openness, honesty, caring, basic elements of human cooperation. Now they're being challenged.... Here in this center I've come to a point I'd never been to before in my life, where the whole picture starts to flicker. Have we gone with the right issues, done the right things, to the right people? When I took these questions to my boss, he was irritated and just snorted back: "My goodness, what else do you need?"

Early in the morning I packed my things together, tensed and wide-awake about the importance of things to come. Together with my equally tensed leadership team—I saw the 260 people wash into the room, all feeling homeless and now wanting to know what's going to happen—who gets to keep their job, and who doesn't, what the sense of the whole thing is. With my nonsense presentation and tail-dragging team leaders, I walked onto the stage.

As soon as I started up the stairs I noticed that my legs were buckling. It seemed like an endless path up to the lectern, I had to struggle to keep going. And I looked into 260 hostile, silent faces. When I was suddenly standing in front of these people, I thought: I'm falling apart. I'm going to die. A moment of total weakness. Minutes went by while the audience and I just stared at each other. Soundless. Timeless.

All of a sudden, though, everything was different. I heard something like a buzzing in the air. All of a sudden there was a strength, which came from being convinced that what we're doing is right. It can only go this way. A member of the works council had reminded me: "We expect a fair trusting relationship with you." Suddenly, a deep inner certainty came over me: We can only help people if we change processes, and our thinking. Maybe you have to have this "death experience" in order to be genuine, I don't know. I was on a whole new playing field. All of a sudden I was strong and sure standing there. The speakers after me also got caught up in how the dynamics had changed. And around me in the room, something there had also completely changed. It was really buzzing. Of course, it wasn't good news, but it was acceptable in the way that I was able to explain it. All at once I was able to speak completely freely, and come up with the right points on the spot in front of the others, hitting just the right nerve. It was an extremely strong force, in harmony with itself, I felt like I was very strong, I can hold out through this.... I let it run...didn't control anything.... It was a very good feeling. Suddenly I felt right: I knew that this was now my job. I'm getting to the point...now the dams are breaking.

What Erik shared as an intentional creative process, happens in Steven's story through a leadership crisis situation: the crack opens—are you ready to die?

The next story also unfolds through an inflection point.

Breaking Through a Membrane

In Houston, Texas, during the first days of June 1999, Joseph Jaworski and I sat in a final team meeting between a group of line managers and external consultants. We were meeting to design an action learning intervention that would help the people at the top of that organization—the result of a big downstream oil company merger—to lead their huge and complex organization more entrepreneurially and more effectively. The room brimmed with tension, anxiety, anger, and frustration.

The level of conversation seemed to be driven by Gresham's law. Sir Thomas Gresham, a sixteenth-century English businessman and public servant, observed that "bad money drives out good."[5] Likewise, I have often seen a pattern in group conversations where bad conversation drives out the good. Bad conversation is annoying and noisy; the same people display their egos and monopolize the airtime, with no sensitivity to process or contributions from others that might move the group in a different direction. Good conversation requires a certain quality of attention, or listening—a "container," as Bill Isaacs would say—that includes some toning down or the elimination of "bad talk." Thus good talk is contingent upon suspending bad talk, but bad talk is not contingent upon good—it just keeps on going and going and further reproducing itself. Our group, it struck me, was a living example of this painful principle.

Almost every kind of birth process involves as much pain as it does joy and magic. Whenever a group achieves a significant breakthrough, first there is plenty of down-and-dirty pain and frustration. So why do we hear so many heroic stories about people accomplishing amazing things without this messy dimension? Because they're fantasies. Soon after our second child was born, my wife said, "That's it. We're not doing this again." But three months later she wondered, "Do we really want to have only two children? Maybe we should consider a third one." If women accurately remembered the pain of childbirth, mankind's future would be in serious jeopardy. And if we all accurately remembered the pain of group work, we would probably change occupations. But our minds clean up and polish our stories. There's an instant figure/background shift, and we start to downplay the "bad parts" and tune in to our joy about what we have accomplished. On that morning in Houston, the Dream Team, as they called themselves, seemed more like the Nightmare Team. Time was running out, and the task of designing a leadership laboratory to help leaders take their organization into the future clearly wasn't being accomplished; the tension and bad feeling in the room escalated, so we decided to take a brief break. The leader of the group stepped out with Joseph and me to talk about how to best use the remaining time.

We'd been meeting periodically for four months and had done a lot of intensive observation, immersion, and learning together. Furthermore, we had created a significant body of shared perception, understanding, and, to a certain degree, aspiration. It seemed we should be doing better. After we reconvened, the project leader pressed on through an endless list of check-off items. I glanced up at David, one of the principal deal makers in the trading division and someone who had initially struck me as probably the most hard-nosed guy in the group. An iron man, he knew about athletics and performing in the zone, but he also was the most focused and serious guy on the team. Now he seemed to be working hard to articulate a question, trying to give voice to something inchoate but clearly present. The conversation moved on, but I saw him still holding on and allowing that question to build up, to take shape in his mind. I watched as his questions seemed to land and crystallize in his mind. The energy field around him seemed to intensify. His question came from his source, and that was the turning point.

He pointed to three or four charts hanging around the room. "These charts seem to be different, but something connects them." One chart was the U model. Another showed the four fields of listening.[6] Others displayed four different levels of organizational change. And then there was one on the structure of our lab process. "We're trying to get our arms around this deep process of creation—of actively participating in creating new worlds—and these four pictures represent images, imprints of this deeper force at work. But what is it that connects these four footprints—what is its common underlying source?"

His question brought the room to attention. The project leader was furious. He wanted to continue with his checklist. But that conversation had been abruptly halted by David's question. Having articulated his question, David and the others looked at me. I looked at him and said—nothing. That silence went on for what seemed to be a long time.

Out of that silence, Joseph slowly rose and put all four charts David had referred to next to one another. When Joseph spoke, we all knew he was speaking from a profound place. With the exception of only a couple of people, everyone in the room could sense it. David's question, the silence, and Joseph opened a door, and the rest of us were caught up in a magical, deep conversational flow. Not everyone spoke up, but you could see the full engagement in their faces. Shining eyes. Some eyes were wet. Something profound suddenly happened in our group, in our room. Time slowed down. The sense of self and connection with the group expanded. We all spoke from that deeper place—a place that connected us to one another and made us one with a larger generative field, allowing us to develop several key ideas very quickly.

In hindsight, I realize that those few hours produced three notable outcomes. Within minutes, the group generated several core ideas that later were implemented in the delivery of the leadership lab. Second, we noticed that after this meeting people were able to tap into the field of generative dialogue much faster and more readily, and without all the pain that had preceded the first "delivery" of that experience.[7]

And third, there was a significant impact on an individual level. When I saw David several years later, he told me that that meeting had been a major turning point in his life. I asked him how he had felt while articulating that question. He said, "It felt as if I was breaking through a membrane." What a wonderful way to phrase it, I thought. A few months later, David became head of a business unit for lease trading that he took from rock bottom to the top of its industry, ranking number one in both volume and earnings.

"Breaking through a membrane." Each birth is a mystery that involves at least three different perspectives: the perspective of the *mother*, the perspective of the *helper* (midwife, father, doctor), and finally the perspective of the *newborn*—the being that is "breaking through" into another world. On that day it wasn't just David who entered a new world. But it was he who midwifed the birth. A friend of mine, Karen Speerstra, who authors and midwifes books (including the one that you are reading now), once told me that she had learned, in part, how to do that from a real midwife, who wisely told her, "You must always honor the spirit of the birth." Sometimes we just have to wait. We may want to grab the forceps, but it's usually wiser to honor the spirit of the birth.

David's remark also reminded me that when I decided to coin and use the term "presencing" for this deeper experience at issue here, I did an Internet search to find out whether anyone else might have already coined and used that word in a different context. Only two hits came up. One was that the word "presencing" had been used by a French translator of Heidegger's work into English. And the other usage was by nurses and midwives, who talked about the deeper aspects of their work. When I saw these two contexts, I knew I had found the right word for what I wanted to express.

A Wedding

The day after the Patient-Physician Dialogue Forum in Germany, the core group of physicians, Ursula, the students, and I met to clean up the schoolroom we'd been using. We were joined by some patients who had shown up to help, unasked. It was like the morning after a party, when you're hanging out, tired but elated and relaxed, and open to anything that happens in the now. One person sat down with a cup of coffee. Another pulled up a chair. Soon the grill was lit and we were eating leftovers from the kitchen. We sat, this circle of friends, in the gentle outdoor light that harbors spring. I asked the woman operating the grill what she thought of the forum the day before. "I was touched by it." "Touched by what?" I asked. "Well, in a way, I experienced the day like a wedding. In the end there was a solemnity in the room, like in a cathedral, and an intimacy, like you only have when you know one another as well as you do in a family." She had found the perfect words to describe a subtle level of experience that we had all felt. The day had truly been about joining two separate fields or bodies in a way that made each stronger and enlarged the possibilities for each.

I turned around and looked at our little "wedding constellation," a circle of friends that united physicians, patients, and students. We had become a community and were totally present to one another. Time slowed down; loving energy radiated through the entire group.

Later that circle emerged as a core group in one of the most successful among the dozens of similar networks started in Germany in the 1990s. In 2000 the network instituted a new emergency control center that includes a 24/7 physician hotline and provides higher-quality emergency service at considerably lower overall cost.

Through the Eye of the Needle

For about ten years, Katrin Käufer and I facilitated the semiannual meeting of a bio-dynamic farming community in Germany. The group consisted of about a dozen people. As always, we used the first night of these three-day meetings for an extended check-in with each participant. Each person talked about where he or she was in their work and in their life. On the following two days we discussed the key issues the group was currently wrestling with. At one of the early meetings, Katrin and I felt that we had made only very little progress during the first day. Things felt unresolved. Something seemed to prevent the group from reaching its real potential. So we invited everyone to share the story of "the journey that brought me here." It soon became obvious how little we had known about one another.

The next morning, a Sunday, a shift happened that deeply affected the group. We started to talk about the larger picture that was emerging through their stories and journeys and how it might relate to the future of this community of farmers and this place—a place that had been founded by a monastery some nine hundred years earlier. One of the farmers began to articulate his felt sense of purpose in very simple but touching words as "taking care of this tiny piece of earth." He spoke from his heart, and people felt moved to an inner place. In earlier discussions they had spoken from their individual perspectives and points of view, but now they talked about the presence and *being* of this place. What might they do as a community to help it realize its best and fullest future potential?

At these moments, when time slowed down and space seemed to open up around us, we felt the power of a subtle presence shining through our words, gestures, and thoughts—as if the presence of a future were *watching* and attending to us, a future that also was totally and intimately dependent on us—and still is.

When the meeting ended later that day, the group had crossed through the eye of the needle. In groups and organizations, this is the point at which the actors begin to see and sense from a different place, a place that allows them to establish a direct connection with a field of the future—and that allows them to begin acting in ways that are informed (inspired) by that future field. For the community of farmers, "going through the needle" created a very productive string of years that gave rise to manifold initiatives, ventures, and collaborative efforts that continued to shape and reshape the farm and its local context.

In a nutshell, all these stories illustrate that in order to move through that eye of the needle, we must look at old issues in new ways and bring our *real selves* into the situation.

The Presence of the Circle Being

Moving into the realm of presencing happens to groups when you go through the eye of the needle. First, they feel a strong connectedness among the group members. Then you sense among yourselves the power of authentic presence. Once a group has experienced that level of connection, there is a deep and subtle bond that remains. The Circle of Seven, for example, has systematically developed the tools and means to move into this place of connectedness and authenticity together. But it takes a fair amount of risk and a willingness to let go of fear. "This may not be true for others," said Glennifer, "but for me it's so hard to release my personal boundary and relax into the circle. It takes a huge amount of inner work and letting go for me to do that. Each of us works differently with how we let go into the collective. Each time it requires crossing a threshold."

I asked Glennifer what it was like to cross such a threshold. "I feel," she responded, "as though I'm going to die if I let go into the circle. So I have to notice and be okay with that feeling. Crossing that boundary is what I imagine it must feel like to die. Who will I be? Because I don't know, I'm not sure how to protect myself."

"So what happens next?" I wanted to know.

"Then I usually step over the boundary. If I step all the way, it's such a relief to have taken the step. I feel freer. Somehow I didn't know beforehand that I would feel freer, even though I've done it before.

"When everyone's done that, we have this collective presence in a different way. We have a new being—the presence of the Circle Being. My experience is that until I've done that, I don't experience the Circle Being. After that, it's beyond me as an individual. I don't matter so much as an individual anymore. Yet, paradoxically, I'm more of an individual at the same time."

After a moment of silence someone else said, referring to Glennifer, "You stepped over the boundary here. If I were to describe this energetically, as you started to speak, your voice was higher. You spoke quickly and breathily. As you pushed into what's on the inside and what's on the other side of that threshold, your rhythm and the pacing changed. Your voice tone dropped. And the energy moved from here (pointing at head) to here (indicating chest and gut). What I saw happening was that you took a risk. There has to be a risk in order for the collective to show up. The risk can be one person's, two people's, or all of ours, but there has to be some kind of risk or vulnerability for crossing the threshold that you're talking about. I felt the whole space shift. Because you took a risk, it shifted the space for all of us."

The Holding Practice

"If we have a dominant circle practice," Ann explained, "it has to do with holding."

I asked, "When you listen to one another, how do you cultivate your listening so that you can function as a collective holding space?"

The women described three different conditions of listening that enable a collective holding space to emerge (see Figure 11.2). The first one they call unconditional witnessing. "The quality of witnessing or holding that we're talking about here is personal identification with the source in the circle. Something like: the eyes through which you see, the heart through which you feel, the ears with which you listen are not personal.

"So there is very little projection onto the situation. There is little intent other than opening to what life wants to have happen right then. There's sensitivity without manipulation. A spirit of nonjudgment and blessing."

The second one is clearing the horizontal space with unconditional love. "The focus of energy drops out of the head and into the heart in the room, because the opening usually happens when somebody's heart really opens, and definitely when the field is identified. The energy field has to drop.

"There is a blessing that comes with impersonal love. It's the impersonality of the love. Your personality isn't in it. And I do think we as a collective somehow manage to just hold that impersonal level," Anne explained.

The third condition has to do with where you put your attention: seeing the essential self. "I see through that wound to the truth of her," Barbara

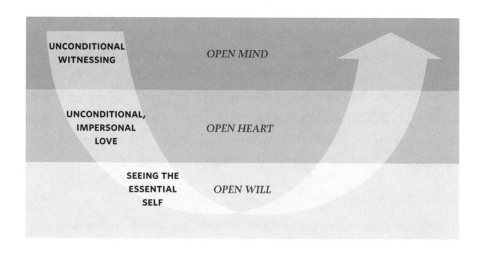

FIGURE 11.2 THREE CONDITIONS OF DEEP LISTENING AND HOLDING

noted. "So it's where I place my awareness that does the work. . . . It's a discipline of attention that has to do with how I see the people who are described by others in the circle."

"We have an agreement," added Leslie, "to see the essential self that we call the no-mess-up clause. No matter what one of us does, she can't mess up as far as the others are concerned. So the intention is placed on the essential self. We have a shared belief that one of the greatest forms of service to people is to see their essential selves—that somehow through my seeing that, they experience more of themselves."

"This may be my own attribution," said Glennifer, "but here's how I experience work in the circle, if I'm the one who's doing the work, being witnessed, or assisted by another person. My experience is that there's a thickness in the atmosphere—an enabling presence—that allows me to go deeper than if, say, Beth and I were working only with one another. . . . I see more. I see more of myself. I see more of what I'm working with. Now, I don't know whether that's because of the skill levels in the group or whether it's because of the quality of attention or a combination of both. But my experience is that I see more; I experience more of myself.

"I feel like a bigger person. I feel fuller in my own being. And I feel empowered or enabled in a particular way. I feel seen. I feel the focus of attention is fine; that it's qualitative, nonjudgmental, and loving. And I feel the presence of the Circle Being, which is different from the sum of the individuals.

"So I can't really describe it any differently than that. When it's not there, I know it. It takes a little time for the Circle Being's presence to be evoked. But when it's present, there's a different quality to my experience. The quality of atmosphere is different. That's one thing. And the other is, I feel more enabled—I feel more powerful."

Being Seen and Witnessed as an Essential Self

Later I asked each of the women to draw two pictures: one that depicts the experience of a normal group meeting and another that depicts the experience of a circle meeting.

"In my first picture," explained Beth, "I thought about a particular new group working together on health care reform. I feel as if everybody's got their own little bubble around them—their identity. So I've drawn what they're walking in with in different colors. In a way, we already have something larger that we're about, but we don't know each other; we don't know if other people are really about the same thing. So there's distance between everyone.

"In the second picture," continued Beth, "there's an impression of the unique gift of each one's inner presence or essential self. What I see happening is more of our essential selves coming through, and at the same time, we're becoming more differentiated in our thoughts and contributions. We are experiencing more of our lives more fully as a result of being seen and witnessed both for who we fundamentally are and for our personality structures and points of view."

"In my experience of working at our highest, I put the same color as essential self on the individual and the collective levels. This basic presence is an aspect of the Great Field. But at the same time, we are all different, so I've also used different colors.

"In my experience, there's a circle around us, permeating and holding us all. That energy informs us if we are receptive, affecting our understanding, our feelings, and our whole expression. Coming through us individually, in a collective, light is shed on complicated challenges, usually characterized by a basic generosity and a comprehensive view.

"When I leave this circle and do my professional work, I bring the continued strength and substance of this space that we've created. I take it everywhere I go. I feel stronger in all those other places. I think people in my work environment feel a sense of their own presence and power as they come into contact with something we've experienced here. They, in turn, go out and take that kind of experience to others."

Looking at the second picture, I was struck how strongly it resonated with the field structure of attention that connects to and originates from "those who are surrounding us," "the beings who surround us."

"So when you say the 'Circle Being,' is that just a concept—just a label?

Or does it denote a living presence?" I asked.

"I will give you an example," Leslie replied. "We have friends who come here to initiate new directions or projects in the circle. I'm thinking of Lexi, for example, who felt drawn to call together a circle of younger women, based on her mentorship work with some of us. She knew that if she sat in our circle, not with us as individuals but in the presence of the Circle Being, that her seed for the young women's circle would grow. So the Circle Being acts on potential.[8]

"There are many things that people have placed in this circle to be cared for by the action of the field."

"How can you tell if the Circle Being is present?"

"It's a change in atmosphere. My ears ring; things slow down; time changes. A quality of depersonalization sets in, and I am urged not to speak casually. I speak when I'm moved by a larger presence that needs a voice. There is always a bit of a mix, but overall it jump-shifts into another zone. Sometimes we note, 'We've dropped into the field.'"

"So, Otto," said Barbara, turning to me. "I have a real-time consideration. I'm wondering if you'd like you and your work to be held by this circle?"

With that question, I felt a palpable presence. I realized that this question actually had crossed my mind earlier in the interview. But of course, I would have never dared to ask. Now, after Barbara raised the possibility, I felt unable to react. My ears were ringing. I suddenly realized how much I'd missed my European community of friends living, learning, and joyfully creating together. I also realized how much I missed the presence of such a collective holding space in my current life. I must have waited a long time before I quietly said, "Yes, I would love to."

When speaking these words I felt the witnessing, loving presence not only of each individual circle member, but beyond. I was held and witnessed in a special space. I felt *looked at* or witnessed by field or entitiy that wasn't me.

Principles of Presencing

Presencing happens in the context of groups, teams, and organizations as well as with individuals. I often encounter the phenomenon in deep listening and dialogue interviews. In these conversations, it's pretty obvious when the conversation drops from one level to another. You can feel it in your whole body. People often describe it as a heart-to-heart connection. I often experience it as a subtle field of presence connecting my interviewee and me, a field that surrounds and holds us in an open, deeply generative, and quieting state of mind. Four distinct principles define this shift:

Letting Go and Surrendering

Letting go of the old and surrendering to the unknown is the first principle. Francisco Varela, Eleanor Rosch, and Brian Arthur all emphasize it as the core element of the journey. "Everything that isn't essential must go," Brian Arthur told us when he described crossing the threshold. When you start to suspend your habitual ways of operating and your attention is grabbed by something that surprises or interests you—something concrete, specific, and unexpected. When that happens, you begin to access your open mind. The burning farmhouse cleared the space and allowed me to move my seeing beyond all the patterns of the past. At such a moment you must let go. What's the point of holding on to a past identity that just went up in flames? In such a case the gesture of letting go is easy. You just surrender to what's obvious. But life doesn't always offer us the mechanism of burning down one's old structures. The challenge is how to access the deep territory without burning down the family farm?

In the absence of a dramatic event like that, we have to perform the activity of letting go and surrendering much more consciously. In the Circle of Seven, Glennifer said it felt as if she were going to die: "Because there's a boundary that has to be stepped over. . . . I imagine that there'll be nothing on the other side and that I won't be who I am now when I cross the boundary." For the participants in the farming community, this involved letting go of their firmly held views about the purpose and identity of the farm, of themselves, and of other participants in the group. For the employees of the oil company in Houston, it involved letting go of enormous group and leadership pressure to meet previously established deadlines and expectations.

For Steven, it involved the process of letting go of his prepared remarks and his fully loaded PowerPoint presentation and to stare into the faces of the 260 hostile people in front of him. It involved his courage to totally die and surrender into that situation.

Letting go and surrendering can be thought of as two sides of the same coin. Letting go concerns the opening process, the removal of barriers and junk in one's way, and surrendering is moving into the resulting opening. When Dave felt that a significant question was beginning to build up within and around him, he had to give it all his attention and simply go with it, surrender to it, whatever it was. When I conduct dialogue interviews, I regularly have to let go of my old intentions, road maps, and lists of questions and simply surrender to what emerges in the conversation.

Inversion: Going Through the Eye of the Needle

"Inversion" is the word I use to describe what happens when a person or a group goes through the eye of the needle and begins to link with an emerging field. The German word for inversion, *Umstülpung*, literally means "turning inside out and outside in." When you pass through the eye of the needle—the threshold at which everything that isn't essential must go—you shift the place from which you operate to "those who are surrounding us"; you begin to see from a different direction, you begin to move toward your self *from* the future.

In the Circle of Seven, Beth described feeling larger, feeling something come *through* her. I also experienced this shift of perspective when I felt witnessed not only by the circle members but also by another presence that wasn't me or the individuals in the room. With the farming community the inversion happened after our Saturday night's conversation was based on individuals' sharing and exchanging their stories and views. The next morning, people started talking from a different point. It was only then that they could ask: What does the *being* of this place mean for fully realizing its future potential?

For the Houston oil company employees, the inversion took place in the moment of silence after David had asked the perceptive question, right before Joseph and the others followed David through "the eye of the needle" and helped to open that space further. All of them, at that moment, shifted their place of operating from inside themselves to a deeper spot from which a collective creativity began to flow through the group. For the participants in the German Patient-Physician Dialogue Forum, an inversion clearly took place somewhere between Saturday morning, when the patients took their places at one end of the room and the doctors grouped together at the other end, and the next morning, when that little group of physicians and patients sat together outside in a circle. One critical turning point was the statement from the heart by the woman who did not want the system to harm the physicians, whom she knew and cared about. In the case of Steven, the inversion took place right after the silence, when he started attending to the buzzing and the profound energy shift in the room: ". . . the audience and I just stare at each other. . . . Total silence. All of a sudden, though, everything is different. I hear something like a buzzing in the air. All of a sudden there is a strength, which comes from being convinced that what we're doing is right." In almost all the examples we see a moment of deep silence before the shifting of the field happens.

The Coming into Being of a Higher (Authentic) Presence and Self

In the Circle of Seven, Glennifer said, "My experience is that I see more, I experience more of myself. I feel like a bigger person. I feel fuller in my own being. And I feel enabled in a particular way—I feel more powerful." When you switch from empathic listening to listening from a deeper source or stream of emergence that connects you to a field of future possibility that wants to emerge. When operating from that deeper presence of a future that wants to emerge, you connect to yet a deeper resource of listening and of intelligence that is available to both human beings and systems—the intelligence of the open will.

I have experienced these kinds of shifts time and again in dialogue interviews. What happens is that you leave that conversation as a different being—a different person—from the one who entered the conversation a few hours earlier. You are no longer the same. You are (a tiny bit) more who you really are. Sometimes that tiny bit can be quite profound. I remember that in one instance I had a physical sensation of a wound when I left a particularly profound conversation. Why? Because that conversation created a generative social field that connected me with a deeper aspect of my journey and Self. Leaving that holding space—the social field—discontinued that deeper connection, which I then experienced as an open wound.

When David articulated his question in Houston, he had, as he told me two years later, actually had a profound personal experience in which he experienced the opening of a whole other dimension of his emerging self.

When the group of farmers had their conversation about the deep and changing identity of their self, their relationship and their place, they also experienced a forward pull from a different kind of opening or possibility that somehow connected with the embodiment of an emerging or different kind of self—the authentic or essential Self.

When Steven came out of the silence, he felt that "I am in a whole new playing field: All of a sudden I am strong and I feel the power of connection and doing the right thing."

In each of these instances we see the same fundamental happening: the arrival, the beginning birth, and the coming into being of a new self, the essential or the authentic self that connects us with who we really are.

The Power of Place: Creating a Holding Space of Deep Listening

The fourth principle concerns the power of place. Presencing happens in places; that is, in some context of holding space. The Circle of Seven described the three conditions in this space: unconditional witnessing or no judgment, impersonal love, and seeing the essential self. When this shift happens, a new type of relationship between the individual and the collective self takes shape. Said Beth, "In my experience, there's a circle around us, permeating and holding us all." In the case of the farming community, the Houston-based oil company, and the Patient-Physician Dialogue Forum, the holding space was consciously created through a process of context sharing, storytelling, and deep listening. In the case of the car company (and in the case of my fire story) this context was created through a real-life crisis that broke up our habitual routines with an existential threat that almost forced us to attend and to let go of the old.

In many cases, nature can also function as a teacher and gateway into that deeper place. How to use and leverage the presence and power of certain places for accessing the authentic dimension of self in individuals and in communities is one of the most interesting research questions for the years to come.

Field Notes

The golden thread that runs through all the stories is about the simple distinction between sensing—acting from the current whole—and presencing—operating from the emerging future whole. There are various leverage points to deepen one's capacity to operate from that deeper source. They are:

Pick a practice. The currency that counts at the bottom of the U is not ideas but practices. Many of the people (interviewees, clients, and others) I have been most impressed by have their own cultivation practices. That is, most of them do something in the morning, such as getting up early and using the silence of the first hour to connect to a source of commitment and creativity. Some meditate. Some use other contemplative practices. There is no standard recipe, just as there isn't a standard practice. People must discover for themselves what works and what doesn't.

Create a circle of presence. Create a context of people that allows you to support one another in the unfolding of your journey and in the pursuit of deeper questions and challenges that present themselves. Think of the Circle of Seven as an example. Theirs is not the only way to do it. But it works for them. The principle here is the principle of a regular holding space. Such a holding space can lend us the wings we need to cross the thresholds our life's journey presents to us.

Develop collective cultivation practices. Develop collective cultivation practices such as intentional silence or generative dialogue that provide access to the deeper sources of communal awareness and attention in the context of everyday life and work. The development of new collective presencing practices is one of the most urgent and important undertakings of the years to come. A collective presencing practice is different from an individual one in that the various sensing and presencing experiences of the individuals are used as *gateways* to connecting with and entering the deeper source of collective creativity and knowing (as exemplified in the farming community story).

Do what you love—love what you do. This is another thing Michael Ray said. It refers to his root question: What is my Work? I have found that there is a very simple formula that explains my sustained level of energy. It doesn't take more than two simple conditions: what I am doing must really matter (connect to my purpose), and it must create a positive difference (feedback mechanism). If these two conditions are met, I am in an ever-increasing positive energy loop.

In summary, each of us is not one but two. Each person and each community is not one but two. On the one hand, we are the person and community that *we have become* on our journey from the past to the present—the current self. On the other, there is the other, the *dormant* self, *the one that is waiting within us to be born*, to be brought into existence, to come into reality through our journey ahead. Presencing is the process of connecting these two selves. To connect our current with our authentic self. To move toward our real self from the future.

When we enter that deeper state of being—as individuals and as communities—we enter a state of fundamental freedom and capacity to create. We step into our real freedom. Hence, the social technology of presencing is a technology of freedom. Operationally that means that the defining feature of entering the field of presencing is the absence of manipulation and manipulative practices. That's the core. In doing this work, all we can do is to open the doors. But we can never ever take away the decision each human being makes: to go through this door—or to stop short of it.

In crossing the threshold, we step into our real power—the power of operating from our highest future Self; the power of connecting with "the beings who surround us."[9] This deep connection has been described by different names in various wisdom traditions: the presence of Source (Daoism), natural state (Buddhism), Brahman (Hindu traditions), Yahweh (Judaism), Allah (Muslim traditions), God, Christ, The Holy Spirit (Christian traditions), or The Great Spirit (Native traditions). All these terms name the same fundamental level of experience and describe a deeper state of being that can become present within us and through us, both individually and collectively. But for this presencing to happen, we must cross the threshold at the bottom of the U.

CHAPTER 12

Crystallizing

The Patient-Physician Dialogue Forum • The Field Structure
of Crystallizing • Principles of Crystallizing • Field Notes

The last chapter described the bottom of the U process, Presencing. Earlier, as you might recall, I described *presencing* as the eye of the needle or the process of *Umstülpung* (turning inside out and outside in). In ancient Jerusalem, there was a gate called "the needle" which was so narrow that when a fully loaded camel approached the gate, the camel-driver had to take off all the bundles before the camel could pass through. Referring to this well-known image of his day, Jesus said, "It is easier for a camel to go through the eye of a needle than for a rich man to enter the kingdom of God."[1] Likewise, at the bottom of the U lies an inner gate, which requires us to drop everything that isn't essential.

What is it that constitutes this eye of the needle at the bottom of the U for groups, organizations and communities? It is the connecting to our authentic or higher self, to our capital-S Self. If this connection is established, the first thing that happens is: nothing. No-thing. It's just a connection. But, when we succeed in *keeping* that connection to our deeper source of knowing alive, we begin to better tune into emerging future possibilities. Acting now, from a "different place," we are able to begin to operate from a different source. We envision, prototype and embody the new.

The term *presencing* can be used as either a noun or a verb and designates the connection to the deeper source of self and knowing. But because we keep that connection alive across the whole right-hand side of the U, we can say that we keep presencing (connecting and operating from source) throughout our entire journey of the right hand side of the U. The term *crystallizing* designates the first stage of that process.

Crystallizing means clarifying vision and intention from our highest future possibility. The difference between crystallizing and normal visioning processes is this: crystallizing happens from the deeper place of knowing and self, while visioning can happen from just about anyplace, even from the place of downloading.

After such a moment of stillness or presencing, in groups, you can notice a subtle shift in identity and a different foundation for working together and moving forward. Up to this point, we have only *felt* the possibility of a future. After a presencing experience, people are now poised to bring this individual and collective potential into reality. "We *can't not* do it." The first step in this journey is to crystallize the vision and intention more clearly. We put into specific language what it is that we want to create.

The Patient-Physician Dialogue Forum

After the group of physicians and patients formed a strong collective conversational field of thinking together, they were ready to move from the sensemaking phase to the action phase. If we did that successfully, the event would produce some activity that could change or even transform the quality of the patient-physician relationships. If we didn't, our efforts would all be wasted.

"We'd like to shift gears this afternoon and invite you to brainstorm about what kinds of actions and initiatives might help us move from here [*pointing at Levels 1 and 2*] to here [*pointing at Levels 3 and 4*]. If you have any practical ideas about how to move our health care system from its current state, symbolized by the blue dots, to where all the white dots are, now is the time to propose it to the rest of us. And just so you know," Ursula and I added, "there will be no afternoon session unless you come up with enough initiatives that excite and engage us to define the agenda for the afternoon."

You could see the skepticism and disbelief in their faces, followed by uncertain silence. No one had left during the lunch break, and it was obvious that the group was engaged and interested. They wanted to move on, but they had never been asked to take over the agenda of an event in an "open space" approach.[2] You could see the wheels turning: *You guys can't be serious. You must be kidding. Aren't you? . . . Well, maybe we'd better get our act together. What could I possibly propose? Wasn't I just thinking about something that might . . .*

After an active silence, one person stood up and suggested an initiative for a group. Then another person rose to suggest a second. Followed by a third, and so forth. Before long we had the group split up into six or seven groups working on different action initiatives. At the end of the day each smaller group reported back to the whole group.

One group wanted to found a *Bürgerforum*, a civic forum that would create a place and voice for the people of the region within the health care system. Another group proposed ways to broaden the support for an existing initiative, the restructuring of the region's emergency care system. A third group suggested a patient initiative to work on the capacities patients and doctors needed to create and sustain a "dialogue relationship." A fourth group was developing steps to "sensitize youth" to chronic disease, planning to take their stories into schools and discuss how they could have taken a different course through prevention.

Dr. Gert Schmidt, the co-founder of the physician network and health care initiative, helped the core group clarify its vision and intent. "Looking at our situation here," he said, "you could get depressed. We have 280,000 inhabitants, 60,000 chronically ill people, 10 hospitals, 15,000 employees, 400 physician practices, plus the whole bureaucracy that comes with all these institutions. Each year we have six million contacts between patients and the health care system in this region. How can we possibly change? But the forum has helped me look at all this in a different way. It can all be reduced to a single simple formula: Patient A has problem B and wants C. It's just like in chaos theory: you reduce the behavior of complex systems to the relationship of three or so variables. When I started to see the essence of the health care system in terms of this equation, I realized that the core axis around which the whole system revolves is the relationship between patients and physicians. Before the dialogue forum, we had never dared to conceive of this fundamental truth. But now, even the insurance companies and other health care providers have come to accept this view. Without an intact patient-physician relationship, no health care system can ever work."

He went on to explain that he now understood that the key to solving many issues lies in focusing on the region. "The health issues are defined through your genes, your biography, your social context, and the structure and processes of the health care system you operate in. You can't change your biology, your genes, but your biography, your context, the structures and processes of the health care system—all of that is enacted locally, all of that you can change in the context of a region. The courage to boil all of this down to the very essence where you start to see what you can create, the courage to boil all of this down to that point where your next action becomes evident, that courage stems from the dialogue forum and from the system analysis we have been doing."

Dr. Schmidt and his colleagues left the Patient-Physician Dialogue Forum feeling a charged inner energy: "We intend to move our system from Levels 1 and 2 to Levels 3 and 4."

Many of the forum's insights became reality because of the group's structured attentiveness to each level of interaction. In 2000, a year after the forum took place, the contracts were signed and the new emergency care system began operation. Now, rather than treating every call to 112 (the German equivalent of 911) as an emergency, physicians can provide comfort, counseling, or a home visit as needed. At the same time, the system lessens the burden on physicians by directing calls to a single center rather than to a hundred individual practitioners. One senior health care executive said that he thought the ideas succeeded because of the "forum's core group whose quality of commitment and intention radiated over time and changed the consciousness of the system's decision makers."

The Field Structure of Crystallizing

Presencing, as we have said, is connecting to source. Crystallizing means sustaining that connection and beginning to operate from it. The first practical aspect of this journey is to clarify what wants to emerge. Crystallizing facilitates the surfacing of a living imagination of the future whole. It clarifies the vision and intent of the emerging future.

In the case of Dr. Schmidt and the German health care network, this resulted in a deeper systemic view and in the clarification of the intention "to move our system from Levels 1 and 2 to Levels 3 and 4," including some tangible initiatives for prototyping this new way of operating.

In the case of a strategy reinvention process with the procurement group of a global company, the key result of the crystallizing phase was a new identity, a new way that group wanted to go about its business in the future. "We are not just service providers to the plants—we are actually the managers of a global business." As a consequence, the group came up with prototyping initiatives that resulted in reducing the number of its suppliers by 80 percent. They did this by making the formerly competing suppliers collaborate with one another, reminiscent of how strategic global networks speak with one voice to the global company and its globally distributed networks of plants.

"What struck me most," said Peter Brunner, who coached the team throughout the whole intervention process, "is that it was so different from a normal visioning process. In a visioning process, you just come up with a dream of the future, even though that might be quite disconnected from what is wanting to emerge. But having gone through the learning journeys, sharing and reflecting on it and a six hour personal field walk in silence, I simply had people share their vision and intention going forward as they returned back from their silent walk. What they came up with was much, much more essential and connected to what they really care about.

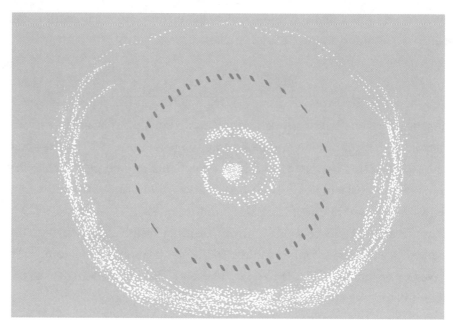

FIGURE 12.1 THE FIELD STRUCTURE OF CRYSTALLIZING

To their real selves. And that helped a lot in coming up with the right prototype initiatives."

Figure 12.1 depicts the crystallizing field structure of attention. The place
from which you operate (the dot) has shifted toward the surrounding sphere
(outside the white circle that represents the boundaries of the observer).
When you operate from that larger holding space, something new begins to
emerge from the center; it begins to crystallize.

I asked Peter Senge to describe what he does when he creates. "To create
music, you have to have violins. You have to have instruments, okay? But the
music doesn't come from the violin. The violin is an instrument. For me, at
an experiential level, giving a talk or working with a group in a workshop can
be the same. I create that reality in my own consciousness, and then I play
the instruments. I just really, really enjoy myself; I kind of fall into my love
of the people. And I know, at some level, when I'm doing those programs
and things begin to operate this way, nothing can go wrong. No matter what
happens, it's exactly what needs to happen right then. Now, I don't always

feel that way, but I know when that kind of state develops. This is what in the Christian tradition we call a state of grace, because I think there is a deep understanding of this in the mystic Christian tradition. It's just so much [about] joy. That doesn't mean it's always happy. Sometimes it's very intense, but you literally have the experience that absolutely nothing could possibly go wrong. That doesn't mean it always turns out according to your plan. It means that *whatever turns out is exactly what is right in that moment, and that is the music.*"

He continued, "When we are leading a program or course, we say a good rule of thumb is that the quality of the relationship between the people will have a bigger impact than the articulateness of the presenters. Say that two people are facilitating. The single most important generative feature is the quality of that relationship. It's not a smooth relationship. It's a relationship with a lot of presence, being, or consciousness that you can be present with whatever is there together. To me, that's the essence of a loving relationship, because love is about presence.

"I think there is a deeper force that's dominant, and has to do with this capacity to live in the world you want to create. . . . If you know what you want to create, then you can to some degree live in that space in your own consciousness. There is no more powerful force than operating from that kind of knowing, from that kind of intention and place."

Principles of Crystallizing

There are four principles that in my observation come into play when moving into the space of crystallizing: the power of intention, letting come, grand will, and venues for waking up.

The Power of Intention

Nick Hanauer has founded half a dozen highly successful companies and was a board member of Amazon.com for many years. When Joseph Jaworski and I interviewed him, he was working with a small group of people to "reinvent" the educational system in the state of Washington. When we asked about the role of intention in his entrepreneurial experience, Hanauer replied, "One of my favorite sayings, attributed to Margaret Mead, has always been 'Never doubt that a small group of committed citizens can change the world. Indeed, it's the only thing that ever has.' I totally believe it. You could do almost anything with just five people. With only one person, it's hard—but when you put that one person with four or five more, you have a force to contend with. All of a sudden, you have enough momentum to make almost anything that's immanent, or within reach, actually real. I think that's what entrepreneurship is all about—creating that compelling vision and force."

The first time I personally encountered the power of intention was during my student days at Witten/Herdecke University in Germany. I was sitting at a large breakfast table with about a dozen other students. With us on that morning was the dean of the Management School, Ekkehard Kappler, and a special guest, Johan Galtung, the Norwegian founder of peace research as a science and the recipient of the Right Livelihood Award, also known as the Alternative Nobel Prize. Galtung, famous for his theory of structural violence, had taught at more than sixty universities on all continents and published over a hundred books. One student turned to him and asked, "Johan, having accomplished all that you have, what's left for you now? What is it that you want to create in the remaining years of your life?"

"I have an idea for a mobile global peace university. Its students would travel the world learning how to see the global system as a living whole and viewing it from the perspectives of different cultures and civilizations."

When he then started to describe in more detail what that global learning journey would look like, I knew this was what I was meant to do. Others at the table that morning had the same feeling. That knowing was a source of enormous energy. As it turned out, Galtung had tried to realize such a global university project with a U.S. college. But the complexity of organizing, financing, and managing it had proved too great. Although as students we lacked any experience in such matters, we knew in our guts that we could do it. And then we did. In record time.

Five of us pulled it together in just a few months: we mapped out the projects, raised a half-million dollars from industry and private sponsors, contracted with twelve partner universities and 290 lecturers, recruited and selected the first class of thirty-five students from ten different countries, including participants from third-world countries and Eastern Europe, raised money for scholarships, and handled the financial and organizational details by putting in time as volunteers. Our joint commitment to this project empowered us in a way that none of us had ever experienced before. We felt part of a larger field, a formative field of creation. When we were operating in that field, we knew that nothing would prevent us from succeeding. Yes, we hit walls and obstacles time and again. But each time we encountered a setback, we knew that we would bounce back by some kind of "predictable miracle," some kind of door would open up or helping hand would show up and lead us onward.

Jaworski describes this kind of coincidental help as "synchronicity" and suggests that the whole U process is about just that: getting into the flow of that deep intention and going with it.[3] Many entrepreneurs concur with Brian Arthur when he says, "Intention is not a powerful force; it is the *only* force."[4]

Letting Come

The inner work of getting into this flow has a lot to do with letting go and letting come. Letting come is the other side of the power of intention. The real question is: How can you tune in to that intention? The answer is: Tuning in to something new requires that you must first let go of something old. If I think about it, almost all of my most successful projects were suggested to me by other people. Galtung's idea for a global peace university is just one example. That is why the U process starts with observation (going into and attending to the world) and not with retreating and reflection. First you go into the world. As you follow your trail, the universe has its way of suggesting to you what to do. Then you listen to it deeply. You pay attention to what is emerging from within. To do that in a really deep way, you have to learn to let go and let come. Old attitudes must die in order for new ideas to move into the picture more clearly and more fully.

Grand Will

As we open up to the new, we gradually tap into our deeper will, the one that Martin Buber refers to as grand will. In his book *I and Thou*, Buber gives a very precise account of the double movement that is involved when accessing one's grand will:

> The free man is he who wills without arbitrary self-will.
>
> He believes in destiny, and believes that it stands in need of him. It does not keep him in leading strings, it awaits him, he must go to it, yet does not know where it is to be found. But he knows that he must go out with his whole being. The matter will not turn out according to this decision; but what is to come will come only when he decides on what he is able to will. He must sacrifice his puny, unfree will, that is controlled by things and instincts, to his grand will, which quits defined for destined being. Then, he intervenes no more, but at the same time he does not let things merely happen. He listens to what is emerging from himself, to the course of being in the world; not in order to be supported by it, but in order to bring it to reality as it desires.[5]

Buber starts by assuming that free human beings believe in destiny—a destiny that stands in *need* of us—yet we don't know where to find it. To find it, we must be willing to move into an unknown territory and to go out with "our whole being." It may demand sacrifice. This is not merely about contemplating—it's about listening to the course of being in the world to what is wanting to emerge with the full intention of acting on it. And, once under way, we must pay careful attention.

The physicist Arthur Zajonc moderated the Dalai Lama–Cognitive Science Dialogue at MIT. He told me he believes that when he moderates, he has more than the visible people present at the table—he also wants to hear what the "invisible" have to say.

"I've developed a couple of little practices. For instance, I'll be in a board meeting where the energy is tough and maybe I'm up against some hot issue. I don't know how to deal with it. I find myself in those times letting go. It's a practice of saying 'Okay, we've had full, bloody attention on this thing. We've really turned over a lot of stuff.' Then I kind of sit back and expand in nonfocal awareness. Empty out. Sometimes I even pretend there's an invisible person next to me. When I was chairing the board of a new school, sometimes I would imagine invisible children at the table. I was actually working for these children who were not yet born or were not yet there. They were my reason for being there. I try to listen into the space. The future is also at the table. There is a wonderful creative moment when everyone present recognizes a special moment. I encourage them to hold on to it, to play it out.

"Those moments give a lot of positive energy to a group. There's a feeling of originality, can-do, and collaboration. Nobody takes ownership, because the idea could have come from somebody else across the table."

Venues for Waking Up

For crystallizing to happen, a certain environment or context is required.

In a farming community workshop in Germany, the core group of farmers invited people from the neighboring communities, people they thought would somehow be connected to the future of that place. The design of the one day event followed the U process. During the morning, about eighty participants checked in and connected with one another on what was emerging in their life's journey and context. During the afternoon we formed five initiative groups around what they wanted to co-create, similar to what Ursula and I had done in the Patient-Physician Dialogue Forum.

About a year later, we learned that four of the five groups had initiated an astonishing stream of activities and events. They had founded a kindergarten-type play group on the farm (which soon after turned into a fully accredited kindergarten); created and co-sponsored a series of concerts and cultural events on the farm; formed and implemented cross-institutional collaborations that include sharing machinery (a great money-saver); and organized several successful seminars on self-leadership as precursor to additional public seminar offerings in the future.

Why had that one-day meeting been so much more effective than many earlier meetings with the core group of the farm?

There probably had been a dormant potential all along. But unless there is an infrastructure that creates a context for sensing and crystallizing together—a one-day workshop in this case—nothing is going to happen.

Field Notes

The golden thread of this chapter identifies and weaves together two types of will: small will and grand will. By tapping into the authenticity and connectedness that emerge from a presencing experience, the group can become aware of its deeper intention or "will." The second type of will, grand will, involves acting on the following principles:

- Clarifying your own intention by "testing" it against the future possibility that has emerged from the presencing experience
- Broadcasting the power of intention to create the opening for creative emergence
- Letting come: listening to what emerges from within
- Acting as an instrument of the emerging future and bringing it into reality as it desires
- Building infrastructures for waking up together across institutional boundaries

Crystallizing means to stay connected to Source and to slowly clarify the vision and intention going forward. As we do this, our image of the future keeps evolving, changing, and morphing. Then we need to take this process of bringing the new into reality to its next level: by enacting living examples or prototypes of the future that we want to create.

CHAPTER 13

Prototyping

Health Care Network • The Field Structure of Prototyping •
Principles of Prototyping • Field Notes

Having established a connection to the source (presencing) and having clarified a sense of the future that wants to emerge (crystallizing), the next stage in the U process is to explore the future by doing (prototyping). Prototyping is the first step in exploring the future by doing and experimenting. We borrow this term from the design industry. David Kelley, founder and long time CEO of the influential design firm IDEO summarizes the approach to prototyping succinctly: "Fail often to succeed sooner."[1] For example, prototyping means to present a concept before you are done. Prototyping allows fast-cycle feedback learning and adaptation.

Health Care Network

Dr. Schmidt and his colleagues left the dialogue forum with the intention of moving their system from Levels 1 and 2 to Levels 3 and 4, but they knew they needed different types of collaborative platforms to make it happen. So they decided to start by holding regional conversations among the key institutional players about practical issues they faced in their work. First, they defined the people who "own" the problems, the people who have the competence and responsibility to make decisions in their own institutional system. "We want to convene groups of practitioners who need one another in order to take effective action," said Dr. Schmidt.

"We talk about all the issues and problems openly and focus on creating actionable solutions and then we implement and review them quickly. When an issue is dealt with, the group dissolves. Currently we have ten of these groups operating. And they all work much more effectively than our groups used to do earlier."

Schmidt said that when they visit their colleagues in adjacent regions, they are very aware of how far they've come. "They're still worried about what the insurance companies will think and do. We've moved past that. Now we focus our time on where we can make the biggest difference." One of Schmidt's action groups focused on chronic diabetes. It convened key practitioners and diabetes patients and together developed a strategy for promoting new eating habits. In this way, they engage people to move beyond drugs and begin to live differently.

Other ad hoc action groups developed agreements for sharing specialized diagnostic equipment among medical groups; a new format for transferring information between hospitals and outside physicians; a jointly run office to coordinate care for patients moving between the two settings; and, last but not least, a new emergency control center. Now, in an emergency, patients have at least three networked options available. They can call a local physician, the center itself, or the emergency number to reach a centralized ambulance dispatcher.

Dr. Schmidt and his colleagues believe that coordinating these three options across the region will not only save money and time but also provide better patient care and make life easier for doctors. It makes an invisible connection to the area's elderly and chronically ill people who live on their own but feel "held" through the center. A physician hotline allows patients to consult a physician after hours and on weekends. This came about because research showed that 70 percent of all emergency calls weren't really about emergencies at all but rather people just seeking advice. Previously, an ambulance would routinely have been sent. But now, with physicians working side by side with paramedics in the new joint control center, taking hotline calls, they reduce the number of unnecessary ambulance trips and the patients are satisfied with their care. This alone has saved four times the cost of running the program.

The journey began with extensive and often frustrating negotiations among the key players—local hospitals, physicians, ambulance services, and insurance companies—each with its own interests, constraints, and turf allegiances. The breakthrough came when the practitioners began to speak about their own experiences, or those of loved ones, with the emergency system. The group soon reached a shared will and vision for more integrated, coherent patient service. That shared will allowed them to stay connected, and to succeed with their negotiation.

The Field Structure of Prototyping

Figure 13.1 is a visual representation of the field structure of attention. It resembles the two earlier ones, presencing and crystallizing. It takes the movement from presencing (connecting to source) and crystallizing (letting an image of the future emerge) to its next stage by deepening the holding space (white outer sphere) and by advancing the letting come process in the center of the figure from envisioning to enacting (emerging white form in the center).

To effectively prototype, we must integrate three types of intelligence: the intelligence of the head, of the heart, and of the hand. As Robert Redford said in the movie *The Legend of Bagger Vance,* "The wisdom in your hand is greater than the wisdom in your head will ever be." When we prototype living examples by integrating different types of intelligence, we always navigate the process between two major dangers and pitfalls: mindless action and actionless minds.

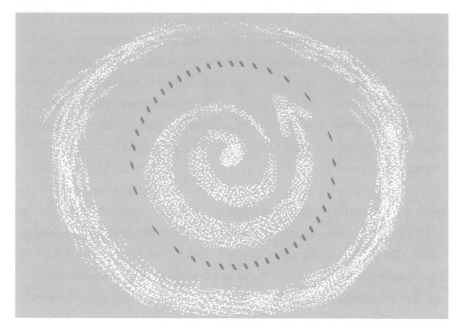

FIGURE 13.1 THE FIELD STRUCTURE OF PROTOTYPING

Principles of Prototyping

Integrating these different intelligences effectively requires connecting to the source as well as to the whole, fast-cycle feedback, and infrastructures for reviewing and awakening.

Connecting to the Inspiration

First and foremost, when moving into prototyping you need to stay connected to the inspirational spark of the future "that stands in need of you" (Buber).

"How do you do that?" I asked Joseph Jaworski, who is a master at establishing this kind of direct link.

"First off," he replied, "you need to do it on a daily basis. As a matter of fact, it's the first thing you do when you get up in the morning." Joseph has a set of personal practices that he does when getting up before dawn. "So the first thing is about practice, practice, practice. You create that place of silence for yourself every day."

As Joseph was speaking, I thought of my parents. By five a.m., when my father started milking the cows, he and my mother had already finished reading a morning meditative text together. I also thought of several of my interviewees who often practiced stillness during the first few hours before dawn.

"The second thing you focus on" continued Joseph, "is staying true and connected with that deeper intention all the time, throughout the whole day or week or year, or even longer."

What does it take to stay committed? Simone Amber of Schlumberger, an innovator in the area of corporate social responsibility, once told me, "It took me many years to take the step from idea to moving into action. What's important is that you don't blame yourself for that. What's important is that you stay true to your intention. But once I took that first step, doors opened, helping hands began to show up. It was as if I have been put on a track."

"The third practice," continued Joseph, is "to sense and seize opportunities as they arise. Whenever the real opportunities arise, it usually is not exactly where you expect it to happen. So you have to be really attentive. You have to pay attention to where that opportunity may arise that goes clunk with what your deeper intention tells you to do. When that happens, then you act in an instant. Then I operate from my highest self, which allows me to take risks . . . that I normally would not have taken.

"For example, I got the feeling, in the middle of a workshop, that we were called to create a larger initiative. I grabbed the CEO of a large multinational corporation, whom I knew only a little, and said: 'Wait here, we need to talk.' Then I went around and grabbed three more people: the head of a foundation, a senior executive of the U.S. National Park Service, as well as an NGO activist. I brought them back to the CEO, pulled five chairs into a small circle, and started the meeting. That moment actually was the beginning of the birth of an initiative that now is known as Synergos Multistakeholder Partnership Program."[2]

This little episode demonstrates several key aspects of acting from the future. First, the new shows up as a feeling, then as a vague sense of being drawn somewhere. It's more a sense of *what* than a sense of *why*. You feel drawn to doing something, but you don't know exactly why. And only then, after practically using the intelligence of your hands and your heart, does your head begin to figure out the why.

Acting, as Joseph did, "from the future"—sensing the feeling, feeling drawn to something, moving into that space, acting from the now, crystallizing what emerges from there, prototyping the new, delivering it into reality—can take years. Social innovators and innovators in business, like Simone Amber, claim that it took them up to five, six, or seven years before moving from a felt sense—feeling drawn to doing something—to crossing the threshold and beginning their journey of discovery and creation. But you also have to be prepared to act fast, as Joseph did. If it takes longer, the important point is not to harshly judge yourself just because you have been sitting with an idea for many years. Only one thing really matters: what you do in the very next moment—now. All the other decision points that are already behind us—all the should-haves and could-haves—no longer matter in any real way.

When acting from the past, we already know *why* before anything happens; that is, we start with the head. The head tells us to follow established routines, and the feeling we are left with is emptiness, at best, or sometimes frustration.

Here is what happened to Dr. Schmidt, the co-founder of the health care network in Germany. In the fall of 1994 he participated in a survey of local physicians about their medical practices and the prospects for the future. The survey showed that many doctors were near despair about their jobs, with little hope that things might change. Sixty percent of the physicians surveyed felt "inwardly resigned" to the stress of their jobs. Forty-nine percent said they had thought about suicide at least once. He himself was also stressed. In fact, a patient told him so. On the very day he finished reading the physicians' survey results, he left his office and ran into a patient who said, "You are so stressed, you don't have enough time for me." When he got home, his frustration was compounded when his ten-year-old daughter told him, "Daddy, I don't ever see you."

That's when he began talking to colleagues about how things might change. And, as we have learned, from those early conversations an entire network of physicians, patients, insurance companies, government, and other officials emerged and initiated a change process that resulted in reinventing the region's emergency care system.

In Dialogue with the Universe

Alan Webber, the co-founder of *Fast Company*, tells a similar story. He left his post as editor of the *Harvard Business Review* to explore an opportunity to co-create a new magazine; the eventual result was *Fast Company*. He began by tapping into his real intention—or intuition or spark of the future—that he felt wanted to emerge. He coupled that with learning to listen to the "feedback from the universe," as he put it.

"The universe," explained Webber, "actually is a helpful place. That means: whatever the response you are getting, you look at it from the assumption that it wants to help you in some way." Webber continued, "If you're open in relation to your idea, the universe will help you. It wants to suggest ways for you to improve your idea."

"Part of the adventure is listening to all the ideas and suggestions and trying to make your own calculations about which ones are helpful and which ones are harmful," Webber explained. He called this process "listening with an honest ear." You have to maintain the integrity of what you're doing, he said, but also maintain a sense of personal conviction that the initial concept you received was in fact an honest and good one. "You listen with an honest ear and you stay true to your inner sense and knowing."

That is exactly what Dr. Schmidt and his colleagues did in presenting their concepts to different parties and players. They took in and accepted the feedback that helped them to tweak, evolve, and iterate their concept of a new emergency care system. And they did not allow themselves to go mad listening to all of the initially discouraging feedback from people interested in preserving the status quo.

Joseph Jaworski did the same things when he co-created the multi-stakeholder partnership. He took in the feedback that helped move the concept forward, but ignored the rest. Such "input" goes in and out at almost the same moment.[3]

Principle o.8: Fail Early to Learn Quickly

At Cisco Systems, the networking equipment company, Principle o.8 says that regardless of how long-term your project is, you have to present the first prototype within three or four months. That prototype doesn't need to work. It's not the 1.0 prototype. But o.8 means you have to show up with *something*—something that isn't finished but that will allow you to elicit feedback that will take you, and it, to its next, improved version.

In the case of the health care network, the early prototype was the meetings, which produced little but led to the next step: creating ideas for joint platforms. In the case of the multistakeholder partnership, the prototype was an early, globally conducted interview project followed by a workshop that convened a microcosm of future core players that helped to both refocus and refine the purpose and approach of the project.

In the case of Alan Webber's *Fast Company*, the production of an initial prototype of the magazine helped to create both excitement and commitment on the part of all core players and sharpened the founders' focus on how to best evolve the approach and concept of the magazine.

Strategic Microcosms: Landing Strips for Emerging Future Possibilities

All prototypes need to be sheltered, supported, nurtured, and helped. From biology we know what happens when the new isn't hosted by a friendly environment: the immune system kicks in and does what it is designed to do: it kills it. Why? Because it is different. Because it threatens the status quo. Because it "doesn't belong here." That's why the fetus needs the womb, why everything new needs a cocoon to foster the right sheltering conditions in order for what's embryonic to be able to sprout.

On a farm you don't go out and pull up a shoot once a day just to check on how things are going. Instead, you water it and give it time. Nor do seeds want transparency or publicity. So, too, in organizations. The last thing you want is to have people constantly checking. You don't launch a new idea with a big public speech from an executive. No, you want to start in some smaller, quieter, and less pretentious place. You want to start with real practitioners dealing with real issues.

The health care network launched its strategy of building new collaborative platforms (ad hoc groups) without public notice. Says Ursula Versteegen, who has been coaching several of the projects of the health care network, "This initiative . . . started as a small, purely physician-driven initiative and then evolved into a set of cross-institutional platforms gathering the key practitioners of the region." And it produced "a whole landscape of new collaborative relationships that now we all take for granted."

Strategic microcosms—fragile living "shoots"—can be either *designed* or *embedded* into the infrastructure. Designed prototypes are wrapped around projects that intentionally focus on launching innovations. Think of the new emergency care control center, which was designed to incorporate and deliver new types of services. Embedded infrastructures, on the other hand, are situated in and wrapped around an ongoing praxis. We asked a group of doctors and patients for examples of new "embedded" relationships developing in the health care system. They pointed us to an NGO that helps patients to complete paperwork, interact with physicians, and navigate the system. It is an excellent example of an emerging innovation that is situated in the context of the old system, in this case in the context of completing a form. Here is one nurse's story: "An elderly woman patient was here this morning asking for a living will, but I told her we don't just hand this form out because it involves a far-reaching decision. The woman rolled her eyes and said, 'I just want to sign my name and be done with it.' I told her the form requires serious consideration. You might write on the form, 'I don't want any life-prolonging measures when I am terminally ill,' which might be interpreted, 'I don't want any infusions,' and that could mean that you would die miserably of thirst. Or this statement could also mean you would not be fed artificially, which would be legitimate while dying.

"These are the kinds of examples I give patients, and once I've managed to get their attention, they are all ears. Then they understand the magnitude of what they are signing. Having trained as a nurse, I have seen many people dying without ever having had such a self-reflective process beforehand, but it was only when my own mother died that I realized what it really meant to have such a patient's will in our hands. I had to fulfill the role of guardian for my mother. She had had a stroke and was on a respirator. I remember watching three doctors standing at her bedside. My mother just lay there. She couldn't remember anything, even though she was still aware. She was like a babbling child, and she kept asking the same questions. At the beginning the neurologist and the senior physician stood there and talked to each other about her, over her head. She was like an object. But when I showed them my mother's living will, they read it and began to see her personality between the lines of the decisions she had made. She was no longer an object. Although she still wasn't clear about what was going on, they respected her because she had given this situation so much thought in advance. Her foresight gave them the capacity to act on an individual level. All of a sudden she was there as a person and I was greeted with a huge amount of respect. And there was deep relief on the doctors' side."[4]

Even a bureaucratic requirement to complete a form can be turned into a vehicle for an embedded infrastructure. In this case, the purpose of the infrastructure is to spark a process of reflection that will have a profound effect on the patient-physician relationship. The infrastructure pulls the patient out of the "fix my problem" behavior and initiates a process of self-reflection that improves the relationship between the physician and the patient. The patient takes responsibility for her life and health. Other health care providers have found that scheduling chronic and acute patients in separate blocks of time allows them to focus on their conditions and as a result provide more personalized consultation and education.[5]

The Sustainable Food Laboratory, initiated in June 2004, also exemplifies cross-institutional prototyping. It's a collaboration among governmental, business, and civil society organizations in Europe, North America, and Latin America. After several workshops, a learning journey, and a wilderness retreat in Arizona, the group formed prototype teams. Seven prototypes resulted from this group's use of the U process in order to create innovations that make food systems more economically, environmentally, and socially sustainable. One of the prototypes linked sustainable food production from Latin American family farmers to global markets, thereby delivering high-quality nutrition from regional farmers to schools and hospitals, among others. Another one focuses on reframing food sustainability for citizens, consumers, and policy makers.

During the prototyping phase, the size of the Food Lab team tripled. Sheri Flies from Costco, who joined the initiative during the prototyping stage, says that three essentials must be considered in order to shift the food system toward sustainability. "The first thing is that you have to have a critical mass of benevolent demand on the side of the consumers. Then you need full economic, social, and ecological transparency across the entire supply chain. And then you need to give a face to the producers, to the farmers; you need to personalize their connection with the consumers, which in turn will strengthen the benevolent demand for high-quality products and processes."[6]

A number of cities and regions in the European Union are presently engaged in another prototyping project called Living Labs. The concept of Living Labs originated with MIT's William Mitchell. Living Labs serve as a research methodology for sensing, prototyping, validating, and refining complex solutions in multiple and evolving real-life contexts. In Sweden and Finland, communities and municipalities are forming Living Labs as hot spots for technological, cultural, and social innovation.[7]

Field Notes

We prototype these landing strips of the future by establishing three types of connection and communication mechanisms:

- The upward connection—that is, connecting to inspiration, to the initial spark of intuition and intention
- The horizontal connection—that is, listening to the feedback that the context (environment) is giving to you
- The downward or local connection—that is, engaging in and learning from locally embedded fast-cycle prototypes

We also establish infrastructures and places that foster the practical integration of these three relational dimensions of bringing the new into the world. And as we go forward, we always navigate our way between the two dangers and enemies: mindless action and the actionless mind. We discover ways to design and embed new actions that use the wisdom of our hands and our hearts, as well as our heads. You will find more details and principles and practices of prototyping in Chapter 21, which outlines 24 principles of presencing.

CHAPTER 14

Performing

We have just spent some time on prototypes, an experimental exploration of something new. A prototype contains some of the essential characteristics of the final product or ecosystem but is only the first of many iterations. The final product successfully incorporates all of the best features of its earlier forms.

Now we focus our attention on how presencing embodies itself into everyday practices. It may be helpful to think of the theater. You're fortunate if you've ever been in a live production because you will recognize how the actors get input from one another as well as guidance from the director and the performance benefits from that refining process. Things are added; things are removed. Theater is a living structure—contained, honed, and refined. Only after many rehearsals is the curtain ready to go up. And still it evolves, but now with the added component of the audience's energy and presence.

Playing the Macro Violin

Performing means to operate from a larger field that emerges from our deep connection with the audience and the place around us. The violinist Miha Pogacnik described this type of peak performance experience as "playing the macro violin."

"When I gave my first concert in Chartres," he remembers, "I felt that the cathedral almost kicked me out. 'Get out with you!' she said. For I was young and I tried to perform as I always did: by just playing my violin. But then I realized that in Chartres you actually cannot play your small violin, but you have to play the macro violin. The small violin is the instrument that is in your hands. The macro-violin is the whole cathedral that surrounds you. The cathedral of Chartres is built entirely according to musical principles. Playing the macro violin requires you to listen and to play from another place, from the *periphery*. You have to move your listening and playing from within to beyond yourself."

The question we are left with, in more mundane settings such as the health care network discussed above, is how to discover and to connect with this type of "macro violin."

Discovering the Locally Embedded "Macro Violin"

Dr. Schmidt said, "In all our feedback, there was one theme and insight that increasingly moved onto center stage. It's the insight that the only sustainable way to take our system to its next level of development is to focus on regional self-governance among all participating actors. This sort of feedback has made me ever more courageous to take concrete steps in this direction. As a consequence, we now have formed a group with key leaders from all sectors in the region we are part of. Our aim with this group is to produce a common vision for where we want to go to as a region and to decide on the next step."

"It's interesting that now we deploy fifteen physicians at night instead of thirty-two, yet things are working much better now," one physician reported. "And we're not alone anymore."

This networked system is still in its early stages. It has, however, become increasingly clear that the larger system still spirals from crisis to crisis and many feel they are "trying to fix a dying system." Some feel that rather than try to keep the larger, "dying" health care system alive, "Maybe we should just pull the plug and let it die." What remains very clear, however, is that, in stark contrast to other regions of the country, the results of the various network initiatives are fewer complaints and lawsuits, while patients' complaints have virtually dropped to zero. And the physicians have no more crisis meetings to attend. Furthermore, there is now a better partnership between patients and doctors. One physician said, "In my case, I have rediscovered the joy of work."

Physicians and patients are now performing differently. They have the formal structures and shared experience to work differently together. The coordination of care and, more broadly, the communication among physicians across the region have improved. But probably the most subtle change is in how the self connects to the whole system and what impact the individual can have on that system. Though still overloaded, physicians feel less isolated, more engaged, and more effective.

When I asked Dr. Schmidt how he would account for all these changes, he responded, "On the one hand, it is the experience of shaping something; that's a source of empowerment. On the other hand, it is to see the context in which you and your colleagues work. That changes your view of the larger system. You learn to see the meaning of your work in the context of the whole region. Seeing that larger whole and how your work relates to it is empowering. Through your better knowledge about how the system works, how the region works, and by getting to know an awful lot of people, you end up having a different access to making things work—things tend to flow more effortlessly."

The Field Structure of Performing

When moving from the field of prototyping to that of performing, the main focus shifts from shaping microcosms to shaping and evolving the larger institutional ecologies. Just as the delivery of a newborn marks the real beginning of parenting, prototyping marks the real beginning of co-creating. What follows is the need to shape a context that allows the newly arrived being to take its next developmental steps.

Once the living prototype is delivered and assessed, the question is how to take it to the next level of its journey—how to embed it in an institutional infrastructure that allows it to evolve by "operating from the larger eco-system" as opposed to operating from each institution's ego-system.[1] In the case of small groups or individuals this institutional infrastructure may be a set of supporting places, practices, peers, processes, and rhythms that allow the new to be developed and sustained.

As the U movement progresses from presencing to crystallizing, prototyping, and performing, the new quality of the collective field that first began to emerge at the bottom of the U—being connected to the source around us—is embodying itself more fully. Figure 14.1 indicates this unfolding through the emergence of a new pattern from the center that increasingly connects with, evolves, and shapes all other aspects of the larger ecosystem.

FIGURE 14.1 THE FIELD STRUCTURE OF PERFORMING

Principles of Performing

Figure 14.2 depicts one way of conceptualizing such an institutional ecology. This triad of three circles depicts three separate fields: business, government, and civil society. Notice how they overlap. In the center are the interfaces.

The key idea is simple. Organizations are not one; they are multiple. And in order to "breathe," they must be embedded in a web of relationships. In this case, that web deals with the supply chain or manufacturing function, with the delivery function or the customer interface, and with the innovation function of the performance system. Each operates out of a different kind of economics: scale, scope, and presencing. While the specifics in organizations of other sectors are different, the general principles are the same. In the case of global NGOs, for example, there is one system that works on the

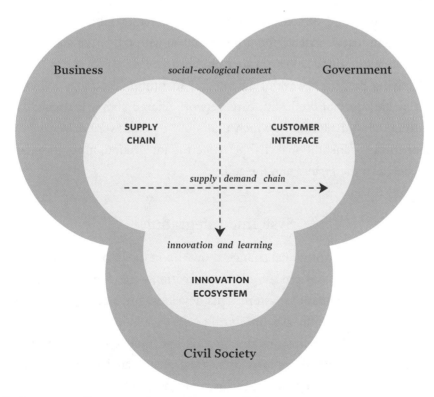

FIGURE 14.2 TRIAD OF INSTITUTIONAL ECOLOGY

ground in order to help and empower the beneficiaries in the field. Then there is the whole infrastructure piece that must be in place to adequately deliver the services to the field. That includes not only funding but also developing logistical infrastructures and so forth. The whole supply chain must be in place in order to deliver services effectively and at reasonable cost. And finally, there is an innovation system to deal with a changing world.

Looking at this figure, you will see three main axes or dimensions that map the major issues and challenges in the world of management and organizations today. The first axis marks the integration along the horizontal dimension—it integrates the seamless stream of value creation as perceived by customers or patients. This horizontal axis is usually referred to as the demand-supply chain.

The second axis marks integration along the vertical dimension: the parallel sphere of learning, innovation, and change.

Finally, the third dimension deals with the relationship of the performance system just described (the inner bubbles) with the larger social-ecological context (the three larger or outer bubbles).

Applying this framework of an integral institutional ecology helps shed light on the story of the health care network shared above. It suggests that the underlying dynamics in which that story evolved were driven by three major forces of institutional change: systemic integration, innovation, and a shift between the system and the self.

Systemic Integration

The first force of institutional change shows up in the imperative of systemic integration in the core process of value creation—the clinical and medical pathways—throughout the system. This development is depicted as integration along the horizontal axis in Figure 14.2.

In the forum's diagnosis-related groups and their disease management programs, this integration shows up in total quality circles and other methods and tools used. The name of the game is to change a functionally driven performance system to a cross-functionally managed performance system.

While this type of change is pervasive in transformations of larger systems across sectors and industries, it is also worth noting that the promise of this type of reorganization usually remains unrealized. For example, when diagnosis-related groups were introduced into the German health care system, a flat-rate case compensation scheme was intended to decrease overall costs by giving hospitals incentives to discharge their patients earlier and thereby increase the "productivity" of the system. Sure enough, the average number of days patients remained in the hospital went down. So far, so good. Except that some people claim that as a consequence, the total costs of the system have been going up.

"How could that happen?" I asked Dr. Florian Gründler from the health care network.

"Let me give you an example from last week. Last Friday the hospital discharged and sent me a patient that I had sent it a couple of days earlier. But instead of being in better condition, his condition seemed worse. When the ambulance driver delivered him to my office, I looked at him and realized that he was having a heart attack. So after providing emergency care I sent him straight back to the hospital, where of course he gets registered as a new patient because he didn't go there with a heart attack when I sent him in last week. So, you see, that's how the system works: as the average hospital days per case go down, the total number of days, along with additional health issues and costs, goes up."

Dr. Gründler's story reminded me of numerous other stories of change efforts that failed because of an insufficient comprehension of the issue of social complexity. Successfully redesigning a medical system requires more than just understanding the technical and medical complexity of the issue. The designers must fully understand and deal with the issues of social complexity, different cultures, interests, and views. Simply imposing another change program on the overworked and underpaid hospital operators won't work.

Innovation Ecosystems

The imperative of the ever-increasing pressure to innovate—that is, pressure to create more value with the same or fewer resources—is the second driving force of change. It evolves along the vertical axis: how to complement and enhance the operational performance system with a parallel structure of constant innovation and learning across boundaries. Examples of this kind of innovation infrastructure include the newly created emergency care control center. This center created a space where "you are right at the pulse of the region" and where the physicians also observed that it "facilitates some important learning processes across physicians, emergency care staff, firefighters, and others."

The driver of this kind of change is not the abstract optimization of clinical pathways but a hands-on exposure of key practitioners to real cases, patients, and issues, and dealing with them in real time.

However, there is still an important limitation to this kind of approach to innovation. It remains more or less bounded by the constraints of the current system. That is, the health care system is designed to deal with the symptoms of sickness. It isn't designed to strengthen the sources of health. Which brings us to the third force.

Field Shift of the Evolving Ecosystem

The third and still incipient force is the subtle shift in the relationship between the system and the self. As Dr. Schmidt noted, "[When you] see the context in which you and your colleagues work, that changes your view of the larger system. You learn to see the meaning of your work in the context of the whole region. Seeing that larger whole and how your work relates to it is empowering. . . . You end up having a different access to making things work—things tend to flow more effortlessly."

How can we make sense of these subtle field shifts at issue here? By turning once again to the U.

Using the four levels of patient-physician relationships, these shifts can now be seen as ways to tune in to a Level 4 relationship. When these moments of presence happen, and when they are connected with the right attention and intention, they can become a positive force in the field and have a tangible impact on the other players in the system. As one of the senior health care executives in Germany observed, "The quality of commitment and intention that this group radiated over time changed the consciousness of the decision makers in the [larger] system."

An Evolutionary View of the Modern Health Care System

Consider the dynamics of the three core dimensions depicted in Figure 14.2. The resulting picture is an evolutionary view of the health system that differentiates four different stages of development (see Table 14.1).

The first column, "Institutional Care," depicts the traditional health care system in Germany, which Chancellor Otto von Bismarck created in the late nineteenth century as a preemptive strike against the rising Socialist Party in Germany. This system, governed by vertical lines of hierarchy, is the backdrop for the current three-core axis of change. Almost everybody agrees that change is necessary, among other reasons because demographics (aging population) and political issues (reunification with East Germany) have made it too expensive. In the United States, the system has already largely progressed from the institutional stage of care delivery to the next stage: managed care.

Column 2, "Managed Care, " shows where the mainstream of the system is currently gravitating, not only in the US, adding the market mechanism to the existing hierarchy. The idea of managed care is to integrate the whole medical pathway alongside the horizontal axis in Figure 14.2.

Column 3, "Integrative Care," adds to the model of managed care by linking the operational level of health care delivery with an innovation ecosystem, as exemplified by the creation of the new emergency care control center. Patient-centered integrative care is organized around concrete patient pathways and life-spaces that allow the Level 3 type of patient-physician relationship to evolve (example: home-based care).

Column 4, "Integral Health," depicts a possible future health care system that incorporates all four levels of patient-physician relationships and focuses on strengthening the sources of health (salutogenesis) instead of battling the symptoms of pathology (pathogenesis). Just as the earlier models introduced

TABLE 14.1 FOUR EVOLUTIONARY STAGES OF MODERN HEALTH CARE SYSTEMS

	Institutional Care	Managed Care	Integrative Care	Integral Health
Organizing paradigm	System centered	Outcome centered	Patient centered	Human centered
Patient-physician relationship	Level 1	Levels 1–2	Levels 1–3	Levels 1–4
Key axis	Functional (institutional structure)	Medical pathways (core process)	Patient pathway (patient-system interface)	Biographical journey
Innovation mechanism	Intra-institutional, functional effectiveness Pathogenesis	Outcome driven, cross-institutional, cross-functional Pathogenesis DRG, DMP, TQC	Patient centered, cross-institutional Pathogenesis New emergency care control center	Human centered, metainstitutional Salutogenesis
Dominant type of complexity	Detailed complexity	Dynamic complexity[a]	Social complexity[b]	Emerging complexity[c]
Coordination mechanism	Hierarchy command	Market price	Dialogue: mutual adaptation	Presence: seeing from the whole
Infrastructure	Social legislation (Bismark)	Rules, norms to make the market mechanism work	Infrastructures for learning and innovation	Infrastructures for seeing in the context of the whole

a. This refers to the integration of different types of functional, technical, and medical knowledge.
b. The integration of different cultures, worldviews, and strategic interests across institutions.
c. Emerging situations where problem, diagnosis, and solution evolve over the course of the project.

additional governance mechanisms, this one introduces a new governance mechanism for coordinating the interrelated health care activities better and in real time: seeing from the whole. Infrastructures that facilitate this kind of shared seeing, sensing, and acting—of which the Patient-Physician Dialogue Forum is an early example—are key to developing this type of system.

Where would the regional health care network be positioned on this map?

The network evolves somewhere between Columns 3 and 4 while its larger systems context happens to move from institutional to managed care (Columns 1 and 2). Just as the four levels of patient-physician relationships aren't good or bad as such—they are only appropriate or not appropriate to a certain health issue or situation—the four health care systems depicted in Table 14.1 aren't necessarily good or bad, either. They differ in their primary focus and level of patient-physician relationship. But this is what we must remember: problems arise when health issues that reside on Levels 3 and 4 are being addressed with mechanisms that function on Levels 1 and 2, and vice versa.

Field Notes

Organizations are not one but three. They evolve along three axes, integrating the stream of current value creation (horizontal axis), the parallel systems of continuous innovation and learning (vertical axis), and the living connection to the evolving social context (third or surrounding axis).

The key to developing Level 3 and 4 institutions is the creation of effective learning infrastructures.

Having seen some learning communities that work and even more that didn't, I have crystallized my observations and lessons learned in eight points. They are as follows:

1. *Core group composition.* The more the composition of the core group reflects the composition of the whole community and context, the better. For example, a learning community of researchers, consultants, and practitioners that is organized by a core group made up only of consultants would defeat the purpose.

2. *Primacy of praxis.* All real learning is grounded in real-world praxis.[2] There are three kinds of praxis: *professional praxis*—striving for performance excellence; *personal praxis*—striving for self-leadership; and *relational praxis*—striving to improve the quality of thinking, conversing, and acting together.[4]

3. *Practice fields and tools.* No symphony orchestra or professional basketball team can achieve world-class excellence without practicing.[3] Likewise, leaders and managers, in order to accomplish their corporate and interactional goals, need (a) tools and (b) practice fields in order to learn to use these tools more effectively.

4. *Parallel learning structures.* Parallel learning structures are the cornerstone of any learning architecture. A parallel learning structure is any setting that allows actors to reflect on their experiences, to share what they learn, to engage in new experiences, and to get help from peers.[5]

5. *Purpose and shared principles.* The quality of purpose depends on (a) its content and (b) its connection to people. A learning community that serves only the future business of its center is a bad example. A learning community that builds on the highest aspirations of all its participants is the counterexample.

6. *Passion, or personal embodiment of purpose.* Usually nothing significant happens unless there is someone who holds it all together, who makes it work. Self-organization does not self-organize. Self-organization needs people to actively create the conditions that allow self-organization to evolve.

7. *Perception-driven participation.* How can one create an environment in which people ask "What can I give?" rather than "What can I get?" Two critical mechanisms are (a) to start with an initial gift such as joint intellectual capital that sets the tone and (b) to establish shared practices of perception that allow contributions to the common knowledge base to be perceived, acknowledged, and appreciated.

8. *Products.* Products that are created using the intellectual and relational capital of the community—such as training courses for new methods and tools—serve as vehicles for both competence and community building.

PART III

Presencing: A Social Technology for Leading Profound Innovation and Change

A t the outset of this investigation, I argued that leaders and people at all levels in all systems are increasingly presented with disruptive challenges and changes that require them to let go of old patterns of thinking and behavior and to sense new future possibilities. These challenges may be techno-economic, relational-political, or cultural-spiritual—or all three.

TOGETHER WE SHARE A universal and deeply felt need expressed in the question: how do we confront these challenges and cross human developmental thresholds? Doing so will require a new quality of awareness and attention: attention not only to *what* we do and *how* we do it but to the inner *source* from which we operate—which for most of us is a blind spot.

Theory U proposes a simple distinction: anything a leader does and everything we do in our professional or everyday life can be performed from at least four different sources: from the center (I-in-me), from the periphery (I-in-it), from beyond one's periphery (I-in-you), and from permeating all of one's open boundaries (I-in-now). And depending on what source we operate from, our actions will effect vastly different outcomes and results: "*I attend* [this way]—*therefore it emerges* [that way]," as we will discuss in greater detail below.

In physics we know that a material alters its behavior when it changes from one state to another. Water, for instance, at temperatures below freezing (32°F), forms ice. If we add heat and the temperature rises above 32°F, ice melts to water. If we continue to add heat and the temperature exceeds 212°F, water begins to vaporize into steam. In all three states, the H_2O molecules are the same. In groups, organizations, and larger systems it is the structure of the relationship among individuals that—when changed—gives rise to different collective behavior patterns. From here on I will call these collective behavior patterns *social fields*.

There are three main scientific field theories: electromagnetic, gravitational and quantum field theory. We know much less about the structural patterns and states of social fields, or about the conditions that can cause a social field to shift from one state to another and about the new patterns of behavior that will result. Yet we have considerable evidence that social fields do exist and do have a major impact on how we live our lives, how we enact individual and collective patterns of behavior.

Why are shifts in social fields so much more difficult to understand? For one thing, they're very hard to observe. We cannot simply stand back and watch them happen in our laboratory. While we can put a block of ice on a burner and watch it melt, we cannot do the same thing in a social setting. When a state shift happens in a social field, the observer is intimately connected with its unfolding. It is as if the observer were watching what's going on from outside and inside a pot of boiling water simultaneously.

Another difference concerns the relationship between *matter, container,* and *mechanism*. It takes the interplay of three things to melt a block of ice: (a) the ice, (b) the container that holds the block, and (c) heat, the mechanism or force that causes the shift. What are the functional equivalents in shifting social fields?

The *matter* in social fields is not a thing but a web of relationships among actors and entities, together with their different ways of thinking, conversing, and acting together. The *container* in a social field is the context in which these relationship patterns unfold—the holding place. And the *mechanism* that causes a field to alter from one state to another is a shift in the source of attention from which the actors and entities relate to one another. That is, the mechanism is a *shift of place* (shift of source) from which the individual and collective perception and action happens.

The capacity to access the subtler and deeper dimensions of social fields in a more reliable and transparent way requires a new *social grammar*.

CHAPTER 15

The Grammar of the Social Field

A Brief Introduction • Our Social Environment and Human
Consciousness • Social Field Theory

A Brief Introduction

When people experience a transformational shift, they notice a profound change in the structure, atmosphere, and texture of the social field. But in trying to explain it, they have to fall back on vague language, and even though people can agree on a surface description of *what* happened, they don't usually know *why*. So we need a new grammar to help us articulate and recognize what's happening and why.

Taking up that challenge, I have devised twenty-one propositions that summarize and name what happens when a social change occurs. Because this actually outlines an advanced social field theory, it could be a book in itself. If you are less interested in learning more about field theory and wish to go directly to our actions, Chapters 16 through 19 are waiting for you. But if you wish to ground yourself in the deeper epistemological and ontological aspects of social reality creation *from the viewpoint of the evolving entity (self)*, you'll find it here. [1]

Our Social Environment and Human Consciousness

All human beings participate in co-creating the complex social networks that we live in and engage with. Still, despite the fact that 6 billion people are busy co-creating this field moment to moment, we don't fully understand the *process of social reality creation* because it is connected to our blind spot. Most of the time we experience social reality as something exterior—as a world "out there" that is doing something to us. Most of us are unaware of the process through which this exterior social reality comes into being in the first place: the source from which our attention, intention, and action originate when we engage with others and with ourselves.

In this investigation of the social field, I build on the work of probably the most innovative social scientist of the twentieth century, Kurt Lewin. Lewin viewed the social environment as a dynamic field that interacts with human consciousness. Changes in the social environment effect particular types of psychological experience and vice versa. In his field theory, a field is defined as "the totality of coexisting facts, which are conceived of as mutually inter-dependent."[2] He believed that, in order to understand people's behavior, one had to look at the whole psychological field, or "lifespace," within which people acted. Lifespaces or fields are constructed under the influence of various force vectors.[3]

Accordingly, human behavior is determined by the totality of an individual's context. This context is a function of the field that exists at the time the behavior occurs. Kurt Lewin also looked to the power of underlying forces (needs) to determine behavior by integrating insights from topology (e.g., lifespace), psychology (need, aspiration, etc.), and sociology (e.g., force fields).[4]

Lewin's field theory was groundbreaking in twentieth-century social psychology and action research and led to the development of numerous experiments and projects. The T-groups of the 1950s and '60s, and the dialogue practices and the organizational learning and systems thinking methods and movements at the end of the century, are all part of this lineage.

As I write about social fields from a twenty-first-century perspective, I am able to draw on major insights and sources of knowing that weren't available to Lewin when he did his pioneering work. Specifically, *neurophenomenology*, as developed in the late work of the cognitive scientist Francisco Varela; *dialogue*, as developed in the Bohm/Isaacs tradition of working with collective fields; and *immersion* social experiments and action research projects.

The social field theory suggested below stands, as I have said, in many ways on Lewin's shoulders. But these 21 Propositions also add a dimension that Lewin, in his time, was unable to clearly explicate and spell out: a differentiated ontological and epistemological grounding of social fields by illuminating the blind spot from which individual and collective fields of attention originate—the four different sources from which fields of attention and behavioral patterns can come into being.

Social Field Theory: 21 Propositions

As you read through these 21 propositions, together with tables and figures and their explanations, you will better understand the breakdown and collapse of our social systems as well as how you might help design future intervention and action strategies.

1. *Social systems are enacted by their members in context.* This first proposition captures the state of the art in social systems and social science theory: (a) social systems are enacted by their members and in turn shape their members' actions; (b) all enactment takes place in a context.[5]

The remaining twenty propositions resonate with this first one. During the Patient-Physician Dialogue Forum, the participants realized that the system isn't simply "out there" (Level 1, Figure 15.1) but is a product of their mutual relationships; they realized that they themselves enact the system in which they operate (Level 2, Figure 15.1).

2. *The blind spot of current social science, social systems, and field theory concerns the sources from which social systems originate.* Social systems and structures are enacted by individuals in a context that in turn is deter-

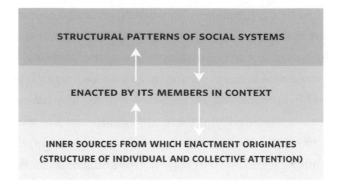

FIGURE 15.1 THREE LEVELS OF SOCIAL REALITY CREATION

mined by how they attend to a situation; and how that happens is determined by the inner source from which their attention originates (Level 3,
Figure 15.1). For example, what wasn't apparent to the members of the
health care network was that the same system could be enacted in different ways with different outcomes depending on the inner source
from which they chose to operate. Whether the health care system was
designed and enacted as a mechanical repair shop for broken parts or
focused on human-centered personal relationships was to a much larger degree a matter of the members' choice than they had expected.

3. *There are four different sources of attention from which social action can
   emerge.* Every social system and every social action can be performed
   and enacted from four different sources. The position of each source in
   relation to its organizational boundary differs accordingly (resulting in
   four field structures of attention):

   - I-in-me: acting from the *center* inside one's organizational
     boundaries (Field 1)
   - I-in-it: acting from the *periphery* of one's organizational bound-
     aries (Field 2)
   - I-in-you: acting from *beyond* one's organizational boundaries
     (Field 3)
   - I-in-now: acting from the emerging sphere *across* one's open
     boundaries (Field 4).

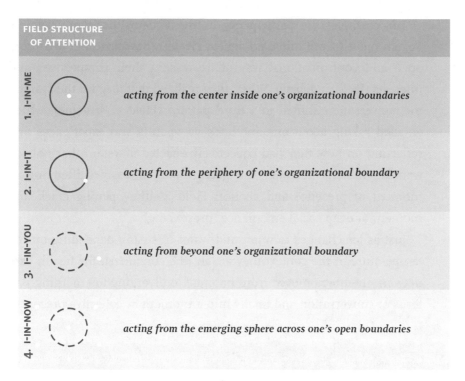

FIELD STRUCTURE OF ATTENTION		
1. I-IN-ME		*acting from the center inside one's organizational boundaries*
2. I-IN-IT		*acting from the periphery of one's organizational boundary*
3. I-IN-YOU		*acting from beyond one's organizational boundary*
4. I-IN-NOW		*acting from the emerging sphere across one's open boundaries*

FIGURE 15.2 FOUR FIELD STRUCTURES OF ATTENTION

Every social action and social structure emerges from one of these four field structures of attention (of which the agents usually remain unaware). Although most actors and systems operate from only the first two, others manage to operate from all four spheres of social reality creation as they evolve on their developmental journey. The point here is that every human actor and social system has *multiple* sources or field structures of attention (or states of awareness and consciousness) to choose from.

4. *The four sources and structures of attention give rise to four different streams or fields of emergence.* Depending on the source of attention and awareness we operate from, we effect and facilitate different social dynamics and patterns. "*I attend* [this way]—*therefore it emerges* [that way]." The same applies to the collective level. Let us use the example of conversation. In my ten years of working with organizations I have observed four basic patterns of conversational reality creation: downloading, debate, dialogue, and presencing (see Figure 15.3).

For example, the participants in the Patient-Physician Dialogue Forum moved from initial politeness (Field 1: downloading) to a more open and confrontational way of expressing their perspectives and interests (Field 2: debate). When they realized that *they* are the system, the conversation shifted to a third pattern (Field 3: dialogue), which entailed asking about one another's viewpoints and experiences and reflecting on how they had collectively enacted a system that nobody wanted. Shortly thereafter the group spontaneously shifted into a moment of presence and silence: Field 4—the opening crack and moment of deep social emergence (presencing).

Just as ice changes to water and water to steam, depending on the temperature of the context they are in (the container), the health care network members moved from habitual to diverging to emerging patterns of conversation and finally into a moment of collective presence.

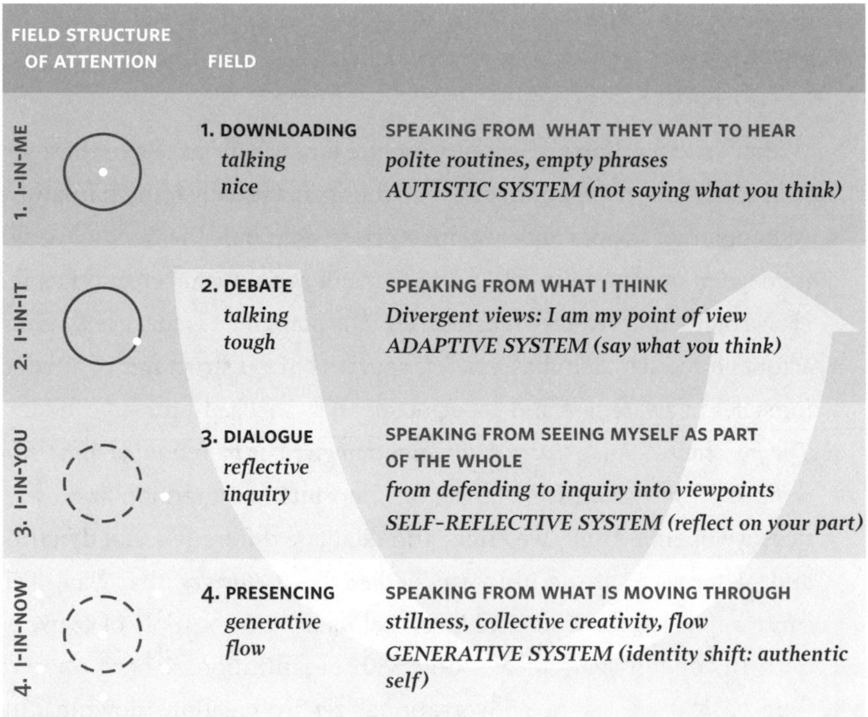

FIELD STRUCTURE OF ATTENTION		FIELD	
1. I-IN-ME	⊙	**1. DOWNLOADING** *talking* *nice*	SPEAKING FROM WHAT THEY WANT TO HEAR *polite routines, empty phrases* *AUTISTIC SYSTEM (not saying what you think)*
2. I-IN-IT	○	**2. DEBATE** *talking* *tough*	SPEAKING FROM WHAT I THINK *Divergent views: I am my point of view* *ADAPTIVE SYSTEM (say what you think)*
3. I-IN-YOU	⊂⊃	**3. DIALOGUE** *reflective* *inquiry*	SPEAKING FROM SEEING MYSELF AS PART OF THE WHOLE *from defending to inquiry into viewpoints* *SELF-REFLECTIVE SYSTEM (reflect on your part)*
4. I-IN-NOW	⊂⊃	**4. PRESENCING** *generative* *flow*	SPEAKING FROM WHAT IS MOVING THROUGH *stillness, collective creativity, flow* *GENERATIVE SYSTEM (identity shift: authentic self)*

FIGURE 15.3 FOUR FIELDS OF CONVERSATION

At each stage of this process the participants operated from a different source and field of emergence and awareness. In downloading, or "talking nice," a group acts from inside the boundaries of its existing language game. "Same old, same old." In debate, or "talking tough," a group begins to deal with and articulate the various diverging views and perspectives on the situation at issue. To do so, the group has to suspend the routines of politeness and enter a tougher and more honest conversation. In dialogue, a group moves beyond the boundary of its members' viewpoints and begins to look at its collectively enacted patterns as part of a bigger picture. The main shift in any kind of dialogue-type of conversation is very simple: you move from seeing the system as something outside to seeing your self as part of the system. The system and each individual begins to see *itself*. In presencing, group members enter—often enabled through a crack or a moment of silence in which the group begins to let go of "the script"—a deeper space of presence and connection with one another. They then move into a generative flow of co-creating and bring forth something profoundly new. How do you know whether or not you have been in such a place? When you participate in such a conversation, you become a different person. You shift your identity and self in a subtle but profound way. You are more your real; you experience your authentic self.

The four fields of co-enacting conversations in a group differ in terms of their first-, second-, and third-person texture as follows (see Figure 15.4).

From a first-person view, the subjectively experienced level of energy by the participants varies from low in Field 1 (same old, same old) to medium in Field 2 (seeing certain new things) to high in Field 3 (seeing through new eyes, gaining new perspectives) to extremely high in Field 4 (shifting one's identity, intention and self: our sense of who we really are and what we are here for).

From a second-person view the participants' intersubjective pattern of connection changes from *conforming* and fitting to a set of given norms, frames, and rules (Field 1) to *confronting* one's diverging views

FIELD STRUCTURE OF ATTENTION	1ST-PERSON VIEW: EXPERIENTIAL OUTCOME	2ND-PERSON VIEW: CONSTITUTION OF THE COLLECTIVE	3RD-PERSON VIEW: PATTERN OF EMERGENCE
1. I-IN-ME	ENERGY: *low*	CONFORMING	RULE-REPRODUCING
2. I-IN-IT	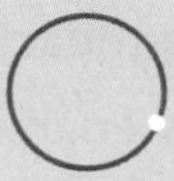 ENERGY: *medium*	CONFRONTING	RULE-CONTEXTUALIZING
3. I-IN-YOU	 ENERGY: *high*	RELATING	RULE-EVOLVING
4. I-IN-NOW	 ENERGY: *extremely high*	COLLECTIVELY CONNECTING	RULE-GENERATING

FIGURE 15.4 FIRST-, SECOND-, AND THIRD-PERSON VIEW

in a process of contextualizing existing rules (Field 2) to *reflecting* and relating to one another in order to incorporate an emerging set of rules (Field 3) to *collectively connecting* and functioning as a vehicle for the future that seeks to emerge (Field 4).

From the perspective of an external observer (third person) the pattern of emergence changes from *rule-reproducing* in Field 1 (repeat the patterns of the past) to *rule-contextualizing* in Field 2 (situate according to the specific facts on the ground) to *rule-evolving* in Field 3 (reflect and co-evolve with the situation that keeps changing) to *rule-generating* in Field 4 (collectively birth and bring forth the future that seeks to emerge).

5. *The four fields of enacting social reality apply to all the spheres of social reality creation.* The four fields and streams of enacting social reality play out across the micro, meso, macro, and mundo levels of social systems

(see Figure 15.5). On the micro level the different streams of emergence show up as discontinuous shifts in the individual field of attention:

- *Downloading:* Perception reenacts past patterns.
- *Seeing:* Perception notices disconfirming data.
- *Sensing:* Perception begins to happen from the field.
- *Presencing:* Perception begins to happen from the creative source.

Each of these different ways of perceiving is based on a distinct structure and source of attention. More downloading doesn't add up to seeing. More seeing doesn't add up to sensing; and so forth.

On the meso level the four streams show up as discontinuous shifts in the field of group attention and languaging, as exemplified by the shifts from:

FIELD STRUCTURE OF ATTENTION	MICRO SPHERE: INDIVIDUAL ATTENTION	MESO SPHERE: CONVERSATION AND LANGUAGING	MACRO SPHERE: INSTITUTIONAL STRUCTURE	MUNDO SPHERE: GOVERNANCE MECHANISM
1. I-IN-ME	DOWNLOADING	DOWNLOADING	CENTRALIZED	HIERARCHY
2. I-IN-IT	SEEING	DEBATE	DECENTRALIZED	MARKET
3. I-IN-YOU	SENSING	DIALOGUE	NETWORKED	DIALOGUE
4. I-IN-NOW	PRESENCING	PRESENCING	INNOVATION ECOSYSTEM	COLLECTIVE PRESENCE

FIGURE 15.5 FOUR FIELDS OF EMERGENCE, FOUR SYSTEMS LEVELS

- *Downloading:* talking nice or exchanging polite phrases to
- *Debate:* talking tough or exchanging diverging views to
- *Dialogue:* thinking together from diverse perspectives to
- *Presencing:* creating collectively from an authentic presence and source of stillness

The same patterns and streams of emergence also apply to the macro and mundo spheres of social reality creation. On these levels a switch from one type of emergence to another shows up as a discontinuous shift of the institutional geometry of power. Accordingly, we can track the evolution of large institutional structures from:

- Centralized machine bureaucracies that operate based on rules and central plans, to
- Decentralized divisional structures that push the decision-making power down the hierarchy closer to markets and customers in order to adapt the rules and strategies to
- Networked organizational structures that shift the geometry of power from hierarchically driven units to evolving networks of relationships that focus on issues that usually remain unaddressed by formal organizational structures and finally to
- Fluid innovation ecosystem structures that form, shape and then dissolve by collectively sensing and realizing needs and opportunities in real time.

On the mundo level the evolution of larger systems coincides with a differentiation of four distinct governance mechanisms:

- *Hierarchy:* coordination through central authority, central planning, or central rules (mechanism 1: the source of power is at the center)
- *Market:* coordination through competition in the context of agreed upon rules (mechanism 2: the source of power moves to the periphery, to the market)
- *Dialogue:* coordination through dialogue among multiple stakeholders (mechanism 3: the source of power resides in the network of relationships)
- *Collective presencing:* coordination through sensing and operat-

ing from an emerging whole (mechanism 4: the source of power resides in the ecosystem's emerging whole)

6. *The inflection points when moving from one field to another are identical at all levels.* The shift from one field to another depends on the inflection points. These inflection points constitute a social grammar. They are:

- Opening and suspension (open mind)
- Deep diving and redirection (open heart)
- Letting go and letting come (open will)

Figure 15.6 shows how these three inflection points apply to field shifts in attending and thinking (micro), languaging (meso), institutionalizing (macro) and global governing (mundo). It illustrates that moving from Field 1 to Field 2 requires *opening up* to the data of the exterior world and *suspending* ingrained and habitual (and often dys-

FIELD STRUCTURE OF ATTENTION	MICRO SPHERE: INDIVIDUAL ATTENTION	MESO SPHERE: CONVERSATION AND LANGUAGING	MACRO SPHERE: INSTITUTIONAL STRUCTURE	MUNDO SPHERE: GOVERNANCE MECHANISM
1. I-IN-ME	DOWNLOADING	DOWNLOADING	CENTRALIZED	HIERARCHY
OPENING AND SUSPENSION				
2. I-IN-IT	SEEING	DEBATE	DECENTRALIZED	MARKET
DEEP DIVE AND REDIRECTION				
3. I-IN-YOU	SENSING	DIALOGUE	NETWORKED	DIALOGUE
LETTING GO AND LETTING COME				
4. I-IN-NOW	PRESENCING	PRESENCING	INNOVATION ECOSYSTEM	COLLECTIVE PRESENCE

FIGURE 15.6 THE INFLECTION POINTS ACROSS LEVELS ARE THE SAME

functional) patterns of action and thought (open mind).

Moving from Field 2 to Field 3 entails taking a *deep dive* into relevant contexts and *redirecting* one's attention such that perception begins to "happen from the field" (open heart).

Moving from Field 3 to Field 4 requires *letting go* of old identities and intentions and *letting come* new identities and intentions that are more directly connected with one's deepest sources of individual and collective action and energy (open will).

7. *The greater a system's hyper-complexity, the more critical is the capacity to operate from the deeper fields of social emergence.* Companies, organizations, and communities face three types of complexities: *dynamic complexity* (defined by cause and effect being distant in space and time), *social complexity* (defined by conflicting interests, cultures, and worldviews among diverse stakeholders), and *emerging complexity* (defined by

FIELD STRUCTURE OF ATTENTION	MICRO SPHERE: INDIVIDUAL ATTENTION	MESO SPHERE: CONVERSATION AND LANGUAGING	MACRO SPHERE: INSTITUTIONAL STRUCTURE	MUNDO SPHERE: GOVERNANCE MECHANISM
1. I-IN-ME	DOWNLOADING	DOWNLOADING	CENTRALIZED	HIERARCHY
COPING WITH DYNAMIC COMPLEXITY				
2. I-IN-IT	SEEING	DEBATE	DECENTRALIZED	MARKET
COPING WITH BEHAVIORAL COMPLEXITY				
3. I-IN-YOU	SENSING	DIALOGUE	NETWORKED	DIALOGUE
COPING WITH EMERGING COMPLEXITY				
4. I-IN-NOW	PRESENCING	PRESENCING	INNOVATION ECOSYSTEM	COLLECTIVE PRESENCE

FIGURE 15.7 TYPES OF COMPLEXITY AND LEVELS OF THE FIELD

disruptive patterns of innovation and change in situations in which the future cannot be predicted and addressed by the patterns of the past). Hyper-complexity is complex in all ways simultaneously. The greater a system's hyper-complexity, the more critical it becomes for organizations, companies, and communities to develop the capacity to operate from the deeper streams of social emergence and to access the power of the open mind, open heart, and open will.

Whenever a process is stuck at one level of operating, instead of continuing to do more of the same it is often better to address the same issue differently, at the next deeper level of complexity and emergence. Figure 15.7 depicts how the three types of complexity relate to the three deeper streams of social emergence as discussed above.

8. *Profound innovation that addresses all three types of complexity requires a process that integrates three movements: opening up to contexts that matter (co-sensing), connecting to the source of stillness (co-presencing), and prototyping the new (co-creating).* Figure 15.8 depicts such a threefold process in a U shape. The process can happen in fractions of a second (as in the martial arts) or over the course of weeks or years.

The three inflection points discussed above (suspension, deep diving, letting go) all apply to the phase of moving down the left side of the U; the mirror process of moving up the right side of the U (co-creating) involves letting come, enacting (prototyping), and embodying (performing) the new in everyday actions and practices.

9. *To access and activate the deeper sources of social fields, three instruments must be tuned: the open mind, open heart, and open will (Figure 15.9).* Deepening the social field requires the appropriate instruments. No musician wants to play a piece of music without a well-built, well-tuned instrument. But that's exactly what repeatedly happens in social fields. Time and again we try to cope with situations using collective instruments that are out of tune. Rather than stopping to tune them, we increase the pace, hire consultants who want to increase productivity by further reducing the time devoted to tuning and practicing, hire new conductors who promise to conduct even faster, and so forth. But the

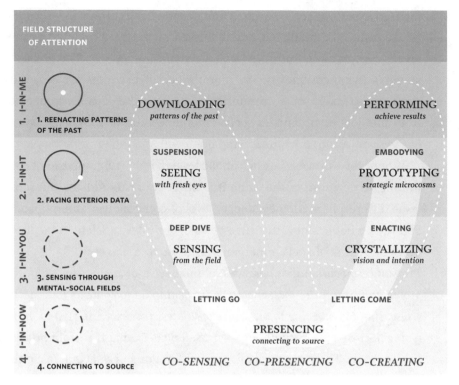

FIGURE 15.8 ONE PROCESS, THREE MOVEMENTS

obvious thing to do—to stop and tune the instruments collectively—doesn't come easily because it requires a shift of the mind to a deeper level of operating.

The open mind—that is, the capacity to see with fresh eyes, to inquire, and to reflect—allows one to navigate the first inflection point, from Field 1 to Field 2 (opening up and suspending habits).

The open heart—the capacity for empathic listening, for appreciative inquiry, and for "exchanging places" with another person or system—enables one to navigate the second inflection point, from Field 2 to Field 3 (deep dive and redirection).

The open will—the capacity to let go of old identities and intentions and to tune in to an emerging future field of possibility—allows one to navigate the third inflection point, from Field 3 to Field 4 (letting go

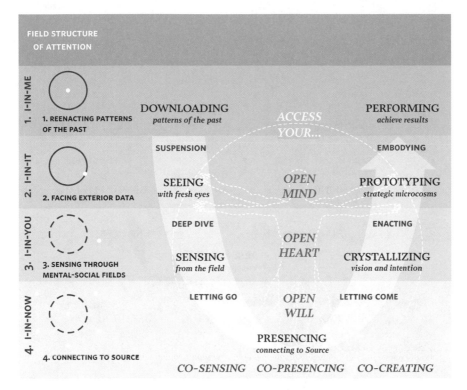

FIGURE 15.9 THE THREE INSTRUMENTS

and letting come).

10. *Opening up these deeper levels requires overcoming three barriers: the Voice of Judgment (VOJ); the Voice of Cynicism (VOC); and the Voice of Fear (VOF).* The reason the journey of the U is the road less traveled has a name: *resistance.* Resistance is the force that keeps our current state distant and separate from our highest future potential. Resistance comes from within. Resistance has many faces and tends to show up where the weakness is greatest. Resistance can operate with stealth and strike largely unrecognized by its victims.

Anyone who embarks on a journey toward the deeper sources and streams of emergence will face these three powerful forces of resistance to the transformation of thought, heart, and will:

• VOJ (Voice of Judgment): Old and limiting patterns of judgment

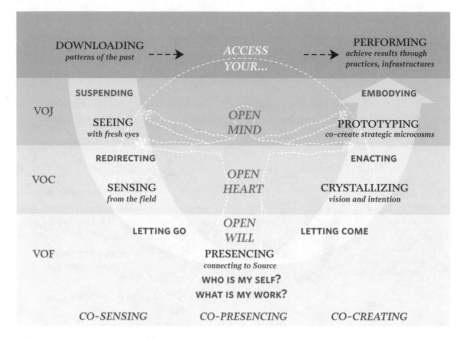

FIGURE 15.10 THE THREE ENEMIES

and thought. Without the capacity to shut down or suspend the VOJ, we will make no progress toward accessing creativity and never reach the deeper levels of the U.

- VOC (Voice of Cynicism): Emotions of disconnection such as cynicism, arrogance, and callousness that prevent us from diving into the fields around us.
- VOF (Voice of Fear): Fear of letting go of the familiar self and world; fear of going forth; fear of surrendering into the space of nothingness.

The capacity to operate from the deeper levels of the U can only be developed to the degree that a system deals with the forces and challenges of resistance. Anybody can have a peak experience. But only those who develop the discipline to face down these forces of resistance will be able to operate reliably from the deeper levels and spheres of social emergence.

11. *Moving up the right side of the U (co-creating) requires a commitment to*

serve the whole and the capacity to reintegrate the intelligences of the head, heart, and hand. Reintegrating the intelligences of the head, heart, and hand happens through the transformation of thought (intention), action (prototyping), and institutional practice (performing). Our challenge lies in keeping any one from dominating the others, which could result in actionless mind (dominance of the head), mindless action (dominance of the hand), or "bla-bla-bla" (dominance of the relational side or conversation).

12. *The bigger the gap between exterior systemic complexity and the interior capacity to access the deeper streams of emergence, the more likely a system will go off track and revert to a destructive space of anti-emergence.* Just as antimatter is composed of the antiparticles of normal matter, the social space of anti-emergence is composed of the anti-practices of normal social emergence. Warren Tignor has called these anti-practices blinding, desensing, and absencing.[6] The normal space of social emergence is based on the cycle of *presencing*, that is, on the activation of the practices of seeing, sensing, presencing, crystallizing, prototyping and performing; in contrast, the social space of anti-emergence is based on the cycle of *absencing*; that is, a cycle of not seeing, desensing, absencing, illusionizing, aborting, and destroying (see Figure 16.1, page 266).

The social space of emergence and the social space of anti-emergence evolve in a dialectical relationship. The tension between these two spaces gives rise to the phenomenon of the social field. This underlying field shows up in everyday social life as resistance to crossing the threshold to the next deeper level of emergence. How we deal with that resistance determines our position relative to the space of emergence or the space of anti-emergence.

In the cycle of absencing, the first stage, *not seeing*, means that we are increasingly blind and unable to recognize anything new—we are stuck in the ideology of a single truth. We isolate ourselves from those parts of reality that don't fit our ideology (think: the Bush administration's search for weapons of mass destruction in Iraq).

Desensing means that our senses don't allow us to move into a new field, into someone else's skin; we are stuck inside the boundaries of our current individual and collective body. Our ability to relate to others and tune in to emerging fields is shut down, and we are isolated from the social fields that are evolving around us (think: the demonization of "the enemy" in large parts of the U.S. media that makes it O.K. to kill "lesser humans," wherever they exist.)

Absencing means that we shut down our capacity to relate to the future that wants to emerge through us. We are boxed into our current self and will, which no longer co-evolve and connect with the source of stillness and the deeper collective social field (think: Nazi Germany being sucked into the space of anti-emergence; blending hubris and an atavistic self-delusion to destroy life on a massive scale—see right-hand side of figure 16.1).

Illusionizing, aborting, and *destroying* mean that the capacities to envision, enact, and embody an emerging future possibility are turned into their anti-practices; the result is that we get stuck in one intention, one worldview, or one truth by becoming fanatics and rejecting anything that doesn't fit our ideology.

In summary: the pathological cycle of absencing exhibits economies of destruction that are based on separating a social system from its embedding field and from its sources of emergence. The results of this cycle are destruction and violence, of which there is no shortage in most societies today.

By contrast, the cycle of presencing exhibits economies of creation and is based on relating a social system to its surrounding social field and its deeper sources of emergence. The results of that cycle are collective creativity and profound innovation and renewal. Moving out of the social space of anti-emergence and reinserting oneself into the creative domain requires a conscious effort, a shift to a deeper level of action and thought (Figure 16.1).

13. *The social space of anti-emergence is manifested in a freeze reaction known as fundamentalism.* The gap between the complexity that a system faces and the ability to enter the deeper sources and streams of emergence

TABLE 15.1 THREE TYPES OF FUNDAMENTALISM

	Religious Fundamentalism	Political Fundamentalism	Economic Fundamentalism
Blinding: stuck in one Truth (and one language)	One almighty, omniscient, and omnipresent God	One almighty, omniscient, and omnipresent agent (state; world history)	One almighty, omniscient and omnipresent mechnanism (the invisible hand)
Desensing: stuck in one collective **There is a lack of empathy for those outside.**	Chosen people syndrome Infidels must be killed (crusade/holy war).	Chosen agent of history syndrome Those who resist the objective laws of history (the opposition) will be annihilated.	Top-tier syndrome The have-nots at the bottom of the pyramid are victims (killed) by structures and policies designed from the people at the top.
Absencing: stuck in one nonemerging self	*Homo pre-modernicus*	*Homo sovieticus*	*Homo oeconomicus*
Destruction and violence: stuck in one will	Direct violence: terrorism Cultural violence: ideologies that legitimize the use of violence	Direct and structural violence: discrimination and annihilation of minorities	Structural violence: people living and dying in daily misery

leads to a freeze reaction called fundamentalism, which is characterized by operating from the shadow space of anti-emergence. Three major types of fundamentalism characterize our world today: religious, economic, and political.

The fundamentalism of our present age is defined by four key characteristics: not seeing, de-sensing, absencing, and destroying:

- *Not seeing:* rigid adherence to certain beliefs and principles: stuck in one language and one Truth

- *Desensing:* intolerance of and a lack of empathy for other views: stuck in one center and one collective (us versus them)
- *Absencing:* a worldview in which the source of problems is exterior, not interior: stuck in one self (the non-reflective and non-evolving self)
- *Destroying:* violence against those who are seen as associated with what is "evil": stuck in one will (fanaticism, violence)

Religious fundamentalism is characterized by four beliefs: the belief in one omnipotent, omniscient, and omnipresent God (one language, one Truth); the belief in belonging to the chosen people (one collective, one center) and, as a consequence, a lack of empathy for those outside this collective (infidels); the belief that the sources of the divine and of evil reside outside rather than inside the human being, from which it follows that the role of the human beings is to subjugate the human to the divine will by battling against the agents of evil; hence the willingness to use violence and destroy life if it serves a higher purpose (see Table 15.1).

14. *The social field is an unfolding whole that can be observed and experienced across five dimensions. They are: social space, social time, the collective, the self, and the holding space (Earth).*

The principle of whole implies that, because all human beings are connected, what happens to other people also happens to oneself. This is not only because we share the same ecosystem and are connected through multiple interdependencies, but, most important, because we are directly connected to one another, as becomes manifest when we enter the deeper states of the social field.

That field of connectedness unfolds through five different dimensions. Think of my demonstration experience in Brokdorf in Chapter 5. I participated, with 100,000 others, in a rally against an atomic power plant in our neighborhood. Reflecting back upon that example, I can now see the five dimensions of the social field as follows: (1) I experienced the social space as dynamic interaction between *us* (the protesters), *it* (the construction site), and *them* (the police force). (2) I experienced social time in the first part in terms of habitual chronological time, but also later as slowing down, stillness, and a moment of *kairos*—when the police force attacked and the crowd entered a state of stillness—that shifted my sense of who I really am. (3) My experience of the collective started with first conforming to the habitual behavior of the group (marching to the construction site) but later moved towards chaos-driven confrontation, connection, and finally a moment of collective presence and stillness. (4) My sense of self started on a more habitual-rational level and then progressed toward relational-authentic as the events of the day unfolded further. When I returned that evening, I was no longer the same person (implying that somewhere along the way I must have had an encounter or connection with my emerging self). (5) And then there is the physical holding space of the earth that often escapes our attention and yet creates the unique sense of place that defines our deeper existential experiences.

15. *As a social field evolves and begins to include the deeper levels and streams of emergence, the experience of time, space, self, the collective, and Earth morphs through a sculptural process of inversion (*Umstülpung*).* Each shift comes with a change in the experiential texture of space, time, self, intersubjectivity, and place or Earth (Figure 15.11). On this journey, the texture of social space morphs from one-dimensional mental images (Field 1) to a two-dimensional exterior connection between observer and observed (Field 2) to a three-dimensional social space where the observer moves inside the field of the observed (Field 3) to a four-dimensional living time-space in which perception becomes almost panoramic. It is as if it happens from an extended clearing or from a distributed source or sphere, as described in Chapter 11, when my search for the source of the river led me all the way up to a place of countless waterfalls streaming off the circle of glaciated mountaintops (Field 4).

The second dimension of this inversion process manifests as a profound change of time. When a social field is moving from Field 1 to Field 4, one first feels disembodied or disconnected from time (Field 1); then time becomes chronological, structured as an exterior sequence of

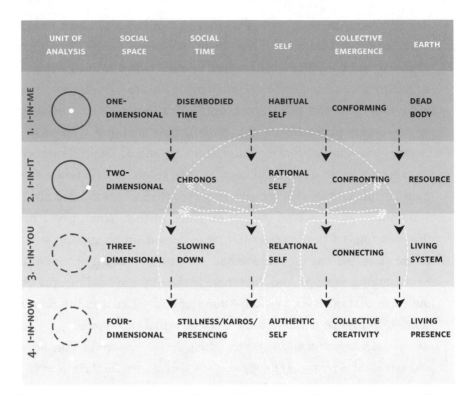

	UNIT OF ANALYSIS	SOCIAL SPACE	SOCIAL TIME	SELF	COLLECTIVE EMERGENCE	EARTH
1. I-IN-ME	○	ONE-DIMENSIONAL	DISEMBODIED TIME	HABITUAL SELF	CONFORMING	DEAD BODY
2. I-IN-IT	○	TWO-DIMENSIONAL	CHRONOS	RATIONAL SELF	CONFRONTING	RESOURCE
3. I-IN-YOU	◌	THREE-DIMENSIONAL	SLOWING DOWN	RELATIONAL SELF	CONNECTING	LIVING SYSTEM
4. I-IN-NOW	◌	FOUR-DIMENSIONAL	STILLNESS/KAIROS/ PRESENCING	AUTHENTIC SELF	COLLECTIVE CREATIVITY	LIVING PRESENCE

FIGURE 15.11 INVERSION OF SPACE, TIME, SELF, COLLECTIVE, AND EARTH

events (Field 2); time then seems to slow down and lengthen, causing one to feel as if an interior dimension of time is opening up (Field 3); finally, one reaches a place of stillness, where the whole universe seems to be holding its breath, where one feels present with something larger that is about to be born and break through (Field 4).

Throughout this process a third dimension of experiential change happens as the sense of self also changes from habitual (Field 1) to a rational self that is anchored and operates from inside the head (Field 2) to a relational self that operates from the heart (Field 3) to an authentic self that is identical to our highest future possibility and that comes into being through the open boundaries of the human body field, both individually and collectively (Field 4).

Another dimension of the social field concerns the experience of intersubjectivity, in which one first interacts with others by fitting into and *conforming to* frames and rules (Field 1). Then one progresses to interacting with others by discussing real issues and expressing diverse views, often *confronting* the views that are already out there (Field 2). By *connecting* and relating to others with empathy and deep understanding one can, through reflection, see oneself as part of a larger whole (Field 3). And finally, one enters a (sacred) space of silence from which a profound sense of connection and *collective creation* emerges (Field 4) (see Figure 15.11).

As we go through these transformations of the social field, we can also notice an inversion of the holding place, of our ways to relate to our planetary body, the earth. At first, we don't notice that there is something right here that is holding us: it's like walking over a dead body (Field 1). Then, as we begin to become aware, we conceive of the place and the earth as a living resource and the place where we interact. (Field 2). Then we can deepen our awareness of place and begin to notice Earth as a living system that interconnects with us and our social interaction in manifold ways (Field 3). Earth, as a global presence, becomes sacred, but is also absolutely unique to the particular *spiritus loci* where your social field happens to unfold in deeper ways. When I remember the battle of Brokdorf, I remember the power of the place and the presence of the universe that was holding us then.

Each of these subtle changes in the texture of experience can be summarized as a generative inversion (*Umstülpung*). What happens is that the sense of space morphs from a single point to a distributed field. The sense of time moves from exterior-sequential to interior-emerging. The sense of self morphs from a closed, habituated ego into an open authentic self. The experience of the collective goes from conforming, to collective stillness and presence. And finally, our experience of place or Earth shifts from a cold, dead body, to a living, sacred space or clearing—a space that invites us to move into the full presence of who we really are and who we are becoming.

16. *The opening of the deeper sources and streams of emergence inverts the relationship between the individual and the collective.* As the structure of atten-

tion shifts and the stream of emergence deepens, a subtle change transforms the relationship between parts and whole, between individuals and the social system in which they participate.

Figure 15.12 depicts the inversion of the collective and the self: from a bounded space, within which the self is framed in the center of its own organization and in the midst of a current reality that keeps it locked into its current mode of identity (left-hand side of Figure 15.12), to a different configuration in which the self is no longer locked into the center of its own organization (right-hand side of Figure 15.12). Here the self functions from its open boundaries and its surrounding sphere as a generative vessel through which a new collective reality is coming into being. Here the self is no longer locked into the center; rather, it co-evolves by participating in the coming into being of a new social collective. An image such as the Grail as the ultimate archetype of a feminine spirituality (or collective holding space) comes to mind.

In this inversion or transubstantiation, the old collective body is transformed by a new relational structure in which the individual

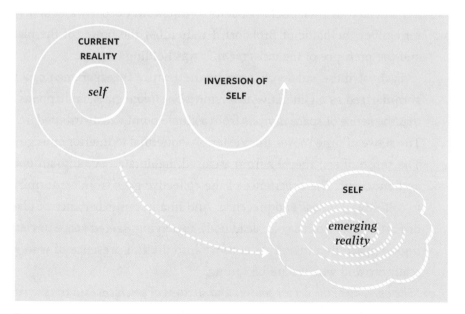

FIGURE 15.12 THE INVERSION OF SELF

actively participates in a communal holding space that allows a new living social field to emerge.

17. *The opening of the deeper sources and fields of emergence transforms the relationship between knower and known.* The same pattern of generative inversion also applies to the relationship between the knower and what is known. Accordingly, we can differentiate among three forms of knowledge: explicit, tacit embodied, and self-transcending knowledge (see Figure 4.5, page 70).[7]

The three forms of knowledge constitute three fundamentally different epistemological stances—that is, three different relationship modes between the knower and the known. Each form of knowledge relates to the reality that it describes from a different point of view as shown in the following table.

Explicit knowledge relates to the reality *outside*, from a Field 2 point of view. Explicit knowledge captures knowledge about things that can be observed (Field 2) (see Table 15.2). Tacit embodied knowledge relates to the reality *within*, that is, from a Field 3 point of view. Tacit embodied knowledge captures knowledge about things we feel and do.[8] This type of knowledge is based on lived experience, which its possessor can observe and reflect on and reproduce.

Self-transcending knowledge is knowledge about the sources or "place" where thought and action originate and from which they come into being (Field 4). The focus is on the primary ground from which human action arises in the first place, before any action manifests.[9] In order to capture this most upstream level of social action, the knower must engage in "reflection in action," or primary knowing. The knower must be able to tune in to and presence it.[10]

Thus, moving from the second to the fourth field structure of attention involves a transformation (an inversion) of the relationship between knower and known from separation (K1) to unity (K2, K3). In the case of tacit embodied knowledge, the self perceives its action *after the fact* (reflection on action). In contrast, in the case of self-transcending knowledge, the self conceives the unity of subject and object

TABLE 15.2 THREE EPISTEMOLOGIES

Dimension	EPISTEMOLOGY		
	K1: *Explicit Knowledge*	K2: *Tacit Embodied Knowledge*	K3: *Self-Transcending Knowledge*
Type of knowledge	Knowledge about things	Knowledge about enacting things	Knowledge about origins for enacting things
Data	Exterior reality (Field 2)	Enacted reality (Field 3)	Not-yet-enacted reality (Field 4)
Experience	Observation	Action	Aesthetic
Action-to-reflection ratio	Reflection without action	Reflection on action	Reflection in action
Truth	Matching reality: Can you observe it?	Producing reality: Can you produce it?	Presencing reality: Can you presence it?

(action) *while acting.* Because aesthetic experiences are often described as being both interior (acting) and exterior (observing), the various types of self-transcending knowing all qualify as genuine aesthetic experience.[11]

18. *The social field is a time sculpture in the making.* Unlike traditional sculptures that exist in space, social fields extend and evolve as sculptures of time.[12] And just as traditional sculpture is defined by a blending of two core elements—matter and form—the social time sculpture is based on blending and integrating two dimensions and streams of time: the manifest time that extends past patterns into the present and a stream of time that pulls from a different direction—from a future possibility that wants to emerge.

Recall, for example, the story of the fire that destroyed my family home when I was sixteen. How did the quality of time change in that story? Up to the point when I returned from school and arrived at the fire site, I was still concerned with the forces of the present and the past. But then, as the experience took me through the next gate, a new time dimension opened up that seemed to pull me toward the source of my future or into a future possibility that was waiting for me. When the direction of time is switched like this, it is as if one is *moving toward oneself from the future (sich selbst aus der Zukunft entgegenlaufen).*[13]

Social time sculptures come into existence when both directionalities of time—from the past and from an emerging future—meet in the now.

The German avant-garde artist Joseph Beuys, who originated the concept of "social sculpture," once said that there were two different types of creativity on Earth: the creativity of the artist, who shapes an exterior reality, and the creativity of woman, who internalizes the concept of creativity by giving birth to a new being. The social time sculpture is about blending these two approaches to creativity. When the two arrows of time meet, people and groups begin to engage in a collective process of giving birth to something new. In this state the participants engage in the process of giving birth from three simultaneous perspectives: the perspective of the mother, which usually is experienced by the group collectively; the perspective of the helping observer, who provides some support and a holding space; and the perspective of the newborn, which "breaks through a membrane." The uniqueness of the social time sculpture is that it probably constitutes the only place in the universe in which participants can actively engage in all three of these perspectives *simultaneously* from within.

19. *Social fielding is a function of scale-free morphic resonance.* The "music" of social fielding concerns the direction and purpose of our movements. Is it something given to us? Is it governed by chance? Or is it something that we collectively co-create? What are the strange attractors (to use the terminology of chaos theory) or the morphogenetic fields (as Rupert Sheldrake calls them in his theory of formative causation) that reinforce and attract patterns of emergence?

Recent advances in network theory suggest that many living systems are organized according to the "small-world" theory. The small-world network theory can be illustrated by comparing a road map of highways with an airline network. The main difference is that a road typically runs from point A to point B, while airlines operate around hubs with many connections that allow passengers to reach any other city in a few steps.

Likewise, in the case of social fielding, the question is, what type of superconnectivity would allow subsets of ecosystems to switch from one way of operating to another? The answer, I believe, lies in creating a network of places that are connected both horizontally and vertically in the sense of including all four levels of wholes and all four fields of emergence. The implication of such a "scale-free" property is that even a limited set of *strategic microcosms* can function as a landing strip and "strange attractor" for the emergence of future possibilities. If these places were well connected and co-evolved as a community, they could eventually function as global landing strips for profound field shifts and tipping points to come.

20. *The future of a system is a function of the Field (source) that we choose to operate from.* Whether or not such microcosms of morphic resonance come into being depends on whether individuals and communities choose to operate from only the first few or all four Fields of emergence that are available to them.

Everyone can choose to operate either from the social space of anti-emergence of absencing or from the social space of deepened emergence and presencing that determines how the future unfolds. Both spaces are available to all people and social systems all the time.

21. *The revolutionary force in this century is the awakening of a deep generative human capacity—the* I-in-now.

Our inquiry so far has uncovered four of the five essentials of a field theory of social emergence:

1. Social field theory is concerned with the quality of *relational space* and the patterns of emergence in a social system.

2. The quality of relational space and the patterns of social emergence are a function of the individual and collective *structures of*

attention. There are four different structures and sources that give rise to four different fields of emergence.

3. To access the deeper sources and fields of emergence, social systems need to tune and activate three different *instruments*: an open mind, an open heart, and an open will.

4. The social space of emergence is mirrored by a dark space of *anti-emergence*. Whether a system functions from a space of deepened emergence or from its shadow space of anti-emergence depends on its capacity to cope with the sources of resistance: VOJ, VOC, and VOF.

The fifth essential concerns the answer to the question: What is the driving force that can trigger a transformational field shift from one space to another by prompting the opening of the instruments and deeper sources of emergence? This is the territory that the final proposition is about.

5. The revolutionary force in our time is the "I-in-now" or the capacity of every human being and social system to switch the structure of attention in a way that begins to connect them to the fourth stream of emergence. The I is not the self. The self is an entity that has a content. Without content, the I is an empty entity. The I-in-now is the primary spark of intentional and attentive attention. It is the spark that can intentionally redirect and shift the field of attention. It acts as if it is an "eye with will."[14] It's a power of presence that we can activate and bring into being wherever we are. It operates from the now. If awakened, this force or spark is the key to unlocking the deeper sources of emergence that connect to the right-hand side of the U. Every human being and social system can wake up and cultivate this deeper source of stillness and becoming. It also helps us to be more practical: The more this source capacity of the I-in-now develops, the greater our ability to deal with the high-pressure, high-complexity situations that life puts increasingly into our face.

These 21 propositions summarize the preliminary findings of our field walk to date. The remaining chapters will illustrate the practical application of this social field theory across all five systems levels (micro, meso, macro, mundo, meta).

In outlining these systems levels from the viewpoint of an evolving self, that is, from the viewpoint of shifting the inner place from which we operate, we will discover four fundamental (but mostly hidden) metaprocesses that create the world we live in from moment to moment. These four metaprocesses shape the reality and life in our institutions and communities much more deeply and profoundly than any kind of functional or institutional core process that is usually talked about. The four universal processes, or metaprocesses, are: thinking (attending), conversing (languaging), organizing (structuring), and forming fields or collective global action (coordinating). The discontinuous shifts in the quality of these meta-processes are mostly hidden by our blind spot. For example: we see the results of our thought process, the outcomes—but we are usually unaware of the fundamental process that is *doing* the creating. That process is the process of thinking. Don't be deceived about this: thinking *is* a creative process. Thinking creates the world. But as long as this happens in our blind spot, we are not really present to this fundamental process of coming into being. We are not fully participating in (and aware of) bringing forth the world. The same could be said in regard to the processes of conversation and of collective action, as we will discuss in more detail soon.

Finally, in the closing chapter I will summarize the principles of presencing as a social technology of freedom that can be used in the real world of social transformation and institutional change.

CHAPTER 16

Individual Actions

Learning from a Three-Year-Old • The Theater Stage and the
Collective Field • Hitler's Secretary

Learning from a Three-Year-Old

One day, as I was filling the dishwasher, I ran out of detergent. I wasn't sure the box next to it was the right kind of soap, but I thought, what the heck, and used it anyway. A few minutes later, foam began streaming from the machine. Damn! I stopped the machine. Wiped up the foam. Inspected the mess: the machine was filled with water, dishes, and vast amounts of soapy foam. Since it seemed impossible to empty the machine of its water, I decided to forge ahead: to let it run and to simply mop up the foam for as long as it continued to pour out. While pre-occupied with my mess, I was joined by our three-year-old, Johan-Caspar, who was fascinated by the show. He began helping me wipe away the end-less white stream. As the rate of the streaming foam began to slow just a lit-tle, Johan-Caspar took some short breaks. During these breaks he started talking to the machine in a low, intense voice. "What are you saying?" I asked him. "I am talking to the foam," he replied. "The foam?" I was surprised.

"Because the poor foam hasn't got eyes to see. That's why he can't find the right way. That's why he keeps coming out the wrong way."

My three-year-old looked at the same frustrating situation as I did, but instead of wanting to kick the machine, he empathized with the streaming foam, communicating with the foam as if it were a sentient being. He noticed that this being had no eyes and believed that was why it had lost its way. It needed our help. One situation, one set of data, two ways of making sense.

From then on we communicated in silence with the streaming white being. Johan Caspar and I didn't exchange any more words. We just got into the rhythm and flow of the work, paying attention to what that "white being" needed us to do to help it find its way.

Now let me deconstruct this story using the field model introduced in Chapter 15.

Filling the dishwasher and mindlessly adding the wrong detergent is a perfect example of downloading. Then, once the foaming started, I jumped from Level 1 (downloading) to Level 2: "Damn!" (seeing the mess). Then I tried to fix the problem. The challenge was to get beyond the Voice of Judgment ("Why can't *they* build dishwashers that have a simple 'empty the water' function?") and to stay cool and analyze the available options. If I had continued on the path suggested by my Voice of Judgment, I would have found many more things to be irritated about and probably would have kicked the machine. That course of action would have taken me straight into the space of antiemergence: the cycle of denial and destruction. First you kick the machine, and then . . . well, we all know the story: the cycle of denial and destruction is filled with feedback loops that reinforce the destructive behavior.

That didn't happen because Johan Caspar entered the plane at a different level, Field 3 (he tuned in to what he saw as an evolving being, and then he started interacting with it). So he taught me to stop kicking and start diving in and feeling from inside. And finally, when we found a rhythm and flow of working together, no more words were needed. We knew what needed to be done and carried it out easily (illustrating, in a nutshell, Level 4).

There are three points about this story that I would like to highlight. One, mindfulness and presence can happen anytime, anywhere, in the midst of our everyday life. It doesn't require us to travel to the moon and back (although for some that has actually been the way into this experience). What it requires is an inward shift of attention.

Two, the greater the pressure of the external challenge (the bigger the mess in front of me), the more natural it feels to enter the dark space of absencing (kicking the machine), which I will explain in more detail below.

Three, the point of moving into Fields 3 and 4 is to stop interacting with objects and start dealing with everything we work and interact with *as if it were a sentient being that we can directly connect to from within* (the foam without eyes).

The Theater Stage and the Collective Field

I still remember the amazing feeling of performing my first major role in a stage play at the age of about fourteen. You do everything you can to prepare, and you've memorized all your lines and stage cues. Then it's time for the opening scene. The curtain is about to rise. The voices of the audience grow softer. Suddenly you feel as if the earth stops turning. Everything, all the months of preparation, shrinks into a little heap of desperation and nothingness. It all vanishes. You forget everything you ever learned. You are frightened. You are alone. Driven more by desperation than aspiration, you hang in there. Not because you are courageous, more because it's now too late to run away (a thought that briefly crosses your mind). Then, before you fully realize it, you see the curtain rising. Too late. No more escape. Time stops.

The colored theater lights blind you and wrap you in an unfamiliar sphere of hot attention and energy. As if in slow motion, you stumble into the first movements, words, sentences, and gestures. You are just getting into it when you suddenly notice that you are not alone. Another "being" seems to be communicating intimately with you. It is the audience. Their attention creates a holding space for you—a place that guides you. You feel it with every fiber of your body. You're now in a place that is watching and communicating with you. And it nourishes you with an energy you have never tasted before. A place that connects your source and being. *Your* place.

In this example, I, as the actor, approach the stage in the mode of downloading, having memorized all 820 of the lines that Shakespeare's Prospero had to speak. Then on stage, as the curtain rises, the resistance shows up as fear: fear of failure, fear of getting stuck, fear of not being able to remember a single line in front of three hundred people. In a mixture of desperation and courage, I stumble across a threshold and simply start moving. After the first few habitual moves my carefully prepared actions move from Fields 1 and 2 to Fields 3 and 4—that is, I enter a flow of deepening/deepened presence and emergence.

What makes that possible? A collective holding space: an audience of three hundred loving parents and friends, sitting there with their minds and hearts wide open, fully present to and in awe of their children's performance.

In this example, the resistance (fear) appears right at the beginning. It is followed by dropping into a deeper flow through the collective holding space provided by the loving audience. The collective holding space makes the shadow space of antiemergence disappear. Collective forces can free us or, as in the following story, keep us locked into the social space of antiemergence.

Hitler's Secretary

Traudl Junge was a simple, humble woman from rural Germany who lost her father early and whose difficult financial situation prevented her from pursuing the artistic career she longed for. More by accident than not, she went to Berlin, got a job through an uncle, and soon stumbled into a typing contest, which she won. Before long she was interviewing with a soft-spoken, friendly uncle type who was looking for a new private secretary. His name was Adolf Hitler, and he hired her to take occasional dictation.

At the end of the war, when Hitler committed suicide in his Führerbunker, she returned to the outside, to the real world—a world that lay in ashes and ruins.

She tried to flee to southern Germany but was captured by the Russians in Berlin. Because she had never been a member of the German Nazi Party, she was released and settled in Munich. Soon thereafter she came across the gravestone of Die Weisse Rose (The White Rose), a small Munich-based group of German resisters who had all been killed by the Nazis. She looked at the inscription and was shocked to see that all the main figures of Die Weisse Rose had been born in the same year she was: 1920. At that moment of seeing she realized that for her and for her generation there was no hiding behind excuses. The Weisse Rose figures were the same age she was, and the difference between them was that each of them had made a conscious choice in their lives, a choice that she had never made. She realized that whatever she had done and participated in was ultimately her full personal responsibility—there was no hiding behind the collective fate of her generation. She gave no interviews until shortly before her death, when she spoke to André Heller, a well-known Austrian artist. A few days before the interview was aired, she told him that only now, fifty years later, could she finally begin to forgive herself. On the day after the interview aired, she passed away.[1] What makes her account of the final weeks in Hitler's bunker so intriguing is the preciseness and clarity of her descriptions. Her mind and memory seemed to work like a supersharp camera. She remembered countless events in great detail. At the same time she was also a gifted second-order observer: she was cognizant of gaps in her memory when she couldn't retrieve exact images or experiences.

Here is how Traudl Junge describes the bizarre company inside Hitler's bunker. They were deep down inside the eleven-meter-thick walls of the bunker, with bombs dropping to the left and right and on top of them. The Red Army was only a few roadblocks away. Hitler's army had collapsed, gone from occupying nearly all of Europe to total defeat. Yet, despite all the "disconfirming data" around them, all the bombs that were being dropped right on top of them, some people inside the bunker were holding on to their hopes and fantasies. They were clinging to their old mental models, unable to let reality sink in. The bombs being dropped onto them were not powerful enough to get the message to penetrate through the thick walls of their minds. Pondering why she didn't simply leave after even Hitler had suggested that she do so, she said, "I was afraid to leave the security of the bunker."

That's what the power of blinding (not seeing) and entrenching (desensing) is about: it keeps us inside the thick walls of our own bunkers so that we are unable to connect with what's really going on outside. Still, her staying is somewhat incomprehensible. What was the real mechanism that kept her locked inside the bunker?

One way to make sense of this puzzle is to imagine that she got stuck in the shadowspace of antiemergence, which froze her deeper resources of intelligence (open mind, heart, will). She lost the connection to her authentic self and ended up participating in the practices of antiemergence (see Figure 16.1):

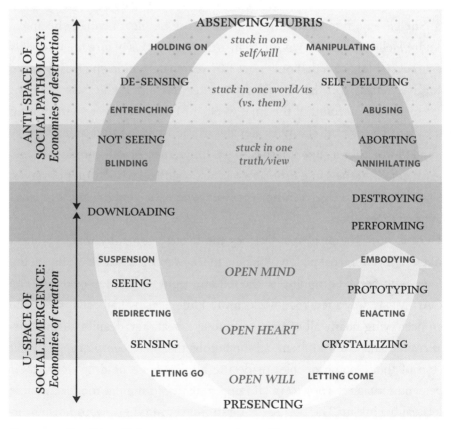

FIGURE 16.1 THE U-SPACE AND THE ANTI=SPACE

Downloading: Traudl Junge described in great detail how life inside the bunker continued, as if the people were automatons. As daily and even special rituals such as the tea ceremony or the wedding between Hitler and Eva Braun (two days before his suicide) continued, they grew into hollow procedures of an absurd disconnect.

Blinding, or not seeing: "I was walled in and separated from the information that I needed to understand what was going on," said Traudl Junge. "First when I got there, I thought that I had arrived at the source of information. But later I realized that I had been in the [system's] blind spot."

Entrenching and desensing: During the final years of the war, Hitler always traveled on a special train with curtains closed so he wouldn't see the war's destruction. When he arrived back at the main train station in Berlin, his driver was instructed to take a route that would expose Hitler to the least destruction. He didn't want any flowers in the bunker because he "didn't want to be around corpses." How ironic. The man whose acts caused the deaths of 55 million people didn't want to be near flowers that were dying.

Absencing: Traudl Junge had the most trouble recalling those final days in the bunker. Her otherwise supersharp camera memory appeared to have black holes when it came to remembering her feelings and emotions during those last days. It is as if these emotions were erased—or deeply frozen inside her experiential body. She described acting like a mindless automaton in her day-to-day routine—disconnected not only from the catastrophic events unfolding outside but also from her real self: "We functioned like automatons, I cannot remember any feelings, it was like an in-between state where I was no longer myself."

Self-deluding: This is a total disconnect between one's images of the unfolding future and reality. Traudl Junge described many meetings and turnaround strategies that all went nowhere because they were grounded in such illusory assumptions. They only deepened the abyss between the world inside the bunker and the course of events outside. "We were so separated from what was really going on outside," reflected Junge, "that we had no idea how the world would continue to unfold."

Aborting: Just as prototyping is about creating microcosms of a future life, aborting is about terminating and killing future life. In the bunker this involved killing first the dog, on whom the cyanide was tested, then all the children, as well as many others, who committed suicide prior to the final victory of the Red Army.

Annihilating: After Hitler killed himself, Traudl Junge said that the remaining characters sat together like a group of lifeless puppets that had just lost their puppeteer.

The group around Hitler was trapped in a space of social antiemergence that revolves around downloading, blinding, desensing, absencing, self-deluding, aborting, and destruction. Figure 16.1 depicts how this shadow space represents the antithesis of the U space of presencing.

Just as the U space of presencing spells out the economics of creation, the shadow space of absencing features the economics of destruction. Each cycle is based on self-reinforcing dynamics. The U space of social emergence is based on the power of activating the instruments of the open mind, open heart, and open will. By contrast, the shadow space of social pathology is based on the dynamics of being stuck in one Truth (rigid ideology), one center or collective (arrogance, hate), and one will (fanaticism and violence)—in short, the space of absencing exhibits all the key features of fundamentalism.

For Traudl Junge, one puzzling question remained: Why didn't I leave?

She didn't leave the bunker because she was caught in a deadly pattern of absencing. The dynamics she was wrestling with are now back in business. Because these destructive dynamics are alive and well, we need a clearer understanding of the process and practices through which the pathological space of social destruction comes into being. That space appears to manifest when human systems face high-stakes situations in which the relationship to their open mind, heart, and will is cut off and frozen out.

Figure 16.1 sums up the individual dimensions of the U:

- Most people on Earth have plenty of experiences across all four levels. When first confronted with the U, many people say: Yes, I do know Level

1 and 2, I do know downloading and seeing, but I am not sure that I know Level 3 and 4, sensing and presencing. But then, on consideration and after going deeper into their life's and work's journey, most people find the hidden gold of their various threshold experiences relatively quickly.

- The movement from Level 1, downloading to the bottom or the deeper levels of the U, can happen in any situation: when doing a four-week meditation retreat or when messing up the dishwasher in your home kitchen.
- Being in the presence of people who operate from the deeper levels can help a lot. In some cases, that can be a three-year-old. In other cases, this wisdom awareness happens some other way, through someone else. Sometimes we call that leadership.
- If you happen to connect to a source once, it isn't good enough. Most people did that already (often without fully noticing). The issue is how to stay connected, how to sustain that connection. Because if you do not, you may be in danger of freezing that single experience into something rigid that catapults you into the antispace of social pathology (one Truth, one Us, one Will). Which brings us to our next point.
- We can flip or revert from the social space of deep emergence into the dark space of antiemergence anytime, anywhere. It can happen whenever we lose our full attention and wakefulness and our firm grounding in a selfless or serving intent. It's easy to see how Hitler's secretary got sucked into a system that finally had her holding on to the informational blind spot behind eleven-meter-thick walls. That's easy to recognize. But isn't that same thing happening to each of us day to day, moment to moment? Aren't we also seduced by situations and systems that take advantage of our not being fully awake, not being fully intentional? As with Traudl Junge, the system hits us right in our blind spot.

So how can we sustain the connection to source? By being and staying awake.

Thinking is an enormously powerful process—one that usually remains untapped, unused and unrecognized. Our thinking creates the world! But instead of discovering the creative power of real thinking, we are socialized into patterns of downloading that relate to real thinking like the shadows inside Plato's cave relate to the actual reality and the sun outside.

The power of this metaprocess of thinking is frozen into fixed forms and shadows in Field 1 (downloading); begins to wake up when we begin to connect with what is really going on outside (Field 2: seeing); begins to get wings that take us out of the prisons of our own mental models when we begin to connect with the others around us and with what the situation looks and feels like to them (Field 3: sensing); and finally turns into the source of fire. In its essence, real thinking is pure fire. The fire of creation. The fire we can tap into when we begin to connect with the fourth field.

Conversational Actions

Clashing Views • Download • Debate • Dialogue • Presencing
• Conversational Fields and Their Antifields • Using Dialogue
Interviews in Organizations • Evolutionary Pathways of
Conversational Fields

A t the beginning of this book, I compared our family farm's agricultural fields to social fields that describe the quality of social interaction. Conversations are the living embodiment of social fields, and they are an important starting point for improving social interaction. In my research in and my work with organizations, I have made two observations that are relevant to improving conversations: (1) conversations are enacted in patterns or fields, and these patterns of conversational interaction tend to remain the same; and (2) there is a very limited set of generic field patterns that you can see in conversations—so far, I have observed four. They are: downloading (Field 1), debate (Field 2), dialogue (Field 3), and presencing (Field 4). The four fields differ in terms of the inner place in which conversation is formed: speaking from "what *they* want to hear" (Field 1), speaking from "what *I* really think" (Field 2), speaking from "*seeing myself* as part of the larger whole" (Field 3), or "speaking from what is *moving through*." A field structure of conversation is a pattern of interaction that, once introduced, tends to be reenacted by all participants in that conversation. When you see a conversation shift from one pattern (such as "being polite") to another (such as "speaking your mind"), it usually does involve all the participants in the conversation, not just a few of them (see Figure 17.1).

Recognizing these patterns of conversation is enormously relevant for leading change. It is in conversation (the second meta-process) that we bring forth the world, moment by moment. Throughout history, different cultures have evolved different rules that govern interaction in groups, communities, and organizations. The sociologist Norbert Elias has called the evolution of these invisible rules that conduct our everyday social interaction "the civilizing process," and it can be traced back many centuries throughout our history.[1] Another sociologist, Erving Goffman, has shown how the evolution of these rules and patterned expectations shapes our interactions with the various audiences of our work and life, the way we construct, present, and enact our selves and our roles in face-to-face group situations.[2] While these studies illuminate the power and deepen our understanding of the genealogy of these patterns, they tell us less about the practical things we can do when we actually face situations where the existing pattern of a group or a team is clearly dysfunctional. By this, we mean when the outcome of the collective behavior is clearly a mismatch with the intentions of the participants.

When we face these issues and situations, the question is: What can we do that might allow us to shift the field of conversation from one pattern to another? What can we do that can help a group to see, assess, and change the patterns that the participants collectively enact?

These and other questions have lead to an increased interest in the art of productive conversation and dialogue over the past ten or fifteen years. The practice of dialogue deals, to a large degree, with seeing and suspending cultural rules of politeness and face saving. Bill Isaacs, drawing on the work of Martin Buber and David Bohm, defines dialogue as the art of thinking together or the capacity of accessing collective intelligence.[3] This now sets the stage for examining the four different field structures of conversation in greater detail.

FIELD STRUCTURE OF ATTENTION	FIELD		
1. I-IN-ME	⊙	**1. DOWNLOADING** *talking* *nice*	SPEAKING FROM WHAT THEY WANT TO HEAR *polite routines, empty phrases* *AUTISTIC SYSTEM (not saying what you think)*
2. I-IN-IT	○	**2. DEBATE** *talking* *tough*	SPEAKING FROM WHAT I THINK *Divergent views: I am my point of view* *ADAPTIVE SYSTEM (say what you think)*
3. I-IN-YOU	◌	**3. DIALOGUE** *reflective* *inquiry*	SPEAKING FROM SEEING MYSELF AS PART OF THE WHOLE *from defending to inquiry into viewpoints* *SELF-REFLECTIVE SYSTEM (reflect on your part)*
4. I-IN-NOW	◌	**4. PRESENCING** *generative* *flow*	SPEAKING FROM WHAT IS MOVING THROUGH *stillness, collective creativity, flow* *GENERATIVE SYSTEM (identity shift: authentic self)*

FIGURE 17.1 FOUR FIELDS OF CONVERSATION

Clashing Views

In 1996 I taught a four-day workshop on art, leadership, and social transformation at Witten/Herdecke University in Germany for students, artists, and some business people. It was all pleasant enough, but then, after my brief talk, one artist said, "I didn't understand a word you said." I felt as if my young lecture career had reached an all-time low. After that, the then CEO of Hugo Boss, a major German clothing company, told how his sponsorship of various art institutions related to their business efforts. A theater director piped up and said that Boss's socially responsible sponsorship was just another example of how the capitalist system exploited people and was actually part of the problem, not the solution. We clearly were in a tough debate, and I was witnessing a vivid and forceful clash of mental models or views of the world.

Moving Beyond the Boundaries of "My Position"

The next day, we started in small groups. Each person took fifteen minutes

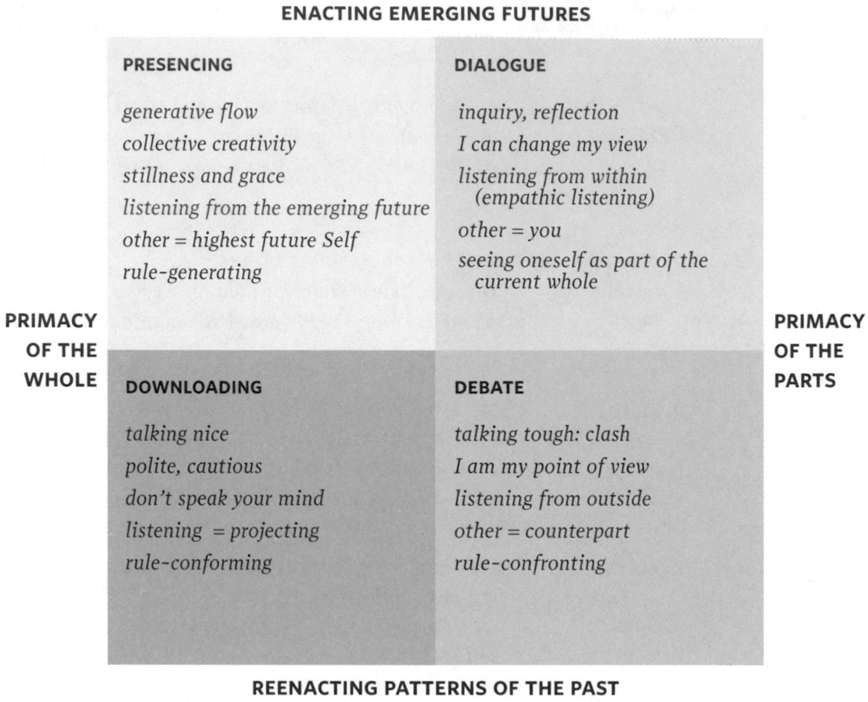

ENACTING EMERGING FUTURES

PRESENCING	**DIALOGUE**
generative flow	*inquiry, reflection*
collective creativity	*I can change my view*
stillness and grace	*listening from within*
listening from the emerging future	*(empathic listening)*
other = highest future Self	*other = you*
rule-generating	*seeing oneself as part of the current whole*
DOWNLOADING	**DEBATE**
talking nice	*talking tough: clash*
polite, cautious	*I am my point of view*
don't speak your mind	*listening from outside*
listening = projecting	*other = counterpart*
rule-conforming	*rule-confronting*

PRIMACY OF THE WHOLE

PRIMACY OF THE PARTS

REENACTING PATTERNS OF THE PAST

FIGURE 17.2 FOUR FIELDS OF CONVERSATION

to build a small sculpture that expressed what he or she wanted to create with his or her work. Then we had a "gallery" tour, during which everyone explained their sculptures. The move to genuine inquiry into one's own and others' ideas allowed us to tap into another field and stream of conversational reality. The difference between this field of appreciative inquiry and the trench warfare of the prior day was palpable.[4]

Talking from the Flow of Pure Presence

On the last morning, we closed the workshop with a large open-forum dialogue. The difference between it and the second day's breakdown could not have been more striking. Yelling at one another was replaced by a deep, calm flow of conversation. The directness, subtlety, and intimacy of the conversation testified to a heart-to-heart connection and collectively felt presence through a moment of spontaneous silence near the end of the event.

In reflecting on that experience, I realized that the group as a whole had operated using different field structures of conversation. I identified four different field structures of conversation that had appeared during the workshop: downloading (talking nice), debate (talking tough), dialogue (reflective inquiry), and presencing (deep co-creative flow). The dialogue model that resulted from this observation is diagrammed in Figure 17.2.[5]

Download: Enacting the Process of Conversation from Field 1

"How are you?"

"I am fine."

Many formal meetings in organizations are conducted using this kind of ritual and set language. Operating effectively in such conversations requires the participants to conform to the dominant pattern of exchanging polite phrases with one another, not to say what is really on their minds. In school we learn to say what the teacher wants to hear. Later, this skill is exactly the one we need to deal with bosses and to get ahead in organizations. If it serves us so well, what's wrong with it?

The problem is that this type of conversation—viewed from an organizational learning point of view—tends to result in dysfunctional behavior: it prevents a team from talking about what's really going on. They talk about the real stuff somewhere else—in the parking lot, on their way home. But at the meeting everyone's time is wasted when they do nothing more than exchange polite comments. If individuals and teams don't talk about difficult issues, what Chris Argyris calls "undiscussables," they won't reflect on them and nothing will change.[6] The higher the complexity of a given challenge, the greater the need to broaden one's conversational repertoire and to learn how to operate from other fields of conversational emergence.

Downloading conversations are center-driven in the sense that they simply reproduce existing rules and phrases. Just as in individual downloading my perception of the world is limited to my existing mental frames and templates, conversational downloading only articulates those aspects of reality (as experienced by the participants) that fit into the dominant frameworks and conversational patterns of the group. The bigger the gap between what is said ("I am fine") and the actual situation ("I am about to die"), the higher the likelihood of some kind of breakdown in the system further down the road.

Debate: Enacting the Process of Conversation from Field 2

"How are you?"

"I am terrible."

The defining feature of Field 2 conversations is that participants speak their minds, such as when the audience member told me that he hadn't understood a single word of my presentation and when the CEO was told that some of his business practices were harmful and stupid. Tension was high. Everybody felt uncomfortable. The group had switched from rule-reproducing language to another tougher type of conversation, where individuals presented their own divergent points of view.

Just as the ticket to enter a Field 1 conversation (downloading) is the (unspoken) requirement to conform, the entry ticket to a Field 2 conversation is the willingness to take a different stance, to suggest a different point of view. To get some airtime in a conversation in Field 1, you must conform with others' views. In Field 2, you suggest a different or even opposing view. Just as in individual perception, the shift from downloading to seeing means being open to disconfirming data (observations that contradict our mental models). Field 2 conversation implies opening up to viewpoints that challenge the dominant views.

And just as the capacity to see with fresh eyes can be developed by suspending judgment and paying attention to disconfirming data (Charles Darwin always carried a notebook in which he would write down observations that didn't fit his theories), the capacity to move from downloading (talking nice) to debate (talking tough) can also be developed by encouraging groups to express divergent views and by developing a culture that values speaking one's mind over being polite.

The structure that results from this kind of interaction is often a debate. The word "debate" literally means "to fight or beat down," which is exactly the pattern in this kind of conversational field structure. People use their arguments to beat or best their opponent, defined as anyone with a different opinion.

The debate style of conversation can be useful in organizations because it allows a team to get all the different views on a subject on the table. I have found that in East Asian and South East Asian cultures the best way to get into Field 2 is not through confrontational debate (as in the West) but by a process that starts by engaging participants in small groups and allows all participants to share their various observations and views on a topic. This avoids face-saving related blockages that prevent the diverse perspectives to come out. Still, it delivers the same fundamental Field 2 bottom line: the expression of different and diverging views.

But if the issue at hand requires team members to reflect on and change their basic habits of thought and guiding assumptions, yet a different type of conversation is needed—one that allows participants to realize, as Bill Isaacs so eloquently put it, that "I am not my point of view." I can suspend and look at my own point of view as well as look at somebody else's assumptions. But to do so, I need to move into Field 3.

Dialogue: Enacting the Process of Conversation from Field 3

"How are you?"

"Not sure. But how are you, my friend?"

"Not sure either. I too arrived with an uneasy feeling."

"Oh, really? How interesting. Tell me about it. What's going on in your life?"

On the third day of the workshop, when each of the group members explained their sculptures, the whole flow of the conversation changed from entrenched warfare to open and appreciative inquiry. People listened to one another with open minds and hearts.

A black South African union leader who once participated in a workshop with a white representative of a mining company described the change from debate to dialogue that happened during the workshop this way:

"He represented this evil capitalist institution, the Chamber of Mines. I represented the National Union of Mine workers. In 1987 we took 340,000 workers out on strike, 15 workers were killed and more than 300 workers got terribly injured. . . . [Back then] he was the enemy and here I was sitting with this guy in the room when those bruises are still raw. This is 1992, it is five years on since 1987.

"Today it is easier for me to say that it is a good thing that he was there because he also had to live a future that he really did not believe in. . . . I think what it [the workshop] did, it allowed him to see the world from my point of view and it allowed me to see the world from his point of view."[7]

Another example comes from a participant in a workshop in Guatemala that was facilitated by my colleague Adam Kahane.[8] The objective of the workshop was to create a dialogue and a common vision of the future among a diverse group of representatives of all sectors in the country, from the military to representatives of the guerrilla movement: "We were capable of understanding each other, of talking to each other; we were capable of respecting each other, of doing this. This is something that I am certain has impressed many people in the country. And one of the conversations heard there was: 'Were the people of the guerrillas there? And if so, were they listening? Yes.' This is something so simple, but I believe that what might be happening in the country may be influenced by one of these processes."[9]

The participants individually and as a group develop an inner observer that helps them focus on what they are doing. They listen more carefully and move away from a debate. One of the participants reflects on this type of conversation: "I think that the greatest impact was to discover to what degree you always engage in conversation without listening to what the other person says. And it is something that was so evident that one begins to put it in practice almost immediately. This is something . . . that I took with me."[10]

Dialogue comes from the Greek *logos*, "word" or "meaning," and *dia*, "through," and can be literally translated as "meaning moving through."[11]

Moving from *debate* (Field 2) to *dialogue* (Field 3) involves a profound shift in the collective field structure of attention based on which a conversation operates. Just as the move from *seeing* to *sensing* on the micro level of the individual involves a shift from facing the world as an exterior set of objects to experiencing the world from (within) the field, the shift from debate to dialogue also involves a shift from trying to beat down the contrary view to inquiring into one another's views, empathically listening from (within) the other."

When this shift toward a dialogic field of conversation happens, your perspective widens to include yourself—you move from seeing the world as an exterior set of objects to seeing the world *and* yourself as you participate in co-creating it. Participants individually and as a group develop an inner observer that helps them to recognize and *redirect* their way and focus of operating. It is as if one is watching not just a movie on a screen but also the cameraman who shot the movie, the director, and even oneself, the observer. One perceives a field of multiple, dynamically interconnected perspectives that constitute a single field. In the Patient-Physician Dialogue Forum this shift happened in the silence when the participants realized that they are the system. When that kind of shift happens, people move from defending their viewpoints to inquiring into viewpoints and speaking from seeing themselves as part of the system at issue.

Presencing: Enacting the Process of Conversation from Field 4

"So, Otto, I'm wondering if you'd like you and your work to be held by this circle?"

When Barbara asked me that question, in the Circle of Seven, I felt a change of atmosphere.

Time slowed down; space opened up. Several times during my interview projects I have encountered this shift to a deeper space of essential emergence. When it happens, time slows down and seems almost to stop, the atmosphere feels thicker, and my sense of space opens up, as if I were in a clearing or in a larger space that opens up and radiates around and through us. The boundary between me and my dialogue partners is now wide open, and we begin to operate in a common field. In these moments, it feels as if something is blessing the communal presence. The conversation shifts from self-reflection to speaking from what is moving through: "I am urged not to speak casually," as Leslie put it in the Circle of Seven: "I speak when I'm moved by a larger presence that needs a voice. . . . We've dropped into the field."

These situations of profound co-creation usually begin by some kind of "crack," of letting-go and letting-come turning point that earlier has been described as "it felt as if I was going to die" or as "breaking through a membrane."

Field 4 conversations differ from dialogue (Field 3) not only in their experiential texture but also in terms of two long-term outcomes: a unique, deep bond among those who participated; and often significant accomplishments by both entire groups and individuals.

Although I admit that the evidence for these claims is more anecdotal than statistically significant, these two outcomes do seem to form a consistent pattern. Both groups and individuals develop deeper bonds of connection. They feel a deeper, timeless quality of connection that will not disappear. You can gloss over it, but it's still there. It's like meeting your best friend after many years of separation and finding that you still "click." And teams or groups who have entered the deep flow of presencing once usually find it much easier to do so the next time.

The initial stage of presencing provides a deeper connection to the essence of our work and who we are, individually and collectively. Tapping into this deeper source can turn into a real force—but it requires a lot of attention and work to bring the new into reality. Sometimes it happens and sometimes it doesn't.

My colleague Adam Kahane tells of one instance when it did happen. As mentioned earlier, he was leading a national scenario project in Guatemala at a time when the country was recovering from a period of great civil strife. The scenario work was designed to help participants see the forces they would be contending with as they moved forward. One evening early in the project, the group gathered after dinner and told stories that they thought would illuminate some of these forces. One businesswoman talked about trying to discover the facts of her sister's assassination by the military. A military official she had spoken with earlier and who had denied any involvement, sat beside her that evening in the circle.

Then Ronalth Ochaeta, a human rights activist, told the story of a time he had gone to a Mayan village to witness the exhumation of a mass grave (one of many) from a massacre. When the earth had been removed, he noticed a number of small bones, and he asked the forensics team if people's bones had been broken during the massacre. They replied that no, the grave contained the corpses of pregnant women, and the small bones were those of their fetuses.

"When Ochaeta finished telling his story," Adam said, "the team was completely silent. I was leading this session and had never experienced a silence like this; I was dumbstruck and had no idea what to say or do, so I did nothing. The silence lasted a long time, perhaps five minutes. . . . At the end of the session, I made an uncharacteristic observation: 'I feel that there is spirit in the room.'" As Adam told it, the normal sense of separation between people lessened; two participants referred to the experience as one of "communion." They moved from appreciating each other's different perspectives to being, for a while, a whole collective "I."

Adam said, "The feeling associated with listening to Ochaeta's story was not empathy toward him. The story was not about him, and he told it with little emotion; several other people in the room could have told similar stories from their own experiences. Instead, Ochaeta was a vehicle for that critically important story to enter the room and be heard by the whole team. Each story is a hologram that contains the whole picture. In Ochaeta's story the team glimpsed the essential whole of the Guatemalan reality: the mystery to which they needed to be connected to do what they had to do."[12]

When communication reaches the point of communion, participants recognize their common ground and deeply sense what they are there for. All interactions and conversations begin to emanate from a different place; a place of deep connectedness and essential emergence begins to open up.

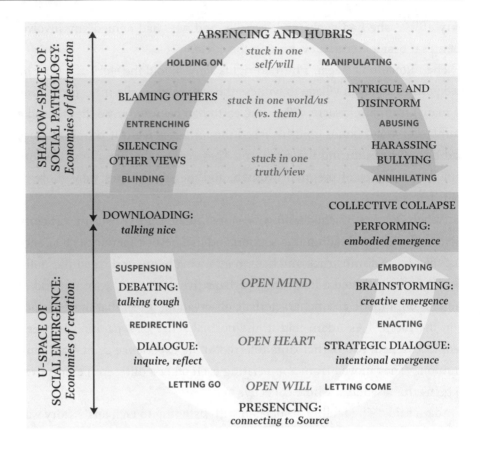

FIGURE 17.3 THE U-SPACE AND THE ANTI-SPACE: CONVERSATIONS

Conversational Fields of Emergence and Their Antifields

Figure 17.3 presents a more differentiated typology of the conversational fields introduced above. It differs in two aspects from the presentation in Figure 17.1. First, it shows three additional fields of conversation on the right-hand side of the U. These three types are: strategic dialogue (intentional emergence), brainstorming (creative emergence), and performing (embodied emergence). They all belong to the larger group of presencing-based conversation (that is, they share the same field structure of attention that is defined by being connected to Source). In all three, one operates from a deeper source. But they are applied in different contexts. They each capture a different stage of the coming into being of the new: as an image and intention, as a living prototype, or as everyday practice.

You'll notice there's something else new in Figure 17.3—a dark space of social pathology in which dialogue does not happen.

Why Dialogue Sometimes Doesn't Happen

Look around, so many systems and institutions have become deeply locked into the mode of downloading. What are the mechanisms through which the grip of downloading takes hold? Why do so many systems get stuck in pathological patterns of behavior?

Social systems can derail into social pathology by what I call the cycle of *conversational absencing*. This is the opposite of the cycle of presencing. Let's now look, at seven debilitating behaviors of conversational absencing:

1. *Downloading:* Reenacting patterns of the past. Downloading is the seed and mother of all the remaining practices of the absencing cycle, just as paying attention and wonder are the seed and mother of all practices in the cycle of presencing.

2. *Silencing other views:* Instead of encouraging diverse views and entering a healthy debate, leaders discourage contradiction, deny disconfirming data, and silence other views. Think of the second CEO in the GlobalHealthCompany case described in Chapter 8: "He was a ruinous leader," recalled one of the company's senior managers. "He sacked people outright if they did not agree with him. You were sacked if you said something about the company that you should not say—your job was to protect the company." Another prominent case in point is the crash of the space shuttle *Challenger*. Conversations at NASA silenced views including disconfirming data exactly when the consideration of those data would have mattered most. Another example of (often unintended) silencing of diverse views was shared by Joseph Stiglitz in his account of the inner workings of the IMF that led to the application of many ill-advised policies in the past: "Those policies weren't questioned by many of the people in power in the IMF, by those who were making

the critical decisions. They were often questioned by people in the developing countries, but many were so afraid they might lose IMF funding, and with it funding from others, that they articulated their doubts most cautiously, if at all, and then only in private."[13]

3. *Blaming others:* Blaming others dims the reality that is most critical when dealing with social complexity and conflict: seeing yourself from the perspective of the other stakeholders and understanding your part in contributing to the issue at hand. The conversational model of blaming others prevents groups from capturing the social complexities that matter most: seeing themselves as part of the system at issue. When pressures rise and a system gets stuck in *blaming others* type of conversations, the outcome will be predictably dysfunctional, too. The anticapacity that underlies this conversation type is to become entrenched in one's own little world rather than crossing the boundaries to the outside. Blaming others means not connecting to others and missing their true view of a situation. This failure often happens in institutional settings in spite of the best individual intentions. Stiglitz, for example, had the advantage of not being entrenched too deeply in the internal politics of the IMF. Therefore it was less difficult for him to connect not only to the institutional IMF view but also to the perspective of the other side: the developing countries. Said Stiglitz, giving voice to this other view, "Today few defend the hypocrisy of pretending to help developing countries by forcing them to open up their markets to the goods of the advanced industrial countries while keeping their own markets protected, policies that make the rich richer and the poor more impoverished—and increasingly angry."[14] This hypocrisy cannot be addressed as a mere individual behavioral issue. It can be addressed only in the context of a collective or group phenomenon in which certain aspects of reality perception are structurally filtered out or switched off.

4. *Absencing and hubris:* If blaming others is about disconnecting horizontally from others, absencing is about disconnecting vertically from oneself—that is, from one's emerging or authentic self. This disconnect is

in some ways both the most subtle and the most dramatic. I was once on a conference call to discuss the design of a high-level gathering of decision makers in one of the world's premier international institutions. As the client and sponsor of this event outlined his ideas and essentials for the meeting, I felt myself silently checking out, because what he was describing was not what he, his core group, and I had envisioned. In an earlier conversation with him I had agreed to participate in an event that would be more courageous and daring, and now I felt that his revised proposal would underutilize people's time and energies and also what I could have contributed. At that moment I simply played by the rules. I was attentive to the client and responded politely to what he was saying. But deep in my heart I knew that going along with the client's current plan would destroy the future possibility that he and the other members of the core group had been hoping for. Knowing this in my heart, I regretted playing by the rules and going with the flow. I felt the need to try to salvage things, but I didn't know what to do.

Later that evening, in a one-on-one conversation with the same client, I expressed some of my concerns. And at that moment the initial connection to the best future possibility began to reappear for both of us, as we again found the common ground of conversing.

Absencing contains a subtle dimension of sabotage, as evidenced by the conference call. It is so subtle that only *you* might notice it when it happens. Who are you sabotaging? Your authentic Self and the relationships it may have with the authentic core of other key players—that is, the highest future possibility for yourself and for your project or group, the one that totally depends on you in order to come into being. Once you have cut that lifeline to your authentic Self, you instantly feel an inner void. That void usually fills up quickly with some dimension of ego and other stuff from yesterday or, if things get worse, the day before yesterday (as in the case of fascim). When that happens, you can quickly lose touch with what needs to happen and end up in some version of collective self-pity or hubris or both.

Hubris and absencing are the opposite of presencing. In presencing, the self serves as a vehicle for the best possible future that wants to emerge for the larger whole. By contrast, when people put their egos, their selves, or their self-pity at the center; the surrounding world becomes a resource that is subject to unlimited exploitation by the ego and its hubris. This distinction does matter because it clarifies, for example, that Nazi Germany was a case of absencing, not a case of presencing. Hitler and his associates may have used several occult practices—but they used them to serve their collective egos. Their hubris placed themselves squarely at the center. They sought to exploit the remaining world as their resource. As a result, they didn't activate the emerging higher Self that would have been in service of the evolution of the larger whole by removing their own egos from the center stage.

The remaining three practices of this collective pathology, the right-hand side of the "shadow U", complete the process of absencing, just as the right-hand side of the U realizes the process of presencing.

5. *Intrigue and disinformation* deepen the disconnect from the highest future possibility of a system by poisoning the collective sources of conversation and thought. They aim at manipulating the views and behavior of others by holding back true and/or inserting false information into a shared conversational space. Both practices have been widely used in the space of institutional and corporate politics, as well as in the sphere of secret agency-based foreign policies as we read in John Perkins' *Confessions of an Economic Hit Man*.

6. *Harassing and bullying* add more poison to interactions and relationships. Harassment and bullying describe a continuous verbal or physical attack against individuals or groups. These behaviors occur on a massive scale, from the kindergarten playground to the boardrooms of organizations to the halls of government. We can see it any day, almost anywhere. And just as creative *brainstorming* is a microcosm for incubating emerging future possibilities, harassment is a microcosm for aborting emerging futures.

7. *Collective collapse* is the final step in the destruction of relational structures. Just as *performing* completes the movement of presencing by

embodying the emerging future, *collapse* completes the movement of absencing by disembodying the future potential.

Summing up, the left-hand side of the dark space in Figure 17.3 depicts the three foundations on which that cycle operates: a system is disabled when it is cut off from the three lifelines of emergence: external context, internal context, and deep source of emergence. *Silencing* cuts a system off from the observable reality outside: that part of the reality that doesn't fit our stereotypes. *Blaming others* cuts a system off from the reality within: the capacity of a system to see itself from the perspective of another stakeholder. *Absencing* cuts off the connection to the highest future possibility. With these three lifelines cut, we are left with conversations that pollute, poison and pathologize our collective thought (through intrigue and disinformation), that poison microcosms of emerging futures (through harassing, bullying, stifling innovation), and that eventually destroy the structural collective ground itself (collective collapse).

Figure 17.3 allows us to make a few diagnostic observations about the current state of the collective body of conversation that happens in organizations and institutions day to day, moment to moment:

1. The individual intention of most participants in most organizations is to operate from the space of creative emergence, not from the dark space of pathology.
2. Yet the collectively enacted outcome is that many conversations in many or most organizations take place in the pathological space of anti-emergence, not the space of creative emergence.
3. Hence, we collectively do what nobody wants: we operate in the toxic atmosphere of pathological patterns of conversation.
4. Such a conversational space is toxic or limiting in two respects: it prevents individual participants from accessing their deeper levels of being and consciousness, and it prevents collective institutions from co-evolving with their environments by accessing the deeper streams of collective emergence.
5. The dysfunctional results of operating from the polluted and patholog-

ical space of conversation are usually addressed by focusing on the right-hand side, but the dysfunctional behavior *originates* on the left-hand side (and the top) of the destruction cycle: it cuts off the lifelines to the worlds outside and within.

So if the dark space or the cycle of destruction is dysfunctional and nobody wants it, why is the world so firmly in its grip? That question is one of the most puzzling questions of our time. We will come back to it later.

The other question sparked by these observations is, of course, how can we move from the destructive space to the creative U space of conversational reality creation? Let's look at some practical issues.

Using Dialogue Interviews in Organizations

Dialogue interviews can be effective in many different organizational settings. For example, in a leadership program for newly promoted directors at a leading global car company, the whole process begins with a kick-off dialogue. This is a ninety-minute or two-hour conversation (via phone) on the current issues and challenges and on the personal leadership journey that brought the interviewee to the place where she or he is now. Ursula Versteegen, who developed and honed this method over the past ten years with me, describes one of her experiences:

"A while ago, I had a dialogue interview with Walter H. For me the toughest challenge in a dialogue is when I have 'to jump off of the bridge.' The moment of pushing myself off the safe ground into a total 'presence' is the most laborious moment of the interview, and I am really scared when I sense it building up. But once I have dared to jump and have overcome my inner reluctance and clumsiness, it's the most effortless, beautiful way of being.

"Walter is an engineer in a global car company. 'I knew at age ten,' Walter started off, 'that I wanted to become an engineer, working with cars. As a kid, I spent more time in junkyards than on playgrounds.' For more than a decade he had been working as a quality expert in different positions and plants. When Walter spoke about cars he was enthusiastic: I enjoyed listening: 'Everyone linked arms with me right from the beginning. I was given responsibility early on.' I could almost touch his pride about building good-quality cars.

"'For a few weeks now,' he continued, 'I've been in HR/Industrial Relations. It's an exotic country for me. There is a huge list of things'—and he started reading the list—'that I am responsible for now: work organization; reorganization; leadership organization in plants; unions; health management; sick-list reports; health maintenance; occupational safety; aging workforce; new employment models; and finally, HIV/AIDS in countries with a high prevalence of AIDS. My challenge is: How do I convince people in the plant to participate in health management? How do I negotiate with the unions, sell them our concepts? How can I make decisions without formal authority about the people who need to comply with all of these rules?'

"After he had read that list to me, I felt knocked out immediately. It took me a moment to realize that my energy level had dropped from one hundred to zero. Why was that? What had happened? Listening to him while he was continuing to speak about his challenge, I noticed that he had changed as well. His voice had become more formal, he was talking much faster, the manner in which he was talking felt more distant, closing up and maybe even more decisive and resolute. My listening was dropping off. It sounded as if he had shifted from the nice, enthusiastic hands-on production guy into the role of a formal bureaucrat who knew exactly what all these plant people needed to do. I felt distant, too. Inside myself I started to slowly ally with these poor production people who were the targets of all of these corporate activities. I asked him about his stakeholders: 'Who would be the most critical people to talk to and get different perspectives from on your new job?' I was silently hoping that the stakeholders would tell him what I felt I couldn't. 'Oh, I have done these already,' Walter quickly said, 'when I did my first-hundred-days inaugural interviews. I told my stakeholders what my responsibilities were and asked them for comments. Do I have to do these again?'

"I saw myself standing on the bridge, and I knew I had to jump to make a difference. But an incredible inner gravity was holding me back. Part of me said, 'Tell him why his way of doing stakeholder dialogue interviews is useless.' The other, the scary part, said, 'Open your heart. Allow him to change you.' In that moment a memory was welling up in me: not long ago, when I was working at the headquarters of a pharmaceutical company, I had been in exactly the same situation as Walter. I had to convince business units and production sites of lots of conceptual positions, statements, and 'to-dos' that didn't relate to my own experience. The more useless I felt, the more my communication style changed to teaching or instructing them.

"I jumped: 'While I'm listening to you, I'm starting to wonder about the difference between working for a plant and working at headquarters.' I heard him nodding. Our distance started melting. I slowed down, speaking out of the inner place of the lost and useless person I felt to be at the time: 'I don't know whether and how this experience may be relating to you at all.' I talked as if I were walking on tiptoes, waiting for the right words to come, not knowing what the next word would be. 'When I, in my case, asked people from production what they needed me for, their answer was 'Honestly, Ms. Versteegen, we don't need you at all for the things you're doing right now, we're sorry to tell you.'

"Silence. I could hear a pin drop. But the silence was pure energy. I heard a sound of very deep relief, and then Walter said, 'That is exactly what they told me.' In that moment, the whole conversation shifted. I asked him, 'Before, you had mentioned that one of your key learnings in production was that things always appear to be different when you look at them from the outside, as compared to when you're looking from within. How does that learning apply to your situation now?'

"Time slowed down, and we got into a flow. Finally he said, 'Well, one interview was different. It was the one where I spoke to a production head who I know well and respect a lot. I wasn't talking to him as an industrial relations person, I spoke to him as if I still was a peer, in my former role of also being a production head. He said, 'Walter, as a corporate person you're bringing answers to questions I don't have. But I have a lot of questions and issues that I need your help on as a peer practitioner, to help me find new and innovative answers.'"

Then Ursula asked him, "Why could he say that to you?" Walter replied, "I guess I put myself into the shoes of my colleague, looking from production to corporate. In the other interviews, I was looking from the outside, corporate, into production. And the difference I see now raises a new question for me: Should corporate organize around production, or should production organize around corporate? As a former plant manager, I can use my new position to shift the conversation from centering around corporate to centering around production."

Identifying Emerging Themes in Large-Scale Change Processes by Using Dialogue

One of the standard challenges of implementing organizational and large system changes is analyzing the input from key stakeholders. Dialogue interviews are effective tools to get this input and at the same time to connect the stakeholders to the process and to each other. In the Patient-Physician Dialogue Forum, for example, we had 130 interviews to analyze and quantify. Other projects may have more or fewer to work with. I have found the following ten steps helpful in analyzing and synthesizing interview data:

1. *Preparation.* The group of interviewers (usually a mix of internal and external people) prepares by reading the full transcripts of the interviews. Everybody arrives prepared and with selected passages from those interviews that seem to express systemic problems.

2. *Opening.* First, each interviewer shares a short anecdote from the interview project that "touched me" or that "touched my heart." This discussion is light and informal, but it sets the tone. Within a few minutes these stories begin to evoke a social field of sparks that stimulate and foreshadow the later stages of the process and that usually get at the heart of the matter quickly. It is important, however, to stick with the data: the point is to share stories, not to ruminate on them at length.

3. *Articulate intention and the core questions* at issue. After that, the real work begins: articulating the reasons whether and why change is necessary, the goal of the project, and the core questions that organize the project.

4. *Jamming: Observe, observe, observe.* The main part of the seeing and sensing activity involves sitting around a large table, everybody with the

transcripts in front of them, and then reading them aloud. In many ways this reading is like a jam session: the instruments are the people you encountered—your interviewees; the sheets of music are the transcripts in front of you; and the piece of music that you are creating is the social art of seeing and sensing the emerging system, the one that you tried to elicit in the thoughts and words of your interviewees.

As in any good jazz session or improvisation, there are rules to be followed. The number one rule at this stage is to suspend judgment. You aren't allowed to say, "I like this" or "I don't like that." You aren't even allowed to say, "I think this" or "I believe that." Nobody at this stage is interested in the interviewers' opinions or beliefs. These sorts of statements could even kill the whole process. At this stage, there is only one currency that counts: real experiences captured in the interviews and stories. Everything else is noise at this stage and should be filtered out.

One person begins by reading a quote that struck her as important. She may also provide a word or two of context. Then, pause. Sparked by that pause, another person is prompted to read another quote that may or may not relate to the first one. She also probably adds a comment to put it into context. Pause. Then the third piece. And so forth. It's like a collage. Each quote is one small piece of the picture. And collectively, out of all those pieces, a picture begins to emerge. This step takes as many hours as are needed. As they read the quotes, the whole group dives deeper and deeper into the stream of reality. They get into a rhythm and learn to listen to the music that speaks from what remains unsaid between the quotes—the empty space in between (deep dive).

5. *Sensing from the field.* As the participants listen to the unfolding collage of quotes, they begin to tune in to some of the emerging patterns, pictures, and polarities. And as the number of stories and quotes accumulates, they begin to shift the place of listening toward listening from the whole, the common ground from which all of the instances, stories, and quotes arose.

On a flip chart, draw an empty circle in the center of the page, write a question or relationship in the center (your focus), and then track everything you hear that relates to that question in bubbles that are grouped around that center. Each of them captures the different manifestations of the core phenomenon at issue. For example, you write *patient-physician relationship* in the center bubble and then around that center in the peripheral bubbles you write all the different manifestations of that phenomenon. You have several of these mind-mapping flip charts, and they grow in parallel as you uncover emerging patterns and themes.

This exercise immerses the group's collective mind in the concrete particulars of the field or system. Each quote can be understood as a "footprint" in a larger *movement* of the field. The collective intuitive mind of the group then connects to the footprint by jointly reading and listening to each quote and then connects to the movement of the field by simultaneously holding and relating the constellation of footprints as a dynamic whole.

When the mind starts to see that movement, when the mind starts seeing reality *from* that movement (redirection), images, ideas, and questions begin to emerge. All you need to do is pay attention to them.

6. *Essential emergence.* As the conversation progresses, you try to deepen and crystallize the emerging patterns and themes. You start to boil down the pictures and patterns to those that strike a chord, that capture and resonate with people's key experiences. And then, you ask: What are the field forces that determine whether a phenomenon is manifested in this or in another space? What are the primary systems and field conditions that cause a pattern to play out one way or the other?

As you crystallize the core themes, patterns, and puzzles, and as you deepen your understanding of the primary field conditions that structure these patterns of emergence, you pay increasing attention to what is coming in through the back door of your mind. It is at this stage that groups begin to function as an instrument for an emerging future. To do this, it is essential to put yourself into the unconditional service of the future possibility that is wanting to emerge. Viewed from this angle, presencing is about entering a dialogue with the future possibility that wants to emerge. Unless you leave the back door of your mind ajar, this kind of dialogue is very unlikely to occur.

And you turn your attention to root questions, such as: What is the deep essence that wants to emerge from these quotes, observations, and formative forces? What is the limiting factor that keeps the dysfunctional system alive? Who are the excluded "voiceless" in the current system? What could reconnect the system/field to its true origin? What other questions come up for us now?

7. *Crystallizing.* Wrap up the crystallization process by identifying the essential features, core themes and questions, systemic issues, and key quotes that bring them alive. This will map the way forward.

8. *Prototyping.* Test your analysis of the system in a mini–stakeholder session, which will provide some instant feedback and suggest improvements on the form and substance of the analysis.

9. *Presenting and performing.* Present, discuss, and deepen the results in a multi-stakeholder or systemic microcosm meeting like the Patient-Physician Dialogue Forum. Read some of the original quotes to trigger and evoke the collective field in the group. Facilitate collective emergence. Use the collective field of this microcosm to generate and launch key initiatives that take the system from the current state to its best future possibility.

10. *AAR.* After-action review: review, reflect on, and document what has been learned.

I vividly remember one interview analysis meeting with a team of about ten people in one of America's most admired companies. The team had conducted a hundred dialogue interviews throughout the organization with everyone from top executives to frontline employees in order to get a sense of where the organization was going from an internal perspective.

Finally, we tried to capture the essence of all of the different views in a single sentence. We had talked about that essence in some detail, but we were not able to boil it down to one sentence. As time was running out and the meeting was about to dissolve, one woman made a final attempt. She said, "I am being torn by two worlds. In one world I am a machine operating under conditions of pressure, power, efficiency, and control. In the other world, I am a being that is entering a space that is open, connected, and evolving in a totally different way. I feel torn between these two worlds."

What she said shifted the energy in the room. She was getting at something. What struck me was that she talked from the "I." Everyone before her had spoken from a third-person perspective. What made what she said so powerful was the ambiguity about who the "I" was. Was it her personal "I"? Or was she articulating the organizational experience from the perspective of the collective "I" of that company?

To sum up: The dynamics between the U-space and the destructive antispace are nonlinear and dialectical. One space can flip to become the other almost instantly. The process is not linear—which is exactly why it is referred to as dark or antispace. The analysis of that space offers us a deepened systemic understanding that often goes unnoticed: in order to address the rampant issues on the right-hand side (manipulation, abuse, and collapse) we have to focus on the left-hand side and the top: on reconnecting with the contexts outside and within. The subtlest origin of dark-space pathologies is probably self-sabotage or absencing. The problem with absencing is that nobody but *you* will likely notice it in real time. So you have to awaken an eyelike organ within yourself that will help you navigate that threshold. It is the eye of your consciousness. This eyelike entity, from which the sparks of our attention and intention originate, is what I call the *I-in-now*. It's the invisible origin of your real presence and power.

Evolutionary Pathways of Conversational Fields

Conversations matter. They constitute the second meta-process of how we bring forth the world. Sometimes it helps me to look at conversations as if they were living beings, living entities, and ask: if our job as participants in these conversations were to help them evolve and to progress from lesser developed to higher developed stages of evolution and consciousness, what would we see and do differently?

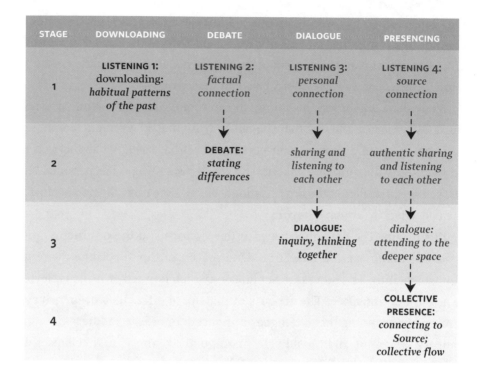

STAGE	DOWNLOADING	DEBATE	DIALOGUE	PRESENCING
1	**LISTENING 1:** downloading: *habitual patterns of the past*	**LISTENING 2:** *factual connection*	**LISTENING 3:** *personal connection*	**LISTENING 4:** *source connection*
2		**DEBATE:** *stating differences*	*sharing and listening to each other*	*authentic sharing and listening to each other*
3			**DIALOGUE:** *inquiry, thinking together*	*dialogue: attending to the deeper space*
4				**COLLECTIVE PRESENCE:** *connecting to Source; collective flow*

FIGURE 17.4 THE EVOLUTION OF CONVERSATIONAL FIELD STRUCTURES

This is exactly what I am trying to get at with Figure 17.4. It shows four developmental journeys of conversational fields, resulting in four different types of conversations. The black letters depict the final stage of each of these four journeys: downloading, debate, dialogue, and presencing (see descriptions in black letters). However, what the black letters don't describe is the mostly invisible journey that leads to that type of conversation. That more hidden journey is captured in the blue colored letters depicting the field's developmental journey. The four journeys differ in terms of how quickly the conversational impulse manifests into speech.

The first column shows us the first conversational field (or being) that arises when a conversational impulse is directly and instantly manifested in a given form—i.e., the only form that happens to be instantly available: the patterns of the past. "How are you? I'm fine."

The second column shows us what happens to the same conversational impulse when the journey between the initial impulse and manifesting into speech is a little more complex. First, we go through the stage of connecting to factual information on the ground (open mind). If that happens first, the resulting conversational field usually manifests in the form of stating differences (debate) or simply coming up with a more differentiated view of the situation at hand: "Let me suggest a different view on this topic."

The third column shows us what happens to the conversational field when the journey between impulse and speech is even more cultivated and enhanced. First, the connection to the context is more personal and more experiential or empathetic (open mind, open heart). Secondly, there is a stage of sharing and listening to one another within the group. This is done with genuine empathy, person to person. Only then, after this phase of intense listening to one another, is the group is ready to move into the space of real thinking together (dialogue). Remember what Walter's manager said after an extended period of listening and friendship: "Walter, as a corporate person you're bringing answers to questions I don't have. But I have a lot of questions and issues that I need your help on as a peer practitioner, to help me find new and innovative answers."

The fourth column depicts yet another evolutionary stage of the meta-process of conversations. It shows the most differentiated journey between initial impulse and manifest enactment of a conversational field. In this case, that journey moves through four stages. The first stage is, again, about connecting to the contextual field. The only difference from the earlier types is that in this case the connection to the field tends to grow even more authentic and deep as the conversation begins to unfold. Then, in the second stage, the situation moves into authentic sharing. This stage can also be labeled blank-canvas imaging, because it involves clearing the space and listening to each other from a complete blank canvas. Pure listening. Think about the jam session, quote by quote. Think about Ursula listening not only to her interviewee but also to her own listening and energy. Then stage three is about moving into dialogue. But rather than just staying with a normal dialogue, in this case the attention and intention are to focus on the deeper source and space wanting to emerge. Think about Ursula staying at the bridge. She knew this was it. She asked herself, "Am I ready to jump?" What you do as a facilitator or participant in this stage is that you constantly monitor the deeper issues or questions or phrases that may begin to show up. In meditation you often use a mantra in order to connect to source; in this kind of conversation, you try to sense which phrase or question or issue that's coming up is the *reality-mantra*. If focused on and enhanced in a moment of spontaneous silence, the reality-mantra allows the group to begin to connect to source. Think of Adam sitting in the group in Guatemala after the story about the mass grave and the unborn children had been told. "The silence lasted a long time, perhaps five minutes. . . . I feel that there is spirit in the room . . ."

Languaging, like thinking, is a meta-process through which we bring forth the world. But just as in the case of thinking, we often do not notice this process and how it shapes the way we collectively create the world. The map in Figure 17.4 is a tool that helps us to see the different field structures that we collectively create. The black written stages of conversation show the more manifest aspect of the four conversational fields: the enactment into the form of speech. By contrast, the blue written stages depict the less manifest developmental aspect of conversational fields. These less manifest aspects matter because they determine whether a given conversational impulse is manifesting in the form of downloading, debate, dialogue or presencing. These four types of conversational fields differ in terms of the journey between the conversational impulse and its manifestation in speech.

Any given conversational field can move across the whole territory mapped in Figure 17.4. For example, the workshop at the university in Germany that I described earlier moved from downloading to debate and then later into dialogue. Yet, the more skillful and cultivated a group is, as in Ursula's dialogue interviews or the Circle of Seven, the more a conversation will gravitate toward the blue pathway depicted in Column 4 (presencing).

In its essence, conversations connect us to the power of collective intelligence. Conversations can be mere shadows, empty phrases (downloading).

They can connect us to the viewpoint of the other (debate). They can connect us even deeper to one another (dialogue). Or they can connect us to our deep source of collective creating and bringing forth the world. When that happens, conversations connect us to who we really are (presencing). When operating from that deeper place, we begin to act as instruments or elements of a whole that is larger than our self. We begin to connect with "the beings who surround us."[14] We begin to operate from what is moving through, from the power of now.

Which brings us squarely back to the puzzle we discovered above: while most people as individuals aspire to operate from the deeper levels of conversation and knowing, the current reality is, that most of our institutions and systems are firmly in the grip of the pathologic patterns of destruction (Figure 17.3). Why?

Because we don't know how to nurture and cultivate the invisible journey that is depicted in Figure 17.4. That journey is about deepening our attention *first* before we start to act on an impulse.

So if that invisible capacity really is the the key (just for the sake of the argument), and if you wanted to prevent mankind from accessing these deeper levels of knowing, what would you do? How would you engineer your assault?

Here are a five ideas: (1) put your children in front of TVs as often as possible (take out interpersonal contact), (2) encourage them to spend hours quickly reacting to video games (killer games help best to reenact the violence that they watched earlier on TV); (3) put them in schools where they are victimized by downloading-based teaching methods that prevent them from developing the capacities of the open mind, heart, and will; (4) as soon as the attention deficit syndrome kicks in (which predictably happens as the result of factors 1-3) use drugs and medication to doze them down; this will make sure that the feedback their body gives them against their unhealthy and inhuman environment, will be responded to on a symptoms level so that the root causes can continue to be unaddressed; (5) make sure that educational policies like quantitative testing (no child left behind) and other methods guarantee, for the years to come, that teachers cannot create an environment that allows our children to experience and explore their deeper levels of awareness, creativity and knowing.

Sadly, these are not just imaginary conditions. They actually describe how we currently prevent our children from connecting to their deeper sources of knowing. But if this is the way we organize the world for most of our children, we also have the power to change it.

CHAPTER 18

Organizational Actions

Organizations • Four Fields of Enacting Geometries of Power •
From Centralized to Decentralized Field Structures • From
Decentralization to Network • From Network to Ecosystem •
Organizational Structures and Pathologies • Collapsing Systems
and Institutional Pathology • Five Observations on Organizations
and Global Institutions • On the Evolution
of Institutions

Organizations: Collective Action

S o far, we have used Theory U to illuminate two of the four fundamental meta-processes of bringing forth the world: thinking (Chapter 16, "Individual Actions") and languaging (Chapter 17, "Conversational Actions"). This chapter deals with the third: structuring, that is, enacting different geometries of power. This discussion will feature and explore the application of Theory U to the organizational-institutional level of social reality creation.

Organizations are a strange species. They take our time and energy and seem to rule much of our lives—or spoil them, many would add. Yet organizations are also in trouble. Even the most powerful organizations—the multinational corporations that in the eyes of many seem to govern the world—have an average life expectancy of a mere forty years. What are we to make of this quickly evolving species that seemingly rules the world but has a life expectancy that is half that of yours or mine?

Henry Mintzberg, a scholar and authority on the subject, defines organizations as collective action for a common purpose, and organizational structure as the "sum total of the ways in which its labor is divided into distinct tasks and then its coordination is achieved among these tasks." According to Mintzberg, "management is just a term for drawing things together and creating some kind of coordination in an organization. . . . Organizations need coordination. Coordination is what management is all about, one way or another."[1]

Let's look at organizations through our four-field-structure lens, as outlined in Figure 18.1. Field 1, where action is based on patterns of the past, describes a centralized machine bureaucracy. Here, organizational attention and coordination manifest through institution-centric sources of power such as hierarchy or central rules.

Institutions and actors operating in Field 2 take an external perspective. In our conversational example, that implies debate and the exchange of different points of view. On an organizational level, it means to push the decision making more into the regions, more to the market. Institutionally, it means that market and competition (that reflect the forces of the organizational periphery) complement the hierarchical coordination mechanism. Decentralized institutions that organize around divisions or strategic business units (SBUs) are typical examples of Field 2 types of organizing. While Field 2 institutions are good at being more flexible and more market driven within their various units or divisions, they are not so good at capturing opportunities that may show up in their blind spot. The blind spot resides in the white space between the units and divisions. Most people can't see this white space because it would involve a deeper collaboration across organizational boundaries.

Which brings us to Field 3. Field 3–type organizations organize around inter-organizational networks and dialogue, around the power of relationships that co-evolve through mutual adjustment by diverse players and partners.

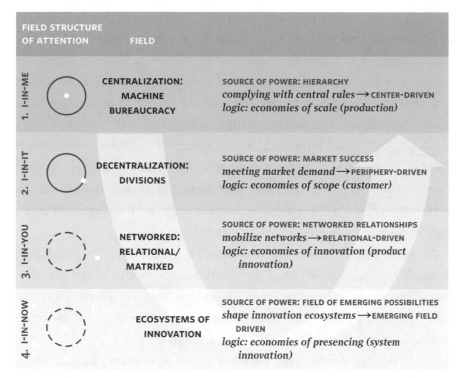

FIGURE 18.1 FOUR TYPES OF COORDINATION, FOUR GEOMETRIES OF POWER

Finally, the fourth field adds the process of deep connection and emergence. It can be experienced in conversations of groups or teams when conversation moves beyond its own boundaries and begins to operate from the surrounding source level of emerging future possibilities. And it can be experienced in organizations if that organization opens its boundaries to the wider constellations of players: the whole surrounding ecosystem, including the customers, users and communities at issue. When this happens, people feel drawn to an emerging future opportunity and begin to see the system from that place.

These four fields of attention originate in different places: *inside*, *at*, *beyond*, or *across* one's organizational boundaries. Similarly, the four types of institutionalizing and coordinating differ in terms of the geometry of power that they embody and enact. Let's think of power, in this instance, in terms of the place where their power originates relative to the boundary of the institution at issue. For example, in a hierarchy the power originates in the center of the system (Field 1). By contrast, in a decentralized market-driven organization, the power originates more in the periphery, in the real demands of the customers and in what the market says (Field 2). In the case of a network-based organization, however, the source of power moves outside its boundaries. The real power, in this case, lies in the network of relationships across boundaries and in the capacity to mobilize these networks (Field 3). And, finally, in an ecosystems type of organizing, we have an example where the real power originates from all across its open boundaries, that is, from the presence of the larger ecosystem and from the opportunities that emerge from there (Field 4).

I'll admit that this fourth field is perhaps the hardest to understand. If you remember my account of deciding to climb to the source of the Inn River, you will recall my amazement when I found that the river's source was manifold. I was surrounded by music from many waterfalls that flowed all around me. In a similar manner, Field 4 opens a system up to boundless "music" and a renewable, free source, a source that wraps, permeates, and surrounds all.

Four Fields of Enacting Institutional Structures and Geometries of Power

Most young companies, founded and driven by one or several pioneers, are simple structures.[2] The coordination and growth of this type of organizing depend primarily on the skills of the founder(s). The more successful the organization becomes, the more its strength (being organized around one person) can become a weakness.

When factors that have led to organizational success in the past begin to become liabilities, at least two options are available: the management can take the company into Field 2 structuring (decentralization) and split into several divisions, or it can choose to remain in Field 1 (centralized structures) and adopt another type of centralized organization, such as a professional or machine bureaucracy.

The source of power in a machine bureaucracy, for instance, resides and originates in the center of the organization. Depending on whether centralism refers to persons, processes, or skills, Mintzberg distinguishes among:

- Simple structures (organized around one person)
- Machine bureaucracies[3] (organized around standardization of processes)
- Professional bureaucracies (organized around the standardization of skills)

Creating a machine bureaucracy requires a reorientation from person-based centralization to process-based centralization. This type of reorganization usually comes with differentiating between person and position, and between ownership and management. Consultants are hired to help develop a new and more rational structure, and the founders of the company hire professional managers to run the rapidly growing organization more effectively.

Professional bureaucracies are based not on the standardization of processes but on the standardization of skills. The more knowledge-intensive a business is, the more the organization will tend to organize around skills (professional bureaucracy) rather than around processes (machine bureaucracy). Today's global consulting companies are a good example of a centralized professional bureaucracy—although they also usually feature some strong elements of decentralization (country offices) and network structures (partnership-driven professional service organizations).

From Centralized to Decentralized Field Structures

When shifting from centralized (Field 1) to decentralized structures (Field 2), the primary source of power moves from the center toward the periphery; in other words, decision-making power moves down the hierarchy and closer to the customer.[4]

An example of a *simple* decentralized structure is the university department, which is often organized around a chair and/or an institute. In

Germany, for example, each chair is organized as a simple structure: a professor is surrounded by a host of administrative, research, and teaching assistants. The coordination among the chairs and institutes is based on two mechanisms: supervision (by a dean) and mutual adjustment (by the faculty).

In the more complex *machine bureaucracy*, the geographic/divisional matrix of an organization is decentralized. This process allows an organization to keep the standardization mechanism and at the same time leverages the mechanism of competition. In a *professional bureaucracy*, a decentralized structure allows regional and local variations within global patterns of skill-based standardization.

During the 1980s and early '90s, most multinational corporations went through waves of decentralization and empowerment, pushing the decision-making power toward the periphery, trying to make heavy and monolithic structures more market-oriented, flexible, and nimble. The epitome of this development may have been the decentralization of the European engineering firm Asea Brown Boveri (ABB) by the then-hailed CEO Percy Barnevik. Another successful and much-admired company during those years was Digital Equipment Corporation (DEC), which rose to become the world's second largest computer manufacturer. In 1986, DEC CEO Ken Olsen was named the "entrepreneur of the century" by *Fortune* magazine, and DEC was named one of the ten most successful U.S. companies by *Business Week* in 1987.

However, even as the CEOs of both companies were celebrated in business magazines across the continents, their companies began, silently and unnoticed by most observers, eroding, faltering, and eventually falling apart (ABB) or ceasing to exist (DEC).

DEC: One Story of Decentralization

The rise and fall of Digital Equipment Corporation are beautifully captured in the book *DEC Is Dead, Long Live DEC*, co-authored by Ed Schein and colleagues.[5] The authors worked with DEC as consultants, managers, and action researchers over more than three decades. Their case study documents the firm's birth, development, and growth into a global technology powerhouse, its maturation, and finally its faltering and death in an episode spanning four decades. DEC made its mark with major innovations, including the minicomputer and the concept of distributed computing and networking. We will use this case to discuss some of the developmental issues and dynamics that companies face as they evolve from a centralized to a decentralized structure and beyond.

In 1957, Ken Olsen, an MIT graduate then working at MIT Lincoln Labs, and his colleague Harlan Anderson founded DEC. With his colleagues, Olsen succeeded in creating an atmosphere and a spirit of innovation that took some of the core elements of the engineering culture, in which he had been immersed at MIT, into a unique company culture organized around the values of technological innovation, human creativity, and personal responsibility. He attracted a long stream of outstanding engineers who, under the direction of Gordon Bell, were eager to join a company that seemed to thrive on an abundance of technological innovation, fun, and human bonding. DEC quickly grew into a multinational company. As a consequence of its success and rapid growth, DEC had to become a more differentiated, decentralized, matrix-type of organizational structure in order to co-evolve with the changing marketplace.

For more than three decades DEC was a very successful organization by all measures. When it peaked during the 1980s as a $14 billion company with more than 100,000 employees worldwide, the seeds of its demise and death were already planted and growing, almost unnoticed in the midst of its award-winning performance and activities (DEC was acquired by Compaq in 1999).

But what caused the decline and death of DEC as an independent company forty years after its founding—almost exactly the average life span of a multinational company today? What challenges did DEC fail to live up to?

According to Schein et al., there were three: (1) the technological and market challenge: a failure to realize the changing nature of the market when the stage of *technology creation* was followed by the emergence of a dominant design and a subsequent stage of *commodification* that gave rise to a new breed of global players ("category killers"); (2) the organizational structure challenge: a failure to evolve an effective decentralized structure that makes divisions fully accountable for their results, establishes clear mechanisms for managing interdependencies, and sets priorities and strategic direction for the best companywide use of resources; and (3) the organizational culture challenge: a failure to evolve the culture when both the changing business context and the changing organizational structure required a different way of operating.

Schein gives an intriguing account of how the same cultural genes first enabled the emergence of a global innovation powerhouse (the technology creation stage) and then, when the context changed but the cultural genes did not, became the very reason for failure (in the commodification stage).

When the DEC organization became more decentralized, the same culture continued to create some breakthrough products, remembers Schein, but at the same time it also developed strong internal animosities:

> Groups would accuse one another of lying, cheating, and misuse of resources. Groups were pulling apart rather than pulling together. And no one was strong enough . . . to pull the diverging strands together into a coherent strategy. . . . Neither strong concepts nor formal hierarchy produced enough consensus to allocate resources and energy wisely in terms of the rapid adjustments that the organization had to make to keep up with the market and technology changes. By the time [CEO] Olsen's style changed to being more of an advocate, the groups had already become too strong, were prepared to ignore what Olsen wanted, and fought among themselves. The culture of empowerment was alive and well, but its negative consequences for DEC the business entity were becoming clearer and clearer.[6]

From Decentralization to Network

When a company shifts from a decentralized structure (Field 2) to a networked structure (Field 3), coordination happens through mutual adjustment in networked relationships. Mintzberg calls the result an *adhocracy*.[7]

Unlike the structures of *hierarchy* and *competition, mutual adjustment* depends much more on the quality of the relationships among the key players. Accordingly, the quality of conversation becomes a central issue when organizations move into this field of coordinating.

When moving from centralized to decentralized, and from there to networked forms of organizing, the source of power moves from the center of the organization (hierarchy support) to the periphery (market success) to networked relationships (network creation and mobilization). Networks often perform additional coordination functions that the other two structures (hierarchy, competition) would be unable to perform. The cultivation of networking events such as "communities of practice" and "DECworld" are examples of organizing by fostering networked communities across institutional boundaries.

As a rule of thumb, the more knowledge-intensive an organization and industry and the more important the issues that fall into the white space between organizational units, the more it will tend to rely on this third field structure of organizing.

It is interesting to note that this third mechanism—mutual adjustment—was frequently used inside the old core group that co-created the initial success culture of DEC. But when the organization grew, the spirit of collaboration remained *inside* the individual groups and units while the relationships *between* groups and units deteriorated.

Why? What allowed the old core group to incubate and grow a culture of creation, while the same cultural DNA failed in the next stage to replicate and sustain this behavior on the large systems level?

Schein's account of the DEC story tells how the old core group, the Operations Committee, successfully used three mechanisms for effective meetings and decision making: (1) an agreed upon agenda, (2) a diversity of interests and viewpoints always ready to enter to debate and "fight it out" (no holding back), and (3) a holding space by the CEO, who participated through listening acutely to the debate. Olsen, the CEO, although present, didn't associate his authority with any of the positions discussed and debated among the Operations Committee members. Yet by carefully listening to all the arguments and weighing all the pros and cons, the risks and rewards, he undoubtedly influenced what happened in the group. Through this sustained listening practice he gradually created a culture in which people began to trust the collective process of debate rather than waiting for the CEO to dictate where to go. This type of holding space embodies the scientific culture at its best: let the data decide.

Although the "agreed-upon agenda" was probably fairly clear and spirited debate was never in short supply, the key piece missing on the large systems level was the eye of the seer, the acute attention of a deeply listening observer. So how could the subtle integrative role that Olsen (and partly also Schein) played in the context of the Operations Committee at its prime have been translated into success in the macro-level coordination? What would have opened the collective pairs of self-observing eyes?

The answer might have been *dialogue*. Dialogue, simply put, results from the capacity to open one's inner eyes, *the capacity of a system to see itself.* As Schein observed: "Reflective dialogue would have required the collaboration of the whole Operations Committee, something that I never saw them achieve."[8] But although the culture of the Operations Committee was that of a small group (due to the presence of an effective holding space), it did not penetrate the organization as a whole (which lacked a holding space). When the organization faced challenges down the road that required a collective response (a Field 3 or 4 response), it continued to operate with Field 2 conversational behavior (debate), and eventually it hit the wall.

From Network to Ecosystem

When shifting from Field 3 to Field 4 coordination, the mechanism changes from *mutual adjustment* through networked relationships to *seeing from an emerging whole*. This fourth type of coordination is called the "innovation ecosystem." In order to tune in to an emerging field of possibility, an organization needs to go beyond itself—to systemically tune in to the relevant emerging contexts, which can be identified only in the collective context of a larger ecosystem.

In hindsight, the ability to make this shift may have allowed Hewlett-Packard to succeed where DEC ended up failing: HP co-evolved with its surrounding ecosystem in a more open and sharing way, whereas DEC tended to focus more on the space within its own organizational boundaries.[9]

Several of today's leading high-tech companies, including HP, Cisco, Google, and Nokia, think in terms of *ecosystems* when creating strategies and cultures of innovation. The difference between the old and new ways of thinking about strategy and leadership is that the old revolves around the boundaries of single organizations while the new revolves around the boundaries of ecosystems, clusters of organizations that co-evolve in a larger space of collective value creation. In networked coordination (Field 3), the cross-boundary aspect unfolds as a mutual adaptation, while in ecosystems coordination functions through a constellation of diverse players that *collectively form a vehicle for seeing current possibilities and sensing emerging opportunities* (Field 4).

The set of organizations that methodically coordinates through Field 4 mechanisms seems empty, yet it is the most interesting area both in coordination theory[10] and in the practice of developing global companies and institutions. It pushes the envelope and holds great possibilities for companies dealing with many of today's most pressing multi-stakeholder issues and problems.

The structure of a co-evolving ecosystem is always inspired and energized by its surrounding field. Accordingly, this kind of structure is fluid and constantly on the move. The common ground of such an ecosystem of organizing is a shared sense of purpose and principles. Visa International, which developed on the basis of what its founder, Dee Hock, calls "chaordic" (a blending of the words *chaos* and *order*) principles of organizing, may have been the first company to attempt to integrate its suppliers and customers into a single ecosystem: a membership-controlled governance system.[11]

One key aspect of DEC's failure, according to Schein et al., was its inability to deal with the emerging complexities of the high-growth 1980s. Why did DEC miss out on these, holding on to its old-style proprietary systems and vertical integration, and then, when it became obvious that those things weren't working, do too little, too late? Why couldn't DEC deal with the emerging complexity in its industry (which it had helped to create) better and faster?

Two things might have provided critical resources for developing a more appropriate response: one, the capacity to engage in *dialogue* across boundaries, both internally and externally; the other, beginning to co-evolve as an *ecosystem*. If there had been such a cross-institutional organ of sense making—which I refer to as seeing from an emerging whole—and if the capacity to engage in dialogue across boundaries had been developed, the story of DEC might have taken a different turn.

Organizational Structures and Pathologies

Figure 18.2 zooms in for a closer view of organizational structures. It depicts the four field structures discussed above, plus three more field structures on the right-hand side of the U. These three are variants of the Field 4 type of structuring (ecosystem). The seven organizational structures are mirrored through another set of seven depicting the shadow space of institutional pathology (institutional ignorance, institutional arrogance, institutional hubris, institutional anomie, institutional sclerosis, institutional collapse).

Viewed from the U, the DEC case can be summarized like this: *When facing the most significant challenges of hyper-complexity in their industry, DEC's leaders couldn't respond effectively because they failed to access Field 3 and 4 types of operating.* This failure applies to both conversation (lack of dialogue) and organization (lack of cross-group integration and ecosystemic structuring). Given that gap between the exterior challenge and the interior capacity to operate from the deeper levels of emergence, the only thing that could have turned the company around would have been a management genius à la Gordon Bell, whose ingenuity might have compensated for the collective leadership deficiency. But Bell had left in 1983, and no one of similar stature had replaced him.

Accordingly, the gap between the exterior challenge and the interior capacity to access the deeper levels of responding to the situation resulted in three predictable leadership failures:

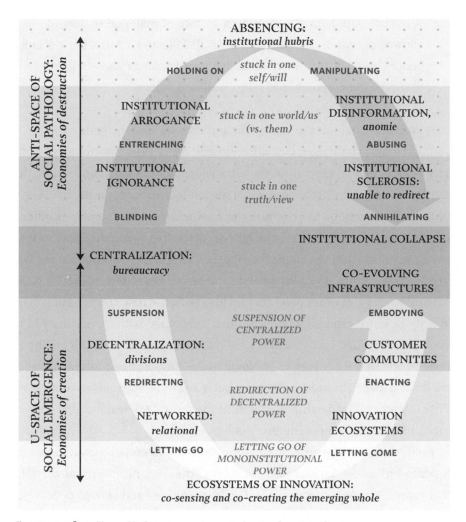

FIGURE 18.2 THE U-SPACE AND THE ANTI-SPACE: ORGANIZING

1. A strategy gap: failing to see the changing dynamics of the industry that would have required an earlier and more forceful reinvention process.

2. A structural gap: failing to differentiate among the three subsystems of a corporate ecosystem: innovation, customer interface, and operations. Instead, marketing and operations became dominated by the innovation subsystem and its specific culture—which worked well as long as the industry moved through the stage of technology creation but didn't work well thereafter.

3. A culture gap: failing to develop a culture of dialogue that would have allowed access to the deeper levels of collective creativity and emergence. Instead, the deteriorating culture began to show all seven elements of the corporate pathology outlined below.

By contrast, at about the same time another technology company, Nokia, faced profound challenges in a different and more effective manner. In the early 1990s, Nokia went through a transformational inflection point that resulted in its selling all but one of its diversified business units, in order to focus all its energy on developing one business unit: telecommunications. Nokia's ability to morph from one type of [diversified] structure and strategy into another [much more single focused] has long been a strength of the fast-paced Nokia culture: to co-evolve with the larger ecosystem of which it is a part and to let go of other parts that no longer fit the new core mission. That capacity to sense emerging opportunities, combined with the capacity to let go of old identities and structures, is what was missing at DEC. When I spoke to one of the key players in Nokia in the early 2000s I asked "What do you do as a leader in order to support such a fast paced innovation process? What is your real leadership work?" And the reply: "My real leadership work is that I facilitate the opening process."

"Facilitating the opening process" presents an interesting contrast to the "holding on" to the various parts of the existing organization that the DEC story represents. As a consequence, DEC was infected and slowed down by all seven elements of corporate pathology shown in Figure 18.2. They include:

- Corporate ignorance: not seeing what changes were happening in the marketplace. Instead, too much time was focused on corporate politics: the "get buy-in" rule and the lack of effective companywide governance mechanisms resulted in too many people wasting too much of their time on internal politics.
- Corporate arrogance: the pathology of entrenchment and arrogance showed up in warfare between organizational units and engineering ("we know what is best").

- Corporate absencing: holding on to existing identities too long and too forcefully; the inability to let go of projects, products, customers, key principles, and core identities that had become dysfunctional.
- Corporate anomie (destruction of values): poisoning of the inter-group atmosphere, strong animosities between groups.
- Corporate sclerosis (destruction of renewal capacity): "the inter-group conflict and loss of confidence in one another had reached levels by the late 1980s that made [strategic shifts and significant innovations] unworkable."[12]
- Corporate collapse (destruction of structure): acquisition of DEC by Compaq in 1999.

Collapsing Systems and Institutional Pathology

The story of DEC is a mild version of how a good company loses its way by getting stuck in the space of institutional pathology instead of evolving. Recent history also provides starker examples of companies that have fallen victim to the virus of corporate or institutional pathology. Enron is a case in point.

Enron was hailed throughout the 1990s by Wall Street, business magazines, business schools, consulting firms, and business gurus alike. In 2001, the year of its collapse, it was listed as America's seventh biggest company.

Ken Lay, the chairman of Enron, was one of corporate America's most celebrated success stories when, in January 2001, he strode onto a ballroom stage at the Hyatt Regency Country Resort in San Antonio and stood between two giant screens filled with his image. Before him, bright light from the ballroom's chandeliers spilled across scores of round tables where Enron executives waited to hear the words of Mr. Lay, their longtime leader.[13]

This meeting of hundreds of Enron executives, wrote Kurt Eichenwald, "was a time of revelry, a chance to celebrate a year when business seemed good—even better than good. At night, according to executives who attended, Champagne and liquor flowed from the open bar, while fistfuls of free cigars were available for the taking. Executives could belly up to temporary gambling tables for high-stakes games of poker."

"Now, as waiters wearing bolo ties scurried about," continued the account, "the executives listened eagerly to Mr. Lay's descriptions of Enron's recent year of success, and the new successes that were within reach. Already, Enron was near the top of the Fortune 500, a multibillion-dollar behemoth that had moved beyond its roots in the natural gas business to blaze new trails in Internet commerce. For 2001, Mr. Lay said, the company would take on a new mission, one that would define everything it did in the months to come: *Enron would become the world's greatest company.* The words replaced his image on one of the screens."

But it was not to be. "For, unknown to almost everyone there," Eichenwald continued, "Enron was secretly falling apart. Even as the celebrations unfolded, accountants and trading experts at the company's Houston headquarters were desperately working to contain a financial disaster, one that threatened—and ultimately would destroy—everything Enron had become. A handful of executives were struggling to sound the alarm, but with Enron's confidence in its destiny, the warnings went unheeded. 'We were so sure of what we were doing and where we were going,' one executive who attended the San Antonio meeting said. 'We didn't know we were living on borrowed time.'"

Practices of Institutional Pathology

When talking with people who participated in the East German opposition movement during the 1980s, I was struck by the parallels between the collapse of Enron in 2001 and the collapse of the East German socialist system a dozen years earlier. Of course, there are many obvious differences between the two systems. But the aspect I am interested in is leadership: in both systems the leaders were unable to change course while heading toward collapse. What kept the leaders of Enron from redirecting the "ship" during the final eleven months of 2001? What kept the East German Politburo from correcting its course during the final decade before the collapse in 1989–90?

Since then, I have realized that the leadership practices in collapsing systems coincide with the anti-space of institutional pathology.

INSTITUTIONAL IGNORANCE: NOT SEEING WHAT IS GOING ON

Most of the Enron executives who attended the January 2001 meeting in San Antonio had no idea what was really happening in their company. Likewise, in East Germany in the 1980s the members of the Politburo had become prisoners of their own ideology and belief system and did not notice the widening gap between those beliefs and reality.

When Erich Honecker, the general secretary of the Communist Party, took a trip to the countryside, his staff and local officials erected colorful facades along the way, creating the impression that he was driving through a thriving country. This practice, of course, is nothing new. When Catherine the Great and her household would travel from Petersburg to the Krim, General Grigory Potemkin erected house-sized facades along her route. Ever since, such deceptive constructs have been referred to as "Potemkin villages." When I recently told this story to the managers of a global oil company, they didn't laugh. They told me that they were doing exactly the same thing. They had a sophisticated warning system that started working the moment the CEO embarked on one of his "surprise" visits to a company site. They mapped out the route the CEO would take, identified the company gas stations along the way that were in bad shape, and dispatched big oil trucks to sit in front of and cover up those ugly gas stations while the CEO's car passed by.

In other words, leaders' perceptions are skillfully "managed" by their environment. The people who surround top leaders often see to it that all of the information that fits the leader's mental model gets through, while information that doesn't fit does not. This distortion explains why, in a collapsing system, the breadth of perception is narrowed to the point where everyone adheres to the existing mental models and belief system. This type of managing the perception of leaders is pervasive.

INSTITUTIONAL ARROGANCE: NO CAPACITY FOR SENSING, REFLECTION, AND DIALOGUE

At Enron the accounting system was distorted through a practice that was once hailed as "aggressive accounting" but that today is referred to as fraud.

Notice the importance that cleverly coined phrases versus accurate language plays here. We know today that several people at Enron were aware of the mistakes that set Enron on the path of self-destruction. So why did those who tried to alert the leadership not get their message across?

In an environment with a nonfunctioning culture of learning, no one paid attention to the early signals. The East German leadership system had the same problem. People who knew what was going on didn't speak up. They continued to play the game. During the 1980s, East Germany put many resources into a microchip factory in Dresden, hoping to beat the Japanese and the Americans in that industry. When the factory produced its first prototype, the Politburo declared it a great success. The accomplishment was perceived as a stunning example of German engineering and received media coverage around the world. Behind the scenes, however, many insiders realized that the factory was in fact performing an elaborate charade for the benefit of the Politburo. When the microchip prototype got media coverage around the world, members of the Berlin-based second-level functional elite clearly knew that the "accomplishments" were fake. While the people at the top still believed in the building up of an East German microchip industry, insiders were talking about "going to the Semper Opera," referring to Dresden's famous musical theater. That's how an inadequate learning culture operates. Only the good news travels up all the way to the top. The bad news gets stuck someplace in the middle.

INSTITUTIONAL HUBRIS: NOT KNOWING YOUR AUTHENTIC SELF

Failing to recognize your authentic self can lead to self-delusion and aggrandizement: "Enron will become the world's greatest company." That's a remarkable mission statement in a year that ended with the company filing for bankruptcy. What about East Germany? The self-image of the Politburo was based on three fundamental "truths": one, that socialism was historically superior to capitalism; two, that the collapse of capitalism was just a question of time before the global victory of socialism as the ultimate stage of history; and three, that the East German socialist system was probably the best-organized and therefore most effective socialist system at the time. This inflated self-image makes even Enron's Ken Lay seem some-what modest. Both images were out of sync with reality and contributed to the deeply ingrained incapacity to realize what was going on.

Institutional Disinformation and Anomie: Not Serving the Whole

Those with a low quality of intention do not serve a larger good. Instead, leaders become self-absorbed, putting their own egos at the center of the universe and then expecting everyone else to support that structure.

At Enron, the missing sense of service was evident in the way the company influenced energy policy and legislation in order to ruthlessly promote its own special interests (for example, by co-fabricating California's energy crisis, which cost taxpayers $30 billion, or by exploiting its local monopoly position in India and elsewhere).[14] By putting its own interests first, Enron took advantage of its real customers—the people who were locked into long-term contracts and forced to pay inflated prices. Those who have a low quality of intention take advantage and exploit the weaknesses of those they are supposed to serve.

East Germany seemed to suffer from another version of the illusion and ego disease. As evidence, consider this story told to me by Heidemarie, an East German social scientist and feminist civic activist: "I still remember a meeting in the early 1980s with a small group of younger high-level leaders of the East German system. They talked and drank the whole evening. And the longer they talked, the more evident it became how rotten the whole system was. At the end I confronted them with what they had said and asked why none of them was doing anything serious to address the real issues. At that moment the entire group fell silent. After a while one of them said what everybody else was thinking: 'We are not going to sacrifice ourselves for this. It's not worth it. We just want to get on with our lives. *We aren't martyrs.*'" Heidemarie paused and then continued, "It was at that moment that I realized that the whole East German system was on autopilot heading toward collapse."

INSTITUTIONAL SCLEROSIS: LACK OF EXPERIMENTATION

This mechanism concerns the lack of fast-cycle experimentation with living microcosms of innovation. In a famous study on the longevity of corporations, Royal Dutch Shell analyzed the key characteristics of companies that had been successful for more than a hundred years.[15] Perhaps its most interesting finding was the identification of "tolerance to experiment at the margin." Experimentation and failure are important today, argued the authors of the study, in order to grow the seeds for tomorrow's successes.

That is exactly what did not happen in East Germany. Everything was centrally planned. The failure to develop prototypes of innovative living microcosms was painfully evident. At Enron, however, this lack is less clear. After all, Enron was the poster child of the innovative company. Yet a closer examination of the Enron case indicates that the actual fields of real experimentation were too narrow, too limited to financial numbers, and too late. In 2001, when the accounting scandal broke, there was no alternative to bankruptcy.

LACK OF AN INFRASTRUCTURE: NOT FOCUSING ON REAL PERFORMANCE

An effective infrastructure for learning lies at the heart of sustained performance. Consider Federal Express, the world's leading courier company. I once had the opportunity to visit its Memphis, Tennessee, hub with my colleague Adam Kahane. At this hub, every night between about eleven p.m. and two a.m., 150 airplanes land, unload, and, after up to a million packages are sorted, are reloaded and take off for their final destinations. Then, after all the planes are on their way again, the whole core team meets to conduct an after-action review at three a.m. At nine a.m. they have a similar after-action review with the managers of FedEx hubs worldwide, and then in the evening the whole team meets again to review what was learned in the previous cycle so that it can be implemented in the next one. When you do that twenty-five years in a row—three after-action reviews on every shift—you become one of the world's leading logistics companies.

By contrast, East Germany and Enron had no infrastructure for this kind of learning. Both systems, interestingly, suffered from a similar defect. At Enron, the CEO and Harvard graduate, Jeff Skilling created a culture that confused ideas with reality: anticipated future earnings were put on the books at more or less fantasy prices. Likewise, East Germany's central planning system assumed that once a central plan was approved and ordered, companies would actually implement it. A plan is a plan. And an idea about future earnings is just that. But real economic value is something different: it is created by collective action, which requires hard work and supporting infrastructures in order to evolve. It requires more than being "the smartest guy in the room."

Five Observations on Organizations and Global Institutions

Let me conclude with five diagnostic observations that highlight some issues and trends in the world of organization and global institutions using the structural map introduced above (Figure 18.2).

1. During the past two or three decades, the organizational mainstream has moved from the first to the second level of the U (from centralized to more decentralized/divisionalized structures). Examples: GE, ABB (during the 1980s and 1990s).

2. At the same time, a smaller group of avant-garde organizations has moved on to more networked and ecosystem-based forms of organizing (levels 3 and 4 of the U). Examples: Nokia, Cisco, Toyota, Google.

3. A parallel third trend pulls organizations into the shadow or anti-space of corporate pathology that is depicted in the upper part of the diagram. Unfortunately, the examples for this type of institutional pathology are not limited to companies like Enron. They are in companies, NGOs (nongovernmental organizations) and they are in government. For instance, how did the Bush/Cheney/Rumsfeld administration move their country into the war in Iraq? First, there was little deep understanding of the real situation in the Middle East (institutional ignorance: not understanding the real complexity on the ground); second, there was a fair amount of post 9-11 trauma and collective entrenchment (institutional arrogance: not understanding how others see you);

third, an inflated self-image of being the world's only superpower and global empire (institutional hubris: not understanding your real role and purpose on this planet); four, add to that a Vice President who actively intervenes in the intelligence community to produce a report on the weapons of mass destruction that isn't based on facts and the best available knowledge but that instead justifies the military intervention in Iraq (institutional disinformation and anomie). If you add up these four items (the first four items on the cycle of destruction), you know what is going to come next: very quickly you find yourself in a situation where you are unable to react to the real issues that suddenly start to unfold in rather unexpected ways (institutional sclerosis: unable to redirect the course once it is clear that Rumsfeld's initial war strategy, "shock and awe," isn't working); which then can result in the final manifestation of the cycle of destruction: institutional collapse. Today we see massive destruction: more than half a million people died in this Iraq war to date (2006); instead of a blossoming democracy we see a breakdown of almost all institutional structures and a civil war that could quickly spread over to the whole region and beyond, and the rise of extremists and fundamentalisms on all sides of the conflict constellation (institutional collapse).

4. The recent waves of globalization, disruptive innovation, and turbulence have all increased the complexity of leading and managing global organizations. Accordingly, the trends listed above (trend towards decentralization, networks, and ecosystems; as well as trend towards being sucked into the anti-space of absensing and institutional pathology) can be found in every organization to different degrees and they define the institutional forces at play. In order to meet the unprecedented challenges many institutions face today, leaders must learn to access and utilize all four levels of coordination and governance of the U. That rarely happens because different levels require different approaches, principles, and practices. For that reason, institutions and companies often become stuck in the anti-space of corporate pathology, the antithesis of the U.

5. The mismatch between Level 3 and 4 challenges on the one hand and predominantly Level 1 and 2 conventional responses from the mainstream of our institutions points at a pervasive leadership failure. Leadership failure is the key issue of our time. How can we help the world's most dominant and yet endangered species to evolve: the species of increasingly globally acting institutions.

On the Evolution of Institutions: A Dominating, yet Endangered Species

Let us close with some observations on the nature of the third meta-process at issue here: collectively enacting institutional geometries of power (structuring). As we did in the previous chapter in the case of conversational fields, let us now look at institutions as *if they were living beings*, living entities.

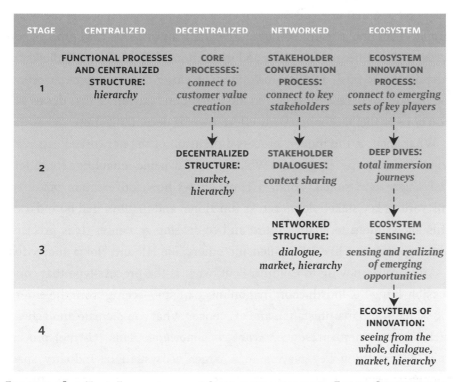

STAGE	CENTRALIZED	DECENTRALIZED	NETWORKED	ECOSYSTEM
1	**FUNCTIONAL PROCESSES AND CENTRALIZED STRUCTURE:** *hierarchy*	**CORE PROCESSES:** *connect to customer value creation*	**STAKEHOLDER CONVERSATION PROCESS:** *connect to key stakeholders*	**ECOSYSTEM INNOVATION PROCESS:** *connect to emerging sets of key players*
2		**DECENTRALIZED STRUCTURE:** *market, hierarchy*	**STAKEHOLDER DIALOGUES:** *context sharing*	**DEEP DIVES:** *total immersion journeys*
3			**NETWORKED STRUCTURE:** *dialogue, market, hierarchy*	**ECOSYSTEM SENSING:** *sensing and realizing of emerging opportunities*
4				**ECOSYSTEMS OF INNOVATION:** *seeing from the whole, dialogue, market, hierarchy*

FIGURE 18.3 THE EVOLUTION OF INSTITUTIONALIZED FIELD STRUCTURES

From this viewpoint the question becomes: What is the invisible process and infrastructure that would help this species—the species of institutional beings—to evolve, to develop, to mature?

Figure 18.3 maps the four different evolutionary pathways of this landscape. The entries in black show the four visible types of institutional coordination that we discussed above (from centralized to decentralized, networked and ecosystem-driven). Yet these types do not tell us the full story about the largely invisible process that keeps these types alive and manifesting.

The blue portions of Figure 18.3 help us decipher the more hidden and underlying process-dimension of structuring. For example, in Column One we see that centralized structures (such as bureaucracy) rely on *functional processes* that, once triggered by some impulse, always react with the same standard operating procedure (SOP).

Then, progressing to Column Two, we see that the decentralization of structure relies on a *core process* of value creation that ends (or begins) at the customer and that links all the prior steps of value creation across the whole supply chain into a seamless flow. Organizing around this core process cuts across all the different functions and institutional boundaries and allows the organization to push decision making much closer to the customer, closer to the market. It is the connection to the market and customer that drives and functions as the backbone of any effort towards decentralization.

What, then, is the hidden process-dimension of the networked organization? What keeps it going? What is its invisible enabling condition? *Stakeholder conversation.* Column Three shows how conversation processes link various key stakeholders across functional and institutional boundaries. This allows them to share context and co-develop strategies. It is precisely why organizations like DEC failed and others like HP and Nokia succeeded.

And finally, moving to Column Four, what is the process-type that could possibly bring the fourth coordination mechanism—seeing from the emerging whole—into manifestation and existence? What could create and activate such an eco-system presence? *Ecosystem innovation.* This (U-type) process links all emerging key players in a larger ecosystem or industry space (including users and customers) that need each other to shape the future, and engages them in deep immersion journeys. They can, as a result, see each other's contexts and issue areas and then progress to a shared understanding of the systemic forces at play and then begin to *see and act from the emerging whole*. Such an ecosystem innovation process engages the various stakeholders as part of an open-ended and transformative journey. If this journey is successful, it can lead to a shift of the intentions and identities of all (or most) key players involved.

So how, then, can we best help the species of the collective social fields to manifest throughout our institutions and the way we enact our institutional structures? We help this species to evolve, to develop and to mature by cultivating this invisible infrastructure (blue portions of Figure 18.3). Cultivation work is the functional equivalent of what the farmers do—what my father and my brother are doing—when they apply their tools to the soil. In the case of people who deal with cultivating the context of *social fields*, we have to do this work by bringing more attention and focus into the various process dimensions of our organizational entities. This includes all four functional processes, core processes, stakeholder conversation and ecosystem innovation processes.

Let me share with you, by way of conclusion, an e-mail written by a DEC alumnus. He tells what DEC alums call *The Sunflower Story*, a story that tries to make sense of the rise and fall of DEC and what it means to the global business ecology:

> In the "strong" version of the story, the end of DEC was planned by Ken, and he somehow put many of the free spirits he had attracted into the company (and helped to develop themselves), under such unpleasant conditions that they chose to leave. In the same way that a sunflower spurts out its seeds at the end of summer, these people [or] seeds took the DEC culture with them and influence the whole of business today. In the "weak" Sunflower story Ken did not do it intentionally but unconsciously. It is evident that the end result is in fact true and the DEC culture continues to influence business worldwide. In systems thinking, DEC outgrew being an enterprise. It emerged to the next level to

become an influence in the world business ecology. The legal entity of DEC had to give up being an enterprise to become an important part of business culture. This point is not made just to have a happy ending but is a serious point and indicates there may be other examples of enterprises that became so successful that they had to emerge to the next level.[16]

Perhaps, as Schein concludes, "a culture such as DEC should have survived as it has in its alumni. Is it worth changing such a culture to preserve the business entity? One aspect of the DEC legacy is to leave us with this tough question. What is, in the end, more valuable—a culture that is ennobling but economically unstable or a stable economic entity that changes its culture to whatever is needed to survive?"[17]

Ed Schein's question gets at the heart of today's discussion about the foundations of business and society. And just as surely as every attempt to drill down to the root issues of scientific disciplines eventually leads to the epistemological and ontological root questions of philosophy, every attempt to drill down to the structural questions in the world of organizations and business eventually leads to the deep systemic questions of our time. These deep questions concern the evolving global foundations of capitalism and democracy.

CHAPTER 19

Global Actions

The Core Developmental Issue in Societies Today • Trying to Solve
Field 3 and 4 Problems with Field 1 and 2 Methods • A Deeper
Societal Shift • Cross-Sector Communication • Four Stages of
Socioeconomic Development in the West • Between
Fundamentalisms of the Past and Emerging Societies of the Future
• The Evolution and Transformation of Capitalism and Democracy

In the spring of 2002, during the feedback session of a health care interview project in Germany, a dozen or so health care practitioners gathered in the meeting room of the town's ancient Schlosshotel. Just as we
were about to begin, one of the participants asked me why I had traveled all
the way from Boston to facilitate the session. I responded by articulating my
personal motivation, something I usually keep to myself: "Well, I happen to
believe that—if current trends and developments continue—our global system will hit the wall within the next ten years. And because of that I try to
focus my time and energy on creating *living examples* that embody new forms
of cross-institutional collaboration and innovation. That's why." When I
ended, I wasn't sure how people would react. Would they share that view or
disagree?

They disagreed. "What do you mean, ten years? There's no way the current system will continue to exist that long. It won't be more than *five* years
before we see the collapse," said one person. The other dissenting group

said, "What do you mean, five years? The breakdown is happening *now*. It's happening as we speak."

I share this with you because I firmly believe the pressure on our frontline practitioners right now is enormous. Nurses and physicians in the hospitals, teachers in the schools, local line leaders in companies, and farmers all tell the same story: the pressure keeps increasing, and they can't take it any longer. They feel that the system is dysfunctional, they feel trapped, and they know that collectively they often produce results that nobody wants. Yet they don't know how to change it or how to get out.

In today's complex systems leaders often feel isolated and trapped. As such the leadership dilemmas in our current global society are not so different from those in the late East Germany or Enron: leaders are forced to operate within stagnant and dysfunctional systems that often strike us as impossible to change. To collectively enact and coordinate our global systems we need to look at the fourth meta-process.

The Core Developmental Issue in Societies Today

"The problem of all attempts to remedy the current societal crisis is that they start with a wrong diagnosis," says McKinsey's Michael Jung. "That's where we need to start anew."

Our schools use teaching practices that do more damage than good to the real creative potential of our kids. Our food systems use unsustainable practices, degrading topsoil while producing more junk food and contributing more to obesity, malnourishment, and hunger than ever before. Our health care systems consume up to 15 percent of GDP (in the United States), although there is no empirical proof of a positive relationship between a country's health care expenditures and its quality of health.

That's what's happening at the symptoms level. But the really interesting question is, why? Why aren't we able, in the twenty-first century, to design more intelligent social systems (of health, education, agriculture, conflict resolution, and so forth) that are more effective, more creative, and more inclusive? Something seems to be holding us back from dealing with the real root issues found in all these systems. To better understand this, let's look at our health care system.

Health Care—Do We Care?

Health care, as an industry, consumes $1.8 trillion a year in the United States alone, or 15 percent of gross domestic product. According to Dr. Raphael Levey, founder of the Global Medical Forum Foundation, which hosts an annual summit meeting of leaders from every constituency in the health system, "a relatively small percentage of the population consumes the vast majority of the health-care budget for diseases that are very well known and by and large behavioral.

"They're sick because of how they choose to live their lives, not because of environmental or genetic factors beyond their control. Even as far back as when I was in medical school many articles demonstrated that 80% of the health-care budget was consumed by five behavioral issues." In a nutshell, they are: too much smoking, drinking, eating, and stress, and not enough exercise.[1]

Dr. Edward Miller, the dean of the medical school and CEO of the hospital at Johns Hopkins University, reviewed the example of heart disease. "About 600,000 people have bypasses every year in the United States, and 1.3 million heart patients have angioplasties—at a total cost of around $30 billion per year. The procedures temporarily relieve chest pain but rarely prevent heart attacks or prolong lives. About half of the bypass grafts clog up in a few years; the angioplasties in a few months." The causes of this so-called restenosis are complex. It's sometimes a reaction to the trauma of the surgery itself. But many patients could avoid the return of pain and the need to repeat the surgery—not to mention arrest the course of their disease before it kills them—by switching to a healthier lifestyle. Yet very few do. "If you look at people after coronary-artery bypass grafting two years later, 90% of them have not changed their lifestyle," Miller said. "And that's been studied over and over and over again. And so we're missing some link in there. Even though they know they have a very bad disease and they know they should change their lifestyle, for whatever reason, they can't."[2]

Dr. Dean Ornish, a professor of medicine at the University of California at San Francisco and founder of the Preventive Medicine Research Institute in Sausalito, California, emphasizes the importance of creating strategies that address four levels of the health issue. "Providing health information is important but not always sufficient," he says. "We also need to bring in the psychological, emotional, and spiritual dimensions that are so often ignored." Ornish has published studies in leading peer-reviewed scientific journals showing that his holistic program, focused around a vegetarian diet with less than 10 percent of the calories from fat, can actually reverse heart disease without surgery or drugs. When the medical establishment remained skeptical that people could sustain the lifestyle changes Ornish recommended, in 1993 he persuaded Mutual of Omaha to pay for a trial study. Researchers signed up 333 patients with severely clogged arteries, helped them quit smoking, and put them on Ornish's diet. The patients attended twice-weekly group support sessions led by a psychologist and took instruction in meditation, relaxation, yoga, and aerobic exercise. The program lasted for only a year. But after three years, the study found, 77 percent of the patients had stuck with their lifestyle changes—and safely avoided the bypass or angioplasty surgeries that they were eligible for under their insurance coverage. And Mutual of Omaha saved around $30,000 per patient.

Trying to Solve Field 3 and 4 Problems with Field 1 and 2 Methods

The health care example demonstrates how we try to solve problems that require profound Field 3 and 4 approaches to innovation and change with technical fixes on Level 1 or 2. Ken Olson tried to do the same thing at DEC, and the company went out of business soon after. Yet the same correcting mechanism doesn't exist in the hyper-complex environments of health care, education, or agriculture—let alone development economics: their quasi-monopolistic situations prevent these societal systems from going out of business regardless of the dysfunctional outcomes they produce.

Unless we crack that nut, to address the real systemic root issues, we will not be successful in solving any key problem that we face as a society today. While we spend $1.8 trillion dollar health care costs and address health issues on a symptom's level, the real systemic causes remain unaddressed.

Nortin Hadler, M.D., and professor of medicine at the University of North Carolina, has done extensive research on the systemic root causes of high mortality risk, and has determined that two factors are key:

1. Are you comfortable in your socioeconomic status?

2. Are you satisfied in your employment? Tell me how happy you are in your work and how comfortable you are in your social status, and I'll tell you your mortality risk![3]

We saw in the health care example in Germany that what people want is to engage in deeper relationships to each other and to themselves. Patients and physicians alike, realized that they were enacting results and relationships that nobody wanted. And yet they found it (almost) impossible to change that. Why? What is holding us back? What would it take to allow us to address the real root issues keeping us from doing what we love and loving what we do?

A Deeper Societal Shift

Although many of us know various positive transformation episodes, often transformed institutions and groups eventually fall back into their old behaviors because the larger institutional ecology in which they operate puts too many constraining demands on them (for example, to meet the expectations of Wall Street analysts). It is obvious, therefore, that our root cause analysis must include the meta-systems that define the current institutional context (mundo). These meta-systems include the economic, political, media, cultural sub-systems, etc. They used to be differentiated, but now are highly intertwined and must be coordinated. How do we do that?

How can we reach that coordination of the whole without reverting back to some model of dictatorship by one of the sectors, for instance, by the priests, by the state, or by business? Can we reach that system-wide coordination through shifting the cross-sector communication from Levels 1 and 2 (downloading and debate) to Levels 3 and 4 (dialogue and presencing)?

The European social model exemplified by Finland, Sweden, Norway, Denmark, or Holland, is a good example of relative balance, autonomy and co-dependence among the three sectors. Historical examples for the three modes of domination have been featured by socialist systems (domination by the state), theocratic systems (domination by spiritual leaders), or neo-liberal economic systems (domination by business) all of which come with their own set of problems and issues that stem from overly reducing the real complexity of our global reality today.

Although the current rise of monocentric fundamentalisms across the board seems to suggest the opposite, I believe that this phenomenon actually is a counterreaction to a deeper and still continuing societal shift towards a deepened co-dependence of the three sectors.[3]

Cross-Sector Communication

Figure 19.1 shows the relationships among the three sectors (public, private, and civic) according to the different types of conversation discussed in Chapter 17: downloading, debating, dialoging, and presencing. The four circles depict the four types and evolutionary stages of communication in the global economic and political system today.

Circle 1: Downloading

The outer circle represents the space of *downloading* and captures the dynamics of pre-democratic and pre-constitutional stakeholder communication. Downloading is a *unilateral* communication structure that sets the agenda and manipulates the other stakeholders to behave in a certain way and that excludes their voices from the discourse. Widely used examples of this type of cross-sector communication are the dissemination of political propaganda, bribery, many types of lobbying, and commercials. Another example of this type from the NGO sector is advocacy groups when they attack a company without any attempt to communicate directly with that organization. All

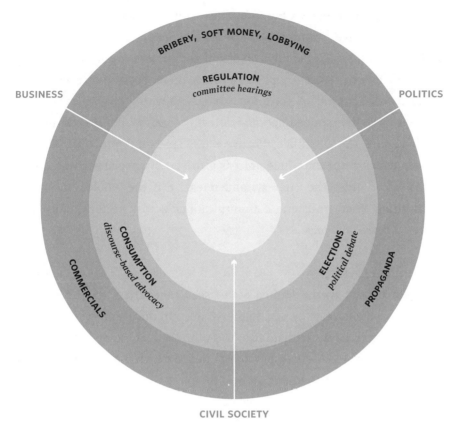

FIGURE 19.1 CROSS-SECTOR COMMUNICATION TYPES 1 AND 2

of these communication structures are *unilateral* (involving only one channel), *noninclusive* (excluding other stakeholders) and except for the case of advocacy, they are *nontransparent* and usually operate behind closed doors. They are designed to influence/manipulate the behavior of the recipient to serve the interests of the sender (usually at the expense of the excluded stakeholders).

If all of these practices are open to anyone, one might ask, what's the big problem? There actually are two problems. One is that there is unequal access to the political and legislative process. Some people and groups have a great deal of economic power, while others have very little. Moreover, we know from Mancur Olson's pathbreaking book *The Logic of Collective Action* that small groups, such as big industries with very few major players, can organize themselves around their special interests much more easily than can larger groups, such as the millions of consumers in the same industry. This is exactly why small groups can leverage their special interests and large groups usually cannot.[4] Accordingly, we end up with a political process that is driven by well-organized special-interest groups, while the rest of us are unable to organize in similar effective ways. That's one problem. The other problem is that since the whole process is driven by special interests, no one group is promoting the interests and integrity of the whole. Examples of downloading-based unilateral communications across sectors (outer circle, Figure 19.1) are pervasive.

COMMERCIAL TELEVISION

The average child in the United States sees more than 40,000 television commercials each year. By age eighteen, our children have viewed 16,000 murders, as well as more than 200,000 other acts of violence. Not to mention the rapidly spreading use of video games in which the observation of violence is replaced by enacting it.

The average high school graduate has likely spent 15,000 to 18,000 hours in front of a television but only 12,000 hours in school. Research also shows a very strong link between exposure to violent TV and violent and aggressive behavior in children and teenagers. Watching a lot of violence on television can lead to hostility, fear, anxiety, depression, nightmares, sleep disturbances, and post-traumatic stress disorder.

PUBLIC DEBATE

The 2004 U.S. presidential election demonstrated the movement of public debate toward the outer circle (downloading), for three reasons: (a) The rules of the presidential debates required audience questions to be submitted and approved prior to the event. In contrast, in earlier presidential debates the candidates' answers to spontaneous nonscripted questions had a major impact on people's impressions of the candidates. (b) When George W. Bush was campaigning, he held town hall meetings to which only Bush supporters were admitted; and the Bush team helped those supporters formulate their questions in a way that would show Bush in the best possible light. (c) In 2004, forty-two percent of Americans believed that Saddam Hussein was behind the September 11, 2001, attacks; this mistaken perception is a disturbing distortion of public perception through political propaganda.[5]

Lobbying

It is estimated that a total of $1.4 billion was spent on all levels of campaign advertising for the 2004 U.S. presidential election. This figure does not take into account all the other money spent on the logistics of organizing an election. A good portion of the money comes from donations. The result is— guess what—policies and rules that favor the people and groups that donate at the expense of the majority who do not have the equivalent means and mechanisms. One glaring example of energy deregulation was not taking action against Enron when it manipulated the California energy crisis in 2001, which ended up costing more than $30 billion to taxpayers.[6]

In short, the dominance of downloading in consumer communication (commercials), public conversation (political propaganda), and legislation (special-interest lobbying and soft-money influence) is like a toxic ingredient that degrades the functioning of the fundamental institutions of democracy and the market economy today.

Circle 2: Debate

The second circle depicts examples of interactive, bilateral, cross-sector communication that I have earlier referred to as "debate." One example is a marketplace that offers a variety of choices to consumers, whose consumption decisions are a means of talking back to the companies (you vote with your money). Other examples are discourse-based stakeholder advocacy in which the better argument wins, political debates and hearings that offer a variety of different viewpoints and perspectives, and elections in which citizens talk back to politicians with their votes. The rise of Web-based political advocacy such as blogging, chat rooms, and other types of Internet groups adds additional channels that people and the civil sector can use to talk back to big institutions such as government and companies. These types of cross-sector communications are interactive, two-way, and advocacy based, as well as more inclusive (because they include more stakeholders) and transparent.

The second circle captures the essence of interactive communication in and between contemporary democratic and economic institutions.

The global challenges of this century require our societies to move from the first to the second circle (restoring market economy and democracy). In addition, they require us to move beyond the institutional status quo (the second circle) into the territory of the two inner circles because there is no way we can meet the challenges of this century with the current institutional setup which dates from the nineteenth and twentieth centuries.

Circle 3: Dialogue

The third circle depicts the type of cross-sector communication that we usually call multi-stakeholder dialogue. Multi-stakeholder dialogue creates a discourse that involves all key stakeholders in a multilateral interaction. Rather than being tightly controlled, the agenda is open, evolving, and transparent to all participants; any stakeholder may raise issues and concerns and co-determine the agendas of the meetings. Most forms of public conversation, stakeholder dialogue, civic dialogue, and empathically designed user interactions[7] are examples of this type of communication, which captures and articulates stakeholders' diverse views.

Multistakeholder conversations introduce a mechanism that allows people's views to be accessible and become part of the decision-making process. Multi-stakeholder dialogue allows a whole new class of actors to actively participate in societal decision-making processes; these actors include non-governmental organizations (NGOs) and civil society organizations (CSOs) that represent "the people."

Still, such dialogue may be unable to turn opposing views into productive co-creation. While the communication forms in the third circle (dialogue) tend to be good at identifying controversial issues and articulating diverse views, they tend to be less effective at turning those views into collective action or at forming new stakeholder constellations around emerging opportunities.

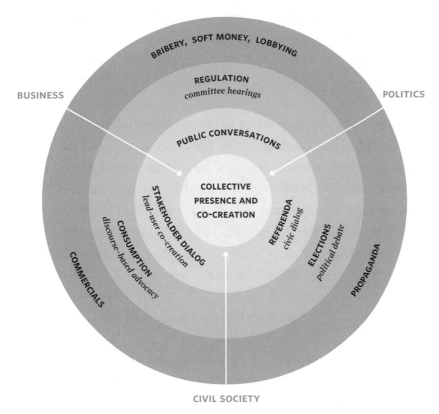

BRIBERY, SOFT MONEY, LOBBYING

REGULATION
committee hearings

BUSINESS

POLITICS

PUBLIC CONVERSATIONS

COLLECTIVE
PRESENCE AND
CO-CREATION

STAKEHOLDER DIALOG
lead–user co-creation

REFERENDA
civic dialog

CONSUMPTION
discourse-based advocacy

ELECTIONS
political debate

COMMERCIALS

PROPAGANDA

CIVIL SOCIETY

FIGURE 19.2 CROSS-SECTOR COMMUNICATION TYPES 1 THROUGH 4

Circle 4: Collective Presence and Co-creation

It is at this point that the generative communication types in the fourth, the inner circle, come into play. Such conversations convene emerging stakeholders in constellations that need one another in order to shape the future collectively. Together they sense and actualize emerging opportunities.[8] Thus the inner circle functions rather like a greenhouse for social innovations of the future. It incubates ideas, intentions, and experimental microcosms that will allow future possibilities to emerge, take shape, and develop.

Of the societal conversation types displayed in Figure 19.2, those in the inner circle are empirically the most rare and the most strategically important. That infrastructure, if in place, would allow whole ecosystems to connect and cope better, faster, and more innovatively with the key challenges at hand. The lack of that infrastructure represents a missing piece of societal hardwiring today.

Four Stages of Socioeconomic Development in the West

Figure 19.3 depicts a historical view of the same fundamental issue: it shows the movement across the four circles discussed above from the U-shaped developmental view. The four levels of the U capture the four different governance mechanisms (and societal sectors) that constitute modern/postmodern societies: (1) hierarchy and central planning, resulting in the development of the public sector, (2) markets and competition, resulting in the differentiation and development of the private sector, (3) networking and dialogue, resulting in the differentiation and development of the civic sector,

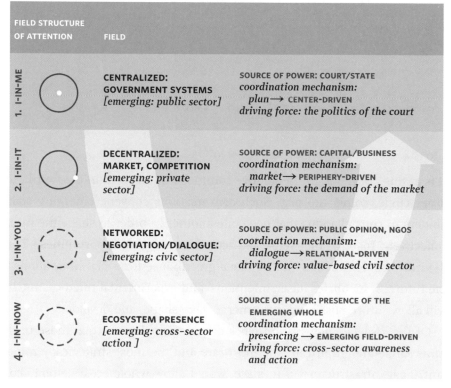

FIGURE 19.3 THE EVOLUTION OF GOVERNANCE MECHANISMS

and (4) a collective ecosystem presence, leading to a generative cross-institutional sphere for reinventing all three sectors and the way they interact.

In a very simplified way, these four types of governance mechanisms capture the developmental logic of social structures in Western society over the past three or four hundred years, usually referred to as modernization (differentiation of Fields 1 to 3) and postmodernity (Fields 3 to 4). Although the stages of societal differentiation and integration play out according to their specific historical and cultural contexts, there are some characteristic elements that the theoretical lens of the four fields can illuminate.

The British historian Arnold Toynbee conceived of societal progress as an interplay of challenge and response: structural change happens when a society's elite can no longer respond creatively to major social challenges, so that old social formations are replaced by new ones. Applying Toynbee's framework of challenge and response to the socioeconomic development of modern economies in the West, we can identify the following four stages.

The Stability Challenge: The Rise of the Public Sector

Think of Europe at the end of the Thirty Years' War in 1648 or the Soviet Union after the October Revolution and World War I in 1918, when the rise of a strong state and public sector provided a central coordination mechanism that allowed the allocation and distribution of scarce resources in line with the strategic developmental priorities as perceived by the elites of each country. In that regard, we can view twentieth-century socialism not as a *postcapitalistic* stage of the economy (according to Marxist theory) but as a *precapitalist* (that is, mercantilist) one.[9] From that point forward, the socioeconomic development of Western economies has been punctuated by three main transformations.

The Growth Challenge: Transformation I: The Rise of the Private Sector

The good thing about a state- and public-sector-driven society is its stability; the bad thing is its lack of dynamism.[10] Accordingly, the more successfully the stability challenge has been met, the more likely there will be a shift of focus from stability to growth and dynamism.

To meet this challenge, what is critical is the introduction of a second coordination mechanism: markets and competition. The introduction of markets and competition facilitated an unprecedented era of growth and industrialization in economic development (which in today's terms may be akin to the economic dynamism in parts of China over the past decade or so). The introduction of markets as a coordination mechanism and the rise of the private sector that came with it has shifted the geometry of power in the society from a center-driven system (governed by the state or the feudal court) to a more periphery-driven system (governed by the demands of the market).

The Externality Challenge: Transformation II: The Rise of the Civic Sector

The good thing about a purely market-driven economy and society is its rapid growth and dynamism, particularly in comparison with the earlier stages of mercantilism and feudalism; the bad thing is that it has no means of dealing effectively with some of the negative externalities that accompany it.[13]

There are two types and generations of negative externalities: those that affect the players within a system and those that affect those outside. System-interior (Type I) externalities include worker poverty (an issue of distribution), prices of farm products that fall below the threshold of sustainability (an issue of protectionism), and fluctuation of currency exchange rates (an issue of capital destruction). In his book *The Great Transformation*, Karl Polanyi described the nineteenth-century transformation from a pure market system to a more tempered market economy. He also argues that the pure market system with its three factor markets (for nature, labor, and capital) never worked because of its underlying "commodity fiction." This "fiction" needed to be tempered through corrective mechanisms such as labor unions, social security, protectionism, and reserve banks, all of which are designed to do the same thing: they limit the market mechanism when its results are dysfunctional or unacceptable and redirect governance by introducing negotiated stakeholders agreements as a third coordination mechanism that complements the two existing ones (markets and hierarchy).[14]

Examples of system-exterior (Type II) externalities include the destruction of nature, the destruction of opportunities for future generations, and the current misery and poverty of the 3 billion to 4 billion people who live at the so called "base of the global pyramid." These Type II issues are much harder to deal with because the stakeholders involved do not have a voice in the normal political process, as workers have when they organize in unions or as farmers have when they lobby for protection. Type II challenges have entered the political process through the mobilization of people-driven movements to deal with each of these problems, resulting in the formation of NGOs or CSOs that focus on issues such as the environment (nature), sustainability (of the world for future generations), development (developing countries), and so forth. The movement around Type II externalities began to show up as a large-scale social phenomenon only in the last third of the twentieth century and began to result in the emergence of global NGO players only during the last decade of the twentieth century and the first decade of this century, along with a massive wave of globalization after the end of the Cold War around 1989. The 1992 Earth Summit in Rio, the 1999 "battle of Seattle" at the World Trade Organization meeting, and the globally orchestrated anti–Iraq War rally in 2003 (before the invasion) were important milestones in the emergence of a new class of global players: globally orchestrated NGOs or CSOs. Today, there are about 28,000 NGOs worldwide that monitor, watch out for and address corporate or governmental misbehavior relating to environmental and social externalities.

The introduction of the third coordination mechanisms (stakeholder negotiation and dialogue) and the rise of the civic sector that came with it has again changed the geometry of power in our society. This relational mechanism functions on a different source of power: public opinion.

Throughout much of the 20th century the various responses to Type I externalities have led to the rise of the welfare state, which helped to alleviate many of these issues. At the end of the 20th century however two realities came together that in many ways marked the end of the traditional welfare state–based approach. One is that the welfare state took care only of the people inside the system, not those outside; the second is that the welfare state worked well only as long as globalization hadn't increased the gap between high-mobility capital and low-mobility labor. With that gap widening and taxation rates decreasing, the old European-style welfare state went into crisis. It needed to reinvent itself to be more efficient, flexible, self-reliant, and creative and less dependent on taxing labor costs as the main source of funding.

The Global Externality Challenge: Transformation III: The Rise of Ecosystem Innovation

The good thing about the European style of social democratic capitalism is that it deals with the classical externalities through wealth redistribution, social security, environmental regulation, farm subsidies, and development aid; the bad thing is that in the age of globalization and changing demographics, many of these mechanisms are no longer feasible in the long run, particularly if applied to Type II global externalities outside one's current system. Therefore, the challenge that most societies face is how to create ecosystems that deal with both Type I and Type II externalities in a way that supports individual and communal creativity and capacity building rather than subsidizing the absence of self reliance and entrepreneurial action. Put differently, the challenge is how to organize, with fewer resources, much more intelligent systems that will allow for widely spread entrepreneurship and innovation in cross-institutional relationships. This is where the fourth (inner) circle comes into play: it serves as a placeholder for an important missing piece of enabling infrastructure.

Table 19.1 summarizes the line of thought throughout the developmental sketch above. A primary challenge defines each developmental stage; each challenge required society to respond by creating a new coordination mechanism (central plan, market, dialogue), which then led to the rise of a new primary institutional actor (government, business, NGO) and source of power (sticks, carrots, norms). Each of these configurations also came with their unique geometry of power from centralized (central plan and hierarchy) to decentralized (markets) to relational (negotiation and dialogue).

Going forward, the same thing needs to happen again: the challenges of this century also require us to innovate, to create a new coordination mech-

TABLE 19.1 FOUR STAGES OF THE WESTERN MARKET ECONOMY, ITS INSTITUTIONS, AND ITS SOURCES OF POWER

	17th–18th Centuries Mercantilist State-Driven Economy	*18th–19th Centuries Liberal Market Economy*	*19th–20th Centuries Social Market Economy*	*21st Century: Global Ecosystem Economy*
Challenge	Stability	Growth	Externalities: internal, external	Externality-driven ecosystem innovation
Response: New coordination mechanism	Central rules/plan	Market/competition	Negotiation/dialogue	Ecosystem presence: Seeing and acting from the whole
Emergence of new institutional actors	State/government	Capital/business	Civil society/NGO	Cross-sector communities of innovation
Sources and mechanisms of power	Sticks	Sticks Carrots	Sticks Carrots Norms/values	Sticks Carrots Norms/values Presence of the whole

anism (seeing and acting from the whole ecosystem) that again will lead to the rise of new institutional actors (cross-sector innovation initiatives) and sources of power (presence of the whole ecosystem).

Between Fundamentalisms of the Past and Emerging Societies of the Future

Let us now summarize and conclude the discussion of the Theory U lens as applied to capitalism and society.

1. The history of Western economies and societies has evolved through

two main transformations: from the feudal/mercantilist system to the liberal market system (Transformation I), and from the liberal market system to the social market system (Transformation II). Each transformation produced a new institutional infrastructure: the liberal market economy during the first transformation (property rights, money, banks), which limited and partly *suspended* the power of the state by adding another governance mechanism (markets); the welfare state during the second transformation (social security, environmental and labor standards, protectionism, independent reserve banks), which *redirected* market forces through the use of negotiated stakeholder arrangements and agreements.

2. As the twentieth-century European-style welfare system—Field 3— fell deeper into crisis, three retro-capitalistic views began to emerge: (1) the mostly European, social democratic view of those who want to hold on to the twentieth-century social welfare state that took root in Europe, North America, and Japan (but that failed to succeed in most other places); (2) that of the mostly Anglo-Saxon neoconservative market fundamentalists, who want to return to the nineteenth-century pure market system that existed before social security and the welfare state; (3) the neo-national ideologies which want to go back to a more or less premodern law-and-order orientation in which one central power (usually the nation-state) controls and directs the strategic resources according to the dominant (occasionally fascist) ideology. In short, the three retrogressive approaches would cause their systems to revert to Field 3, 2, or 1 of the evolutionary framework shown above, accordingly.

3. While the three retro-approaches seem to pull the current social system backward, another set of forces appears to pull the system forward, toward Field 4. These forces help innovate the way people and their institutions collaborate and coordinate across the whole ecosystem (such as health care in a whole region) by moving from the two outer to the two inner circles (see Figure 19.2).

4. Just as new infrastructures were necessary to establish market- and

negotiation/dialogue-based coordination mechanisms, the next transformation will also requires a new institutional infrastructure to facilitate the emergence of another coordination mechanism: the ecosystem
presence of "seeing and acting from the whole" (Figure 19.3). I believe
that such new infrastructures would be among the highest leverage
innovations of our time.

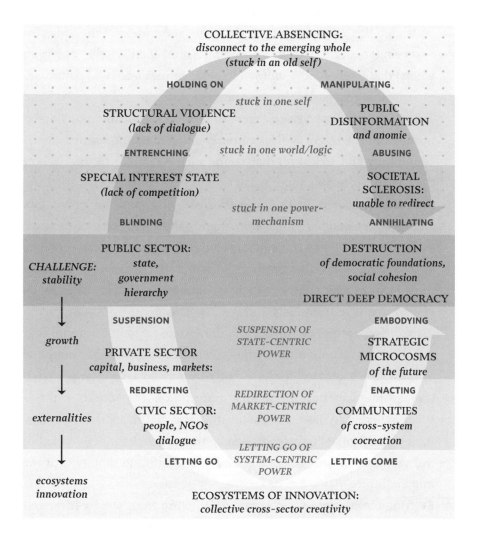

FIGURE 19.4 THE U AND THE ANTI-SPACE: COORDINATION MECHANISMS

5. Figure 19.4 demonstrates how the ecosystem innovation challenge, if responded to from the retromovements (Fields 1 to 3) instead of Field 4, will result in the larger system being sucked into the shadow space of societal pathology.

In such a scenario, society will gravitate toward a special-interest-driven state (resulting from a lack of transparency and competition) that is *blinding* the system to the needs of other groups in society; structural violence (resulting from a lack of stakeholder dialogue) that *entrenches* the divides among the various stakeholders; and collective absencing (resulting from a missing connection to the emerging whole) that freezes the *holding-on* to old identities and rigid patterns of the past that increasingly get out of touch with the real issues at hand. This will then lead to the three-part syndrome of anomie (loss of norms, values), sclerosis (lack of renewal), and atomie (destruction of community and structure) that seems such a familiar picture in both the Global North and South today.

6. Approaches that try to fix the pathologies of anomie, sclerosis, and atomie by reinstalling proper norms and values and restructuring will inevitably fail. They must fail because they do not address the problems at their root. Instead of treating the symptoms, a systemic response must focus on creating *innovations in infrastructures* that will allow the system to evolve from Field 3 to Field 4. This is precisely why current global crises cannot be solved with the recipes of the past: more market, more regulation, more major-stakeholder negotiation. Though all of those are necessary, they are not sufficient to take a large system through the deep transformational transition at the bottom of the U. What is necessary now is a subtle shift of social fields that will allow multiple networked individuals and communities to function as collective agents of an emerging whole and to innovate and prototye our way into the future.

7. Evolving the Western socioeconomic structure from Field 3 (twentieth century) to Field 4 (twenty-first century) would transform the foundations of both capitalism and democracy by institutionalizing the fourth

governance mechanism: seeing and acting from the whole that connects players and stakeholders that need each other to take their system
into its best future.

The Evolution and Transformation
of Capitalism and Democracy

The left-hand side of the U reflects the three field structures and stages of
modernization (Field 1-3) as well as the debate between modernists (system-
centric) and postmodernists (experience-centric) in the transition from Field
3 to Field 4. The space at the bottom of the U suggests a deep transformational shift toward accessing a deeper source of individual and collective
knowing. On the right-hand side, the U depicts some innovations in infrastructure that will assist in moving forward. This way forward does not simply continue the linear path of the past (as Western-style development concepts tend to suggest) but focuses on transforming and transsubstantiating
the old bodies of collective behavior.

In this transformation, the old market sector, that had been blind towards
externalities, opens up more and more toward internalizing externalities.
Secondly, the old state-centered public sector opens up toward participatory
decision-making in which the citizens directly manifest their will through
referenda and informed public dialogue. And lastly, the old NGO sector
opens up toward pioneering and co-creating new forms of cross-sector innovation initiatives rather than fighting against the symptoms of the system
downstream.

What infrastructure innovations would enable the global system to evolve
from Field 3 to Field 4?

Figure 19.5 shows four types of innovation in infrastructures that may be
worth considering: infrastructures for the renewal of democracy, markets,
culture, and the power of place.

1. *Innovation in Democratic Infrastructures.* Infrastructures that support
   the shift from a state-centric to a citizen-centric public sector would

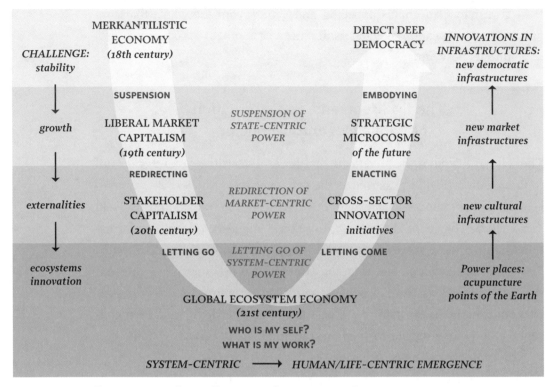

CHALLENGE:
stability

↓

growth

↓

externalities

↓

ecosystems
innovation

MERKANTILISTIC
ECONOMY
(18th century)

SUSPENSION

LIBERAL MARKET
CAPITALISM
(19th century)

REDIRECTING

STAKEHOLDER
CAPITALISM
(20th century)

LETTING GO

*SUSPENSION OF
STATE-CENTRIC
POWER*

*REDIRECTION OF
MARKET-CENTRIC
POWER*

*LETTING GO OF
SYSTEM-CENTRIC
POWER*

DIRECT DEEP
DEMOCRACY

EMBODYING

STRATEGIC
MICROCOSMS
of the future

ENACTING

CROSS-SECTOR
INNOVATION
initiatives

LETTING COME

*INNOVATIONS IN
INFRASTRUCTURES:
new democratic
infrastructures*

↑

*new market
infrastructures*

↑

*new cultural
infrastructures*

↑

*Power places:
acupuncture
points of the Earth*

GLOBAL ECOSYSTEM ECONOMY
(21st century)
WHO IS MY SELF?
WHAT IS MY WORK?

SYSTEM-CENTRIC ⟶ *HUMAN/LIFE-CENTRIC EMERGENCE*

FIGURE 19.5 FOUR TYPES OF INNOVATION INFRASTRUCTURES

include a ban on corruption and manipulative disinformation and focus on the creation of high-quality platforms of conversation that convene microcosms of key stakeholders in their respective systems (schools, health care regions, or cities, for example). A good example is the city of Porto Alegre, Brazil, which has received worldwide attention and recognition for its development of participatory processes of decision making on budgets and planning. *Orçamento participativo* (participatory budgeting) and *plenárias temáticas* (theme-oriented meetings) are innovations in public management.

2. *Innovation in Market Infrastructures.* Infrastructures that support the shift from externality-blind to externality-aware price mechanisms would include global standards that better internalize social and environmental costs. To make these standards practical, several radical reforms are necessary.

The current welfare system is still based on nineteenth-century thought, that is, taxing labor for funding welfare services (instead of taxing all factors). The German entrepreneur Götz Werner recently suggested linking welfare and tax reform by introducing a simple flat *basic income* for every citizen (as a basic human right) and by changing the tax system through abolishing all direct (income) taxes. This would shift the whole system to a simple *indirect (consumption) tax.*[15] These two changes would not only get rid of a great deal of government bureaucracy (for both the welfare and taxation bureaucracies), it would also allow each country to internalize social and environmental costs without being penalized in the global market place (because indirect taxes are reimbursed in the case of exports and are added in the case of imports). A simple basic income for everyone would also eliminate the welfare state bureaucracy by facilitating a new culture of self-reliance and entrepreneurship.

Another reform that needs further exploration and refinement is the use of parallel currencies to better internalize externalities. Between 1992 and 2002, some four thousand communities across the globe adopted parallel or complementary currencies based on the barter system.[16] While the global economy works well for certain products and markets (such as information technology), the strengthening of local and regional production–consumption cycles may be favorable for some other domains of the economy (such as local food cycles).

3. *Innovation in cultural infrastructures.* As we come to the cultural foundations of society, we encounter three interconnected systems and reforms: education, media, and public conversation. Reinventing our entire educational system to emphasize the lifelong process of cultivating all the deeper learning capacities—the open mind, open heart, and open will—would put whole societies on a different playing field (as will be discussed at greater length in the Epilogue).

Likewise, by transforming our current media system, we could shape new collective patterns of awareness and conversation. Current media products are firmly in the grip of the downloading paradigm, making us passive recipients and polluting the minds of hundreds of millions of children, as well as adults, every single day. What's missing are innovations for media products that revolve around a Field 4 presence and could inspire viewers to become aware of their deeper levels of knowing. This idea will be explored further in the Epilogue under a discussion of the Social Presencing Theatre.

Furthermore, we have no places in a given community or ecosystem that intentionally connect leaders across institutions and sectors. Frontline practitioners cannot easily build shared understanding and conversations to better sense and seize emerging opportunities that cut across institutions and sectors. This obvious deficiency brings us to the other aspect of the root system of society: the grounding of the social field and its meta-processes in nature, in the power of place.

4. *Power Places: Innovations in the Sacred Presence of Earth.* One of the most significantly underutilized resources societies have for accessing the bottom of the U is our presencing relationship to nature and the earth and what that relationship can teach us about who we are and why we are here. For example, when I visit Finland, I see people who have a deep, heartfelt relationship to nature, which Finnish children are encouraged to develop. Across the board, people spend more time in nature as a regular individual and collective practice. When parents go with their children to simple cabins in the woods, for example, they teach their children how to listen to the forest— because the forest is a *living being.* That special—even sacred—relationship with the presence of places in nature, as opposed to seeing nature as merely a resource, may very well play an invisible, enabling role in the high rates of educational excellence and successful social and technological innovations that Nordic countries like Finland repeatedly demonstrate.

I have also noticed that certain farms that have been cultivated over many years with an intentional set of ecological, social, and spiritual practices, can turn into powerful holding places for people and communities, allowing them to connect to the presence of earth in practical as well as contemplative ways. Maybe future farms will not only deal with the production of food but also will provide places where both children and adults can reconnect to their deepest source of inspiration and Self. The farm where I grew up serves both of these functions.[15]

At its core, deepening and transforming democracy and capitalism according to Field 4 of Theory U will also expand the use of capitalism's quintessential medium: money. Today we use money in four different ways: to *calculate economic value* (Field 1: downloading); to purchase products, in which case we exchange money for the product of our choice (Field 2: making a purchase means eliminating or "suspending" all other possible options of using the money); to *provide credit* to support other ventures, in which case we *redirect the immediate* use of the money from consumption to investment in an entrepreneurial venture (Field 3); to *advance the foundations of community and creativity* by donating or letting go of it (Field 4). We see this in some examples of philanthropy, when successful entrepreneurs give away most of their money and wealth as a gesture of giving back to society.[18] But then, when we look at the actual practices of how foundations give away their money, we often see that these practices lack the capacity of really letting go. Instead, they hold on to their control and force the grant-takers to adopt a set of targets and objectives that is often more designed to please donors rather than address real problems on the ground. Field 4 money should be given to the not-for-profit sector with no strings attached in order to stimulate and enable innovation and change that benefits the whole ecosystem and prototyping new ways of living, learning, and working together.

So how can we grow a healthy economy? Every economist knows the answer: by shifting resources from Field 2 (consumption of current products) to Field 3 (investing in future products and capacities). What we currently need to learn is that societies must shift their use of resources more toward Field 4. There, money can be invested freely in the sources of the future, in the foundations of future creativity, and in the health of the whole ecosystem. The lack of significant Field 4 money is a serious impediment to shifting capitalism and democracy to Stage 4.

To sum up: This chapter applied the Theory U lens—that is, four different fields of social emergence—to the fourth meta-process at issue: the collective enactment of global coordination mechanisms. We saw that four different voices respond to this crisis by suggesting differing pathways forward: the first three are the retro-voices, which suggest returning to the global field structure of Field 1 (autocratic and state-driven: regulation, law and order), Field 2 (market-driven: deregulation), or Field 3 (stakeholder negotiation-driven: dialogue), respectively. The fourth voice, however, suggests that there is no way back. Retreat is impossible because circumstances have changed. This is why we need to go forward to the next evolutionary stage of the global economy (ecosystem-driven: seeing and acting from the emerging whole).

However, moving forward is extremely difficult because we're missing a piece of hardwired infrastructure. All the earlier transformations of the socioeconomic system came with a new set of institutions and infrastructures. But we don't yet have our new ones. The creation of these innovations in infrastructures are among the highest impact leverage points of our society today. Examples include innovations in democratic infrastructures, market infrastructures, cultural infrastructures, and the cultivation of power places that could function as planetary "acupuncture points" in the process of shifting the field of global consciousness.

That's the major thing that's missing in our infrastructure. But the other missing piece and leveraging factor is leadership—the capacity to collectively sense, shape, and create our future. For that leadership capacity to develop and grow, we must cultivate all four meta-processes of the social field. They are: thinking, languaging, structuring, and evolving the coordination mechanism of ecosystem presence which means sensing and acting from the whole.

Viewed from outside, it is a surprise how little the central issue of this chapter—the evolution and transformation of democracy and capitalism— happens to be a topic in our scientific and public discourse today. The few discussions that we have can usually be subsumed among the retro-movements: thinking about new issues by applying old patterns of thought (Field 1-3). And yet, I am convinced that the questions at issue here will inevitably move center stage over the course of the next decade. While only a first beginning, I hope that this chapter will contribute to the broadening and deepening of this much-needed conversation.

The final two chapters and the Epilogue explore, in more depth, how we can catch those sparks and move forward. Together.

CHAPTER 20

Catching Social Reality
Creation in Flight

Field 1: Autistic Systems • Field 2: Adaptive Systems • Field 3: Self-Reflective Systems • Field 4: Generative Systems • The Grammar of the Social Field • Transforming the Causal Mechanism • The Leader's Journey • Catching the Sparks of Social Reality Creation

As our *Feldgang* across social fields draws to a close, let us pause and reflect on the whole that has emerged. As we discussed the four metaprocesses of the social field and how they unfold across systems levels from thinking (micro), "languaging" (meso), and structuring (macro) to global governance (mundo), we were able to see that on all these levels the social process can happen in four field structures of attention (Fields 1–4). Just as a musical tune can be performed in different keys, a social tune—that is, an individual or collective social act—can come into being through any of four different field structures of attention. Learning to recognize these various keys is like catching social reality creation in flight—just by *noticing* their differences, we can begin to alter the structure and direction of these sparks of social reality creation as they manifest in the here and now. The capacity to catch and redirect these sparks at their moment of inception, the capacity to illuminate our blind spot and become aware of that primary point of creation, our point of freedom, is when we experience the *I-in-now*.

We now focus on the *systemic whole* that we have seen emerge throughout the last couple of chapters in which we discussed the four metaprocesses of social reality creation (Chapters 16–19). I would like to take you back to the thought experiment that I invited you to contemplate earlier in our discussion: what if the social field structures of attention that we discussed throughout this book (Fields 1–4) were living entities? What if these fields could actually go on a developmental journey? What if our jobs (as managers, leaders, teachers, facilitators, farmers, health professionals, educators) were to help these fields to become aware of themselves and to advance to the next evolutionary stage?

By asking these questions and by also inquiring into the different qualities of relationship across levels (from micro to mundo), we will explore a fifth level of systems thinking, *the meta-level*, to help us better understand the larger system as a whole.

Field 1: Autistic Systems

The first stage of all four meta-processes has the same basic characteristic: it is an *autistic system*.[1] That is, what a system (or person) picks up from its environment or outside world is limited to the frames, concepts, and structures it already has. Nothing new gets in. Examples include downloading (listening while confirming your judgments), talking nice (using polite language), centralized institutional structures (a machine bureaucracy), and centralized societal structures (governmental policies, plans, and rules).

All of these examples share the same basic feature: the system is autistic in the sense that whatever impulse is trying to penetrate the boundary between the outside (the world) and the inside (the system), it will always trigger the same kind of response: a level 1 snap response that is programmed or hardwired into the system through the patterns of the past. We refer to this hardwired stuff as cognition on the micro level, as conversational habits on the meso level, as standard operating procedures on the institutional level, and as government bureaucracy on the societal or mundo level. But it is basically the same kind of beast at each level: a beast that limits your reaction to the habits and routines that the experiences of the past have hard-wired into your memory.

In the Field 1 system, how do the different levels (from micro to mundo) relate to each other? Through hierarchy. The mundo level defines the frame of the macro level, the macro level defines the boundaries of the meso level, and the meso level defines the boundaries of the micro level of evolution. Each level is distinct and separate from the others. Each higher level defines the boundaries of those below it.

The separation of levels sounds clean and logical. It fits nicely with how we divide the world into social science disciplines and professional communities: psychology looks at individuals; group psychology deals with group interactions; social systems theories and consultation practices focus on institutions; and economics, political science, and sociology consider the mundo sectors of society (business, politics, civil society). But no discipline looks at the variables and dependencies *in a truly holistic and integrative way across all levels from micro to mundo, all fields and all interdependencies.* This is a critical blind spot in the social sciences today, as Master Nan's words pointed out earlier in our field walk.

Instead, much of social science looks at social systems from a Field 1 point of view, as if the levels were orderly and separate from one another and as if the modern tri-sector differentiation didn't need to be explored in a more methodical way.

Field 2: Adaptive Systems

The second stage of thinking, languaging, structuring, and the evolution of global governance also has a number of shared characteristics: the characteristics of an *adaptive system.* In Field 2, what a system (or person) picks up from its environment or the outside world is no longer limited to the frames and patterns of the past; you can pick up new stuff from what is going on around you and then adapt to it. Examples include factual listening (listening from an open mind: opening up to the real data around you); debate (encouraging the articulation of diverse views that help a group to open up to what people really think); decentralized institutional structures (opening up to what our customers really want); and private sector-driven market economies (opening up to what the markets actually want us to do). All of these examples share the same systemic feature: the system is adaptive in the sense that whatever impulse is trying to penetrate the boundary between the outside and the inside (between the exterior world and the interior system), it will always trigger one of two responses: a level 1 response (reacting based on old habits) or a level 2 response (adapting to a situation by changing the structure of the system). We refer to this second type of response with different terms across levels (micro to mundo), but all of these terms refer to the same basic capacity: the capacity of a system to adapt to the changes in its environment.

In such a Field 2 living systems approach, how do the different levels (from micro to mundo) relate to each other? Through "structural coupling." Structural coupling is a term in living systems theory that denotes the co-adaptation of an organism with its environment.[2] Structural coupling differs from hierarchical integration à la Field 1 in that it is open to two-way interaction, co-dependence, and co-evolution. That is, the upper levels not only influence the lower ones (as they do in the context of Field 1) but also, at least to a certain degree, the lower ones influence the upper ones.

The most influential living systems theory in recent years has been the autopoietic systems theory that sociologist Niklas Luhmann introduced to the social sciences (based on Humberto Maturana's and Francisco Varela's pioneering work in biology and cognition). Luhmann's approach to sociology is a good example of a Field 2 approach. Luhmann argues that social systems are autopoietic entities; that is, they are constituted through elements that create and recreate themselves. Accordingly, researchers in this tradition usually do not pay much attention to the other levels. For example, you look at patterns of communication; you don't look at what happens *inside* an individual.[3] Although the focus of the autopoietic living system can be (and has been) applied to all levels (micro to mundo), little attention is paid to the interdependence across levels or to the conditions under which the separation of levels and systems may actually collapse.

Thus, two principal differences between presencing and autopoietic theory are that (a) presencing theory looks at *all levels and all four metaprocesses* in an integrative way, while autopoietic approaches have tended to look at them separately, and (b) presencing looks at the developmental journey of systems across *all four field structures of attention (Fields 1–4)*, while autopoietic approaches look through the lens of a single framework and field structure (Field 2), which doesn't change throughout the developmental journey of the system.

Field 3: Self-Reflective Systems

When a system moves from Field 2 to Field 3, a fundamental shift takes place. It's a shift that changes the worldview of each system in the most fundamental way. There is a clear and simple test that you can run to determine whether you or your system is running before or after such a shift to Field 3: when you see the system, do you see yourself as part of the picture? Does your perception include your self—the seer? Does the system have the capacity to see *itself?*

Remember Figure 10.2 (page 146). That figure shows how you begin to see the situation through the eyes of another stakeholder or player, and how the system begins to see itself. We explored that fundamental shift across all metaprocesses: as a shift from factual to empathic listening with an open heart, that is, to a listening that allows you to see the world and your self through another person's eyes (micro level); as a shift from debating differing views to engaging in dialogue—that is, to a process of thinking together that helps a group to see itself (meso level); as a shift from a divided structure where each division competes with all the others to a more collaborative and networked structure of stakeholder dialogues that allow the stakeholders to see themselves as part of a larger whole (macro level); and as a shift from a liberal market economy system that is blind to the externalities that it produces to a more externality-aware social market economy in which policy making involves multi-stakeholder dialogues that allow the policy makers to reflect the impact of their rules onto groups and stakeholders, including the stakeholders on the periphery of the system. In all of these examples there is a shift from seeing the system from *my* point of view to seeing the system through the eyes of *other* stakeholders—that is, to a seeing that will help the system to begin to see *itself*.

Thus the key feature of a Field 3 system is that a given impulse that penetrates the boundary from the outside world will trigger one of three responses: reacting (level 1), adapting (level 2), or self-reflecting (level 3). According to the level of response chosen, different action strategies and systems outcomes will result.

Although a Field 3 response (self-reflecting) is referred to with different terms by the various professions that deal with this shift from micro to mundo (psychologists on the micro, dialogue people on the group level, organizational development people on the institutional level, and global development people on the mundo level), it is crystal clear that they deal with the same fundamental phenomenon on each level. It is a field shift of utmost significance. A failure at this level means—given all of the disruptive changes taking place around us—that the system at issue will most likely be sucked (back) into the anti-space of social pathology (see Figures 16.1, 17.2, 18.2, 19.4).

Switching the meta-perspective from Field 2 to Field 3, we begin to see the boundaries between levels and entities open and partially collapse. Whereas structural coupling means that entities influence one another across existing boundaries, when boundaries open and partially collapse entities are influenced more fully by the collective social fields in which they operate. An example of this Field 3 approach is the biologist Rupert Sheldrake's theory of morphic resonance and the psychoanalyst and family systems expert Bert Hellinger's application of this theory in his "constellation work" in family systems as well as its application to organizational work. The focus is on collective mental-social fields that are rooted in the experiences of the past and that, if evoked, are experienced as real and powerful forces that show up in the present moment and offer us different ways of dealing with a situation.[4]

While the levels and entities are separate in Field 1 and structurally coupled in Field 2, they are more directly connected in Field 3: what individuals in constellation practices articulate and enact is the direct result of experiencing a collective field.

Field 4: Generative Systems

When a system moves from Field 3 to Field 4, another fundamental shift happens. It's a shift from being connected to the current field to connecting with the deepest presence and source of the best future possibility that is seeking to emerge. We tracked that fundamental shift across all metaprocesses: as a shift from empathic listening (open heart) to generative listening (open will) that activates the capacity to connect to your best future Self; from a dialogic-reflective conversation to a presencing-based group conversation that connects a community to its deeper sources of inspiration and purpose; from a networked to an ecosystem coordination that activates the capacity of seeing and acting from the whole among diverse constellations of players. In all of these examples we see a shift from connecting with a current field to connecting and acting from an emerging future field.

Thus the key feature of a Field 4 system is that a given impulse will trigger one of four responses: reacting (level 1), adapting (level 2), self-reflecting (level 3), or presencing the emerging future (level 4). Depending on the approach chosen, different action strategies and outcomes will manifest according to the principles discussed above: "*I attend* [this way], *therefore it emerges* [that way]."

I personally believe that the shift of a system to a Field 4 state of operating is *the* central phenomenon of our time. And it's starting to happen all around us: on the individual, group, and macro levels, and even on the mundo level, as we have explored throughout the field walk of this book. Operating according to the principles of Field 4 is also a key condition that we must meet in order to deal with many of the most pressing local, regional, and global challenges. And yet, despite its significance, and although it is starting to happen all around us, we don't yet have a word for it.

The issue is not (as in Field 3) that different communities use different terms for the same phenomenon. The issue is that most people tend to confuse Field 3 and Field 4. That means they confuse the current field with the emerging field of the future. But they are two different realities. They have different causalities and flows of time (as we will discuss in more detail below). They also feel different. When you have experienced both, your body knows the difference. And so does our collective (social) body. These fields activate different parts of who we are.

For these reasons, I believe it is appropriate to introduce a new term, a word for the process that occurs when human systems begin to operate from Field 4: *presencing*. It is a term that points at the heart of the blind spot in our consciousness: it points us to the possibility of a deeper way of operating. It points us to the essence of leadership—that is, to our capacity to shift the place from which we operate. The place of presencing is our deepest source of knowing and being, from which we navigate our way forward in situations when all other navigation instruments have failed.

When switching the meta-perspective from Field 3 to Field 4, the boundaries between the various system levels collapse to co-originate from the deepest source. The relationship across system levels differs from that of Field 3 in that the boundaries collapse fully (rather than partially) and the different levels and entities form a vehicle for the future to emerge.

Accordingly, the four fields not only originate from different sources—that is, inside, at, beyond, or surrounding the boundary of the organization; they also result in different cross-level relationships (that is, vertical separation, structural coupling, and partial or full collapse of boundaries, respectively). Hence, there is an increasing participation of the individual in co-creating the conditions for enacting social systems: from reenacting known patterns (Field 1) to adapting (Field 2), to co-evolving (Field 3), and to collective origination (Field 4).

As we move down the left side of the U, progressing from Field 1 to Field 4, the degree of interconnectedness and fusion goes up, as does the participation of the individual in shaping the whole.

At the same time, we see the system moving through a phase of differentiation that results in a more loosely coupled set of subsystems. That is true for the individual (where we can see the differentiation of the open mind, open heart, and open will), but it also applies to the group (where we see it in the collective equivalents of the open mind, heart, and will); to the institution (where we see it as a differentiation among structure types, centralized, decentralized, networked, and ecosystem and among the performance systems: customer interface, supply chain, innovation system); and to global governance and society (where we see it as a differentiation among the coordination mechanisms: hierarchy, markets, dialogue, the presence of the whole, as well as among the subsystems of society: the economy, the political system, and culture).[5]

So as one progresses down the left arm of the U, the degree of connection and fusion across levels goes up, while at the same time the system as a whole starts to differentiate in more loosely coupled subsystems.

Think about this for a minute. This is challenging, because the loose coupling and the fusion levels at the bottom of the U go against conventional wisdom.

To illustrate, Peter Senge once told about a meeting he had with the astronaut Rusty Schweickart:

> Rusty was on the Apollo mission that preceded the first moon landing, where they tested the lunar lander in orbit. He gave a presentation about ten years after he had come back. He said it took him ten years to figure out how to talk about what had happened. He said: "You know, all the engineers and technical people who are astronauts, they just talk about things technically. I just didn't know any words for it."
>
> But then he gave this talk at Lindisfarne, which is a spiritual community founded by William Irwin Thompson on Long Island. He told me later, "I had this flash of insight that I would describe what happened to me in the second person." The whole presentation was given in the second person, present tense—"Now you see this; now you see that." He said he did this because he realized that who he was as an astronaut was an extension of the sensory organs of humankind. "I was there," he said; "I could see something with my eyes, but it wasn't just me seeing. It was humankind seeing." So he tried it. And as he got into

telling this story in the second person, he realized that it was a very pow-erful experience—because a lot of his earlier experience started to make sense to him in a very different way.

In giving the talk in the second person, he had given himself per-mission to see as a collective, but also to see as another—"Now you wake up in the morning. Now you see this." The latter part of the talk is very moving, because he says, "Now you're near the end of the mission, and you're very fortunate because the mission has gone very well tech-nically. And so you have free time that you really had no right to expect. So the last days you actually spend much of the time just looking out the window. And as you look out the window, you realize that your identity has shifted—that for the first several days, whenever you had the chance to look out the window, you looked for the west coast of California, or you looked for Texas, or you looked for the Florida peninsula. You looked for the things that were familiar to you. And then you suddenly realize that you're now looking forward to the west coast of Africa. And you're looking forward to the Sinai. And you're looking forward to the Indian subcontinent. You realize that your identity has shifted, and you are now identifying with all of it."

"And now you're well into the last day. And you find yourself just looking. And you're drifting over that very familiar piece of geography that we call the Middle East. And you're looking down at this, and sud-denly it hits you that there are no boundaries. Every time you've seen this before, from the time you were a little child, there were always lines. And you realize there are no lines. The lines do not exist. Lines only exist because we hold them in our mind as existing. Then you realize, at that instant, that people are busy killing each other over those imagi-nary lines." And that's where his talk ended at Lindisfarne.

A couple of years later, Rusty participated in a three-day leadership course I was co-conducting. When it was over, we invited him to say whatever he would like to say. He got up and told a little bit of the same story. Then Charlie Kiefer, the other facilitator, said, "So, Rusty, what was it like up there?" By this time most of us had read his Lindisfarne talk. He stood there for a long time, and then he said, "It was like see-ing a baby about to be born."

Rusty Schweickart's experience exemplifies the fusion of levels at the bottom of the U. At first he was looking for what was familiar (Field 1). Then he moved into seeing with fresh eyes (Field 2): "you're now looking forward to the west coast of Africa." Then his perception shifted again: he saw that there were no lines between nations. This shift illustrates some of the key features of sensing (Field 3), including the fusion of system levels: "I was there, I could see something with my eyes, but it wasn't just me seeing. It was humankind seeing." And finally, he moved to yet another level (Field 4) when tuning into the deep essence of encountering the sacred presence of the planet earth: "It was like seeing a baby about to be born."

This intimate encounter and profound fusion of levels is a key characteristic of all the other examples of sensing and presencing we looked at in the earlier chapters. For instance, when the participants in the Patient-Physician Dialogue Forum began to see themselves as a system, the whole group started operating from a new collective sensory organ of perception. Rusty Schweickart's seeing made him participate in a subtle, collective birthing process that, without his presence and attention, might not have happened.

While the individual (micro level) in constellation work seems subordinate to the collective level (the social field and its impact), this isn't the case in Rusty Schweickart's story (or in other stories of presencing).[6] Rusty wasn't forced by an external force to say this or that. Instead he was going through a deep process of quieting, stillness, and grace through which he encountered a higher level of awareness and presence.

The Grammar of the Social Field

If the behavior of social systems is a function of the field structure of attention (and consciousness) from which a system operates, and if this applies to all levels in all systems, the following questions arise: According to what rules do these shifts happen (from one field structure to another)? And what driving force triggers such a shift?

The rules or social grammar of these shifts are summarized in Table 20.1. The table depicts the footprints of the U transformation from ten different

TABLE 20.1 THE SOCIAL GRAMMAR OF EMERGENCE: TEN CATEGORIES

Categories	Downloading	Seeing	Sensing	Presencing	Crystallizing	Prototyping	Performing
1. Gesture of paying attention	Projecting habitual judgments	Suspending and paying attention	Redirecting and diving or tuning in	Letting go and connecting to stillness	"Letting come" the future that wants to emerge	Enacting and improvising microcosms	Embodying and embedding in larger ecologies
2. Place of operating	From the center of one's own organizational boundary	From the periphery of one's organizational boundary	From beyond one's organizational boundary	From the deep source of one's emerging future	From being in dialogue with the future that wants to emerge	From being in dialogue with the emerging future and current contexts	From being in dialogue with co-evolving ecologies
3. Seeing the world as:	A projected mental image	A set of interacting objects	A current collective field/whole	Highest future possibility	An emerging field of the future	A living microcosm of the future	A co-evolving ecosystem
4. Knowledge	Opinionated judging	Explicit: "know-what"	Tacit: "know-how"	Self-transcending knowledge	Self-transcending knowledge co-imagining the emerging future	Self-transcending knowledge co-inspiring new microcosms	Self-transcending knowledge co-intuiting collective action
5. Social space	One-dimensional spaceless mental images	Two-dimensional exterior point-to-point distance between observer and observed	Three-dimensional interiority: observer moves inside the observed; boundary collapses	Four-dimensional reversed time-space: perception from Source	4-dimensional space: connect to Source to envision the emerging future	4-dimensional space: connect to Source and context for situational co-creation	4-dimensional space: connect to Source and the co-evolving ecosystem
6. Social time	Disembodied boredom	Chronos	Slowing down	Presence in sacred stillness	Presence in emerging imagination	Presence in situated co-creating	Presence in everyday practices

TABLE 20.1 THE SOCIAL GRAMMAR OF EMERGENCE: TEN CATEGORIES (continued)

Categories	Downloading	Seeing	Sensing	Presencing	Crystallizing	Prototyping	Performing
7. Collective social body (complexity) as:	Collective "dead" body (linear complexity)	Autopoietic living system (dynamic complexity)	Collective phenomenological fields (social complexity)	Presence of deep emergence (emerging complexity)	Crystallizing deep emergence (emerging complexity)	Enacted deep emergence (emerging complexity)	Embodied deep emergence (emerging complexity)
8. Primary causal mechanism	Exterior causation (determinism)	Primarily exterior causation	Largely interiorized causation	Fully interiorized (Self-) causation	Fully interiorized (Self-) causation	Fully interiorized (Self-) causation	Fully interiorized (Self-) causation
9. Episteme	Primacy of *subjectivity*: naive constructivism Wilber: Zone 3	Primacy of inter/*objectivity*: naive realism, rationalism, systems theory Wilber: Zone 4	Primacy of *intersubjectivity*: phenomenology, hermeneutics (Husserl, Heidegger, Habermas, Hellinger) Wilber: Zone 1, 2	Primacy of *trans-intersubjectivity*: developmental schools (Nishida, Wilber Nan, Torbert, Cohen, Steiner)	Primacy of *trans-intersubjectivity*: integral collective phenomenology of emerging systems (Bohm Cooperider, Cohen, Wilber)	Primacy of *trans-intersubjectivity*: integral aesthetics integral pragmatism of co-creation	Primacy of *trans-intersubjectivity*: intersubjectivity integral aesthetics integral pragmatism of social sculpting
10. Self	Center self: I-in-me Beck: 1st Tier: blue: order — Kegan: impulsive-imperial Torbert: impulsive-opportunist Wilber: mental self-concept	Rational self: I-in-it Beck: 1st Tier: orange: achievement — Kegan: formal-institutional Torbert: diplomat-achiever Wilber: role-self, rational	Relational self: I-in-you Beck: 1st and 2nd Tiers: green/yellow: sensitive/integrative — Kegan: post-formal, inter-individual Torbert: existential Wilber: rational-reflexive/exisstential	Authentic self: I-in-now Beck: 2nd Tier: turquoise: holistic — Kegan: post-formal, inter-individual Torbert: ironist Wilber: integrated/psychic	Authentic self: I-in-now/you — Wilber: integrated/subtle	Authentic self: I-in-now/-it — Wilber: integrated/causal	Authentic self: I-in-now/-us — Wilber: integrated/nondual

angles (categories). Nothing in the table is new; it just summarizes the journey described in this book.

Since I have covered the first seven categories at length in earlier discussions, I now suggest that you take a few minutes to read and reflect on those categories before I resume the discussion. Think of the table as an archaeology of the U process: the footprints of the deep process of collective human creativity that offers us an inside view of life's evolutionary grammar. These ten categories—although their descriptions vary according to cultural, situational, and personal context—are universal. When discussing these ideas with audiences and practitioners across cultures and continents, I have always been struck by the universality of the deeper shifts at issue here. The ten categories capture some key aspects of these shifts that a workshop participant once suggested that I refer to as the *epistemology of the human spirit*. It's that deeper epistemology that connects us across cultures. And because it relates to a collective global field, such a grammar can help us to navigate deeper transformations with greater transparency and ease.

Transforming the Causal Mechanism

Now let us turn to the last three rows and categories of Table 20.1 (rows 8 to 10). From micro to mundo, most of our systems are currently stuck in Field 1 and Field 2 behavior—we react and firefight against the issues of the past, unable to redirect our attention and intention toward connecting with and realizing emerging future possibilities.

One reason this shift often seems so difficult and unattainable is that people lack an understanding of the mechanisms that *cause* social systems to behave the way they do. Twenty-three hundred years ago, Aristotle suggested a framework of four different types of causation that I want to use to illustrate the profound transformation of causal mechanisms that occurs as a social system moves through the U.

Figure 20.1 depicts the four levels of the U as four concentric circles: the outer circle represents Field 1 (I-in-me) or downloading; the next circles represent Field 2 (I-in-it) and Field 3 (I-in-you); and the inner circle represents

Field 4 (I-in-now) or the bottom of the U. Furthermore, the four axial arrows that meet in the center circle depict the four types of causation that Aristotle distinguished. They are:

1. *Causa materialis:* the material cause
2. *Causa formalis:* the formal cause
3. *Causa finalis:* the final cause
4. *Causa efficiens:* the efficient cause (agency or the beginning of movement)

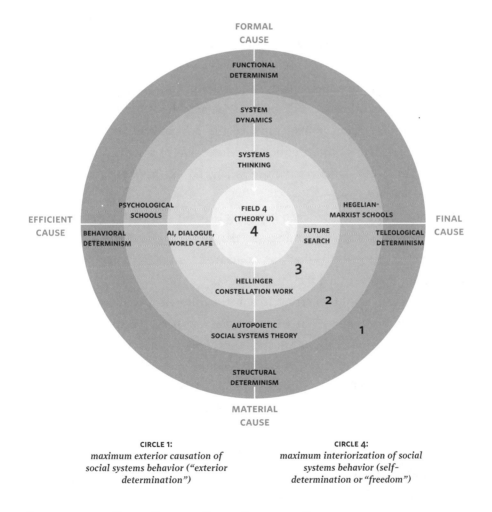

CIRCLE 1:
maximum exterior causation of social systems behavior ("exterior determination")

CIRCLE 4:
maximum interiorization of social systems behavior (self-determination or "freedom")

FIGURE 20.1 FOUR CAUSES, FOUR TYPES OF CAUSATION

In mapping these two distinctions (field structure of emergence and type of causation), Figure 20.1 depicts the landscape of different schools of thought in social systems theory today. The outer circle captures the traditional schools of social systems theory. These theories conceive of the cause of change as *exterior to* the boundaries of the system. By contrast, the innermost circle conceives of the cause of change as something that is connected to a deep opening process and a collapse of boundaries and that emerges from within. The two middle circles map the intermediary space between the two poles. While the four circles map the increasing interiority of causation from the outside to the inside, the four axial arrows represent the four Aristotelian types of causation: material cause, formal cause, final cause, the efficient cause.

An example of the material cause and exterior causation (outer circles) is the autopoietic social network theory that social systems are a function of the communication structures that produce the system and reproduce themselves (independent of the attention and intention of the participating individuals). This focus on the structure is a good example of what Aristotle called the material cause.

Another example of the second circle (primarily exterior causation) is the methodology of system dynamics: social systems are analyzed in terms of their patterns or the forms that they collectively enact. This approach focuses on what Aristotle called the formal cause.

Another example of this same circle is the different psychological schools that conceive of social systems in terms of the personal motivations that drive people to behave one way or the other. This is what Aristotle called the efficient cause—that is, the actor or the beginning of movement.

And finally, the Hegelian-Marxist way of looking at the process of history as the gradual realization of a final cause that manifests itself according to objective historical laws is a good example of a theory that focuses on the final cause as the key driving force.

While each approach emphasizes a different type of cause, their locus of causation is largely the same. The locus of causation and change is, by and large, *exterior to* the attention and intention of the people that live in and enact the system at issue. This is true across all these theories, including the communication patterns that, according to autopoietic social systems theory, drive and reproduce the system; the collectively enacted patterns that, according to system dynamics theory, drive the behavior of social systems; the psychological patterns that, according to the various psychological schools of thought, drive people's behavior; and the objective laws of history that, according to Marxist theory, drive the historical process toward its final stage. All these theories share a common feature: the causal variables that shape the change are exterior to the attention and intention of the people who collectively enact the system. It happens right in their blind spot. This points up the principal difference between the theories of the two outer circles (exterior causation of change) and those of the two inner circles (interior causation of change). The main difference is that in the two inner circles we are dealing with social systems or social fields (as the totality of relationships among actors in a system) that begin to *see themselves*, that is, that begin to illuminate their blind spot.

Such a self-reflective turn of a social field is exactly what happened during the Patient-Physician Dialogue Forum when it dawned on people that "we *are* the system." Everything stopped, and then the conversation continued from a totally different place (the mayor stood up, the teacher stood up, the farmer stood up). This turn also happened in the case of the car company when the engineers analyzed their system, looked at the resulting map, and exclaimed, "Oh, look what we're doing to ourselves!" In both of these cases we see the *interiorization* of the collectively enacted pattern (formal cause). This and similar systems thinking-based intervention work clearly show how the collectively enacted patterns of a system can be interiorized through seeing one's jointly enacted patterns and collectively reflecting on them. Once visible, they can be acted upon in different ways.

Another example and method of interiorizing the mechanism of causation in a social field is the Hellinger-based constellation work, which focuses on what Sheldrake calls the morphic resonance of a field or what Aristotle called the material cause: it focuses on the historical memory and structure of the roles and relationships among the key players of the system. If done in the right way, constellation work can enable clients to make another move, to interiorize and change the causation of the system.

A third angle from which to look at the interiorization of the causal mechanism is that of the efficient cause: the change-makers and people who actually move, create, and enact the system. Examples of this type of interiorization include David Cooperrider's method of appreciative inquiry, Bill Isaacs's method of dialogue, and Juanita Brown's World Café method.[7] All of them focus on the individual and collective agents and how the gold of their best experiences can be surfaced, harnessed, and leveraged in moving forward. These approaches deal with accessing the positive energy that moves through and empowers people to take action.

A fourth angle from which to examine the interiorization of change is from the perspective of the final cause. A method that exemplifies an approach from that angle was articulated by Marvin Weisbord, widely recognized as one of the founding fathers of organizational development. In his Future Search conferences he focuses on discovering common ground by creating a shared vision of the future, which then begins to function as a catalyzing force of change.[8]

And last, there is the innermost circle, which is about fully interiorizing and integrating all types of causation, such that the social field opens up to forming a holding space for the future that is seeking to emerge. Think of Rusty Schweickart's words: "It was like seeing a baby about to be born." When that deep existential opening and encounter happens, the different types of causation and levels all merge into a single field of self-causation or noncausation that connects the respective human or social system with its deepest source of becoming and freedom.

Thus, by going through the U, we can shift and transform the causal mechanism of human and social systems and their evolution. When operating from the outer two circles—represented by Field 1 and Field 2 of Theory U—the behavior of social systems is driven by the past and/or exterior mechanism and events. As the process of moving through the U unfolds and social systems begin to access their Field 3 and Field 4 ways of operating, we enter the territory of the two inner circles, where the behavior of social systems is self-reflected (Field 3) and Self-caused (Field 4). As discussed earlier, it is the nature of this century's global challenges such as climate change that will force all of us—the entire global system—to interiorize our patterns of social causation. These challenges will force us to become aware of our collectively enacted patterns, to illuminate our blind spot, and to shift our level of operating from the outer to the inner circles of (self-) causation.

The Leader's Journey

The journey from being driven by past patterns and exterior forces (the outer circles) toward the place that allows us to shape the future from within (the inner circle), we call the journey of leadership. Leadership in its essence is the capacity to shift the inner place from which we operate. Once they understand how, leaders can build the capacity of their systems to operate differently and to release themselves from the exterior determination of the outer circle. As long as we are mired in the viewpoint of the outer two circles, we are trapped in a victim mind-set ("the system is doing something to me"). As soon as we shift to the viewpoint of the inner two circles, we see how we can make a difference and how we can shape the future differently. Facilitating the movement from one (victim) mind-set to another (we can shape our future) is what leaders get paid for.

The journey from the outer circle to the inner one is the journey of the U. We move through a full inversion (*Umstülpung*) of the old system's view of exterior causation toward a different system's view of interior opening or self-causation. Rusty Schweickart described this shift in terms of moving from seeing something in the outside world that is familiar (California) or new (the west coast of Africa) toward a different way of operating in which he participates in a larger process of a collective opening ("It was humankind seeing") and then to acting as a holding space for a profound evolutionary process ("It was like seeing a baby about to be born").

The shift from sensing exterior causation to sensing something collective that is emerging from within brings us back full circle to Master Nan's point: the core issue of our time is the split between matter and mind, between the exterior and the interior world. It's the same split that Ken

Wilber's integral theory focuses on when, in his "all-quadrants, all-levels" approach, he differentiates between the interior and the exterior on the one hand and the individual and the collective on the other.[9] This split between matter and mind, as discussed earlier, applies only as long as we view the world through the lenses of the outer two circles (Figure 20.1). To the degree that we progress to the inner two circles, we gain access to a deeper participation in the process of social reality creation. The journey of the U is a journey of integrating all the levels and quadrants that Wilber talks about in his integral theory. While on the first level of the U all four quadrants are separate and exterior to each other, the closer we get to the bottom of the U, the more these quadrants and levels become intertwined, until at the bottom of the U they all collapse into a single point—the point of stillness and creation.[10]

Catching the Sparks of Social Reality Creation

Let us now return to the thought experiment: What if the social field were a living system, a living and evolving entity? Viewed from that angle, our inquiry surfaced the following points:

1. The four circles of Figure 20.1 capture four different evolutionary stages of that evolving entity. These four stages coincide with the first four columns in Table 20.1. If we look at all the circles (Figure 20.1) and all the columns (Table 20.1) we can see them as the *footprints* of an evolutionary process. Each column and circle captures a particular stage or state of that process. We can see these different states and stages across all aspects of social life, from micro to meso, macro, and mundo. We have seen them across all four metaprocesses. The different social systems and their different current position in terms of Fields 1–4 are all around us and often create a great deal of confusion because people usually do not recognize these different states and their implications for leadership and action.

2. If the evolution of the social field can be described as footprints, the

question is: *Who* is creating these footprints? Who is the seer or the self that is emerging, and what can trigger the evolutionary process of jumping from one level of operating to another (as captured in the various circles or columns)? The capacity to shift that field state lies within the blind spot of the seer. It's a hidden capacity that all human and social systems can uncover and unleash. I call this capacity the *I-in-now*, the capacity of the seer (the system) to switch on a higher field structure of attention.

3. This is why "Self," the tenth category in Table 20.1, represents the most fundamental grounding condition. While going through the U movement, we not only journey through seven gestures of attention (Row 1) that differ in terms of the place from which we operate (Row 2), but we also activate the presence of a different part or aspect of our self (Row 10). The different types and developmental stages of the self are described with different terms in different traditions and cognitive theories. However, as Ken Wilber shows in his book *Integral Psychology*, most of these developmental approaches agree more or less on the stages and/or their subsets. The tenth category basically says that *each and every human being* and community is *not one, but many*. And as we evolve our individual collective capacities, we begin to access and develop these other aspects of our self. As a consequence, our thinking and acting progresses through stages and states that shift from emphasizing the subjective, objective, intersubjective, and trans-intersubjective realm as the primary *metacategory* of action and thought (Row 9).

4. Theory U acts as a practical lens and framework to explain why and how groups can drop into a Field 4 state. The "U" complements existing developmental theories and differentiates various states of attention and consciousness. In our research, we have found that groups can achieve this state even though individuals within the group, according to developmental theory, would have been unlikely to get there. In other words, the collective serves as a gateway to access the deeper states of awareness and knowing.

5. The global social field is likewise not one, but many. It is many in terms of its functional differentiation: the global economic, political, and cultural sub systems have differentiated into loosely coupled systems, each of which needs a great deal of autonomy in order to function well. But it is also many in terms of its different field structures of attention (Fields 1–4). What's necessary today is that we develop small microcosms of the social field in which we can develop new forms of Field 4 ecosystems that function by seeing from the emerging whole. Once we have developed a couple of them it might not be too difficult to create similar shifts in the larger system, given that the larger system is on the global threshold (the door is open just a crack) as we speak.

Summing it up: The different columns of Table 20.1 capture the footprints of the evolving social field. Each footprint corresponds to a different state of the social field, of the self, and of its structure of attention and consciousness. What links these footprints is *movement*. Movement cuts across these evolutionary states. That movement is powered and triggered by the I-in-now: the hidden capacity of all human and social systems to become aware of their own blind spots, their source, and to redirect the sparks of social reality creation in real time.

The next and final chapter is a field manual that outlines the principles of presencing and describes how to do this type of leadership work in practical situations.

Principles and Practices of Presencing for Leading Profound Innovation and Change

Co-initiating • Co-sensing • Co-presencing • Co-creating •
Co-evolving • Root Principles

To lead profound change is to shift the inner place from which a system operates. This can be done only collaboratively. Throughout this book, we've referred to this practice as a "social technology." Having discussed various aspects of this social technology, we now turn to looking at it as a whole and from a practitioner's point of view: what are the principles and practices that will help me and others to link with and realize our best future possibility? The social technology at issue is based on five major movements. Each of the movements is grounded in a host of principles and practices that we will discuss below. The five movements are (Figure 21.1):

- *Co-initiating:* listen to others and to what life calls you to do
- *Co-sensing:* go to the places of most potential and listen with your mind and heart wide open
- *Co-presencing:* retreat and reflect, allow the inner knowing to emerge.

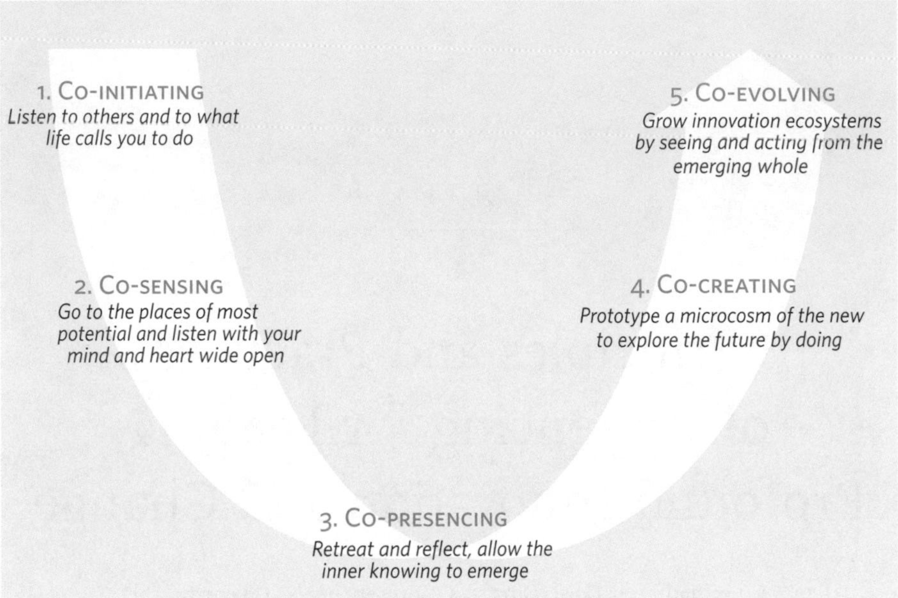

1. CO-INITIATING
Listen to others and to what life calls you to do

5. CO-EVOLVING
Grow innovation ecosystems by seeing and acting from the emerging whole

2. CO-SENSING
Go to the places of most potential and listen with your mind and heart wide open

4. CO-CREATING
Prototype a microcosm of the new to explore the future by doing

3. CO-PRESENCING
Retreat and reflect, allow the inner knowing to emerge

FIGURE 21.1 THE FIVE MOVEMENTS OF THE U PROCESS

- *Co-creating:* prototype a microcosm of the new in order to explore the future by doing
- *Co-evolving:* grow innovation ecosystems by seeing and acting from the emerging whole

Finally, we will conclude this "how-to mini-manual" by identifying three root principles that underlie the social technology of the U.

Co-initiating: Listen to Others and to What Life Calls You to Do

The first movement, co-initiating, focuses on beginning from nothing and uncovering some common ground. We start by creating a field or container from which the remaining four movements can come into being. How? By listening. By listening to other core players in the field (listening to others), by listening to what life calls you to do (listening to oneself), and by listen-

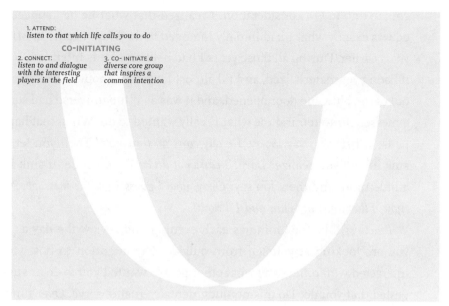

FIGURE 21.2 THE FIRST MOVEMENT: CO-INITIATING

ing to what emerges from a forward-oriented constellation of core players in the larger system (listening to the common ground).

1. **Attend: Listen to what life calls you to do.** All great ideas are triggered by something. The essence of the U process is to strengthen our presence and active participation in the world. Just as Ed Schein's approach to process consultation starts with the principles "Always try to be helpful" and "Always deal with reality,"[1] the U process of presencing also starts with the primacy of perception and attention: "listen to what life calls you to do." As such, the U approach is firmly grounded in process consultation (PC) as one of its principal parent disciplines.[2]

   Example: The idea to develop what would become my most popular class at MIT was suggested by a first-year MBA student, Neil Cantor. One day he walked into my office and proposed that I offer a class on corporate social responsibility. Because my teaching schedule for the coming term was already set, my first reaction was that I couldn't do it. On consideration, I realized that what he had suggested was exactly what I had initially intended to do when I came to MIT years earlier. During all those years I had held on to this intention, but it hadn't yet materialized, and I'd almost forgotten about it. And then, out of the blue, the door opened, and it was as if the universe had sent a messenger to remind me what I really wanted to do. When that happens, at first you say: *Sorry, I really can't do that now!* Then you let it sink in and you realize: *Darn! I can't not do it.* Then you let it sink in a little more and then you say: *Okay, now I guess I get the message. All right, I'll change my plan and I'll do it!*

Practice: Take four minutes each evening and review the day as if you are looking at yourself from outside. Pay attention to how you interacted with others and what other people wanted you to do or suggested that you do. Do this nonjudgmentally. Just observe. Over time, you will develop an internal observer that allows you to look at yourself from someone else's point of view.

2. **Connect: Listen to and dialogue with interesting players in the field.** The second domain of listening takes you out of your normal world and to the interesting edges and corners of the field that you feel drawn to: you talk to some of the most interesting players and listen to them in order to learn what it would take to move the current situation toward its best future possibility. Talk to both the highly visible core players and to the less visible ones—the people without a voice who may be shut down or shut out by the dysfunctionality of the current system. As you proceed on your mini-journey, you let yourself be taught, enchanted, and guided by the field. The most important players, helpers, future partners, and guides often turn out to be different from what you expect; therefore, your inner work is to stay open to suggestions and stay tuned to the help and guidance that the universe offers you.

Example 1: During the class on corporate social responsibility, mentioned above, I went with one of the student teams for a sensing journey to the UN Global Compact offices in New York. Inspired by the people they talked with, the students returned to Boston with an idea: MIT could develop a leadership development program that would help executive leaders to transform their companies through more sustainable and socially responsible business practices. The students created a joint student and faculty action team at MIT to explore the idea, and during the first meeting one of the senior faculty members turned to me and said "Otto, couldn't you try to develop such a program?" I thought, "Dammit, I can't do that now" and responded, "Not sure, but I will think about it." The next morning I had made up my mind: I couldn't *not* do it. So I began to think about what would spark my own best energy. I realized that it would be to work with the next generation of executives, the people who in five to seven years would be in executive leadership positions in their respective global organizations. I realized that if everything continued on its present course, the world would see major global breakdowns and disruptive changes within the next five to ten years. No one was preparing future CEOs or executives for their roles; they wouldn't know what lay ahead of them or how to respond to the major breakdowns that probably lie ahead.

That idea, with its energy, fueled my own mini-learning journey. I approached ten global institutions—international organizations, global companies, and nongovernmental organizations (NGOs)—and asked all of them essentially the same question: If we created a joint project to help the next generation of executives in leading global companies, NGOs, and international institutions to focus on some of the global challenges ahead, to develop the practical skills for innovating across systems, and to prototype these innovations in hands-on projects—would you play? Very much to my surprise, all of them responded, "Right, that's what's missing today—so yes, we probably would want to play. We would consider giving you some of our very best people for that. At minimum, we would be seriously interested. So who else have you got on your list?"

Example 2: What are ways to make this work within the world of organizations? One way is to do it through stakeholder dialogue inter-views. For example, in the case of a global car company, I developed and delivered a leadership capacity building program for its newly promoted directors (the second level below the CEO). Newly appoint-ed directors begin this program by engaging in three activities: a kick-off dialogue, which is a 90-minute conversation about their leader-ship journey and challenges; a shadowing practice, where they follow an experienced director from another part of the organization for a full day (see a more detailed description below); and a series of dia-logue interviews with their most important stakeholders.

Bill G., one of the participants and then the global leader for IT strategy, recalls: "One of my main challenges has been that country managers don't talk to each other. The regions of the U.S., Europe, and Asia don't coordinate their actions." When doing the stakeholder interviews with his most important stakeholders he posed to each of them a set of four questions that helped him to see his own job through their eyes.[3]

Says Bill: "As a newcomer, I sensed that there wasn't a lot of trust in the organization. With all these questions in mind, I was asked to do 'stakeholder interviews' as a preparation for a leadership seminar. The first thing I realized was that stakeholder interviews are 180 degrees different from *normal* conversations. No checking out and bargaining over my pre-prepared plans and trying to convince the other person. On the contrary, I had to shift my perspective and put myself into the stakeholders' shoes: "How does *she* or *he* look at my job? I had to find out how I could serve my stakeholders so that *they* could be successful. What did they *need* me for?

"At the beginning I was a little bit concerned: These guys had hired me in as an expert, and here I come, walking around and asking ques-tions rather than giving bright answers or offering solutions to prob-lems. But then it was amazing: The interviews were incredibly help-ful. They saved me months of work and communication! I learned things from the perspective of my stakeholders in this open way that

I would never have heard in 'normal communication.' Shortly after the interviews, people I didn't know came along and said, 'We've heard about these open communications you've had. We must tell you that they've created a lot of trust. How did you do that?' And all I did was try hard to just be *not knowing*! Forgetting about who I was and what my job was about. Usually, I would have 'sold' my work program and convinced people to collaborate. But now, obviously, being in the shoes of my stakeholders, I couldn't do that. It was my open mind that created insights and months' worth of work. No plan could have ever come up with that level of understanding. And the biggest surprise to me: it created not only insight but trust. That's even more amazing."

Practice 1: The most important practice at this stage is listening. Listening not only to your inner voice but also to what other people around you really tell you. Ursula and I once did a one-day dialogue interview training session with a group of health care practitioners in Germany. A year later Ursula asked one of them what had been her most important takeaway. The practitioner said: "What I took away from that day was that listening is the critical prerequisite for any reasonable interview. That means, for me, that I as a listener need *to build a space for the 'Other' within myself.* It is this inner space that creates the possibility for my counterpart to come into appearance—rather than just myself with my preconceived ideas." So the practice here is about intentionally building that space for the "other" within us.

Practice 2: The other key practice that matters at this early stage has to do with perseverance. That means not giving up in the face of rejection or (disconfirming) data that the world puts in front of you. I am talking about the many years that often lie between forming an initial idea and finally moving it into action, bringing it into reality. So what was it that helped me to survive that period?

Answer: A handful of people who knew and supported me and who held similar intentions. The practice here has to do with forming and maintaining your initial holding space, the handful of people who connect with your intention and provide you with the staying power to keep going. This initial incubation period may continue for five, six, or seven years, or more. In fact, many seed ideas for the future never get beyond this stage. So what does it take?

First: Nurture and maintain your initial holding space. Second: Never give up. Third: Once you sense the invitation to your calling— once a "messenger" shows up with an invitation to something you can't *not* do—respond with "yes" first and only later figure out how to do it (follow your feeling, not your rational mind).

3. **Co-initiate a diverse core group that inspires a common intention.** The essence of co-initiating is to convene a constellation of players that need one another to take action and to move forward. You will need to convene the right folks at the right time and in the right place. The opposite of co-initiation is marketing—to try to get people to "buy in" to your idea. That almost never works because it's just your idea. So part of the art of convening these players is to loosen your own grip on the idea—without necessarily giving it up. You lead by painting a picture that is intentionally incomplete; you make a few strokes; and you leave lots of blank space that others can add to and participate in. By operating this way, you shift the power dynamics from ownership to belonging, to seeing your part in a larger social field or whole.

The barriers to co-initiating are needs for (or attachment to) power (control), ownership, and money. This is exactly why most projects go wrong at an early stage. And if they go wrong at this stage, you don't need to waste your time microengineering the process that follows. It's already too late. The biggest leverage any project has is at the beginning, when you can clearly spell out your intentions and convene the right collaborators.

Although probably most of us have been trained and socialized *not* to let go of power, ownership, and money, I have come to realize that the net impact of my ideas seems to be positively correlated with my ability to let go of those three things. The result is that I get back a whole lot more than I gave up in the first place. That said, I also know (and have experienced) that this way of operating can backfire if people start to exploit you. Then, of course, you need to confront that problem.

Example 1: When I had completed my mini–learning journey about my idea with the ten global organizations and institutions, we held a core group meeting in London at the headquarters of one of the participating companies. It was just a one-day meeting, and the agenda was pretty open. The participants were all the people who had expressed a strong interest, including the MIT-based core group that had co-inspired it. We started with a personal check-in about what was happening in each organization, in society, and even in the participants' own lives. Then we took it from there. There was no formal presentation; instead, we talked freely about our real work and what we felt was at stake in our communities and society, and somehow along the way we found common sparks of interest and inspiration. Some of those sparks ignited during the first two hours of the meeting.

By the end of the meeting, we had decided to design a pilot program for that initiative with a design team composed of one person from each of the seven core institutions. That group included global players from government, NGOs, and civil society. We called our pilot ELIAS (Emerging Leaders for Innovation Across Sectors). Six months later, that team presented its proposal to a group of executive sponsors—where it was unanimously approved. At that point, the center of gravity for power and ownership of the initiative shifted from a small MIT core to the larger core group, which collectively functions as a vehicle for bringing their intentions and vision to light. That shift in the center of gravity required the old center (the MIT core) to begin operating differently: doing less telling and teaching and more learning and inquiring; less conventional problem-solving and more collectively owned prototyping.

Example 2: When I came into the meeting room at the R&D center of one of today's leading global car companies, I hadn't the faintest idea what was about to happen. There were seven of us: the head of the Research Center and the head of a Development Center, who happened to be his most important customer; three people who reported directly to them; one external consultant (formerly an employee of that company); and me. The head of the Research Center opened the meeting and suggested that I make a short presentation. I suggested that he go first. He presented his challenge and described the existing R&D process at his company. He outlined where that process didn't work, where he wasn't getting the results that he needed in order to succeed. Then I presented the U process as an alternative approach to addressing the same innovation issue. It all went very quickly. Time flew, and we had an easy and inspiring conversation and brainstorming. At the end of the meeting we had agreed on the focus, time frame, and rough schedule of the project (six months), the size of the full-time core team (six mostly younger high-potential future leaders), a commitment from each of the two center heads to give some of their best younger team members to the project team, a personal commitment from each person at the table to help as sponsors for the project, a commitment by the consultant and me to support the project team over the following six months (on a low budget that allowed the center heads to engage in this project without much visibility and noise in the organization), as well as the dates for the kickoff and the final presentation to the project team. Duration of the entire meeting: four hours.

Creating a common spark of intention doesn't necessarily require a lengthy process. What it requires is meeting the right people at the right moment in the right place. In this case it was a single meeting masterminded by the other consultant who brought things together; his earlier work experience and personal connections with most of the key players provided the right timing and place for this idea to move forward.

Practice: Checklist for co-initiating or sparking common intention among diverse core players:

- An intention to serve the evolution of the whole.
- Trust your "heart's intelligence" when connecting with people or exploring possibilities that may seem unrelated to the strategic issue at hand. Be open- minded to other ways of framing the real issue or opportunity (different key stakeholders will emphasize different aspects and variables).

- Connect with people professionally and personally: try to connect with their highest future sense of purpose (Self and Work), not just with their institutional role and responsibility.
- Include, when convening a core group meeting, executive sponsors and key decision makers who have a deep professional and personal interest in exploring and shaping the opportunity.
- Include activists in the core group: people who would give life and soul to make it work. Without this personal passion and commitment, nothing radically new will ever come into being.
- Include people with little or no voice in the current system: patients in the case of health care, students in the case of schools, customers or NGOs in the case of business organizations, future participants in the case of the leadership development project (ELIAS).
- Include key knowledge suppliers to the degree necessary to build a support team and infrastructure (helper/consultant, internal or external).
- Shape the time, place, and context to convene this constellation of people for co-inspiring the way forward (sense and seize opportunity).

Co-sensing: Go to the Places of Most Potential and Listen with Your Mind and Heart Wide Open

Having initiated a common future intention with the core group, the next challenge is to put that intention onto its feet by forming a prototyping action team that goes on a journey of sensing, discovering, and learning by doing.

4. **Form a highly committed prototyping core team and clarify essential questions.** It is important for the prototyping core team to reflect the diversity of players and stakeholders mentioned above and to commit itself to making the prototype projects the number one priority over a certain period of time (for example, four, six, or nine months).

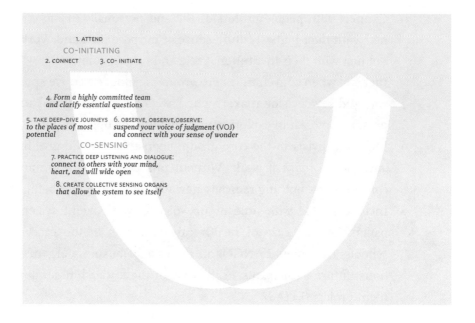

FIGURE 21.3 THE SECOND MOVEMENT: CO-SENSING

Example 1: At the car company project we assembled a team of five. Many of them were up-and-coming leaders in the organization who were now approaching their early or mid-thirties. The team also included a more seasoned engineer who had an outstanding reputation for competence in many of the key knowledge areas at issue and who proved to be key to the implementation success of the project later.

Example 2: In the case of multistakeholder projects such as the Food Lab, the project team includes thirty to fifty people.[4] Usually smaller, more focused teams work better than larger, less focused ones. The bigger the group, the more you need to rely on forming smaller subgroups of five to seven people, which become the primary units for sharing context, generating ideas, and getting things done.

Practice: Here is a checklist for a foundation workshop, the kickoff event that for the first time convenes all the prototyping team members and connects them with the core group of champions that initiated and is sponsoring the project initiative. As always, there is more than one possible design that can make the foundation workshop a success. But this checklist of desired outcomes may be useful for testing the design you come up with. To create focus and commitment, clarify:

What: what you want to create
Why: why it matters
How: the process that will get you there
Who: the roles and responsibilities of the players involved
When, where: the road map forward

Additional goals:

To uncover common ground by sharing the context and story that brought us here.

To spark inspiration for the future that the team wants to create.

To use "Minitraining" in dialogue interviews and deep-dive best practices.

To plan the action for deep-dive journeys: by identifying core people, organizations, and contexts that need to be explored and visited (a target list of the places with the most potential).

To give people an experience that embodies a first *feel* of the future that the project wants to create.

5. **Take deep-dive journeys to the places of most potential.** Deep-dive learning journeys connect people to the contexts and ideas that are relevant to creating the possible future. The deep-dive journey moves one's operating perspective from inside a familiar world—one's institutional bubble—to an unfamiliar world, one that is outside, surprising, fresh, and new. A deep-dive journey is not a benchmarking trip. It is designed to access a deeper level of emerging reality by observing hands-on practices through total immersion. It incorporates a combination of shadowing, participation, and dialogue.

Example 1: The focus of the car company project mentioned above was on solving key quality problems concerning the electronic control of the car. After the kickoff workshop, the participants began to generate a list of people, organizations, and contexts, both internally and externally, to visit during their deep-dive journey. Three activities were performed simultaneously: a Web-based learning journey, internal learning journeys, and an external learning journey. Over time, the key focus shifted from the Web to the internal and from the internal to the external learning journeys. After the first month the internal interviews were completed, and the team of six split into two groups of three to begin their external global learning journey (for a period of three weeks). Both started in Europe, with one going east and the other west. Three weeks later we planned to meet in Shanghai for the sense-making session. The deep-dive journeys took the team to R&D departments in other industries, engineering labs at MIT, or other development centers, but also to seemingly less relevant places, such as the offices of two healers and experts on traditional Chinese medicine.

Example 2: Another tool that can be used for taking deep-dive learning journeys is the shadowing practice. In the global car company program for directors, the participants spend a day shadowing another director in a different part of the organization, prior to the workshop. Bill G. describes his experience:

"As an IT businessperson, I chose "production" for my shadowing day. I wanted to experience that part of the organization where a product finally gets onto the street.

"Mr. B., the head of the assembly line, is known as a "nonmainstream," creative man and a master at putting innovation into practice. I was wondering: What is he doing when he innovates?

"Usually, work in the financial services business doesn't start before 9:00 a.m. But my shadowing day at the plant would start at 7:00 a.m. For such an early start, I had to get ready the night before—another difference. The plant was huge! 'What a difference,' I thought, 'between a virtual financial service business and a real plant.' I got off the bus at the wrong stop and got to Mr. B.'s office five minutes late. He'd already left for his first meeting.

"One of his people took me to their morning circle, where they review all the problems of the previous day. Fascinated, I listened to how intensively they discussed and worked on improving a car model that, in my mind, was "old" already: the new model would be introduced to the market in spring 2007. Why still worry about this one? Where did their passion for quality come from?

"In our one-on-one conversation later in the day, Mr. B. shared his personal story. I was impressed by his quiet, supreme ease. Obviously, his capacity as a leader was much greater than his formal responsibility for running an assembly line. I realized that what I had observed in the morning session was the result of a painful and systematic process of building a culture of co-creation and continuous improvement, which drives the plant's success: Within six years, the plant had been able to cut *50 percent* of the length of its assembly line! How? "At the beginning I found a lot of resistance to change. Change," Mr. B. said, "is not something that is expected to create any value for people themselves."

Mr. B. realized that it wasn't people he had to change, but rather his relationship to them: How could *they* become the source of change? What would it take to help them to become the drivers of change, rather than making them react to his efforts? He created management rules that actually turned out to be personal rules, guiding himself.

"When you become a director, you will be confronted over and over with one thing: 'Listen. *Listen and learn to listen more.*' That's the first rule. Managers," he said, "cannot listen. I couldn't listen when I started to be a manager. I had to learn listening. Once I started listening, I got my call: I have to create an opportunity for people to tap into their best potential to co-create the future change. When I listen deeply, I come to an inner place, where I am full of appreciation for the person I listen to. The best ideas for progress and change are rooted in the people themselves. I just have to 'listen them into appearance' and something mystical will happen. I once had a works council member who deeply objected to the introduction of a new standard assembly process. We went through a lot of listening. At the end, at a big works reunion, he stood up and spoke to his people. He presented to them what he had come up with as the most valuable next step to be taken. Guess what he presented? The new standard assembly process!"

Bill concluded his shadowing experience reflection: *"Listen and learn to listen* will be burned into my mind for the rest of my life."

Practice: Ask yourself: Given the sense of the future that you want to create, what are the people and places of most potential that could teach you most about that future and how to make it work?

Deep-dive journeys are usually best when conducted one-on-one or in small groups of up to about five people (so that the team can fit into one car). It works through the practices of shadowing, dialogue conversations, and if possible, in ongoing activities. The preparation and debriefing are done in a disciplined, structured, and timely fashion. Each team member of a deep-dive journey keeps a journal; each team has digital cameras, cell phones, and Web space for real-time documentation and cross-team sharing; to speed up the process, the teams should also receive both strategic and operational support in setting up their learning journeys (which does tend to consume some time).

Before each visit:

- Gather relevant information about the site you will be visiting. (Use the Web.)
- Make it clear that you want to talk to/shadow/work with people and not get a standard presentation.
- Prepare a questionnaire as a team (but feel free to deviate from it).
- Conduct a mini–training session on effective observation and best sensing practices.
- Prepare a thank you gift and assign roles (speaker, time keeper)

After each visit:

- Do not switch on cell phones or PDAs before completing the after-action reflection.

- Plan a time for immediate reflection as a group.
- During this reflection, each participant should describe his or her observations but try not to reach any conclusions in the first round. Stay focused on what emerges from the flow. Here are a few sample questions:

  1. What struck me most? What stood out?
  2. What was most surprising and unexpected?
  3. What touched me? What connected with me personally?
  4. If the social field of the visited organization were a living being, what would it look like and feel?
  5. If that being could talk, what would it say (to us)?
  6. If that being could develop, what would it want to morph into next?
  7. What is the source that allows this social field to develop and thrive?
  8. What limiting factors prevent this field from developing further?
  9. Moving into and out of this field, what did I notice about myself?
  10. What can this field tell us about *our* blind spot?
  11. What can this field teach us about our future?
  12. What other ideas does this experience spark for our initiative (our way forward)?

6. **Observe, observe, observe: Suspend your Voice of Judgment (VOJ) and connect with your sense of wonder.** Without the capacity to suspend your Voice of Judgment, all efforts to get inside the place of most potential will be in vain. Suspending your VOJ means shutting down (or embracing and changing) the habit of judging based on the experiences and patterns of the past in order to open up a new space of exploration, inquiry, and wonder.

   Example: In 1981, an engineering team from Ford Motor Company visited the Toyota plants that operated on the "lean" Toyota production system. Although the Ford engineers had firsthand access to the revolutionary new production system, they were unable to "see" (recognize) what was in front of them. The reaction of the engineers—seeing something staged and not a "real" plant because there was no inventory—reminds us how difficult it is to suspend our judgment even when we find ourselves in the place of most potential.

For many entrepreneurs, the "observe, observe" immersion often requires leaving behind an environment that in the past has provided a sense of security. That very security begins to feel constrained and inspires the need to cross the boundary from the known to the unknown. Some people take the step with trepidation, some with glee, but the move always opens up a new world of activity, connection, and "magic." Alan Webber, the co-founder of *Fast Company*, recalls, "I remember vividly my sense of liberation when I left the *Harvard Business Review*. All of a sudden I started meeting a whole new group of people. The basis for personal interaction was completely different: 'What are you working on that is interesting and who are you and how does it feel?' I was seeing the world with fresh eyes. I was learning at a rapid clip, going places I had never been before, and meeting people I would never have met before. It was as though I had escaped the boundaries of a walled city."

Practice: Take an object (such as a seed) or a situation and observe with undivided attention for at least five minutes. When you notice your mind wandering to other ideas or thoughts, correct your course and return to the task of pure observation.

7. **Practice deep listening and dialogue: connect to others with your mind, heart, and will wide open.** When connecting to other people and contexts, activate and open up all four "channels" of listening: listen from what you know (Listening 1), from what surprises you (Listening 2), from empathizing with the interviewee (Listening 3), and from the deepest source (Listening 4).

    Example 1: Of all the interviewers I have met, Joseph Jaworski stands out for his ability to create a trusting connection with the interviewee even in high-stakes political contexts. I once asked him how he managed that. His response was that the most important hour is the hour *before* the interview starts. That is when he centers himself in order to open his mind and his heart to the interview about to take place.

Later, as I gained more experience conducting deep-listening and dialogue interviews, I began to notice that interviewees often don't want to stop the conversation when time is up. They want to remain in the field. Sometimes they remark, "Boy, this was really interesting. Can I have the tape? I must have said things today that I never said before." They seem to sense that upon leaving the conversation, they will take with them a timeless element of connection from the conversation—something that won't disappear, no matter what. The interviewer feels the same way. It is as if he or she has entered a field that is more closely connected to a true authentic presence. Some special connection became present during the conversation. And finally, when I became even more aware of these subtle shifts in conversational fields, I could tell almost exactly *when* a conversation shifted from normal reflective discourse to a deeper flow of meaning and essential emergence. When that happens, voices get softer, the conversation slows, the texture of light seems to thicken, a sense of enhanced warmness seems to radiate from the interpersonal space, and at the same time I often hear a high-frequency ringing in my ears. When these changes happen, we enter the fourth field and the conversation deepens to a profound presence and flow.

The most important conditions on the side of the interviewer for such a deep conversation to occur are an open mind (genuine inquiry and interest), an open heart (appreciation and empathy), and an open will (attention to the emerging future and authentic self).

Can this type of listening and dialogue be learned? My experience suggests: absolutely yes. It can because it's already there. Because the Field 3 and Field 4 ways of operating are dormant capacities in all human and social systems, small or large. They just need some triggering or awakening.

Example 2: In 2004, Ursula and I conducted a one-day dialogue interview training session for a group of teachers and principals in northern Germany. Anna M. decided to apply some of our dialogue practice to her own leadership situation in her school in Hamburg, so she asked Ursula to give her some minimal coaching support.

Says Anna: "After one year as a principal in this public school, I was in despair: Teachers didn't approve of what I was proposing to do. Parents pushed, believing that I wasn't moving fast enough on strategy, funding, and quality of teaching. The kids were my only source of energy. I found myself comparing this school with the school I used to work in before: great fun, lots of innovation, perfect team. But now, new concepts and ideas felt like they were just being boycotted. I tried so hard to do the right thing, to please them, but I was stuck. Finally, the teachers would stop talking when I entered the teachers' lounge."

Listening to Anna, Ursula suggested she do a round of stakeholder dialogue interviews. Anna later recounted, "That meant I had to change my approach. Rather than giving to them what *I thought* they wanted from me (and which obviously was wrong), I instead asked them what *they needed me for*. A total shift. I was horrified. This was probably going to turn into a nightmare: they would use the conversation to tell me that I was just not good enough, that they wished they had another principal, and that the projects I was suggesting were just garbage.

"Nothing close to this actually happened. They were so generous in sharing what they *really* needed. I was deeply touched, relieved and shaken at the same time: In some ways, it was so much less than I had expected. In other ways, so much more that I needed to do. This is what they said they needed: Patience. Support. Not–too–high expectations. See me. Treat me like everyone else. Trust. Openness. Listen. Help us to do things ourselves. Consultation when we ask for it. Peacefulness. Confidence. Encouragement. Clear objectives. Rules.

"They were asking for the same things that I had been asking them to do for the kids! There was a mind-set of *not being good enough* at work that I was probably the source of. It determined our relationship and in turn their relationships with the kids. Looking at it from my own perspective, I didn't have a clue what to do next. But looking from *their* perspective, a whole array of new opportunities presented themselves to me. The table was set—I just hadn't been able to see it. A few weeks later, a young teacher said she was planning to have stakeholder interviews with a couple of parents and kids. Could I help her on how to do them?"

Practice 1: Spend four minutes each evening reviewing when during the day you engaged in Listening 3 (open mind and heart) and Listening 4 (open mind, heart, and will). If you cannot identify a single instance of deep listening, take note of that too. If you do this exercise for a month, your effectiveness as a listener will rise dramatically— without a single dollar spent on further training or coaching. All it takes is the discipline to focus on that four-minute review process every single day.

Practice 2: Pick your various key stakeholders and have a dialogue conversation in which you put yourself into their shoes and look at your own job from their point of view. Before each interview, take your moment of stillness and intention–setting to open up. Here are the four questions that I have used in the case of the global car company mentioned above, and that you could use as a starting point for your own list of questions:

1. What is your most important objective, and how can I help you realize it? (What do you need me for?)
2. What criteria will you use to assess whether my contribution to your work has been successful?
3. If I were able to change two things in my area of responsibility within the next six months, what two things would create the most value and benefit for you?

4. What, if any, historical tensions and/or systemic barriers have made it difficult for people in my role or function to fulfill your requirements and expectations? What is it that is getting into our way?

8. **Create collective sensing organs that allow the system to see itself.** Maybe the biggest institutional gap in seeking profound systems innovation is today's lack of collective sensing mechanisms. We have lots of collective downloading mechanisms (commercials, TV, and, unfortunately, much of our education system). By contrast, collective sensing mechanisms use the power of shared seeing and dialogue to tap an unused resource of collective sense making and thinking together.

Example: The Patient-Physician Dialogue Forum described earlier in the book is an example of a collective sensing organ: when individual sensing activities (in that instance, 130 dialogue interviews and several weeks of shadowing) are convened, they gradually begin to function as a collective sensing organ of the whole: "Look what we are doing to ourselves."

Practice: One enormously useful practice for creating collective sensing organs is the World Café method, developed by Juanita Brown and her colleagues David Isaacs and Toke Moller, among other World Café pioneers. Larger groups sit together as in a coffeehouse, around small round tables with four or five chairs. Rather than limiting the interaction to a single table, the World Café method focuses on interaction on multiple levels (threaded conversations from table to table and whole-group conversations) using seven simple café principles: clarify the context; create a hospitable environment; explore questions that matter; encourage everyone's contribution; connect diverse perspectives; listen—deeply—for insights and further questions; and then harvest or collect discoveries and share them with the larger group. For more details, see www.theworldcafe.com.[5]

Co-presencing: Retreat and Reflect, Allow the Inner Knowing to Emerge

After deeply immersing yourself in the contexts and places of most potential, the next movement focuses on accessing a deeper source of knowing: connecting to the future that wants to emerge through you (co-presencing).

9. **Letting go: Let go of your old self and "stuff" that must die.** The biggest obstacle to moving through the U comes from within: it emerges from your *resistance* (individually and collectively). Dealing with resistance is essential when you move down the left side of the U. Don't be surprised when your resistance shows up again and again. It happens to everyone. But as you become a pro, you know in advance that it will pop up at certain stages and that your job is to be prepared to meet and deal with it through calmness, appreciation, and focus. Moving down the U invites you to *suspend* your Voice of Judgment, VOJ, *reverse* your cynical view of a

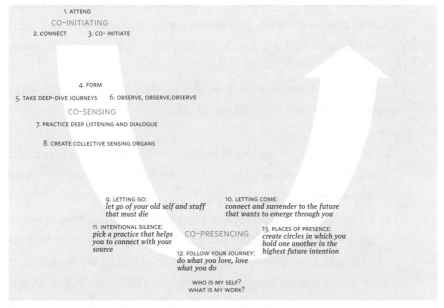

FIGURE 21.4 THE THIRD MOVEMENT: CO-PRESENCING

situation, VOC, and *overcome your fear*, VOF, *of letting go* of your old self—that part of you that must die in order for the new to take shape. Dealing with these three forms of resistance requires—to use the classical language of virtue—commitment to truth (living with an open mind), to love (living with an open heart), and to courage (living with an open will).

Example: The letting-go principle is about letting go of everything that isn't essential. Alan Webber recalled what kept him going on his journey to co-create *Fast Company* despite all the obstacles he encountered: "People who have genuinely been taken over by an idea or a belief usually can't answer the question 'Why are you doing this?' in rational terms. Years ago my father bought me a collection of interviews of great fiction writers. The interviewer was George Plimpton. He'd say, 'Why did you become a writer? Why do you get up in the morning and write?' The answer invariably was 'Well, I can't not.'

"People would ask me 'Why are you doing *Fast Company*?' At first, the answer was very rational: 'Well, you know, it's a magazine about this and that, and the world doesn't have one.' But I soon realized that those reasons weren't the real ones. The reason you do it is because *you can't not do it*. But it's hard to explain that to people without sounding like a lunatic."[6]

Practice: Go through the following four-step meditation (by way of reflective journaling or visual imagination):

1. What in your life and work are the situations, practices, and activities that connect you most with your best sources of energy and inspiration?
2. Consider these activities and situations as small seeds and building blocks of the future: what might a possible future look like in which these small seeds and building blocks are interconnected and grow into an inspiring whole that resonates with your best energies?
3. If you were to take this on, to bring that future into the world, what do you need to let go of? What is the old "stuff" that must die?

4. If you took the risk and your project failed—what would be the worst case, and would you be ready to face it?

Courage comes from the willingness to "die," to go forth into an unknown territory that begins to manifest only after you dare to step into that void. That is the essence of leadership.

10. **Letting come: Connect and surrender to the future that wants to emerge through you.** The most important leadership tool is the leader's *Self*—*your* Self. At the foundation of this principle—and at the foundation of the whole presencing approach—lies this simple assumption: every human being is not one but two. One is the person who we have become through the journey of the past. The other one is the dormant being of the future we *could become* through our forward journey. Who we become will depend on the choices we make and the actions we take now. That being of the future is our highest or best future possibility. Both these beings are real in the sense that each one constitutes a specific body of resonance— the field of the past and the field of the future. I can evoke an active resonance with either field. Usually these two fields of resonance—and the different dimensions of our evolving self that they represent—are poles apart. The essence of presencing is to get these two selves, these two beings, *to talk and listen to each other*, to resonate, both individually and collectively.

Example: The authentic self can be experienced each time you engage in a deep generative conversation that enters the fourth field of emergence. When you finish such a conversation, you leave it as someone different from the person you were when you entered it a few hours earlier: you leave that conversation closer to your real, your authentic Self.

Practice: Such an experience could be likened to a germinating seed. Just as a seed needs a nurturing place and loving attention to germinate and grow, this inner seed also needs a sustained nurturing place and loving attention in order to evolve to its highest potential.

Thus, the question is how to create such places in our everyday life. One approach is simply to always attend to the deeper social field from which a situation arises when two or more people connect. Try to be acutely attentive to the deeper dimensions of presence and self, and *hold* the field so that the deeper flow can be sustained.

In addition, three practical leverage points can help to sustain the capacity to access the bottom of the U. These are explained in Principles 11 to 13.

11. **Intentional silence: Pick a practice that helps you to connect with your source.** The currency that counts at the bottom of the U is not ideas, words, or insights. Here, you must use a different currency: practice. Practice is what we do every day. Thus this principle is about picking a personal practice that will help you connect to your future resonance.

Example 1: In conducting interviews with 150 thinkers and practitioners of innovation and leadership, I realized that many of those who impressed me most seem to be doing a similar thing: they all practice something in their everyday lives that helps them access their best source of creativity and self. For example, many rise early in order to use the silence of the early morning hours to connect to their own purpose or essential self. Some use the evening. Some, midday. What people do, when they do it, and for how long differs widely. Some people seek the silence of nature. Some people meditate. Others pray. Some people practice an exercise that gives them energy and control, such as *qi gong* or yoga. Some simply drop into a space of silence that helps them to reconnect to their sense of purpose. Many people practice a combination of the things mentioned here. Whatever the activity, the principle is the same: that sometime during the course of the day you create for yourself a place of deep reflection and silence that helps you to connect with that what is most essential (for you).

Practice 1: The morning practice can be likened to the moment after the last note of a symphony and before the applause begins. At that moment your whole being is resonating with the music. Likewise, when you wake up, your whole being is still resonating with the tacit music of the night's deep sleep. Alarm clocks occasionally destroy (or disturb) this precious time space. The trick is not to lose it right away. You start developing that capacity by listening, by paying attention to the "music of that moment" so that it resonates throughout the day.

Morning Practice (an example: 10–30 minutes)

- Rise early (before others do), go to a place of silence that works for you (a place in nature is great, but you also may find other places that work for you), and allow your inner knowing to emerge.
- Use a ritual that connects you with your source: this can be a meditation, prayer, or simply an intentional silence that you enter into with an open heart and open mind
- Remember what it is that has brought you to the place in life where you are right now: Who is your Self? What is your Work? What are you here for?
- Make a commitment to what it is that you want to be in service of. Focus on the outcome that you want to serve (the larger whole).
- Focus on what you want to accomplish (or be in service of) on this day that you are beginning right now.
- Feel the appreciation that you are given the opportunity to live the life that you have right now. Empathize with all of those who have never had all of the opportunities that led you to the place you are now. Feel the responsibility that comes with those opportunities, the responsibility that you have to others, to all other beings, to all of nature—even to the universe.
- Ask for help so that you don't lose your way or get sidetracked. Your way forward is a journey that only you can discover. The essence of that journey is a gift that can come into the world only

through you, your presence, your best future self. But you can't do it alone. That's why you ask for help.

I have found a few things that help me. Once I took a two-week course in awareness training with John Milton, a pioneering ecologist, educator, and meditation master who founded the Way of Nature Fellowship and Sacred Passage. Over the years, he has distilled a twelve-principle practice from his many years of solo time in the wilderness and combined that with what he has learned in deep training across multiple wisdom traditions. Part of the training he offers is a seven-day solo retreat in a special spot in nature. I found that week of silence, fasting, and meditation helped me to sustain and deepen my daily practice. It also helps one to forgive small failures. Like most people, I have often started a practice and failed to keep it up, ending up feeling bad and blaming myself (enacting my VOJ). Only years later did I realize how dysfunctional such a pattern was. The trick is to pay attention to the small things that you *do* accomplish and to correct your course instantly when you deviate from it—that's where the energy needs to go, not into the blame game. It is also useful to have a partner with a similar (or a different but consistent) practice. Finally, the busier your life is, the more mileage you may get out of even shorter periods of intentional silence. If you really can't afford more than ten minutes a day without violating your core commitments to the other people in your life, these ten minutes can have the same positive impact that thirty to sixty minutes would have for those with a more flexible schedule.

In short, this practice is the opposite of waking up and turning on the radio, computer, or television. Clicking on an outside stimulus during one's first waking hour kills the inner space of silence that the practice described here is supposed to cultivate. (I used to turn on the radio as soon as I woke up.) Regardless of our profession—manager, physician, farmer, educator, inventor, entrepreneur, venture capitalist, architect, artist, or parent—after that first hour of the day, most of us face the same situation: chaos, change, and unexpected challenges. It's a part of living in this century. The question is how to deal with it. Panic? Freak out? Get defensive? Or would it be better to meet the events of the day from a different kind of place, from the field of the future that you want to create? Grounding oneself in that field of the emerging future is what the morning practice is about.

While we have many good examples for using silence in individual cultivation practices, we have far fewer good examples of situating intentional silence in collective work settings. Yet, going forward, the development and refinement of practicing collective silence will prove to be one of the most important leverage points for future leadership work. The example and practice below are first steps into that territory.

Example 2: A core team that was charged with the task to develop a new business strategy for the procurement group in a global car company had just completed their learning journey. They did not have the time or resources to go on a long retreat in nature, so they went to a golf resort near Detroit for a three-day workshop during which they engaged in six hours of silence. Having completed the debriefing and sense making from their various learning journeys on the first day, they entered a group meditation and dialogue conversation on possible futures for them as persons and for them as a team and organization. The next morning, after a joint intention setting, they moved into a six-hour period of silence in which the participants simply took a walk across the beautiful nature retreat area. "These six hours," says Peter Brunner, who coached the team through this process, "became a breakthrough experience for the group. When they reconvened, they together easily defined the core elements for a new vision that later led to a new strategy definition. As a result their complete purchase volume today is done by reducing the number of vendors by 80 percent."

Example 3: When the global ELIAS group met near Shanghai after their deep immersion learning journeys in small groups, each team arrived with some key stories and with numerous artifacts gathered along the way. The presencing retreat session took in this case four days. The first day was focused on sharing everything that was learned throughout the learning journey. The second day focused on moving into the space of silence. The group spent five hours in silence. Before and after that silent period we met in a circle where each shared what came up for him or her before or during the learning journey or the period of silence. The third and fourth days focused on crystallizing prototyping initiatives and action planning for taking these initiatives forward. Throughout, we worked with various types of reflective and contemplative practices (starting with 7:00 a.m. sunrise seminars) to increase awareness and attention to one's life's and work's journey. The middle day with the five- hour period of silence and the dialogue circle before and after, turned out to be a real turning point for many in the group, both in terms of their individual leadership journey as well as in terms of the journey that the ELIAS group had taken collectively.

Example 4: The retreat workshop functions as a space of reflection and contemplation that allows participants to tie together various loose ends from their learning journeys and prototyping ideas. For example, when I facilitated the presencing workshop of the global car company project team, it turned out that a learning journey visit with traditional Chinese medicine experts in Cambridge sparked some further interest in the whole group. As most members of the group joined an optional 6:00 a.m. *qi gong* session with Chinese residents in a nearby park, it was not a surprise that one group developed a prototyping idea that focused on creating a dream state for the car. They speculated that just as human beings have different states of awareness—waking, dreaming, dreamless sleep—the same could apply to vehicles. The car might run through certain stages of self-analysis and self-repair, just as the human body does during the stages of sleep. At the conclusion of the workshop, the sponsors chose this initiative as one of the two most promising and selected it to be prototyped in the next stage of the U cycle.

Practice 2: Running a presencing retreat workshop. The flow of a retreat workshop follows the U: sharing key insights and ideas from the deep-dive journeys; moving into the space of silence; crystallizing ideas for prototyping initiatives and action planning.

The location of the presencing workshop must be carefully selected and prepared: physically and logistically, mentally and emotionally, and intentionally and spiritually. It cannot be an office. It should be a remote space with a centered and focused energy, with windows on two (or three) sides and access to nature for extended (if possible overnight) solo retreats, and it should be spacious enough for the whole team to live and work there more or less nonstop for a full week. A presencing workshop, if conducted in the right way, always is a deep personal and collective experience that touches and profoundly resonates with the whole being. The facilitators throughout that week need to be in full awareness of the deeper change that this process activates. They need to hold the space and align their intention with fully serving the highest future possibility of that group or the community that is going through that eye-of-the-needle process.

12. **Follow your journey: Do what you love, love what you do.** For many people, the gateway to accessing the deeper sources of knowing involves a deep dive into the essence of their work. Michael Ray of Stanford University frames this principle as "Do what you love, love what you do." His motto captures what I have heard many successful creators and innovators say: In order to access your best creative potential, you have to go on a journey—a journey in which you follow your bliss, your feeling, your felt sense of the emerging future. You trust that sense more than all the good advice you get from other people, which may also be valuable. But at the end of the day, the essence of your creativity is about accessing a *deeper source* that is unique to you, your life, your future. To unlock that deeper source, you need to take a journey through the eye of a needle—and that eye of the needle is your Self—it is your capacity to access the uniqueness of *your* journey *now*.

Example 1: Joseph Campbell described this journey as a call to adventure, crossing the threshold, following the road of trials, making the supreme encounter, and returning with a gift. It is the Grail quest. Whatever we choose to call it, it is our underlying developmental path of accessing the full power of our own creativity, which is dormant in every human being in different ways. Unlocking it requires going on a deeper type of journey than most of us travel. It is where we follow *our own* path.

Example 2: When I was completing my Ph.D. thesis, I received some good job offers, but none really grabbed my heart. What spoke to my inner self was the idea of leaving Europe and joining the MIT Learning Center in Boston. Not having any connections there, I simply applied to do that. No one responded. Then I called. They said they needed to discuss whether to invite me for an interview. No one called back. I called again. Then someone said, "Oh yes, come interview with all the principal researchers at the Center." I had to borrow money for a plane ticket to the United States. At the end of my last interview, Bill Isaacs, the founder of the MIT Dialogue Project, explained that MIT had a hiring freeze in effect and that the only possible position would be that of a visiting scholar (without compensation). "Can you provide your own funding?" Bill asked. "Sure, I can," I heard myself responding, knowing that the door that I felt was open a crack might close again in an instant. Then he asked whether I could start September 1. Although I knew I couldn't finish my thesis by then, I heard myself say, "Sure, not a problem." And sure enough, the first week of September I started my postdoc project at MIT, working on that during the day while completing my thesis at night and living happily on maxed-out credit cards. Only years later did I realize that the project that first took me out of my funding crisis, the global dialogue interview project, would have never happened if I had started with a "real job" at MIT. And that project, as mentioned earlier, was probably the best thing that ever happened to me in my entire professional life.

Example 3: Another time I chose to follow my inner instincts, rather than the unwritten rules of conduct, was when I applied to the founding class of Germany's first private university, Witten/Herdecke. Getting my education in the founding class of the Management School at that university was, in retrospect, an invaluable formative experience. However, when I applied to the university, I was turned down. I remember how shocked I was when I read the rejection letter because I had felt such a strong sense of my emerging future related to that university. I felt that I was losing my way. My life was going in the wrong direction. So after a day of deep depression, I called the university admission office and asked why I had been turned down. Because, they said, I hadn't completed the requisite amount of in-company work. That same night I wrote a letter to the dean of the Management School, Professor Ekkehard Kappler. I told him about my experience in formal (company) and informal (social movement) systems, as well as about other work experiences (on the family farm). I also told him what initiatives I would launch as a student if they would admit me to the first class. I wrote the letter because I had to do something (not because I thought I could change the school's decision—I knew that my chances were less than slim). The next morning I mailed the letter, and the following day Dean Ekkehard Kappler called. I almost fell off my chair. He said, "Okay, if you can satisfactorily complete the two missing months of company experience in a textile company in western Germany, we will invite you to join the founding class of the school. Can you start that job next Monday?" "Sure, not a problem," I heard myself responding. "Okay, let's do it," the dean said and hung up. I looked at my watch: Friday, 4:00 p.m. Two more hours to get into the city and buy a suit to wear on Monday morning. When I hung up, I knew that this one-minute conversation with Ekkehard Kappler had put my life back on track. It may sound strange, but that was my felt-sense—then as well as now.

Practice: As always, much of the credit should be given to one's parents. My parents never gave their children money for work and always encouraged us to follow our inner motivations rather than the promise of exterior rewards. We had to figure out what we wanted to do and were encouraged to follow that path. By contrast, much of today's environment for kids is focused on dragging them through back-to-back activities (that others organize for them) and socializing them to a system that rewards "good behavior." This poisons their capacity to act from an inner source, to act out of intrinsic motivation and love.

The road to accessing one's creativity includes the stages of (1) nothing much happening, (2) boredom, and then (3) noticing and responding to an inner impulse that evolves within yourself. It is difficult to learn how to do these things when you are managed by a tight system of exterior activities, rewards, and controls.

The same goes for companies: much of corporate motivational and reward system is probably more dysfunctional than helpful because it imposes a culture of reward-driven behavior rather than a culture of doing the right things *because* they are right. So the practice here is about creating environments that allow people to do what they love and love what they do. Both things are important. Love what you do; fully appreciate what life offers you. Do what you do with love—and you will be amazed what life gives back.

13. **Circles of Presence: Create circles in which you hold one another in the highest future intention.** There is an invisible movement going on in the world. It's a movement that is manifest in a variety of forms and practices. These practices rest on the same underlying principle: to form a safe collective holding space in which the participants support one another in making sense of and advancing their life and work journeys. It's not actually new, for it's what the bond of real friendship has always offered. But it's more vigorous and vital today than ever, because our social norms and structures are disintegrating and dissipating left and right. As the world turns into "a burning platform" (referring back to my German farm home experience) we also need to somehow progress with the ordinary business of life. In the midst of chaos and breakdown, we must develop the ability to stay calm and discern the path forward—even when that path seems ill

defined and fragile. Developing the capacity to operate from the nothing-ness of the now, the ability to discern and take the next step in situations where old structures have broken down and new structures haven't yet emerged is perhaps the most important core capacity of navigating work and life in this century.

Example: The most advanced example of this that I know of is the Circle of Seven (see the detailed description in Chapters 10 and 11).[7] That circle of women has cultivated the practices of deep listening and presence over many years. The result has been a collective field of presence that can be activated during circle meetings as well as out-side them, a field that functions as a gateway to deeper professional and personal presence and proficiency.

Practice: Having seen how some of my student and executive groups succeed and fail with this concept, I offer the following notes on place, people, purpose, and process for use in exploring this prin-ciple with your own group.

Place: Form this circle in a meeting space that is hospitable and yet cocoonlike and provides a sense of intimacy away from exterior dis-ruptions. Apply all the well-known criteria of good meeting spaces: spaciousness, natural light, windows on at least two sides of the room, simplicity, beauty. Introduce whatever makes the place feel alive, whatever makes you feel at home

People: A group of five or six people is probably ideal, although sometimes a "group" of two can also work. It's not necessary (or even helpful) for this circle to be limited to your established (old) friends. What matters most is that you personally feel some bond or (possible future) connection. The group should consist of people who are interested in regularly exploring some of the deeper issues of their personal and professional journeys and how they relate to organizational and societal transformation—people who share this interest because of a *deeply felt need* to pursue this deeper inquiry, not just out of purely intellectual curiosity. You want people who are willing to put themselves on the line, not those who would limit their role to sitting in the audience to criticize others. You want people who may be connected to your future journey; you don't want to get stuck in the mud of past karma (although sometimes you need to work through some of that to uncover the deeper common ground).

Purpose: As you pull your first meeting together, uncover a common intention that is larger than yourself. Create or discover a purpose that connects the being of your circle to the larger global field that you and the members of your circle feel a part of. Connect the presence of the circle to serving the larger whole: the Circle Being, as the Circle of Seven describes it.

Process: Develop a process that works for you and your group. As the circle evolves, that process is likely to change. Yet you may want to consider some basic building blocks such as inviting intentional silence, using a personal check-in, holding a speaking object for as long as you talk, story sharing about the golden thread in one's life's journey, cultivating deep listening, and developing the personal courage to raise issues and discuss challenges that are current and require real trust to be shared.

Co-creating: Prototype a Small Microcosm of the New in Order to Explore the Future by Doing.

The movement of co-creating focuses on putting ideas onto their feet by prototyping microcosms of the future that you want to create—and by fast-cycle learning that constantly iterates the existing prototype based on the feedback from all key stakeholders.

14. **The Power of Intention: Connect to the future that stays in need of you— crystallize your vision and intent.** The philosopher Martin Buber made the distinction between two types of will: the small will, or one's instincts, and the Grand Will, which is the future that needs us to come into reality. There is something deeply magical about tapping into our deeper creative

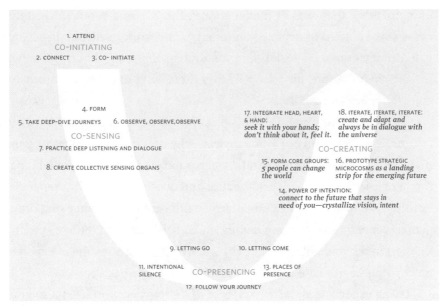

FIGURE 21.5 THE FOURTH MOVEMENT: CO-CREATING

force. It has to do with a different kind of energy economics. It's not the sort of neoclassic economics that you learn in school. It's a creative or spiritual economics that describes a quality of energy dynamics that highly creative people and high-performing teams are able to activate and thrive on. It functions on a simple principle: *If you give all you have and all you are to your essential project, everything will be given to you.* But notice the sequence: first you have to give everything away, and only *then* will everything you need be given to you—maybe. That's a different kind of economics. It has nothing to do with exchange value. What it describes is a gift economy: the more you give, the more amplified you get. But it works only if you fully let go of what you give without the certainty of getting anything in return. This kind of creative or spiritual economics is at the heart of every profound innovation in science, business, and society.

The spiritual energy economics at issue here can be summarized in a simple equation: $E = D\,m$. Personal energy (E) is a function of making a difference (D) in something that matters to me (m).

If your work doesn't make a difference, that's a problem. Or if you work on something that doesn't matter to you, that's also a problem. In those cases you will tend to deplete your energy. The work itself won't recharge you. But if you make a real difference, doing something that truly matters to you, then you are on a loop of ever-increasing energy: the more you give, the more you get back.

The practical bottom line of this equation: If we are going to spend a lot of time and energy on our work anyway, why not focus on something that matters? By contrast, many of our systems today are designed around paying people for work that doesn't matter and doesn't make a difference. For example, we have an institutionalized health care bureaucracy that drains people's energy, makes them depressed and sick, and encourages them to fill their inner void with material things, which in turn results in exponentially rising health care costs and environmental degradation.

Having experienced the dynamics of this energy economics, I also know how easy it is to lose it. Just because you have it today doesn't mean you will have it tomorrow. So what does it take to make it last? What practices would help people reconnect to that deeper source and flow? Here are two that I have found to be helpful: practicing creative tension and prioritizing.

Practice 1: Creative tension exercise: This practice was devised by Peter Senge and Robert Fritz, composer, filmmaker and organizational consultant. In its classical form, it works as a meditation in three steps: First ask (1) What do I want to create? and (2) What does the current reality look like by contrast? Then (3) Picture both images together (e.g., as a split screen) and note the creative tension between them.

This practice is an excellent tool to use as you start up the right-hand side of the U (crystallizing). I have found it useful to modify this exercise slightly in the U context this way: during the first step, focus on your future state in your journey. During the second step, do not only concentrate on how the current reality differs from your desired future, but try to figure out where in today's reality you find the *seed elements of the future*. Then, in the third step, picture the creative tension in a three-dimensional space. Move between the poles. Go into the seed elements (with your mind and heart) and evolve with them toward the desired future state, and return from there to current reality, and so forth . Many practitioners use this exercise successfully.

Practice 2: Setting priorities and managing time: What is the larger project that I am here for? How can I create conditions that will allow me to focus on and serve it? And how can I prioritize my time so that it is spent on projects and outcomes that matter, rather than on reacting to issues that do not? This practice is all about using the different qualities of the day, week, and year in a more intentional way.[8] First thing in the morning, ask yourself: "What are the one or two most important things for me to do today? How am I going to use the best quality time of the day?" The underlying principle here is that *energy follows attention*. This means that the biggest leverage we have is what we pay attention to and how we attend to a situation.

The flipside of course is the question, What do we ignore and where do we accept a delayed response time? In the age of instant communication technologies it is important to remember that any kind of real time management will translate into *not* responding right away to a whole bunch of people. Spending your most valuable time making sure that you always respond to all people right away suggests that your method of managing time (and filtering noise) doesn't work. Hence, you are likely to get stuck in reactive patterns of behavior.

Energy follows attention: so what matters is to create quality spaces for those activities that matter most, that directly link to our felt purpose—particularly if these activities happen to be important but not urgent.[9]

15. **Form core groups: Five people can change the world.** Whenever you look behind the scenes of stories about successful and inspiring projects, regardless of size, you will find a key person or a smal core of people who are deeply and fully committed to the purpose and outcome of the project. That committed core group then goes out into the world and creates an energy field that begins to attract people, opportunities, and resources that

make things happen; then momentum builds. The core group functions as a vehicle for the whole to manifest.

Example: In an interview, Nick Hanauer summarized his experiences founding half a dozen highly successful companies: "One of my favorite sayings, attributed to Margaret Mead, has always been 'Never doubt that a small group of committed citizens can change the world. Indeed, it's the only thing that ever has.' I totally believe it. You could do almost anything with just five people. With only one person, it's hard—but when you put that one person with four or five more, you have a force to contend with. All of a sudden, you have enough momentum to make almost anything that's immanent, or within reach, actually real."

Like Hanauer, I have also seen that five or six people can accomplish amazing things, sometimes almost effortlessly. When this happens, you become part of a much bigger stream of emergence and energy. "Effortless," of course, doesn't mean that there is no work involved. But it is work that flows. Progress happens only if you make a huge commitment (to avoid the term *sacrifice*): you basically have to give everything you have. That's not something that people like to talk about because it often means putting the work ahead of other people. How to reconcile these two aspects—work and life—will remain a constant tension.

Practice: Ask yourself these questions: Who in my current life and work are the four or five people with whom, when connected in the right way, I could change the world? What do I need to do to really connect to them? What obstacles or barriers do I need to remove in order for this core group to function more effectively? Once you do that, you realize that much of the other "B.S." just fades away.

16. Prototype strategic microcosms as a landing strip for the emerging future.
A prototype is an experiential microcosm of the future that you want to create. Prototyping means to present your idea (or work in progress) before it is fully developed. The purpose of prototyping is to generate feed-

back from all stakeholders (about how it looks, how it feels, how it connects with people's intentions, interpretations, and identities) in order to refine the assumptions about the project. The focus is on exploring the future by doing rather than by analyzing. As the folks at IDEO have put it, as we read in Chapter 13, the rationale of prototyping is "to fail often to succeed sooner" or to "fail early to learn quickly." Prototyping is not a pilot project. A pilot has to be a success; by contrast, a prototype focuses on maximizing learning.

The key idea in prototyping strategic microcosms is to create a landing strip for the future. A strategic microcosm is a small version of the future that you want to create that includes all core elements of your vision. It requires you to have the confidence to move into action before you have figured out the entire plan forward. You have to trust your capacity to improvise and to connect to the right places and communities, and through them to the right individual people. The process of prototyping strategic microcosms itself is a mini U that starts with clarifying intention, forming a task team; taking deep dives to connect to and engage with other practitioners, partners, and places that matter; returning and sharing everything that has been learned; reflecting and listening to the inner source of inspiration and knowing; jointly crystallizing the immediate next step; and then going back to involve other players in the practical next steps forward.

The trick is to move through the U not once but many times, maybe even daily. Establish a team practice of beginning the day jointly (if possible with the use of intentional silence) by checking in on overnight insights and reviewing and adapting the agenda for the day; then go out and do it and reconvene in the evening to share what has been learned. Process it overnight, wake up with a new idea, and do it all again. The key is not to overplan and overschedule the prototyping. You must be able to go with what emerges from the process. That said, you also need to have some tough milestones for progress review and stakeholder feedback; these will help you stay focused and provide useful input.

What differentiates social innovations from product innovations is usually three things. First, with social innovations we need to pay more attention to the context in which some of the innovations may already exist. Second, we need to be mindful that social innovation always deals with human life; the "fail early to learn quickly" principle must be situated in a fast-cycle learning process that almost allows you to correct mistakes before you make them. And third, we need to deal with a deeper layer of social and emerging complexity that involves letting go of old identities and letting new ones come (by going through the bottom of the U). Particularly in situations of massive direct, structural, and cultural violence that has been inflicted on certain communities over several centuries (and there are plenty of these places across the continents), going down the U involves a kind of healing of massive wounds that have been inflicted on the collective body. (A good example is the work of the South African Truth and Reconciliation Commission.) That healing of the collective social body will be one of the central activities of such a process. It's not just a sidelight of project work. It's the real thing. And everything else is the context for the healing to take place.

Example (of prototyping in a corporate context): At Cisco Systems, the world leader in networking equipment, the prototyping imperative begins with what that company calls principle 0.8: regardless of how long term the project, engineers are expected to come up with a first prototype within three or four months—otherwise the project is dead. The first prototype is not expected to work like a 1.0 prototype—it is a quick-and-dirty iteration that generates feedback from all key stakeholders and leads to the 1.0 version.

Practice: To create a strategic microcosm requires you to focus on three areas: players, project, and infrastructure. Here is a checklist for each item.

Convening the players: A strategic microcosm connects key players across boundaries who need one another in order to take their system into the best future way of operating. For a microcosm constellation to be productive, it usually needs five types of practitioners: (1) practitioners who are accountable for results (problem owners, such as the CEO of the hospital); (2) practitioners on the front line who know the real problems first hand (e.g., physicians); (3) people at the bottom of the system who normally have no voice and no say about how others spend their money and who bring a different view and focus that can help to reframe the overall issue (e.g., patients or citizens); (4) people outside the system who can offer a view or a competence critical to the success of the project (creative outsiders); and (5) one or a few activists who are wholly committed to making the project work (who have the right heart and who are willing to give their lives to make it work).

Another view of these five categories is to determine who should *not* be involved: you don't want 90 percent "experts" (who tend to be the world champions in downloading—exceptions confirm this rule); you don't want people who are only interested in defending the status quo—in short, you don't want people who, when they use the word "change," mean that only *other people* need to change. You want to link and convene players who have the networks, knowledge, power, and intention to co-create change across boundaries for the benefit of the whole. And you want to keep the group small enough to get the work done. Larger groups may need to set up subgroups in order to work efficiently. As a rule of thumb, the more comprehensive the representation of all current stakeholders, the slower the process. The more selective the microcosm, the faster you can move to rapid-cycle prototyping. In the business of innovation, it is a mistake to involve everyone and his uncle before you move into action.

Comprehensive representation of the status quo can quickly turn into an enemy of innovation. Innovation is based on the courage to act on the basis of selected data and players. The trick is to select correctly. In social innovation we of course have to be much more inclusive. But still the same principle applies: you want to focus on the stakeholders in the system that is about to be born; you don't want to simply reproduce another gathering of special-interest-group-driven stakeholder interaction.

Selecting the project: Here are seven questions to ask as you select and evolve an idea for prototyping.

1. Is it relevant—does it matter to the stakeholders involved? Select a problem or an opportunity that is relevant individually (for the persons involved), institutionally (for the organizations involved), and socially (for the communities involved).

2. Is it revolutionary—is it new? Could it change the game?

3. Is it rapid—can you do it quickly? You must be able to develop experiments right away, in order to have enough time to get feedback and adapt (and thus avoid analysis paralysis).

4. Is it rough—can you do it on a small scale? Can you do it at the lowest possible resolution that allows for meaningful experimentation? Can you do it locally? Let the local context teach you how to get it right. Trust that the right helpers and collaborators will show up when you issue the right kinds of invitations.

5. Is it right—can you see the whole in the microcosm that you focus on? Get the dimensions of the problem or project definition right. In a prototype you put the spotlight on a few selected details. Select the right ones. For example, when doing the patient-physician study we didn't focus on all the stakeholders. We started with two: patients and their physicians. You have to be courageous in making these choices, and you have to be right—right in the sense that you clearly see the core axis or core issue of the system. Ignoring the patients in a health study, the consumers in a sustainable food project, or the students in a school project (just to name a few examples that I have encountered recently) misses the point.

6. Is it relationally effective—does it leverage the strengths, competencies and possibilities of the existing networks and communities at hand?

7. Is it replicable—can you scale it? Any innovation in business or society hinges upon its replicability, whether or not it can

grow to scale. In the context of prototyping, this criterion favors approaches that activate local participation and ownership and excludes those that depend on massive infusions of external knowledge, capital, and ownership.

Creating the infrastructure: Prototyping teams need different types of help: (1) a place (a cocoon) that helps the team focus on its creative work with minimal distraction; (2) a timeline with strict milestones that forces the team to produce preliminary prototypes early on and generates fast-cycle feedback from all key stakeholders; (3) content help and expertise at important junctures and process help that enables the team to go through the U cycle of rapid experimentation and adaptation every day (after-action reviews); and (4) regular prototyping clinics in which to present the prototypes and to benefit from peer coaching that focuses on the key challenges of the way forward.

17. **Integrate head, heart, and hand: Seek it with your hands; don't think about it, feel it.** As the master coach puts it in the novel and 2000 movie *Bagger Vance* when helping a golfer who has lost his swing: "Seek it with your hands—don't think about it, feel it. The wisdom in your hands is greater than the wisdom of your head will ever be." That piece of advice articulates a key principle about how to operate on the right-hand side of the U. Moving down the left-hand side of the U is about opening up and dealing with the resistance of thought, emotion, and will; moving up the right-hand side is about intentionally reintegrating the intelligence of the head, the heart, and the hand in the context of practical applications.

Just as the inner enemies on the way down the U deal with the VOJ (Voice of Judgment), VOC (Voice of Cynicism), and VOF (Voice of Fear), the enemies on the way up the U are the three old ways of operating: executing without improvisation and mindfulness (blind actionism); endless reflection without a will to act (analysis paralysis); and talking, talking without a connection to source and action (blah-blah-blah). The three enemies share the same structural feature: instead of balancing the intelligence of the head, heart, and hand, one of the three dominates (the head in endless reflection, the heart in endless networking, the will in mindless action).

In summary, the key virtue required on the right-hand side of the U is the practical integration of head, heart, and hands that prevents one's becoming frozen into one of the three one-sided ways of operating (mindless action, actionless mind, blah-blah-blah).

An interesting detail during this stage is that the sequence in which the new shows up in the human mind is contrary to conventional wisdom, as follows. (1) It usually begins with an unspecified emotion or feeling. (2) That feeling morphs to a sense of the *what*: the new insight or idea. (3) Then the *what* is related to a context, problem, or challenge where it could produce a breakthrough innovation (the *where*: the context). (4) Only then do you begin to develop a form in which the *what* and the *where* are framed by a rational structure and form of presentation (the *why*: rational reasoning). This sequence can be traced in almost any type of breakthrough innovation. The biggest mistake when dealing with innovation is to put the cart before the horse by first focusing on the rational mind. In order for a new insight to emerge, the other conditions must already exist.

In short, connecting to one's best future possibility and creating powerful breakthrough ideas requires learning to access the intelligence of the heart and the hand—not only the intelligence of the head. The rational mind is usually the *last* participant on the scene.

Example: The economist Brian Arthur told me he reached his most important scientific insight this way.[10] He was doing his thesis at Berkeley on a difficult math problem that several mathematicians had failed to crack. Arthur tried hard for many months, but, with no breakthrough imminent, he gave up. His adviser then suggested a less difficult problem, which he solved swiftly. Soon after completing his thesis, he was reading in the department library with no specific agenda when his mind suddenly apprehended an image. He could see it. But at first he couldn't fully recognize it. He could see what it was—a topographical presentation of a solution. He thought: Okay, that's the solution. But the solution to what? What's the problem that it belongs to? Then he realized that it was the solution to the mathematical problem he had given up on. At that point he was able to begin embodying the idea as a mathematical equation.

This story, of course, is a beautiful demonstration of the U: create the intention to solve a problem, dive into it, work like crazy, break the flow (stop), pay attention to the ideas that start to slip in through the back door of your mind; then develop and embody that idea.

Practice: Focus on what really matters. Work a lot. Take a shower. Get an illuminating idea. Dry yourself off and prototype the idea.

We all know this sequence. It has happened to most of us. What's important here is that all the elements work together. Just taking a shower won't get you anywhere if you haven't taken the two previous steps: focusing on what really matters and immersing yourself in the work. These two steps are necessary but not sufficient. Taking a shower means you break the flow by switching the context; you relax your body by sensing the water, you relax your mind by taking it out of the problem-solving mode; and finally you pay attention to what is coming through the back door of your mind (sheltering yourself from distractions).

Maybe half of why the shower is such a functional place for getting great ideas has to do with eliminating distractions: you can't watch TV (yet), you can't read a newspaper, and you can't talk on the phone as long as the water is pouring down on you. Accordingly, a practice that accesses this deeper source of intelligence would integrate four activities: (1) focusing (clarifying intention), (2) working a lot (immersing yourself in the task), (3) breaking the flow, switching context, relaxing, and paying attention to what emerges (shifting the locus of attention), (4) following the spark that begins to emerge, prototyping it quickly, and learning by doing (iterate, iterate, iterate). Which brings us to Principle 18.

18. Iterate, iterate, iterate: create, adapt, and always be in dialogue with the

universe. Don't get stuck with the initial form of your idea. Maybe that initial form was just to get you going. Always learn from the world and hone and iterate your idea from each interaction. The trick is to operate *as if* the world is a helpful place. For if you do, it actually is, and if you don't, it isn't.

Example: This principle has been effectively described and framed by Alan Webber, the co-founder of *Fast Company.* Says Webber, "The universe actually is a helpful place. If you're open in relation to your idea, the universe will help you. It wants to suggest ways for you to improve your idea. Now, that said, the universe sometimes offers suggestions that suck. Part of the adventure is listening to those ideas and suggestions and trying to make your own calculations about which ones are helpful and which ones are harmful. You don't want to be closed and say, 'No, this idea came from my mind fully hatched, and if we can't do it the way we've conceived it, I'm not going to do it at all.' On the other hand, if you listen to everybody else's suggestions, you go mad."[11]

Practice: Here is a practice that may help you connect to a larger perspective:

Step 1: Take three minutes at the end of each day to write down the suggestions the world has made to you during the day without judging them as good or bad.

Step 2: Write one or two core questions that follow from these observations and that relate to current challenges in your work.

Step 3: The next morning, take five or ten minutes to write down the ideas that come to mind regarding the core questions (and observations) you put on paper the night before. Go with the flow of writing when a stream of ideas comes through.

Step 4: Complete the "journaling" by exploring the possible next steps: What would it take to further investigate/test/prototype these possibilities?

This practice is a safe place to explore new or challenging ideas and will significantly increase your capacity to read weak signals and to evolve your concepts.

Co-evolving: Grow Innovation Ecosystems by Seeing and Acting from the Emerging Whole

In Figure 21.6 you can see the integration of all the U steps. Once the prototypes are reviewed and assessed by the various key stakeholders, the next movement focuses on piloting and evolving the new in the right kind of institutional ecosystem and supporting infrastructure. To date, we know about many episodes and stories of great transformational change and breakthrough. But at the end of day they remain merely that: *episodes.* Sooner or later the larger system snaps back into the old way of operating. The trans-

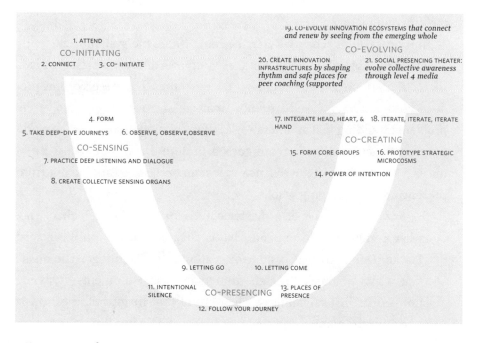

FIGURE 21.6 THE FIFTH MOVEMENT: CO-EVOLVING

formational episodes almost never spread the (positive) "virus" like a wildfire across the remaining system. Why not?

I believe that it is mainly because of two things. One: we have not fully developed our ability to operate from the generative Field 4 of social emergence, both individually and collectively. Two: the institutional infrastructures that would bring together the constellations of players who need one another in order to transform the system are currently missing. The final, fifth movement of the U is about putting these infrastructures into place. To date, we are only beginning to figure out what it really takes. Principles 19 to 21 preview the front line of that territory. Welcome to exploring this territory of the future!

19. **Co-evolve innovation ecosystems that allow people to see and act from the emerging whole.** To deal with the enormous institutional challenges of our time, organizations and larger systems need to embrace and activate a fourth governance mechanism: seeing and operating from presencing the emerging whole.

In most systems today, we face the same issue: the system is currently governed by a blending of the three existing coordination mechanisms—markets, hierarchy, networking—yet the outcomes that these systems produce are insufficient. And we know that we are not going to solve the problem by adding just another overlay of regulation, market, or networking infrastructure. What's required is a profound innovation that introduces a fourth type of governance mechanism: seeing, and acting from presencing the emerging whole.

Example 1: Think of a master conductor like Zubin Mehta, who, when conducting, focuses on what is *about to emerge* from his soloist Plácido Domingo. The conductor is at one with Domingo. The music that wants to break through from that special moment—from the now—rests in total stillness. Then out of that magic stillness, music bursts forth, manifesting the energy that is flowing through Plácido, Mehta, and the whole field surrounding them. It is as if the music continues to rise up through the ground, connecting everyone involved in this creative energy field: the soloist, the orchestra, the audience, the place, and the conductor, who in these moments seems to function as a *condu-it* (*condu*-ctor) for the creative energy of the field.

Example 2: Think of a master educator who looks at her student, who is at one with her and the presence of her highest future potential, and then acts very quickly in ways that help the student to progress on her journey of realizing that potential. Or think of a farmer who takes a walk in his field on Sunday and who uses that as a mechanism to establish a direct connection to the living presence of his fields and then tries to tune in to what that living ecosystem wants him to do next. Think of a physician who takes into account not only the technical-scientific aspects of her patient-physician relationships, but also the deeper mental, social, and spiritual layers of those relationships, connecting to the authentic presence of each patient's self, and then starts to act from that, trying to be in service of that authentic self. Think of leaders who, like Mahatma Gandhi or Nelson Mandela, have operated by connecting with a much larger collective field and who through their actions began operating from the presence of that collective field, serving as a vehicle for the best future possibility of that field to come into being.

All of these examples are performed by individuals. But the fundamental challenge of our time is to learn to do exactly the same thing: operate from the presence of the evolving whole—*collectively*, not just individually. Almost all of the major challenges of our time require us to operate this way. Yet we haven't yet learned how to do it.

Many leaders confronting difficult challenges realize that those challenges require new ways of operating, a Field 4 approach to organizing: seeing and operating from presencing the emerging whole (or ecosystem).

Example 3: Oxfam Great Britain (OGB) is a very influential global NGO. Structured as a confederation of thirteen organizations, Oxfam works with others to overcome poverty and suffering. Judith Flick is the regional director for OGB's southern African region (Angola,

Malawi, Mozambique, South Africa, Zambia, and Zimbabwe). When she took the job, the region was considered "dysfunctional," with low morale, low adherence to organizational standards, and an internal reputation for not getting the work done. During her first eighteen months on the job, Judith orchestrated the organizational part of the turnaround by systematically upgrading the systems while refocusing her staffs' energies on what had brought them to the organization: a desire to help alleviate poverty and suffering.

In her additional capacity as the organization's global lead on HIV/AIDS, she realized that the existing approaches to the problem were inappropriate and ineffective: "The HIV pandemic is—as the word says—an epidemic with a global spread and with worldwide consequences; it should be addressed through and as a worldwide system, but it is not." Continuing the old Oxfam programs no longer made sense with whole communities and even societies in the process of collapsing. It would have been like repairing the staircase of the World Trade Tower just moments before the whole building collapsed. Although the goals were noble, the processes were out of sync with the circumstances. Says Judith, "The pandemic is not only a health issue: it is an economic, social, and political issue; it needs a multidisciplinary approach, including technological solutions to the disease, social changes in people's behavior, new economical systems nationally and globally to decrease vulnerability and to increase access to health care, and true leadership that is accountable to a diverse group of citizens at local, national, and global levels. The pandemic cuts across all sectors: the civil service, corporate sector, and civil society; and the effect of the pandemic is different at each level; it needs an analysis and approach at each of these levels."

There is an extreme urgency, she says, because "according to the latest (2006) UNAIDS report more than 38 million people are infected by HIV, 2.8 million people are dying of AIDS yearly, in southern Africa alone 2,550 daily. The pandemic has created 15 million AIDS orphans so far; it has eroded community safety nets; it will absorb unrecoverable amounts of revenues of the most affected nations, while destroying their productive forces."

When your job confronts you with such a challenge, what should you do? Should you turn to traditional approaches, or should you stop, let the reality sink in, and come up with responses that do not replicate the patterns of the past?

Choosing to do the latter, Judith saw three immediate stakeholder issues. First, she had to encourage her staff to internalize the HIV/AIDS reality. She elaborated by drawing an analogy between the behavior of people living in "slow-onset emergencies" like the unfolding AIDS pandemic and that of a frog in boiling water. "If you put a frog into a pot of boiling water, it will jump out. If you slowly heat up the water with a frog in it, the frog will boil to death because it does not detect the gradual increase in temperature. We needed our staff to jump up to see the bigger picture, and they needed to realize that this is about each and every one of us."

Next, she had to empower her staff to propose responses that they believed would work, given the cataclysmic and long-lasting effects of the pandemic. They would have to stop downloading corporate models and instead propose responses that would make a real difference without being afraid of "stepping out of line." She did this by carefully listening to her staff and trusting them to "read" their reality.

Third, she needed to work with her boss and her boss's boss (the CEO) at the headquarters in the United Kingdom to make the wider organization respond more appropriately to the HIV challenge. This would require a strategic shift in fund-raising, resource allocation, campaigning, and program development. In effect, this meant that the organization would make HIV/AIDS part of its core portfolio. They also needed to bring the other members of the confederation and key stakeholders across other sectors on board.

While the first three items were difficult but doable, the last shift is proving to be the most challenging. To achieve this, the organization needs to quit organizing around standard processes and programs (Fields 1 to 2). Instead, it must organize around the ecosystem, or "whole," that it wants to address and transform (Fields 3 to 4).

That clearly is the challenge on the ground.

Whether it is doable is a different matter. But if it is, the only way of getting it done is by approaching it as a generative multistakeholder process (see the inner circle on the multistakeholder interaction map in Figure 19.2, page 337; there, the institutional power moves from the center of the organization to the emerging whole of the ecosystem).

Although Oxfam has always understood that poverty is a systems issue, it has not usually worked to change the ecosystem in a multistakeholder way. This has become imperative with HIV/AIDS, and the organization has recently started to experiment with this new approach.

Practice: Use the framework of Figure 19.2 to assess your current system: First, draw four circles; then identify each of the key stakeholders in your ecosystem outside the circles; in the circles themselves list the communication qualities of the key stakeholder relationships; notice which communication qualities (channels) are activated, and which ones are not. If possible, use this stakeholder communication assessment as a starting point for thinking together about how to move the system from the outer to the inner circles of communication and governance.

20. **Create innovation infrastructures by shaping safe places and rhythms for peer coaching (supported through social technology).** Innovation happens in specific places. Much has been written about innovation networks, but what gets lost in all the excitement about networks is that the creative process also relies on the opposite of networked sharing. Creative processes need a *cocoon*—a sheltered interior place for the collective—from which something new can emerge. Just as a seed needs a place and time to grow and a child needs a place and time to develop, innovation needs a place and time to evolve and come into being on its own schedule.

For several years, the Japanese management scholar Ikujiro Nonaka has focused on how to better understand the environment of successful knowledge-creating companies.[12] He argues that the power of place in organizations includes physical place, virtual place (the World Wide Web), social-mental place (shared context, trust), and a shared purpose and intention.[13]

In every developmental process these four aspects of place are foundational. For a seed to develop, it needs a physical place (soil), connectivity (water), nourishment (nutrients, sunlight), and an organizing presence (the farmer's field). A child's development requires the same four conditions: a physical place (home, school), connectivity (movement and touch), social nourishment (loving attention, friends, challenges), and the developmental space in which the Self can come into presence (formative field).

The same four conditions also apply to successful innovation in organizations. Innovations happen in a physical place. But most of the physical office space in organizations lacks any cultivation or intelligent design. Hence, its impact on the psyche of the workforce is depressing rather than uplifting and stimulating.

Example 1: A good example of creative workplace design is the space of IDEO, the international design company, which combines elements of design, technology, and creativity with an industrial-style functional and open layout; each team also has its own cocoon, which grows or shrinks according to the needs and requirements of the project it is working on.

Innovations often also need virtual space and connectivity, which of course rapidly evolves as new technologies come into the marketplace. Innovations also need a shared social space and context, which in the case of IDEO is created by a highly committed and focused core project team that is co-located in one or a very few places. And last, profound innovation requires a spiritual place—a sense of purpose for coming into being, which is often the inspiration and motivation for the core team.

While companies such as IDEO create a culture of innovation supported by all of the dimensions of place mentioned above, companies and organizations that are less innovation-centered may find it harder to do so. For those organizations the challenge is to innovate while at the same time running the organization efficiently. The leverage points for dealing with this challenge are *rhythm* and *place*: create a pattern of quality time and quality place that allows core groups of players to interweave efficiency and innovation.

Example 2: Ikujiro Nonaka describes the practice at Kao, a leading Japanese health consumer products company, where executives meet daily from 8:00 to 9:00 a.m. for conversation over a cup of tea. During these conversations they share success-critical context information informally; then they pass on the information to their management teams later in the day. In this case the rhythm is daily, and the place is an informal lounge that allows relaxed discussion. The result is that critical information is disseminated across the organization very quickly without keeping too many people away from their work or in meetings.

Practice 1: Close your eyes and imagine that your area of responsibility—your core team—is a living organism. What would that organism want you to do? What breathing rhythm would be appropriate for the group of key players? Would it be the daily rhythm used at Kao? Would it be weekly, monthly, or quarterly, or some combination of the above? Once you have identified the appropriate rhythm, where should it take place? And what processes and structures do you want to put into place that would make the most of cross-team peer coaching and consultation?

Once you have answered these questions for your core team, try to answer the same questions for the extended network of stakeholders and players that matter most to the future of your project or organization: What is the best way to convene this constellation of players in order to cultivate the presence of the collective field among them?

What rhythm, context, and place will be most helpful in developing this ecosystem?

Practice 2: Peer-coaching case clinics: Case clinics and peer coaching need a structure in order for teams to work together successfully. The structure below outlines one example.

Imagine you have 70 minutes per session and four persons per team. Here are some specific parameters you could use to construct your clinic.

1. Select a case giver and a timekeeper.
2. *10 minutes:* Intention statement by case giver: Situation/ Problem/Opportunity/Project = What do you want to address?
   - Current situation: What are the symptoms of the current difficulties/issues?
   - What are my personal development edges in this?
   - My intention: What would I like to see? What do I want to create?
   - Help = Where do I need input and help?
   - Consultants ask clarifying questions if necessary.
3. *5 minutes:* Consultants suspend their urge to give instant advice. Instead, they enter a brief moment of silence, and then each reflects back to the case giver:
   - What images does the case bring to mind?
   - What feelings and emotions do I sense?
   - What questions come up for me related to that?
4. *40 minutes:* Reaction by case giver + generative dialogue by all.
   - Coaches ask questions to deepen understanding.
   - Conversation to brainstorm solutions.
5. *10 minutes:* Recommendations by consultants:
   - What is the key issue to be addressed? [diagnosis]
   - What solution/action do I propose?
6. *3 minutes:* Concluding remarks by case giver:
   - What new insights/answers do the solutions offer to me?

- How could I use/combine these ideas going forward?
- What are my next steps?
- Thank you!

7. *2 minutes:* Journaling: Key takeaways (all).

21. **Social Presencing Theater: Evolve collective awareness through Field 4 media productions.** Mechanisms for leveraging a deep transformational experience in one part of the system so that other parts can jump-start and leapfrog their development are still missing from the infrastructure on a societal level. Although various mechanisms purport to do this, most of them belong to the category of downloading, reproducing patterns of the past. Ninety-plus percent of our media and media production is firmly in the grip of downloading practices. The biggest void in today's culture is Field 4 cultural productions that would use the deep transformational experiences in one part of the global field for inspiration and healing in another.

Example 1: Ralf Schneider and his team at PricewaterhouseCoopers, the world's largest global services company, designed a leadership development program that takes deep-dive action learning journeys to some of the current spots of societal crisis and breakdown. Every year he convenes a group of twenty to twenty-five of the company's high-potential younger partners. After an intensive preparation phase (some virtual, some in the form of a face-to face residential experience) he splits them into teams of three and sends them on a two-month deep dive into a developing-country development project. During that time, each trio works full-time on an existing development initiative such as HIV/AIDS. Their goal is to make the best possible contribution to the community that hosts them, while pursuing a couple of agreed-upon individual and team development objectives.

At the completion of these two months, the partners reconvene as a group for a one-week retreat to engage in deep reflection and sense making and to crystallize the key learnings and their implications. Although most of the participants have profound experiences in the field, it is mostly through this one-week retreat that they learn to mine the gold of their experience and to integrate it into their personal and professional lives. For the past four years I have worked with these groups both prior to their two-month field immersion and then after they have returned, during the reflection retreat. I have been always amazed how deep the changes are that this seemingly simple intervention—exposing people to the real world—creates, if supported in the right ways. Meeting with them a year later for a third time also convinced me that a significant number of them had translated this life-changing experience into new kinds of projects, ventures, and behaviors—such as setting up a foundation for social innovation and community work or founding a new school in India by donating, among other things, all of their personal savings.

What we don't know, at this time, is what it would take to distill such life-changing experiences and make them accessible to others. That is the idea behind the Social Presencing Theater we are, at this writing, in the midst of creating.[14]

As we envision it, the Presencing Theater will synthesize all creative arts, theater, social change techniques, energy awareness methods, contemplative practices, and dialogue. Using a minimalist "blank canvas" and performing discipline, it will turn the audience into co-creators of the event.

The assumption underlying this approach is simple: because of the oneness of the global field, what happens to or heals one part of the collective social body (in one part of the world) must have the possibility to trigger healing in another part of the world. In reality, these communities are already connected through the global social field. The social-presencing performance only provides the mechanism for these communities to become aware of that deeper connection more fully. By using these combined elements, a social-presencing theater production would take the actors/audience through the stages of the U in about two hours.

Root Principles: The Three Groundings of the Social Field

The U process can be applied to practical situations in three different ways: as process, as a set of field principles, and by operating from the presence of source.

First, as a *process*: you follow the sequence of initiating, sensing, presencing, prototyping, institutionalizing. That's a beginning. But for that process to work you need to connect to the two deeper levels: principles and source. Otherwise it is just another mechanical process tool that some people use to put other people into straightjackets (and charge money for it).

Second, as a set of *principles* and *practices* (as outlined throughout this chapter): you no longer follow a mechanical process blueprint; instead you apply the wholeness of the 24 principles to the situation at hand. You situate and adapt the process as needed in a context.

And third, as connecting to and operating from the presence of your deepest *source*, that is, from the bottom of the U. At this level, even the scaffolding of the principles falls away. The connection to this source level is articulated in the three root principles below: intentional grounding, relational grounding and authentic grounding. I call them root principles because they relate to and support the other 21 remaining principles like the root system of a tree relates to the visible parts of a tree. They establish a foundation to evoke the presence of a social field—an intentional grounding that serves the whole; a relational grounding that connects to the collective body of the social field; and an authentic grounding that connects you to your essential self as a vehicle for the emerging future.

22. **Intentional grounding.** Some of the most important variables that determine the quality of a situation—say, a meeting—are the ones that are least visible: our quality of attention and intention. They profoundly influence how a situation unfolds: "*I attend and intend* [this way]—*therefore it emerges* [that way]."

   Example: As described earlier, when I asked Joseph Jaworski how to best conduct deep-listening interviews, he told me, "The most important hour of the interview is the hour before you begin the interview."

Practice 1: On the evening before facilitating or leading a workshop or gathering, take a few minutes to align your intention with the best future possibility of the group or community that you will be working with the next day. Establishing this relationship will help you to improve the quality of intuitions that slip through the back door of your mind when you have to respond to real-time situations.

Practice 2: When conducting large-group events, I have found it useful to hold a collective intention-setting session the evening before the event begins. It usually takes no more than five or ten minutes. When the room setup is complete and most of the preparations are done, you call the core group together and stand in a circle; everyone then says one or two things about what they personally consider to be the event's purpose or goal: What should this event accomplish, and what future possibility do they want to facilitate and serve? I have found that groups that engage in intention setting the night before are likely to establish a better field and holding space throughout the event than groups that do not.

Another aspect of intentional grounding deals with *covering our currency*—that is, grounding what we *say* in what we *do* in our everyday lives. As the saying goes, "For every word you say about change, take one action. For every word you say about ethics or spirituality, take two or three actions." It is through what we *do* that we gain the legitimacy we need, not through what we *say*.

Sometimes our initial success can get in the way of serving the whole. The more you apply the above principles, the more successful you may seem and the more you are in danger of falling into one of the following traps: fame (I did it), money (I deserve it), or empire building (I should own it). This trio of pitfalls tries to attack our weak spots. Once they have us in their grip, they put a spin on our perception, and soon our interactions are driven by that terrible trio instead of by our essential intentions.

Practice 3: Go through your life story in reverse (starting today and going back as far as you can remember) and think about the people who have influenced you along the way. Ask yourself what gift you received from connecting to that person. Complete that exercise back to the very beginning, to your parents and your early family experiences. Then, in your mind, add up all the gifts you have received and subtract those from who you are today. Note that there is almost nothing in yourself that you do not owe to someone else.

23. **Relational grounding.** Whenever two or more people meet and truly connect, something special happens: they participate in the presencing of a social field. That social field not only connects us to one another—it also connects us to ourselves. It's the medium through which we can wake up to who we really are. The nature of that field at first seems to be bounded by the group we are present with in a particular situation. But as we learn to pay attention to the more subtle aspects of the social field, we realize that the social field is both locally grounded and nonlocally connected—it is the medium that directly connects us with all other human beings on the planet. Just as the air that we breathe is a shared medium that literally connects all of humankind, the social field is a tacit medium of connection. It is a collective body of resonance that we can tune in to and cultivate.

Example: The current collective body of humankind that was described in the first parts of the book is like an old social body that is about to die. It has absorbed the blows of direct violence (people killed by the actions of other people), structural violence (people killed by structures such as the socioeconomic divide), and cultural violence (people killed by cultures that legitimize the use of structural or direct violence against others they view as lesser beings). We are experiencing the dominance of that dying body, the old social field, in all social systems and on every level. The dying of that old body and the birth of a new social field are the central events of our time. The essence of the U deals with deciphering this central set of events. They happen every day around the globe. Whenever two or more persons meet and attend to what emerges from the subtle connection between them, it opens a gateway to that deeper process and mystery.

Practice: Move with your mind and heart around the globe and empathize with people in each community and region. Empathize both with people you know personally and with people you don't. Develop an intimate relationship with them by "inhaling" their suffering and "exhaling" healing energy. Develop a sense of the global field of mankind that connects all of us such that it would be impossible to be happy as long as a single person is suffering.

24. **Authentic Grounding.** The U process can be thought of as a social breathing process. The left-hand side of the U is the inhaling part of the cycle: total immersion in the current field, taking everything in. The right-hand side of the U is the exhaling part of the cycle: bringing the field of the future into reality as it desires. Between these two movements, breathing in and breathing out, there is a small crack of nothingness. That silent pause is the mystery or source at the bottom of the U. It's where the letting go (of the old) connects with the letting come (of the new). That crack can be thought of as the eye of a needle: the Self. It's the capacity of our I-in-now to link with our highest future possibility—a future that is in need of us and that only we can bring into reality. At the very moment we begin to operate from that place, we evoke the presence of a different social field—a social field that enables its participants to connect to the deeper sources and streams of generative emergence.

The transition from the dying collective body of the past to the coming into being of an emerging social field is based on a profound shift of the state based on which the individual and collective self (Self) operates. While the self in the old collective body is imprisoned by the patterns of the past, the self in the generative social field functions as a holding space for a future possibility to emerge and manifest. The shift from the former (being a prisoner of the system) to the latter (giving birth to a new world that emerges from within) is like an *inversion* of the self/Self.

Example: An example of this inversion process is the sculpture *7000 Oaks* by the German avant-garde artist Joseph Beuys. Like the process of authentic grounding, *7000 Oaks* is a time sculpture. It deals with two fundamentally different streams of time: one that emerges from the past, and another that emerges from the future. Accordingly, the sculpture goes through a process of transformation in which the old body is dissolving and dying while another body of life is coming into being.

You see here the initial form of the sculpture, a gigantic heap of 7,000 basalt stones in an arrow-shaped column. At the top of the column is a single stone next to a single oak tree, which Beuys planted at the official unveiling of the sculpture in Kassel, a city in northern Germany. Beuys's vision was to disassemble the column of 7,000 stones piece by piece, pair each individual stone with an oak tree, and plant the tree/basalt pairs throughout the greater city. In its initial form the sculpture was just a heap of stones (Sculpture 1), but in its final form it had morphed into the greening of a city (Sculpture 2). The transformation took five years and the work of many volunteers.

THE SCULPTURE "7000 OAKS" BY
JOSEPH BEUYS
photo by Dieter Schwerdtle

The last tree was planted in 1987 during the opening of the "Documenta" (an exhibition that takes place once very five years), after Joseph Beuys himself had passed away. The transformation from Sculpture 1 to Sculpture 2 is a perfect representation of the inversion process (*Umstülpung*): a process in which one body ceases to exist in order to allow another, a new living field to manifest.

Practice: Review the current challenges in your life and work and how they resonate with your past journey. Do this as if you were looking down from above. If someone had designed your current

rent challenges in order to teach you an important lesson that is connected to your forward journey, what would that lesson be? If someone had intentionally designed your past journey and current challenges to prepare you for your future work and life, what do you think might be the central theme of that future journey?

Figure 21.7 completes the field walk of our "U Tour," summarizing Principles 1 to 24. With that we are at the end; that is, back to the beginning. We started our field walk with a question: What does it take to learn from the future as it emerges? What it takes, we found, is a profound shift—a shift in the inner place from where we operate. The journey of the U is the journey of performing that shift—and performing it in a more intentional and con-

1. ATTEND:
listen to that which life calls you to do

CO-INITIATING

2. CONNECT:
listen to and dialogue with the interesting players in the field

3. CO- INITIATE *a diverse core group that inspires a common intention*

19. CO-EVOLVE INNOVATION ECOSYSTEMS *that connect and renew by seeing from the emerging whole*

CO-EVOLVING

20. CREATE INNOVATION INFRASTRUCTURES *by shaping rhythm and safe places for peer coaching*

21. SOCIAL PRESENCING THEATER: *evolve collective awareness through level 4 media*

4. *Form a highly committed team and clarify essential questions*

5. TAKE DEEP-DIVE JOURNEYS *to the places of most potential*

6. OBSERVE, OBSERVE,OBSERVE: *suspend your voice of judgment (VOJ) and connect with your sense of wonder*

CO-SENSING

7. PRACTICE DEEP LISTENING AND DIALOGUE: *connect to others with your mind, heart, and will wide open*

8. CREATE COLLECTIVE SENSING ORGANS *that allow the system to see itself*

17. INTEGRATE HEAD, HEART, & HAND: *seek it with your hands; don't think about it, feel it.*

18. ITERATE, ITERATE, ITERATE: *create and adapt and always be in dialogue with the universe*

CO-CREATING

15. FORM CORE GROUPS. *5 people can change the world*

16. PROTOTYPE STRATEGIC MICROCOSMS *as a landing strip for the emerging futur*

14. POWER OF INTENTION: *connect to the future that stays in need of you—crystallize vision, intent*

9. LETTING GO: *let go of your old self and stuff that must die*

10. LETTING COME: *connect and surrender to the future that wants to emerge through you*

11. INTENTIONAL SILENCE: *pick a practice that helps you to connect with your source*

CO-PRESENCING

12. FOLLOW YOUR JOURNEY: *do what you love, love what you do*

13. PLACES OF PRESENCE: *create circles in which you hold one another in the highest future intention*

WHO IS MY SELF?
WHAT IS MY WORK?

22. INTENTIONAL GROUNDING: *always serve as an instrument for the whole*

23. RELATIONAL GROUNDING: *connect and dialogue with the global social field*

24. AUTHENTIC GROUNDING: *connect to your highest self as a vehicle for the future to emerge*

FIGURE 21:7 TWENTY-FOUR PRINCIPLES AND PRACTICES OF THE U

scious way—as an individual, a group, an organization, or a globally distributed system. And as we go through that journey in any kind of social system,
we transform the social body in exactly the same way as Joseph Beuys' sculpture of 7,000 oaks (Sculpture 2) transformed the initial formation of the
7,000 column stones (Sculpture 1). That transformation is the real threshold
event going on in the world today. It is what is arising from the rubble.

Throughout our field walk we have stopped every now and then to look at
some of the details that belong to this transformation of the global sculptural field. The ten categories of transformation, as outlined in Table 20.1, function as our logbook of these various observations. When you read this logbook, you look into the grammar of our own evolution—into the grammar
of our individual and collective journey that brought us here. When you read
the 24 principles, you delved into the manual of the evolutionary process *at
work*. It's the same fundamental process but viewed from an action perspective, not a theory perspective. So we saw the footprints of evolution from the
perspective of theory (evolutionary grammar) and from the viewpoint of
practice (24 principles). But where is the perspective of the creator?

The key to accessing the perspective of the *artist* lies in the sculpture *7,000
Oaks*. It lies in the phenomenon of *Umstülpung* (inversion), of transubstantiat-
ing the old body (Sculpture 1: 7,000 stones) into a new one (Sculpture 2: 7,000
pairs of stones with oaks). Which is exactly what we observed along the four
metaprocesses of the social field. In Chapters 16 to 19 we looked at the profound transformation of thinking, languaging, structuring, and constituting
the global whole. In each of these cases, we have an old body that is crumbling
and exhausting itself, while something else is thrusting up from the rubble.

We might ask, so what? What are the implications for moving forward?
Everything we encountered in our field walk now brings us to the Epilogue.

Birthing a Global
Presencing-In-Action School

The Battle of Our Time • Inspiring a Global Shift • Innovations in
Infrastructures • The Presencing Institute •
The Power of Place • Born in a Blizzard •
Flying on the Wings of Others

The Battle of Our Time

With the beginning of this millennium we have entered a phase of increased tension between two principal sets of conflicting forces. On the one hand, we see a dramatic acceleration of the forces of fundamentalism, manipulation, and destruction. Day by day, symptoms of this drama play out on the front pages of our morning papers. We see the acceleration of the dying process, the disintegration of the old social body (Sculpture 1). On the other hand, we witness the deepening of a profound opening process that happens around the world when more groups of people begin to become aware of and connect with the deeper meaning of their life journeys. New social networks and fields of living presence are coming into being (Sculpture 2). Day by day, week by week, both of these forces seem to amplify at the same time. The difference between them is that the first one—the forces of fundamentalism, manipulation, and destruction—works by *decreasing* the degrees of freedom for the people involved. We see this happening, for instance, when bombs are dropped with the intention of blowing people into a future that looks more like a caricature of the past.

By contrast, the other set of forces at work *increase* freedom by shifting the inner place of operating and showing people additional ways to attend and respond to situations at hand. The difference, simply put, is that the first looks at a human being as an object that is determined by its environment and conditioned by its past. As a consequence, it can be influenced, manipulated, and controlled through exterior mechanisms. The second view sees human beings as subjects—carriers of a dormant capacity to connect with a deeper source of creativity and knowing. Through this capacity, people can link with and realize a future that depends on each of us in order to come into being. As a consequence, the essence of this view of the human being is to create through connecting to one's highest future possibility, one's authentic Self.

The stakes in this battle are high. The very direction of our evolutionary pathway forward is at risk. Are we, as a species, heading toward a mechanization of the collective global field—as illustrated in the movie *Matrix*—where the evolutionary project gets frozen in the dark space of antiemergence? In such a scenario, we cut ourselves off from the sources of goodness, beauty, and truth. Or shall we deepen our connection to and co-create the world from our source?

It has been often said that in the face of the utmost destructive forces—such as Hitler at the height of his power—it's not good enough to keep focusing on Gandhian types of nonviolent strategies of conflict transformation. But that is exactly what hundreds of unarmed German women did for a week in February 1943. In Berlin's Rosenstrasse, they stood toe to toe with machine-gun-wielding Gestapo agents, demanding the release of their imprisoned husbands.

Charlotte Israel was among the women who waited in freezing temperatures outside Rosenstrasse 2–4, the Jewish community center, desperate for news of her husband. She had been coming each day since the police arrested Julius Israel along with hundreds of other factory-working Jews, the last of the Jews to be taken. She recalled, "Without warning, the guards began setting up machine guns. Then they directed them at the crowd and shouted: 'If you don't go now, we'll shoot.' The movement surged backward. But then, for the first time, we really hollered. Now we couldn't care less. . . . Now they're going to shoot in any case, so now we'll yell too, we thought. We yelled, 'Murderer, murderer, murderer, murderer.'"

The protest by the women from the Rosenstrasse was successful, says the historian Nathan Stoltzfus in his recent book on the event, because women such as Charlotte Israel were so deeply motivated that they risked their lives even though there was no central organization.[1] "We acted from the heart, and look what happened," another woman, Eliza Holzer, told Stoltzfus nearly half a century after she protested the arrest of her husband, Rudi.

In the end the women's courage and passion prevailed; as thousands of other Berlin Jews were crammed into cattle cars and transported to Auschwitz, the 1,700 Jews who had been locked in at the Rosenstrasse were set free.

Inspiring a Global Shift

What if more Germans had "acted from the heart," as the women of the Rosenstrasse did? This story is uncomfortable for Germans, because it proves that successful resistance against Hitler was possible—even at the height of his power and even right in the center of Berlin.

What can this little story teach us about how to deal with today's challenges? How can we learn to begin to act from the heart?

We do know from systems theory that when a system hits a bifurcation point, very small differences can determine the future pathway of the system. If our current era is marking such a threshold point for the global system, how many committed people acting from the heart would it take to co-inspire a profound global shift one way or the other? The Renaissance, it is often said, was created by a core group of approximately two hundred people. The core group of the Bauhaus was much smaller than that—maybe a dozen committed people with only half a dozen at the inner core. We don't know how many people it will take at the beginning of this century to co-inspire another profound global shift. But it probably wouldn't take more than fifty or a hundred people if these people were really committed and supported by the right kind of infrastructures.

If the social technology outlined in the chapters you've just read is the lever, what is the leverage point where we can best apply it? In my view, we have to remove both of the limiting factors that keep the current system locked into its old patterns: the lack of *innovations in infrastructure* and the lack of a committed global *core group* for inspiring and supporting these innovations in the context of a global movement for conscious evolution and change.

Innovations in Infrastructures

Whenever the global or societal system has moved from one developmental state to another, such a shift has come with distinct innovations in infrastructures (see Chapter 19). In our current situation, what are the innovations in infrastructures that are necessary to take us to the next level?

I see at least three of them. They connect and empower the frontline people and leaders across institutional boundaries in order to *see and act from the emerging whole*. They are:

1. *Innovations in economic infrastructures:* Together we can co-create platforms to help players across boundaries connect, sense, adapt, and innovate more effectively. Such platforms would convene players across the supply chain, including consumers and user communities. While usually the communication between business and user communities is tilted by billion-dollar marketing budgets applied against consumers and citizens, in this case the conversation would happen on a more equal footing and in a more open and dialogic way, in order to contemplate the system as a whole and to adjust and reconfigure one's current ways of operating accordingly.

   Another innovation in economic infrastructure would be a guaranteed basic income, as discussed in Chapter 19. Such basic economic security would empower people to better follow the journey of their own work and life, putting them more into an entrepreneurial driver's seat and making them less vulnerable in the context of the rapidly changing global economy.

2. *Innovations in political infrastructures* that create places for *deepening democracy* through advanced methods of participatory decision making. These places would bring together diverse stakeholders that are already de facto connected through operating in the same larger system. The goal would be to replace their current downloading type of communication and interaction by more open, transparent, and distributive processes of observation, sense making, collective presence, and rapid innovation prototyping. If that were to happen, special-interest group identities would be abandoned in favor of broader and deeper views of oneself in the context of the larger system.

3. *Innovations in cultural infrastructures* that reinvent our institutions of education. Table 22.1 below spells out nine knowledge and learning contexts that a prototype twenty-first-century school (and university) would need to provide for its students and faculty.

Table 22.1 maps the landscape of current approaches to capacity building by combining two distinctions: the three leadership capacities (open mind, open heart, open will) and the three types of knowledge (K1: knowledge without self-reflection; K2: reflection on action; K3: reflection in action) that I have spelled out in the earlier chapters of this book.

The crisis in our current educational system can be stated simply: we are sending our kids into a world that requires them to open their minds, hearts, and intentions in order to cope with and thrive on the challenges they will face as individuals, in groups, and in society. Yet we do nothing to help them develop these capacities during the most formative stages of their early development. That's like putting a seed on a concrete floor and saying "I want you to grow strongly and quickly, but I am not going to give you any water, nutrients, light, or soil."

That approach to "educating" our children is one of the starkest irrationalities of our time, an irrationality that paradoxically is committed in the very name of rationality and reason. We probably spend more

TABLE 22.1: NINE LEARNING ENVIRONMENTS...

Knowledge/ Intelligence	K1 Non-reflective knowledge: *knowledge without self-reflection*	K2 Self-reflective knowledge: *reflection-on-action*	K3 Self-transcending knowledge: *reflection-in-action*
Open Mind **IQ** Explicit Dynamic complexity	*Lecturing:* explicit knowledge learning is to fill a barrel	*Training:* Practice+feedback Reflection on exercise	*Creative Practice* Improv, Theater Imagination-in-action
Open Heart **EQ** Embodied Social complexity	Experiential action, projects, immersion, empathy walk, tacit-embodied knowledge	Case Clinics, action-reflection papers, dialogue walk, reflection-on-embodied knowledge	Embodied Prescence Performing authentic speech Aikido, inspiration-in-action
Open Will **SQ** Not-yet-embodied Emerging complexity	Deep immersion practice: existential storytelling, total immersion journeys	Deep inversion practice: Guided journaling, Generative dialogue	Deep presence practice: room of silence, contemplative practices

than 90 percent of our educational resources on lecturing: downloading old bodies of knowledge without self-reflection (OM, K1). Of the remaining 10 percent, most is spent on exercise-based training (OM, K2). The remaining seven squares in the table are largely unaddressed by the mainstream of the current educational systems.

We need a small cultural revolution on a global scale that illuminates these seven blind spots in the current system of education. In addition, we need to turn the curriculum of the school inside out, reconnecting the learning agenda with the real world outside, as well as with the deeper inward journey of discovering our authentic sources of creativity and knowing. We need to reinvent our schools and institutions of higher education around the interplay of all nine knowledge and learning environments, not just one or two of them.

The Presencing Institute: A Global Transformation Living Lab

So what could such a small cultural revolution or movement look like? What might happen if we could integrate science, consciousness, and profound social change?

Imagine a global network of places and communities that co-inspire and serve a worldwide movement of change makers. Each of these places would regularly host a circle of leaders and grassroots activists for a couple of days, maybe three to four times a year. During these gatherings, circles of committed people would deepen the personal and collective sources of their capacity to co-inspire and hold the space for others to connect with their emerging self and purpose in life. These places would function as a hub for a globally distributed community. And then, when the few days or the weekend is over, everyone would return to their home base to continue their servant leadership on the ground level of their various contexts and communities.

So the main image is this holding space for the movement: coming together (breathing in) from all corners of the world, locally and globally, connecting to the source, and then going back to each individual's home organization or context in order to do one's work (breathing out).

There are three concrete elements that make this image actionable and concrete:

The first element is that such a globally distributed community would enable cross-cultural, cross-sectorial, and cross-generational dialogue, and action. One important core group would be composed of the ELIAS (Emerging Leaders for Innovations Across Sectors) Fellow group (see Chapter 21 on ELIAS). ELIAS Fellows are already in important leadership positions today but are expected to move into the most senior executive positions within five to seven years. Most ELIAS Fellows are now in their late thirties or early forties. The members of this group will continue to connect with one another across boundaries to discover the key challenges and possible breakthrough innovations for the years to come. As they identify key systemic innovation possibilities and begin to undertake prototype initiatives aimed at exploring actual opportunities, they will need hands-on support from highly motivated, practical yet out-of-the-box-thinking younger people who would run some of these experiments.

Here is where the second element of this vision comes into play: The Global ELIAS Classroom. This is another global action platform that I prototyped recently with my students at MIT. We co-developed this protoype in cooperation with the World Bank Institute and tested an early version of it with student groups from China, Japan, South Africa, Indonesia, Russia, Europe, and Mexico. The main focus is on composing a global microcosm of players and people across cultures, training the student participants in the skills of deep listening, dialogue, and fast-cycle prototyping, and then throwing them into the hot application phase of the ELIAS prototyping projects. Just as the community of ELIAS leaders is a globally distributed cross-sector and cross-cultural community, students in this virtual classroom also come from and link across contexts, cultures, and socioeconomic spheres. If such a Global ELIAS Classroom could be done on a larger scale (along with the ELIAS Fellows prototyping platform and program), I am sure that these systemic innovation initiatives could scale up, quickly spread, and blossom around the earth.

The third element I envision for this cross-institutional project and place is a supporting infrastructure for all global-sensing, global-presencing, and global-prototyping activities. This infrastructure would consist of three different types of places: virtual places (a Web-based infrastructure), urban places for cross-institutional sensing and prototyping, and rural places that would serve as holding spaces for presencing gatherings using nature as a gateway.

Stepping back, we might ask: What is being proposed here? Is it a prototype platform for systemic innovation? Is it a leadership lab inside and across powerful global institutions in all three sectors? Is it a cross-sector think tank and action lab for profound systems innovation? Or is it all of the above?

What struck me most about the early global classroom prototypes was the power that these few sessions unleashed on the part of the students. When doing our after-action review I asked my MIT students why, with all the countries on earth represented in the MIT student body, they spend their time in these global classroom sessions trying to hook up via Skype with student buddies in China and South Africa instead of hanging out with their friends on campus? Their answer: "Because the global classroom allows us to meet totally different people. People we would never meet on campus." That response was really eye-opening to me: *If* you connect the diversity of the global social field in the virtual classroom, and *if* students are enabled to explore that space through deep listening, dialogue, and collective action, *then* globalization can be a real source for authentic empowerment—very quickly.

The three elements—ELIAS, the Global Classroom, and the infrastructures for co-sensing, co-inspiring, and co-creating—are the seeds for a larger project, a globally distributed Presencing-In-Action Leadership School. Such a new school, elements of which have already begun operating through some of the projects mentioned above, would prototype a twenty-first-century educational environment (Table 22.1) in ways that inspire and enable a maximum amount of replication and learning. It would reinvent the old, established learning environments (characterized by running on two out of nine "cylinders") and build the capacity to lead profound innovation and change through the social technology of presencing. Such a project would be more global than a normal university (incorporating global classrooms and global field projects), more practical (all students would be required to engage in organizational and community prototyping projects), and more personal (with individual and collective cultivation practices). The faculty of this virtual school would include frontline innovators and leaders of profound social change across all cultures, sectors, and strands of life.

For such a Presencing-In-Action School or movement to be successful—that is, to inspire a shift on a global scale—seven enabling conditions would need to be in place. They are:

1. A *set of living examples* that prototypes profound innovations by shifting the social field in a local, regional, or global system.
2. A *theory* that provides a language to reflect on what happens and why, as well as published research that documents what has been learned from projects and applications.
3. A *social technology* that helps dispersed communities to collectively sense, realize, and scale up innovations in their own systems easily and cost-effectively.
4. Various open-source-based *capacity-building mechanisms* that allow the dissemination of the social technology to people across cultures and communities—regardless of their ability to pay for training or support.
5. A new social art form I call *Social Presencing Theater* that stages media events and productions to connect different communities and their transformational stories by blending action research, theater, contemplative practices, intentional silence, generative dialogue, and open space.
6. *A global core group of leading practitioners* and researchers who intentionally act as a vehicle for advancing a movement around the practice of inspiring change through presencing the emerging future.
7. A *constellation of power places* that is dedicated to serving all of the above by establishing an infrastructure for global sensing, presencing, and prototyping.

Together these seven elements would act as a living laboratory to connect change leaders across sectors and would be grounded in the integration of science, consciousness, and profound practical change.

The Power of Place

Among the 150 interviews I conducted for the research that led to this book, two of them stand out in terms of illuminating the blind spot of the interviewer. The first one was an interview with the physicist Arthur Zajonc. At the end of the conversation he turned it around and started to draw out the story that had brought Katrin and me to the place in which we now find ourselves. Then he said something I will never forget: "Think of everything that you experienced in the past as preparatory building blocks for your future journey and task." It's like jumping backward into a pool: you look down at where you stand—but only in order to find out and navigate the territory that unfolds behind your back. I have found this to be a very useful way of viewing one's past. You don't get attached to something which was particularly good or bad, but rather look at the journey of the past from the viewpoint of exploring the future. What can the stories of the past teach us about our journey forward?

The other interviewee was Eleanor Rosch. At the end of the interview I asked her about the qualities of real places. She suggested that I should contemplate the places I had lived over the years. With that suggestion she turned the camera onto my own blind spot. Taken by surprise, I thanked her deeply—and didn't do much with her suggestion. Until now. Now I see her suggestion as an opportunity to decipher certain qualities of place that may be helpful for facilitating the way forward.

The first place that comes to mind is our family farm. What I learned growing up there is that a farm is not just an enterprise; it is first and foremost a living organism, a community that extends from the visible parts above the surface of the soil to the invisible parts below. The community includes minerals, plants, animals, farmers, consumers, children, and friends who hold the farm in its social and economic space. Together, this community hosts and participates in the spiritual presence of the place, which also needs constant cultivation. Coming back to the farm, where I am writing these concluding lines right now during a visit, I feel some of the sacred presence that special places in nature like this one can provide.

Living in this place gave me a sense of the *vertical grounding* of the social field: a connection among nature, the human community, and the presence of the whole. That is the essence of a farm: you realize that you are the guardian and the servant of a larger community of animals, plants, the earth, and people who depend on you and your servant leadership. As my elder brother once put his sense of purpose: "caring for this little piece of earth."

The next place that comes to mind helped me to become aware of the *horizontal grounding* of the social field. I found that grounding in the streets of Brokdorf, Berlin, Budapest, and Bonn, all of which staged major antinuclear, antiwar, peace, and civil rights events in Western and Central Europe during the late 1970s and early 1980s. That was when I started feeling another connection—a more horizontal type of connection that bonded me with a web of like-minded and like-hearted folks across generations, classes, countries, and cultures. Having this global connection awakened me to a new level of awareness of and participation in the global social fielding: the temporary oneness with an emerging collective social body—sparked by the *resistance from the heart*—that otherwise appeared to be fragmented by class, race, gender, age, culture, and system.

The third place that comes to mind is much smaller—a place called the Villa on the shore of Germany's Ruhr River. The Villa, a once beautiful and later crumbling Victorian-style house build for Krupp directors in the early twentieth century, was about to be torn down when a fellow graduate student and I came across it. The owner gave us a one-year lease, but after that he planned to tear the building down (in fact, he ended up renewing the lease every year for fifteen years before finally demolishing it). We moved in with ten other students who loved and inspired one another in ways that I hadn't known were possible. Living in that place and cultivating our community may have been the happiest time in my young professional life.

The university I attended was sponsored by German industry to develop and teach better ways of learning. It was greatly inspired by the concept of Ekkehard Kappler, who served as the founding dean of the Management School during the 1980s. Ekkehard Kappler's idea of co-creating a new school based on action learning, self-reflection, and student-centric learning environments was powerful and simple: "Studying" he told us, "is the prax-is of freedom." I happened to be in the first class of the Management School, and my housemates at the Villa were founding-year students in some of the university's other schools. Our core group during those years often func-tioned like the heart of that young university. When important visitors came, the president or Ekkehard would bring them to the Villa, where we would provide a good dinner and inspirational conversation.[2] We inspired one another on multiple levels, from reading Plato to staging postmodern par-ties. I remember that my friend Kai and I took long walks after reading and studying Plato and Aristotle, during which we applied and improvised con-temporary versions of philosophical dialogues that dealt with the foundation-al questions of knowing and being. He argued as Plato, and I fell in love with taking the role and viewpoint of Aristotle.[3] Once a term we held a party at the Villa where we performed original cabaret skits, played music, and danced until dawn. The Villa was always an open place. Visiting faculty like Johan Galtung, the founder of peace research and recipient of the Alternative Nobel Prize, stayed regularly at the Villa when they taught on campus. In Galtung's autobiography, he later referred to those visits as the most inspiring univer-sity experiences of his life (he had taught in more than sixty universities on all continents). We, the students who were his hosts at the Villa, shared exact-ly the same deep transformational experience.

While the Villa was open to others, it also functioned as a secure cocoon for breeding new ideas, many of which were cooked up and launched at our breakfast table. What stood out in that place was the enchanting rhythm and presence of a living field that extended from our core group to other people around us. There was nothing that our group couldn't have accomplished. Whatever we launched, we accomplished with ease and increasing levels of energy. It was strange, but fun. Thus, the third quality of place at issue here has to do with the *generative cocoon*: with grounding the social field in a core group that is connected across all three channels of intelligence: the open mind, the open heart, and the open will.

The fourth place that comes to mind is not a single place but rather a *dis-tributed network* of places. It includes my current family home in Boston as well as places and communities in other countries and cultures that I visit on a more or less regular schedule. Today I find myself traveling—maybe too much—in my work with a dispersed constellation of core groups and initiatives.

Not long ago I attended a two-day conference at MIT that convened His Holiness the Dalai Lama along with some eminent Western cognitive scientists and Buddhist cultivators to discuss issues in cognition research.[4] At the end of that conference I was filled with energy and excitement about the power and possibilities of investigating a field that linked the worlds of science (the third-person view) and changes in the structure of consciousness (the first-person view). During those two days I felt, though, that the conversation was ignoring a third dimension that was necessary to co-define and frame the inquiry: the dimension of social transformation and change.

When I left the MIT auditorium, I could see, in a flash, everything that was *wrong* with my current life. I was going in too many different directions, pursuing far too many projects in too many places, each of which made sense individually, but which, viewed as a whole, lacked *focus*.

Just as that message *You need focus—you must change your life!* was sinking in, I saw in the same flash what I should be focusing on as I moved forward. I should concentrate my energy on a single project: creating a place and a vibrant community dedicated to investigating and cultivating the common ground among science, consciousness, and leading profound social change.

I left Kresge Hall at MIT needing to talk with Katrin, Peter, and Arthur Zajonc (who facilitated the Dalai Lama session) about ways to make that idea work. We decided that the next step would be to convene a group of individuals for whom this question—how to integrate science, consciousness, and social change—is central to their life's journey and work. That group now includes a dozen participants and has met three or four days a year over the past few years.[5]

Born in a Blizzard

In December 2005 we felt that the time was right to take the next step. We invited a small core group of practitioners, researchers, and activists of Field 4 change to begin to co-initiate a platform for such a global presencing-in-action school that would integrate science, consciousness, and leading social change. We currently call this initiative the Presencing Institute, but our intention is to create the seed for a global Presencing-In-Action Lab or University.

About a dozen people met at a hotel in Cambridge, Massachusetts, on December 9 and 10.[6] From there, we decided to walk the short distance from MIT to the SoL offices on the Charles River, a walk that usually doesn't take longer than ten minutes. But that day the snow piled up deeper and deeper and the visibility grew worse. No cars passed us. It was as if we were lone actors in a Siberian slow-motion movie. The blizzard offered us a special form of walking meditation. Later that day, as the storm intensified, we heard thunder and saw lightning strikes fairly near our venue. That was the first time that any of us had experienced that rare combination: a blizzard with lightning and thunder all at the same time. We took it as Mother Nature's way of welcoming us.

I opened the meeting by recognizing and reconnecting all of the streams—the scientific, the organizational change and social liberation movements, and the various wisdom traditions—that had provided the three contexts for this gathering (science, consciousness, social change). These held the space around us as we met to germinate a seed for the future, and of the future.

Several people couldn't attend this first meeting in person. One of them was Judith Flick from South Africa. So she joined us for the opening session via phone. One of us asked her to tell us about her work and about her highest hopes for the initiative we were about to create.

Judith described her current role as global leader of the HIV/AIDS-related work within Oxfam GB and how her immersion in this context had affected and transformed her professional and personal life and identity. When

Ursula asked her to give an example, she told the story of a staff member who had gone to the funeral of a family member who had died of the virus. When the funeral ended, it was time to deal with practical matters: how to divide up the deceased's material belongings and, most important, what to do with the two small children who were now left without parents. The room grew silent. No one offered to adopt or care for the two kids. During that silence Judith's colleague turned her head and looked at her husband. Their eyes met, and they knew that they had the same thought: they couldn't simply walk away. So they took the two children with them, increasing the size of their family from two children to four. A few weeks later, at the next funeral, the same events were repeated. Again, after another painful silence, they returned home with two additional children. A couple of months later they took in three more children. Finally they found themselves with ten instead of two, and it became increasingly difficult for them to deal with the complexity at home. When, at the next funeral, the same situation came up again, what to do with the children, they behaved like everyone else: they remained silent and did nothing because they had reached the limit of their coping capacity—like everyone else at the funeral, like whole communities in some southern African countries and maybe whole nations to come.

Why, asked Judith, isn't there a global system that connects us in such a manner that makes global care and responsibility part of our lives? Why do we obey global rules that take away our humanity? When confronted with human suffering at an individual level, we connect, but when it is systemic, we disconnect. Why?

Judith's question and the silence that followed struck a deep chord in our group. It made us even more aware of the need for the profound systemic healing and change and more determined to be a vehicle for it. (Resulting from this conversation, the first Presencing Institute project on HIV/AIDS in Southern Africa was launched within less than six months, even before the formal launch of the institute.)

Another member of the core group who couldn't attend this first meeting was Nicanor Perlas, the civil society activist and recipient of the Alternative Nobel Prize in 2002 for his "trisector" approach to policy making and social transformation in the Philippines. In a letter, Perlas shared his hope that the Presencing Institute would give him and his fellow activists in the Philippines and other countries of the global South access to research, methods, and tools to co-create new forms of "strategic partnerships between visionary elements in civil society, business, and government." He said that he hoped that we could develop "new forms of social movements and human or leadership development that are based on the latest advances in science, arts, and spirituality."

He also pointed out that important design elements for the Presencing Institute from the global South would include open-source capacity building, affordable five-day presencing programs and master classes, documentation, and dissemination of research on living examples because "it is too expensive to fly to the global North," as well as a globally supported infrastructure for study and work groups on presencing. "If personal meetings were required," says Nicanor, "then travel-related assistance for the participants from the South would be key."

Flying on the Wings of Others

A few weeks after the December meeting in Boston, I co-facilitated a workshop in South Africa with my colleague Beth Jandernoa, who lives half the year in South Africa. When Beth and I started talking about presencing and what it takes to operate from one's deeper source of knowing, we asked participants for some examples. A young man stood up and shared his story.

Martin Kalungu-Banda was born and raised in a small village in Zambia. Through many amazing turns during his young life he wound up in a career that included leadership positions in a global energy company; the position of special consultant to the president of the Republic of Zambia, responsible for establishing the position of chief of staff in the State House (the president's office); as a facilitator and consultant in the Global Learning Center of Oxfam; and as lecturer at several universities in Africa and Great Britain, including Cambridge University. He has also written a wonderful book on Nelson Mandela's approach to leadership.[7]

When Martin ended his story, people were stunned by his truly amazing journey. I asked him, "Martin, what kind of knowing allowed you to navigate and move from one stage of your journey to the next one?" He responded by sharing the story of an interview that he had given recently to a radio station in Zambia. During that radio show on his new book, some of the listeners called in. One of them happened to be a young rural kid, who said, "Martin, tell me what did you do that allowed you to begin as a young boy from a rural area in Zambia, as I am, and end up lecturing at famous universities, advising the president and working for major international institutions. How was that possible? What allowed you to do that?" Martin paused for a long time and then replied, "You know, you will probably be very disappointed by what I am going to tell you now. But the truth is that I didn't know what I was doing. I didn't have a plan. Rather than planning my future, I often have found myself drifting into situations. I drifted into situations as they unfolded. But I always trusted that if I were drifting into some new situation and if I had the right deep intention, that somehow the right help would be given to me. As I drifted, I realized that I was also flying on the wings of other people . . .

As I now think about it, I wish that going forward I would be able to drift in a somewhat more intentional manner."

I was struck by Martin's description. I realized that his term "drifting" also applied to much of my own journey. Over the past ten years I have been drifting into a whole new set of projects, players, and possibilities that I never rationally planned out.

As I now look back on the past ten years, I realize that without specifically planning to, my colleagues and I have been prototyping several core elements of the Presencing-In-Action School. As a result, there is a whole set of emerging *living examples* that not only include the examples we discussed, but also several new projects, including those in Zambia and Washington, D.C., on beating HIV/AIDS and the Indian Bhavishya Alliance, which addresses the huge problem of malnutrition.[8]

I have also "drifted" into a whole host of projects in which the U process is applied to *capacity-building* programs that I have been creating for a variety of mostly global institutions.[9] Other examples include the launch of a platform that integrates both the Global Classroom at MIT and the ELIAS program. It brings together twenty-five to thirty key leaders from global institutions across all sectors who are working on seven different prototype initiatives addressing how to create profound systems innovations across the three sectors.[10]

While this drifting into emerging opportunities has worked in some cases, in others it has not. Among the most important missing pieces are:

- *A consolidated global core group* of a few people who are essentially willing to give their lives to further the larger goal; a core group that would intentionally function as a collective vehicle for serving the whole.
- *A set of hotspots and power places* that could host and support all of the above-described activities by providing the infrastructure for global sensing, presencing, and prototyping activities. These places would function as "acupuncture points" for the global social field. They would host workshops for up to 100 or 150 people, and they would have the simplicity and openness of an empty warehouse or a Zen temple; they would be linked with each other to allow for high-quality multi-site virtual dialogues, while at the same time they would also have the feel of an artists' place and incorporate a multimedia studio and a science lab for visualizing global trends and issues. A flexible stage, in the center of the room, would be the stage for social presencing theater performances.

These future possibilities depend on others—on all of us—in order to come into being. Throughout this book I occasionally tried to put some of that into words. I confess that this sense of the future at times *feels* more clear and more real than it actually *looks* as I read the words emerging from my keyboard now. So you, too, are probably wondering how all this will work. But, like me, your heart probably already knows. So does your gut. And if we've learned anything from going through the U together, we know that's precisely where the future will show up first.

As the crumbling of the old structures continues left and right, I am thankful that I have the opportunity to be around at this point in history, to connect to other fellow drifters who share some of the same concerns. We are now called to step up, as the women of the Rosentrasse did, to learn to act from our heart in a more intentional, conscious, and collective way, to act from the power of our emerging authentic self. Or as Martin Kalungu-Banda put it: to fly on the wings of those around us.

Glossary

Aesthetics: The term "aesthetics" comes from the Greek *aistesis*, "sensual sensing"; activating all our senses (including the one for sensing beauty).

Anomie: Destruction and loss of social norms and values.

Archemedian point: The leverage point that, if focused on, could enable us to shift the whole system.

Atomie: Fragmentation, destruction, and loss of social structure; a term coined by the peace researcher Johan Galtung.

Autopoietic: Autopoiesis literally means "auto (self)-creation" (from the Greek *auto*, "self-" and *poiesis*, "creation"). The term was originally introduced by the Chilean biologists Francisco Varela and Humberto Maturana in 1973. The notion of autopoiesis is often associated with that of self-organization; that is, with a system in which the elements create and re-create themselves. Niklas Luhmann introduced this theory to the social sciences.

Ba: The Japanese word for a "place" (or "field") that is not only a physical place but also a social, mental, and intentional place. The Japanese philosopher Kitaro Nishida made this term a cornerstone of his work. The Japanese management scholar Ikujiro Nonaka introduced this term as a central concept in his theory and practice of knowledge in creating companies. *Ba*, in his view, is context-in-motion.

Blank canvas: The place or state where we connect with our sources of creativity and inspiration and create from nothing.

Blind spot: The inner place (source) from which our attention, intention, and action originate. This dimension of our reality can be accessed only if we redirect the beam of our observation to begin to see the seer, the self.

Causa efficiens: The efficient cause or the beginning of movement or agency (one of the four types of causation Aristotle differentiates).

Causa finalis: The final cause or the final goal or purpose that drives what we create in the now (one of the four types of causation Aristotle differentiates).

Causa formalis: The formal cause or the pattern, form, or shape into which something comes into being (one of the four types of causation Aristotle differentiates).

Causa materialis: The material cause or the material, physical, or structural conditions that shape the way reality unfolds (one of the four types of causation Aristotle differentiates).

Co-creating: The movement of the U that enables us to explore the future by doing; enacting prototypes of the future by linking the intelligences of the head, heart, and hands and by iterating through the guidance of fast-cycle feedback from all stakeholders in real time.

Co-evolving: The movement of the U that helps us interweave and link with the larger ecosystem around; by co-evolving, we begin to see, strategize, and act from presencing the emerging whole.

Co-Initiating: The movement of the U that helps us listen to what life calls us to do in order to crystallize an initial sense of intention and direction. We co-initiate by attentive listening to others, to ourselves, and to what emerges from constellations or circles of people that we help bring together.

Co-presencing: The movement of the U that helps us connect to our deepest sources of inspiration and stillness—and to the place from which the future possibility begins to arise. This movement merges three different types of presence: of the future, the past, and the authentic self. It shifts the place from which the self emerges to the highest future possibility—to our Self.

Co-Sensing: The movement of the U that helps us connect with and tune in to the contexts that matter; moving into a state of seeing in which the boundary between observer and observed begins to collapse and in which the system begins to see itself.

Community of Practice: A group of people that engages in a learning process based on a common interest in some subject or problem and collaborates over an extended period to share experiences and ideas, and to find solutions. The term was first used in 1991 by Jean Lave and Etienne Wenger.

Crystallizing: Envisioning the future that seeks to emerge from a deep connection with source.

Deep dive: Connecting deeply to a context by putting yourself into the shoes of the other; going on a total immersion journey. The term is used by IDEO in the context of a total immersion in a problem at hand.

Downloading: Reenacting habitual patterns of action, conversation, and thought.

Double-loop learning: Learning that goes beyond the single loop and reflects on the governing variables and deep assumptions that guide the normal action learning process. The term was coined by Chris Argyris and Don Schön.

Dynamic complexity: Situations characterized by a delay or distance between cause and effect in space or time.

Embodying: The capacity to bring the new into an institutionalized level of reality by embedding it in new practices, processes, and infrastructures while maintaining a connection to source.

Emerging complexity: A situation characterized by emerging profound or disruptive change; the ambivalent feeling that something is going to change but you have no idea what it is and how you should respond; the solutions are unknown, the problem is still unfolding, and the key stakeholders are not clearly defined.

Enacting: The capacity to bring the new into reality by improvising and prototyping while maintaining a connection to the source of your inspiration; linking the intelligence of the head, heart, and hands.

Explicit Knowledge: Knowledge that can be expressed, for instance, in spreadsheets and e-mails.

Feldgang: A field walk.

Field: The total set of connections that are mutually interdependent.

Field structure of attention: The relationship between observer and observed, the quality of how we attend. That quality differs depending on the place or position from which our attention originates relative to the organizational boundary of the observer and the observed (I-in-me, I-in-it, I-in-you, I-in-now).

Global economy: An economy with the capacity to work as a single unit in real time on a planetary order.

Holon: From the Greek *holos*, "whole," with the suffix *on*, which, as in "proton" or "neutron," suggests a particle or part. The term was coined by Arthur Koestler to describe the hybrid nature of subwholes/parts in real-life systems; holons are simultaneously self-contained wholes of their subordinated parts and dependent parts when seen from the inverse direction.

IDEO: An influential international design company that successfully applies the (first three levels of the) U process onto the subject of product innovation. www.ideo.com.

I-in-it: The second field structure of attention in a social or cognitive system: the source of attention originates from the boundary between the observer and the observed; I see the world from outside, that is, as a set of exterior objects.

I-in-me: The first field structure of attention in a social or cognitive system: the source of attention originates from inside my own boundaries; I see the world as a confirmation of my own mental models and structures.

I-in-now: The fourth field structure of attention in a social or cognitive system: the source of attention is operating from the source of the future that is seeking to emerge; the boundary between observer and observed is fully inverted (*umgestülpt*) or transcended; I see the world from a surrounding sphere, that is, from a holding place that allows the emerging future to come into being. The I-in-now is the capacity of the seer to redirect the beam of attention and intention across all levels and fields; the capacity of a system to shift the place from which its attention, intention, and action originate.

I-in-you: The third field structure of attention in a social or cognitive system: the source of attention is shifting beyond my boundaries into the field, my perception begins to happen from the whole; the boundary between observer and observed collapses; I see the world from within, that is, from the place where the manifest world is coming into being—from the field.

Intersubjectivity: The web of collectively evolving relationships.

Leadership: The capacity of a system to sense and shape its future. The Indo-European root of the word "leadership," *leith*, means "to go forth," "to cross a threshold," or "to die." That root meaning, which suggests that the experience of letting go and then going forth into another world that begins to take shape only once we overcome the fear of stepping into the unknown, is at the very heart and essence of leadership.

Learning: There are two types and sources of learning: learning from the past and learning from the future as it emerges. Learning from the past is based on the normal learning cycle (act, observe, reflect, plan, act), while learning from the future as it emerges is based on the process and practice of presencing (suspending, redirecting, letting go, letting come, envisioning, enacting, embodying).

Letting come: The capacity to crystallize and envision the future that you want to create while staying connected to the source of your inspiration.

Letting go: The capacity to let go of your old self and your old identities and intentions in order to create an open space for your emerging or authentic Self to manifest.

Macro: The institutional level.

Meso: The group or face-to-face level.

Micro: The individual level.

Morphic field: A field within and around a morphic unit that organizes its characteristic structure and pattern of activity. Morphic fields underlie the form and behavior of holons or morphic units at all levels of complexity. (The hypothesis of morphic fields has been proposed by the biologist Rupert Sheldrake and is not generally accepted by the mainstream scientific community at this point.)

Morphic resonance: The influence of previous structures of activity on subsequent similar structures of activity organized by morphic fields. Through morphic resonance, formative influences pass through space and time, but they come only from the past.

Mundo: The global system level.

Objectivity: The it-world of quasi-objective facts and things (third-person view).

Open heart: The capacity to redirect attention and to use one's heart as an organ of perception ("seeing with the heart"); to shift the place from which your perception happens to the other or to the field/whole; to access our sources of EQ (emotional intelligence).

Open mind: The capacity to suspend judgment and to inquire; to see something with fresh eyes; to access our sources of IQ (intellectual intelligence).

Open will: The capacity to let-go of one's old identities and intentions and tune into the future that is seeking to emerge through me or us; to let-go of our old self and to let-come our emerging authentic Self; to access our sources of SQ (spiritual intelligence).

Organization: Collective action for a common purpose; organizational structure is the "sum total of the ways in which its labor is divided into distinct tasks and then its coordination is achieved among these tasks" (H. Mintzberg).

Management: From the Latin *manu agere*, "to lead by the hand"; the process of coordinating to getting things done.

Pathogenesis: The mechanism by which certain factors cause disease; (pathos = disease, genesis = development).

Presencing: To sense, tune in, and act from one's highest future potential—the future that depends on us to bring it into being. Presencing blends the words "presence" and "sensing" and works through "seeing from our deepest source."

Prototyping: To create microcosms that allow us to explore the future by doing. Prototypes function as landing strips for the future. They work through the principle of "failing early to learn quickly" (IDEO).

Redirecting: The capacity to shift your attention from an object to the source from which that object is enacted and coming into being moment by moment.

Salutogenesis: An alternative medicine concept that focuses on factors that support human health and well-being rather than on factors that cause disease; (the term salutogenesis comes from the Greek salut = health, and genesis = development).

self: Current self, ego.

Self: One's highest future possibility; higher self.

Self-transcending knowledge: Not-yet-embodied knowledge, such as inspiration in action or intuition in action.

Sensing: The view from within—when seeing and perception begin to happen from the field. When you enter the state of sensing, you experience a collapse of boundary between observer and observed.

Single loop learning: When we reflect on our actions (but not on our deep assumptions that govern them).

Social complexity: The differences in interests, cultures, mental models, and history that the various stakeholders of a situation bring into play.

Social fields: The totality of connections through which the participants of a given system relate, converse, think, and act together.

Social grammar: The hidden rules, structures, and inflection points that enable certain types of evolution and emergence to happen. This term comes from a conversation the author had with Reinhard Kahl.

Structural coupling: In Living Systems theory, this denotes the co-adaptation and co-evolution of an organism within its environment; it allows for two-way interaction, co-dependence, and co-evolution.

Subjectivity: The I-world of the first-person perspective.

Suspending: The capacity to suspend one's Voice of Judgment (VOJ) and to attend to the situation at hand.

Structure of attention: The quality of our attention, which differs depending on the position from where our attention originates relative to the organizational boundary of the observer (I-in-me, I-in-it, I-in-you, I-in-now).

Tacit Knowledge: Embodied knowledge.

Theory U: A theoretical framework for the analysis of principles, practices, and processes that differentiate among four types of emergence and antiemergence: the four types differ in terms of their source (or their structure of attention) with respect to where their activity is enacted or performed from. Theory U illuminates the source level of enacted systems (or social systems).

Trans-subjectivity: The world of Self; of living presence (Husserl).

VOC: Voice of Cynicism.

VOF: Voice of Fear.

VOJ: Voice of Judgment.

World economy: An economy in which the flow of goods, services, and capital proceeds throughout the world.

Notes

INTRODUCTION

1 President Václav Havel, speech in Philadelphia, July 4, 1994. I am indebted to Göran Carstedt for calling this speech to my attention.

2 World Hunger Education Service, "World Hunger Fact Sheet" (http://www.worldhunger.org).

3 Combining the world figures for strong and extreme degradation gives the best estimate of land that has been largely, and for most practical purposes irreversibly, destroyed by land degradation. This survey was conducted in the late 1980s. More current information can be found by doing an Internet search for "land degradation assessments" to see various countries' assessments.

4 "The State of the World's Children 'Childhood Under Threat'" (www.unicefusa.org)

5 I owe this point to the peace researcher Johan Galtung. see Galtung 1995.

6 See, e.g, Argyris, 1993; Argyris and Schön, 1995; Senge, 1990; Senge et al., 1990; Schein, 1987.

7 Scharmer, 2000a.

8 Scharmer, 2000b, 2000c; Senge, Scharmer, Jaworski, and Flowers, 2004.

9 Among those valued colleagues are Beth Jandernoa, Joseph Jaworski, Michael Jung, Katrin Käufer, Ekkehard Kappler, Seija Kulkki, Ikujiro Nonaka, Ed Schein, Peter Senge, and Ursula Versteegen.

10 See the full interview with Jonathan Day conducted by Claus Otto Scharmer, July 14, 1999, at Dialog on Leadership (www.dialogonleadership.org/interviewDay.html).

11 Reason et al., 2001.

12 Aristotle, *Nicomachean Ethic*, Book VI, Ch. 3.

13 For more information, see www.presencing.org.

14 *Und kennst du nicht dies stirb und werde, so bist du nur ein trüber Gast auf Erden.*

Chapter 2

1 Artistotle, *Nicomachean Ethics*, Book VI, Chapter 3.

2 The label for the fourth level, "regenerating," was suggested to me by Adam Kahane.

3 Kolb, 1983.

4 Argyris and Schön, 1995.

5 Scharmer, 1991, 1996.

6 Steiner, 1894 (original), 1964.

7 Scharmer et al., 2002.

8 Senge, Scharmer, Jaworski, and Flowers, 2004.

9 Co-edited with Natalie Depraz and Pierre Vermersch, 2003.

10 Depraz, Varela and Vermersch, 2003, p. 25.

Chapter 3

1 Strebel, 1996.

2 See, e.g., Argyris, 1993; Argyris and Schön, 1995; Senge, 1990; Senge et al., 1990; Schein, 1987; Wanda Orlikowski, interview by Claus Otto Scharmer, September 7, 1999, transcript, *Dialog on Leadership*, www.dialogonleadership.org/interviewOrlikowski.html.

3 This large project, conducting dialogue interviews with thought leaders in the areas of management, knowledge, and change, grew into a body of 130 interviews, which are now being published in *Reflections: The SoL Journal for Knowledge, Learning and Change* (MIT Press). Many are also available on the website www.dialogonleadership.com.

4 Gendlin and Wiltschko, 2004.

5 See Schein, 1987c, 2001.

6 Kolb, 1983.

7 See also some related earlier work on the subject: Senge, Scharmer, Jaworski, and Flowers, 2004; Kahane, 2004; Torbert et al., 2004.

8 See Weick, 1996.

CHAPTER 4

1 Kahane, 2004.

2 The content of the wheel in Figure 4.2 can be displayed in two ways: moving "upstream" can be depicted as moving into the center of the circle, or it can be reversed, with movement leading out toward the edges of the circle. The advantage of the latter would be to show graphically that many functions that have been internal and fairly constrained are now becoming functionally dispersed and decentralized. On the other hand, the "outside-in" movement is a better conceptual match with the growing interdependency among the twelve different management functions. That they seem to merge into a single field in the center of the wheel is precisely what the following chapters address. Ultimately, both ways are limited because they can capture only two dimensions of something much larger, more complex, and more dynamic.

3 Porter, 1998.

4 Prahalad and Hamel, 2000.

5 Hamel and Prahalad, 1994.

6 See Hamel and Valikangas, 2003, p. 52.

7 Wenger et al., 2002; Wenger, 1998.

8 See Nonaka, 1994; Nonaka and Takeuchi, 1994; Nonaka, 1991.

9 Nonaka and Takeuchi, 1995.

10 Scharmer, 2000.

11 See Nonaka and Konno, 1998; Nonaka, Toyama, and Konno, 2000; Krogh, 1998, 2000.

12 Womak et al., 1991, 1996.

13 See the full transcript of the interview with Thomas Johnson, conducted by Claus Otto Scharmer on August 20, 1999, at www.dialogonleadership.org. For further reading, see Johnson, 2006.

14 Normann and Ramirez, 1998.

15 For the distinction between management and leadership, see Krauthammer and Hinterhuber, 2005.

16 Peters and Waterman, 1982.

17 Quoted in Alan Webber, "Trust in the Future," *Fast Company*, September 2000, p. 210.

18 See Collins, 2001, p. 66.

CHAPTER 5

1 President Václav Havel, July 4, 1994, Philadelphia. I am indebted to Göran Carstedt for making me aware of this speech.

2 I owe the point on the three poverties to my colleague Ursula Versteegen. She articulated this observation at the first Presencing Institute meeting in Cambridge, Mass., on December 10, 2005.

3 Castells, 1998, p. 336.

4 Ibid., p. 340.

5 Ibid., pp. 92, 93.

6 Ibid., p. 343.

7 Capra., 2002, p. 140.

8 Castells, 1998, p. 475.

9 Personal conversation with Gary Hamel in Detroit in 1996.

10 For example, over the past couple of years Novartis has shifted much of its R&D activity from Europe to the greater Boston area in order to participate in the networked ecosystem of innovation that is flourishing there.

11 Arthur, 1996.

12 Bill Joy, "Why the Future Doesn't Need Us," *Wired Magazine*, April 2000 (www.wired.com/wired/archive/8.04/joy.html).

13 Pinchbeck, 2006, p. 102.

14 Shiva, 2000, p. 2.

15 Perlas, 2003, p. 64.

16 Perkins, 2004.

17 Castells, 1996, p. 386.

18 Beck, 1986, 1996.

19 "Sins of the Secular Missionaries: Aid and Campaign Groups, or NGOs Matter More and More in World Affairs," *The Economist*, January 29, 2000, pp. 25–27.

20 Eni F. H. Faleomavaega, U.S. representative at the Global 2000 Symposium hosted by Counterpart International, Washington, D.C., April 24, 2000.

21 Florida, 2002, p.8.

22 Ibid., pp. 10–11.

23 Ibid., pp. 11–12.

24 Michelle Conlin, "Religion in the Workplace: The Growing Presence of Spirituality in Corporate America," *Business Week*, November 1, 1999, pp. 150–58.

25 Personal conversation.

26 Putman, 2000, p. 148; Wuthnow, 2000.

27 Csikszentmihalyi, 1990.

28 Scharmer, 1999, 2000; Isaacs, 1999.

29 Isaacs, 1999; also, personal conversation with William Isaacs.

30 Ray and Anderson, 2000, p. 4.

31 Michael Shellenberger and Ted Nordhaus, 2004. "The Death of Environmentalism.

Global Warming Politics in a Post-Environmental World," see www.thebreakthrough.org and www.evansmcdonough.com.

32 Galtung, 1977.

33 Weber, 1998, pp. 203–204.

34 Habermas, 1981, p. 522.

35 Scharmer and Senge, 1996.

36 Examples of organizations that produce excellent scholarship on social and ecological issues are the United Nations Development Program and the Club of Rome. On the cultural divide between East and West, Samuel Huntington and others have done important work; see, e.g., Huntington, 1996.

37 Habermas, 1981.

38 William McDonough and Michael Braungart, *Cradle to Cradle: Remaking the Way We Make Things* (New York: North Point, 2002); for more information, see also The Natural Step (www.naturalstep.org), which does great work in the field of sustainability and has concrete tools and frameworks for measuring the impact of organizations on the environment. Likewise, see the Wuppertal Institute (www.wupperinst.org), which also does great work in sustainability and has a method of measuring impact on the environment called MIPS (Material Intensity Per Service Unit), invented by Friedrich Schmidt-Bleek and explained in a document at www.wupperinst.org/Publikationen/Wuppertal_Spezial/ws27e.pdf; see also Weizsacker, 1994.

39 Michael Shellenberger and Ted Nordhaus, 2004. "The Death of Environmentalism. Global Warming Politics in a Post-Environmental World," see www.thebreakthrough.org and www.evansmcdonough.com.

40 Capra, 2002.

41 Beck and Cowan, 2005.

42 In the spirit that real intellectual appreciation expresses itself through criticism, two questions may be allowed. One question that Wilber's work raises is whether his all-quadrant approach is exhaustive. One could argue that it lacks the most important dimension: the I-Thou world Martin Buber wrote about. Wilber, of course, would argue that the I-Thou is included in his category "We" (intersubjectivity). But then one could object that a real I-Thou encounter is a category *sui generis* and hence different from Wilber's We-experience (or, for that matter, from Habermas's notion of intersubjectivity).

CHAPTER 6

1 Capra, 2002.

2 Brown et al., 1989.

3 Nishida 1990, pp. 174–175.

4 Hawkins, 2002, p. 90.

CHAPTER 7

1 Pokorny, 1994, p. 672.

CHAPTER 8

1 Watzlawick, 1983, pp. 39–40.

2 The GlobalHealthCompany story is based on a case study written in 1997 by a Harvard case writer who was hired by the GlobalHealthCompany. When the managers who had ordered the case study read the result, they decided that this was too dangerous and that the case study should be locked away in a poison cabinet so that nobody would ever read it—which is why it was never published or used.

3 Schein, 1989.

4 Up to this point, the story of GlobalHealthCompany is based on the case study mentioned above. From this point on, it is based on my interpretation of the data.

CHAPTER 9

1 This was quoted by Charles Flinn in *The Golden Mean* (New York: Doubleday, 1974), but is representative of Alexander's thinking throughout all his prolific writing; the latest works include the *Phenomenon of Life* series.

2 Before joining PARC, Whalen worked as a senior research scientist at the Institute for Research on Learning in Menlo Park and at the University of Oregon, where he was an associate professor of sociology and department head.

3 Kaeufer, Scharmer, and Versteegen 2003; for a free download of the paper see www.ottoscharmer.com/downloads2.htm; for more details, please see www.humedica.org.

4 www.humedica.org (my translation).

5 I advised the students on this thesis project; it was published in Jung et al., 2001.

6 For more information, see http://ocw.mit.edu/index.html.

7 More information about the half-day dialogue training of the students can be found at the MIT OpenCourseWare Web site: http://ocw.mit.edu/OcwWeb/Sloan-School-of-Management/ 15-974Leadership-LabSpring2003/StudyMaterials/index.htm.

CHAPTER 10

1 The *Steelen* were developed by Professor Emeritus Nick Roericht of the HDK Berlin; see www.roericht.net.

2 See more about setting intentional space in the description of the Circle of Seven, later in this chapter.

3 To learn more about Deep Dive, you can see a film clip of a TV report that aired on ABC in February 1999 at www.ideo.com/media/nightline.asp.

4 "How does that relate to and differ from Kurt Lewin's notion of field?" I asked her, referring to the great pioneer and founder of social psychology, learning, and action research. "Lewin had an intuition about field as I'm talking about it," replied Rosch, "but when he described it, he made it very clear that it was the field as known to a given individual at a given time. What he meant by knowing and the individual seemed to be the individual locked inside his skin looking out through his eyes that we take for granted. And certainly that's how other people have taken him and how he has been used in education and in therapy systems. So that's one difference."

"So the field that you described is not a thing, it's not an 'it,' you wouldn't find it in the exterior domain?" I asked Rosch. She nodded. "Right. That's right."

5 This version of the Parsifal story is based on Wolfram von Eschenbach's (1980) *Parzival*. The story is, in part, retold from Catford and Ray, 1991.

6 The full version of the interview can be found at www.dialogonleadership.org.

7 Bortoft, 1996.

8 Ibid.

9 Senge, Scharmer, Jaworski, and Flowers, 2004.

10 Goethe, 1823, quoted in Crotell, 1998. (Italics by the author.)

CHAPTER 11

1 Heidegger (1993) talks in paragraph 65 of *Sein und Zeit* about future as follows: ""»Zukunft« meint hier nicht ein Jetzt, das, *noch nicht* »wirklich« geworden, einmal erst *sein wird*, sondern die Kunst, in der das Dasein in seinem eigensten Seinkönnen auf sich zukommt. Das Vorlaufen macht das Dasein *eigentlich* zukünftig, so zwar, daß das Vorlaufen selbst nur möglich ist, sofern das Dasein *als seiendes* überhaupt schon immer auf sich zukommt, das heißt in seinem Sein überhaupt zukünftig ist" (italics in the original), p. 325. Thanks to my colleague Professor Walther Dreher, who made me aware of this paragraph.

2 Peter Ross, "The Most Creative Man in Silicon Valley," *Fast Company*, June 2000, p. 274.

3 This is an interesting reflection of this field structure of attention, which originates from the surrounding sphere. See also Pokorny, 1994, p. 341.

4 Interview with Eleanor Rosch conducted by Claus Otto Scharmer, October 15, 1999, transcript, *Dialog on Leadership*, www.dialogonleadership.org/interviewRosch.html.

The following definitions from Rosch can also be found on page 19 of the interview:

> *Wholeness:* "There is a powerful intuition of wholeness which goes beyond conceptual analysis into isolated units. Analytic detail is included but must be seen in proper perspective."
>
> *Causality:* "Humans bear the suspicion that causality (and/or contingency) is not the one-on-one relationship between separate units which the conceptual mind finds it easy to imagine, but rather a basic interdependence of phenomena."
>
> *Time:* "There is the sense that time may not be merely the linear flow we take for granted. Instead, supposedly lasting objects and experiences may be made up of the momentary, and the momentary can have a sense of timelessness."
>
> *Action:* "Humans have the experience of action that appears to arise without intention, effort, self referential motivation, or conscious control—even without the sense of 'me' doing it."
>
> *Knowing:* "There is a strong sense that there is a kind of knowing not captured by our models, a fundamental knowing not explicit or graspable. This is the kind of knowing that senses wholeness, interconnectedness, and so on, in fact, all of the other intuitions. Our psychology and culture have attributed this knowing to a variety of sources (such as the unconscious) which may actually be sidetracks, rather than aids, in exploration of knowing."

5 For example, when gold and silver coins have circulated together at legally established values that have come to differ from the relative commodity values of the two metals, then the one with the lesser value (silver) would drive out the one with the higher value (gold).

6 See Chapter 17.

7 One notable event was a meeting at the Stanford Park Hotel in Palo Alto among Gary Jusela, Joseph Jaworski, and myself shortly after the meeting in Houston I described above. At this meeting in Palo Alto, which happened at the end of several days of joint interviews throughout Silicon Valley, the three of us had an experience very similar to the one described above. These two meetings account for the better part of all the creative ideas and concepts for the Leadership Laboratory that we developed that year.

8 A process that the Circle of Seven developed for this deeper coaching work is The Symbols Way. This process was developed to draw personal and collective potential out of the mesh of current reality. The Symbols Way kit is available to individuals, consultants, and leadership teams by contacting its designer, Barbara Coffman-Cecil, at bcecil@mind.net. It is a product of The Ashland Institute (www.ashlandinstitute.org).

9 Pokorny, 1994, p. 341.

CHAPTER 12

1 The Bible, Mathew 19:24

2 See Owen, 1997.

3 Jaworski, 1996.

4 Scharmer et al., 2002.

5 Buber, 2000. The German original of this key section from I and Thou reads like this:

Der freie Mensch ist der ohne Willkür wollende. Er glaubt an die Wirklichkeit; das heißt: er glaubt an die reale Verbundenheit der realen Zweiheit Ich und Du. Er glaubt an die Bestimmung und daran, daß sie seiner bedarf: sie gängelt ihn nicht, sie erwartet ihn, er muß auf sie zugehen, und weiß doch nicht, wo sie steht; er muß mit dem ganzen Wesen ausgehen, das weiß er. Es wird nicht so kommen wie sein Entschluß es meint; aber was kommen will, wird nur kommen, wenn er sich zu dem entschließt, was er wollen kann.

Er muß seinen kleinen Willen, den unfreien, von Dingen und Trieben regierten, seinem großen opfern, der vom Bestimmtsein weg und auf die Bestimmung zu geht. Da greift er nicht mehr ein, und er läßt doch auch nicht bloß geschehen.

Er lauscht dem aus sich Werdenden, dem Weg des Wesens in der Welt; nicht um von ihm getragen zu werden: um es selber so zu verwirklichen, wie es von ihm, dessen es bedarf, ver-wirklicht werden will, mit Menschengeist und Menschentat, mit Menschenleben und Menschentod. Er glaubt, sagte ich; damit ist aber gesagt: er begegnet.

CHAPTER 13

1 Kelley, 2001, p. 232.

2 www.synergos.org/partnership/.

3 For a more comprehensive presentation of the Global Leadership Initiative, see Senge et al., 2004, and www.globalleadershipinitiative.org.

4 Kaeufer, Scharmer, and Versteegen, 2003.

5 In addition, physicians and their staffs have examined ways to improve the patient experience (for example, by reducing waiting times); doctors in the emergency center log the patient's problem after each call, note how they responded and what they learned from it—and share that learning with colleagues; women in one rural area have created a "regional kitchen" to teach diabetics and their caregivers healthier eating habits and lifestyles.

6 For more information on the Sustainable Food Laboratory, see: www.sustainablefood.org.

7 www.frappr.com/networkoflivinglabs.

CHAPTER 14

1 Personal conversation with Miha Pogacnik in New York, 1999.

2 I owe the distinction between eco-system and ego-system to a speech by Maurice Strong in Beijing, October 23, 2006, during the deep dive journey of the ELIAS program.

3 Kolb, 1984.

4 See Senge, 1990.

5 See Bushe and Shani, 1990; Schein, 1995.

CHAPTER 15

1 For an overview on contemporary methods of action research, see Reason and Bradbury, 2001.

2 Lewin, 1997, p. 240.

3 For more information about Kurt Lewin, see the following Web pages: Mark K. Smith, "Kurt Lewin, Groups, Experiential Learning and Action Research," *Encyclopedia of Informal Education* (2001), www.infed.org/thinkers/et-lewin.htm; "Force Field Analysis," www.accel-team.com/techniques/force_field_analysis.html; Julie Greathouse, "Kurt Lewin" (1997), www.muskingum.edu/~psych/psycweb/history/lewin.htm; Edgar H. Schein, "Kurt Lewin's Change Theory in the Field and in the Classroom: Notes Toward a Model of Managed Learning," *Reflections*, 1995, www.solonline.org/res/wp/10006.html.

4 See Hall and Lindzey, 1978, p. 386.

5 Orlikowski, 1992; Weick, 1995.

6 I owe the term "absencing" to Warren W. Tignor, who in his excellent paper suggests that a cycle of absencing is an inversion of the U; see Tignor, 2005.

7 Scharmer, 2001, pp. 137–150.

8 Nonaka and Takeuchi, 1995; Polanyi, 1966.

9 Scharmer, 2000; Fichte, 1982; also see interview with Eleanor Rosch conducted by Claus Otto Scharmer, October 15, 1999, Dialog on Leadership, www.dialogonleadership.org/interviewRosch.html.

10 Schön, 1983; Rosch, 1999; Scharmer, 2000.

11 The term "aesthetic" refers to those kinds of experiences that meet three conditions: the subject of experience (a) sees something (seeing 1), (b) observes her observing at the same time (seeing 2), and (c) closes the feedback loop between "seeing 1" and "seeing 2" ("seeing 3"). Hence, in an aesthetic experience, the subject is within (watching something) and outside of herself (watching herself) at the same time. Technically speaking, we refer to those experiences as aesthetic experiences that have the property of synchronicity between action and reflection,

i.e., zero feedback delay.

12 See Beuys, 2004.

13 Heidegger, 1993, p. 325.

14 See Lauenstein, 1974; Fichte, 1982.

CHAPTER 16

1 The interview, available at www.amazon.com, is *Blind Spot—Hitler's Secretary*, a 2002 German documentary DVD and video starring Traudl Junge, directed by André Heller and Othmar Schmiderer, and produced by Sony Pictures.

CHAPTER 17

1 Elias, 1978.

2 Goffman, 1999.

3 Isaacs, 1999.

4 For more information on appreciative inquiry, see *Appreciative Inquiry Commons* at http://appreciativeinquiry.case.edu.

5 It and others can be found in Isaacs, 1999.

6 Argyris, 1994.

7 Glennifer Gillespie, *The Footprints of Mont Fleur* (2000) www.democraticdialoguenetwork.org.

8 See Kahane, 2004.

9 Gillespie, 2000, p. 155.

10 Gillespie, 2000.

11 See Bohm 1996; Isaacs 1999.

12 Kahane 2002.

13 Stiglitz 2002, XIV.

14 Ibid., XV.

15 This is an interesting reflection of this field structure of attention, which originates from the surrounding sphere. See also Pokorny 1994, p. 341.

CHAPTER 18

1 Mintzberg, 1983, p. 2.

2 The remainder of this discussion of organizational structures also draws on Mintzberg, 1983.

3 See Adler and Borys, 1996.

4 The elemental structures discussed above relate to Mintzberg's famous "Structure in Fives" as follows. The first three structures, (1) simple structure, (2) machine bureaucracy, and (3) professional bureaucracy, are reflected in Field 1. Mintzberg's fourth structure, the divisionalized form, comes here in not one but three versions: as a divisionalized version of all three forms of centralization. Finally, Mintzberg's fifth structure, adhocracy, also comes in three different versions (networks of makers, traders, and thinkers). The last quadrant of organizational structures (community or ecologies) does not exist in Mintzberg's concept of structure in fives.

5 See Schein et al., 2003, p. 128.

6 Ibid., pp. 220–221.

7 Mintzberg, 1983.

8 Schein et al., 2003, p. 87.

9 See Saxenian, 1994.

10 See the full interview with Thomas Malone, conducted by Claus Otto Scharmer, May 31, 2000, in *Dialog on Leadership*, www.dialogonleadership.org/Malone2001.html.

11 See Hock, 1999.

12 Schein et al., 2003, p. 236.

13 All of the following quotes about Enron's collapse are from Kurt Eichenwald with Diana B. Henriques, "Enron's Many Strands," *The New York Times*, February 10, 2002.

14 Paul Krugman, "Delusions of Power," *The New York Times*, March 28, 2003.

15 See de Geus, 1997.

16 Former DEC employee Mike Horner, quoted in Schein et al.,2003, p. 256.

17 Ibid., p. 254.

CHAPTER 19

1 Quoted in Alan Deutschman, "Change or Die," *Fast Company*, May 2005, p. 53.

2 Ibid.

3 Hadler, 2005. I thank Richard Brush and Jeff Doemland of Cigna for making me aware of this remarkable study.

4 Perlas, 2003

5 See Olson, 1965.

6 www.aap.org/healthtopics/mediause.cfm.

7 See *Time*, November 15, 2004, for more details about the 2004 U.S. presidential election.

8 See *Time*, November 15, 2004, for more details about the 2004 U.S. presidential election.

9 These include, for example, lead-user developments, which are innovations jointly generated with an interested user who contributes critical ideas, experiences, and feedback.

10 See Scharmer and Jaworksi, 2000.

11 I owe this point to Johan Galtung.

12 I owe the basic argumentation about Transformations I and II to Johan Galtung.

13 Galtung, 1977.

14 Polanyi, 2001.

15 www.unternimm-die-zukunft.de/; http://www.iep.uni-karlsruhe.de/grundeinkommen/.

16 Brunnhuber and Klimenta, 2003.

17 www.dannwisch.de.

18 For example, in June 2006, Warren Buffett directed nearly $1.5 billion of his Berkshire Hathaway fortune to the Bill and Melinda Gates Foundation to address the world's most challenging inequities. This gift roughly doubles the Gates' yearly gifts focusing on world health issues, including fighting malaria, HIV/AIDS, and tuberculosis — and on improving U.S. libraries and high schools. The Gates' philanthropic lifetime gifts total $30 billion at the time of this book's publication. *Newsweek*, July 10, 2006, lists its "Philanthropy's All-Star Team" on page 86. Included there are Oprah Winfrey's Angel Network, Al Gore's green awareness, Lance Armstrong's cancer survivor work, Tiger Woods's Start Something program, Ted Turner's global aid, Rosie O'Donnell's foundation for children, Jimmy Carter's home building and disease prevention, Veronica Atkins's obesity prevention, Paul Newman's camps for kids, Michael J. Fox's Parkinson's disease research, and many more.

CHAPTER 20

1 I am unhappy with the term *autistic system* because it may sound as if I am disparaging children and others with autism. But the reality is that autistic children have an innate capacity that they can activate to overcome the limitations that they were born with (the use of music therapy has led to amazing successes in this regard, and may mean that a key to unlocking the autistic world is to find the right language). We can think of autistic systems in the same way: it may seem that no real communication is possible, and yet, if we can find the right language, we will be able to communicate and cross boundaries.

2 See Maturana, 1987.

3 Luhmann, 1995.

4 Helen Wade, "Systemic Working: the Constellations Approach.," *Industrial and Commercial Training*, August 2004, pp. 194–199.

5 On the parallels between differentiation in the individual and in society, see Steiner, 1980.

6 I say that with a caveat: I have not yet had occasion to participate in a constellation work session myself. So what I am saying here is based on second-hand knowledge, not on my own experience.

7 Cooperrider et al., 2000; Brown et al., 2005; Isaacs, 1999.

8 Weisbord et al., 1995.

9 Wilber, 2000. See also the discussion of his work in Chapter 6.

10 On the right-hand side of the U, we would see an inverted version of the four-quadrant model, through which a new world is coming into being.

CHAPTER 21

1 Schein's book *Process Consultation Revisited* (1998) is one of the most useful books I have ever read. It helped me to become a much better process consultant.

2 The first U process principle, however, starts before any kind of external client relationship has been built. It starts at the moment when we try to figure out what our real work is. The U process is based on many of the same philosophical assumptions that process consultation is grounded in. One of the main differences is that the U process starts with building a relationship to an important element of our existential "client system," so to speak: our own highest future Self. Other elements that the U process slightly broadens from the process consultation approach include the use of deep-dive journeys, rapid prototyping projects, and individual and collective practices for accessing the authentic self.

3 The four questions are: (1) What is your most important objective, and how can I help you realize it? (What do you need me for?) (2) What criteria will you use to assess whether my contribution to your work has been successful? (3) If I were able to change two things in my area of responsibility within the next six months, what two things would create the most value and benefit for you? (4) What, if any, historical tensions and/or conflicting demands have made it difficult for people in my role or function to fulfill your requirements and expectations?

4 www.sustainablefood.org.

5 Brown et al., 2005.

6 Scharmer and Jaworski, 2000.

7 See www.dialogonleadership.org/interviewC07.htm.

8 Example: getting the most important things done during the first eight hours of the day, from 4:00 a.m. to noon.

9 Covey, 1990.

10 Arthur is the founding director of the economics program at the Santa Fe Institute.

11 Quoted from: Senge et al., 2004, p. 158.

12 Nonaka, 1994, 1995, 1998.

13 Nonaka, Toyama, and Scharmer, 2001.

14 See www.presencing.org.

EPILOGUE

1 Stolzfus, 2001.

2 Konrad Schily was the president of Witten/Herdecke University during the 1980s and 1990s. See also Konrad Schily, *1993*

3 Kai Reimers is today professor of IT and economics at RWTH Aachen and visiting professor at the School of Economics and Management, Tsinghua University, Beijing. He talks about our dialogue walks in a recent article by Johannes Wiek: "Macht doch, was ihr wollt!" *Soziale Innovation*, Folge 6. in: brand eins, June 2006.

4 web.mit.edu/newsoffice/2003/dalailama.html.

5 The participants in this group include: Jon Kabat-Zinn, the founder of clinics that promote stress reduction through mindfulness; Arawana Hayashi, an educator of embodied presence; Rose van Thater, the co-founder of the Native Science Academy; Diana Chapman Walsh, the president of Wellesley College; Reverend Jeff Brown, the co-founder of the Boston Ten Point Coalition; Sayra Pinto, the head of the Twin City Latino Coalition; Dayna Cunningham, director of the ELIAS Project; Richard Noel, an organizational consultant to Diana Chapman Walsh at Wellesley; Katrin, Peter, Arthur, and me.

6 Thanks to the Fetzer Foundation, which funded this and two related other meetings for the co-initiation of the presencing institute.

7 Martin Kalungu-Banda, "Leading Like Madiba: Leadership Lessons from Nelson Mandela." Double Story Books, a Division of Juta & Co. Ltd. To order the book, contact: Bimpey@juta.co.za.

8 For detailed references, see www.ottoscharmer.com. Detailed information on the Food Laboratory and the Child Nutrition Laboratory can be found at www.synergos.org/partnership/about/initiatives.htm.

9 Recent capacity building programs I have been running include programs for leaders at DaimlerChrysler, Fujitsu, PricewaterhouseCoopers, BASF, Nissan, Royal Dutch Shell and the United Nations Development Programme.

10 ELIAS stands for Emerging Leaders for Innovations Across Sectors. For more information: www.elias-global.com; www.ottoscharmer.com.

11 www.tsiba.org.za.

Bibliography

Adler, Paul S., and Bryan Borys. 1996. "Two Types of Bureaucracy: Enabling and Coercive." *Administrative Science Quarterly* 41: 61–89.

Aguayo, Rafael. 1991. *Dr. Deming: The American Who Taught the Japanese About Quality*. New York: Simon & Schuster.

Alexander, Christopher. 2004. *The Luminous Ground*. Vol. 4 of *The Nature of Order*. Berkeley, CA: The Center for Environmental Structure.

———. 1979. *The Timeless Way of Building*. New York: Oxford University Press.

———, Sara Ishikawa, and Murray Silverstein. 1977. *A Pattern Language: Towns, Buildings, Construction*. New York: Oxford University Press.

Alexander, Jeffrey C., and Steven Seidman, eds. 1990. *Culture and Society: Contemporary Debates*. New York: Cambridge University Press.

Ancona, Deborah, Thomas Kochan, Maureen Scully, John Van Maanen, and Eleanor Westney. 2005. Managing for the Future: Organizational Behavior and Processes. 3rd ed. Mason: South-Western College Publishing.

———, Henrik Bresman, and Katrin Kaeufer. 2002. "The Comparative Advantage of X-Teams." MIT Sloan Management Review, 43: 33-39.

Anderson, Rob, and Kenneth N. Cissna. 1997. *The Martin Buber–Carl Rogers Dialogue: A New Transcript with Commentary.* Albany, NY: State University of New York.

Argyris, Chris. 1994. "Good Communication That Blocks Learning." *Harvard Business Review*, July 1.

———. 1993. *Knowledge for Action.* San Francisco: Jossey-Bass.

———. 1992. *On Organizational Learning.* Cambridge, MA: Blackwell.

———. and Donald Schön. 1995. *Organizational Learning II: Theory, Method and Practice.* 2nd ed. Englewood Cliffs, NJ: Prentice Hall.

———. Robert Putnam, and Diana McLain Smith. 1985. *Action Science: Concepts, Methods, and Skills for Research and Intervention.* San Francisco: Jossey-Bass.

Aristotle. 1985. *Nicomachean Ethics.* Translated by Terence Irwin. Indianapolis and Cambridge, U.K.: Hackett.

Arthur, Brian. 1996. "Increasing Returns and the New World of Business." *Harvard Business Review* 74, no. 4: 100–109.

Atlee, Tom. 2003. *The Tao of Democracy: Using Co-intelligence to Create a World That Works for All.* Cranston, RI: Writers' Collective.

Austin, Rob, and Lee Devin. 2003. *Artful Making: What Managers Need to Know About How Artists Work.* Upper Saddle River, NJ: Financial Times–Prentice Hall.

Bache, Christopher M. 2000. *Dark Night, Early Dawn: Steps to a Deep Ecology of Mind.* Albany: State University of New York.

Barnard, Chester I. 1938. *The Functions of the Executive.* Cambridge, MA, and London: Harvard University Press.

Bateson, Gregory. 1999. *Steps to an Ecology of Mind.* Chicago and London: University of Chicago Press.

Batstone, David. 2003. *Saving the Corporate Soul.* San Francisco: Jossey-Bass.

Beck, Don E., and Christopher C. Cowan. 1996. *Spiral Dynamics: Mastering Values, Leadership, and Change.* Malden, MA: Blackwell Business.

Beck, U., A. Giddens, and S. Lash, 1996. *Reflexive Modernization: Politics, Tradition and Aesthetics in the Modern Social Order.* Cambridge: Polity Press.

———. 1986. *Risikogesellschaft. Auf dem Weg in eine andere Moderne.* Frankfurt aM: Suhrkamp.

Beckhard, Richard, and Reuben T. Harris. 1987. *Organizational Transitions: Managing Complex Change.* 2nd ed. Reading, MA: Addison-Wesley.

Benedikter, Roland, ed. 1997. *Wirtschaft und Kultur im Gespräch: Zukunftsperspektiven der Wirtschaftskultur.* Meran: Alpha & Beta Verlag.

Bennis, Warren. 1989. *On Becoming a Leader.* Reading, MA: Addison-Wesley.

Berger, Peter L., and Thomas Luckmann. 1967. *The Social Construction of Reality: A Treatise in the Sociology of Knowledge.* New York: Doubleday.

Bernasconi, Robert. 1993. *Heidegger in Question: The Art of Existing.* Atlantic Highlands, NJ: Humanities Press.

Beuys, Joseph. 2004. *What Is Art?* Edited by Volker Harlan. Translated by Matthew Barton and Shelly Sacks. Stuttgart: Verlag Freies Geistesleben & Urachhaus.

Block, Peter. 1993. *Stewardship: Choosing Service Over Self-Interest.* San Francisco: Berrett-Koehler.

Bohm, David. *On Dialogue.* 1996. Edited by Lee Nichol. London: Routledge.

———. 1994. *Thought as a System.* London and New York: Routledge.

———. 1983. *Wholeness and the Implicate Order.* London and New York: ARK Paperbacks.

Bond, Patrick. 2004. *Talk Left, Walk Right: South Africa's Frustrated Global Reforms.* Scottsville: University of KwaZulu-Natal Press.

Bortoft, Henri. 1996. *Wholeness of Nature: Goethe's Way of Science.* Edinburgh: Floris.

Brand, Stewart. 1988. *The Media Lab: Inventing the Future at M.I.T.* New York: Penguin.

Brown, John Seely, Alan Collins, and Paul Duguid. 1989. "Situated Cognition and the Culture of Learning," *Educational Researcher* 18, no. 1 (January–February), pp. 32–42.

Brown, Juanita, David Isaacs, and the World Café Community. 2005. *The World Café: Shaping Our Futures Through Conversations that Matter.* San Francisco: Berrett-Koehler.

Brunnhuber, Stefan, and Harald Klimenta. 2003. *Wie wir Wirtschaften werden: Szenarien und Gestaltungsmoglichkeiten für zukunftsfühige Finanzmärkte.* Frankfurt: Redline Wirtschaft Ueberreuter

Buber, Martin. 2000. *I and Thou.* First Scribner Classics Edition. New York: Scribner.

Bushe, Gervase R., and Abraham B. Shani. *Parallel Learning Structures: Increasing Innovation in Bureaucracies.* Reading, MA: Addison-Wesley.

Campbell, Joseph, with Bill Moyers. 1991. *The Power of Myth.* Edited by Betty Sue Flowers. New York: Anchor.

Capra, Fritjof. 2002. *The Hidden Connections: Integrating the Biological, Cognitive, and Social Dimensions of Life into a Science of Sustainability.* New York: Doubleday.

Carr, Nicholas G. 2003. "IT Doesn't Matter." *Harvard Business Review* 81, no. 5: 41.

Carter, Robert E. 1997. *The Nothingness Beyond God: An Introduction to the Philosophy of Nishida Kitaro.* 2nd ed. St. Paul, MN: Paragon House.

Castells, Manuel. 1998. *End of Millennium,* vol. 3. Oxford: Blackwell.

———. 1997. Castells, Manuel. *The Power of Identity: The Information Age—Economy, Society and Culture.* Oxford: Blackwell.

———. 1996. *The Rise of the Network Society.* Oxford: Blackwell.

Catford, Lorna, and Michael Ray. 1991. *The Path of the Everyday Hero.* New York: Tarcher.

Chaiklin, Seth, and Jean Lave, eds. 1993. *Understanding Practice: Perspectives on Activity and Context.* New York: Cambridge University Press.

Chandler, Dawn, and William R. Torbert. 2003. "Transforming Inquiry and Action: Interweaving Flavors of Action Research." *Action Research* 1, no. 2: 133–152.

Chatterjee, Debashis. 1998. *Leading Consciously: A Pilgrimage Toward Self-Mastery.* Boston: Butterworth-Heinemann.

Childre, Doc, and Bruce Cryer. 1998. *From Chaos to Coherence: Advancing Emotional and Organizational Intelligence Through Inner Quality Management.* Boston: Butterworth Heinemann.

Chrislip, David D. 2002. *The Collaborative Leadership Fieldbook: A Guide for Citizens and Civic Leaders.* San Francisco: Jossey-Bass.

Christensen, Clayton M. 1997. *The Innovator's Dilemma: When New Technologies Cause Great Firms to Fail.* Boston: Harvard Business School Press.

Clegg, Stewart R., Cynthia Hardy, and Walter R. Nord, eds. 1996. *Handbook of Organization Studies.* London: Sage.

Coase, R. H. 1998. *The Firm, The Market, and the Law.* Chicago and London: University of Chicago Press.

Coleman, James S. 1998. "Social Capital in the Creation of Human Capital." *American Journal of Sociology* 94: S95–S120.

Collin, Finn. *Social Reality.* 1997. London and New York: Routledge.

Collins, Jim. 2001a. *Good-to-Great: Why Some Companies Make the Leap . . . and Others Don't.* New York: HarperBusiness.

———. 2001b. "Level 5 Leadership: The Triumph of Humility and Fierce Resolve," *Harvard Business Review* 75, no. 1: 66.

———, and Jerry I. Porras. 1994. *Built to Last: Successful Habits of Visionary Companies.* New York: HarperBusiness.

Confucius. 1971. *Confucian Analects, The Great Learning & the Doctrine of the Mean.* Translated by James Legge. New York: Dover.

Cooperrider, David L., Peter F. Sorensen, Jr., Diana Whitney, and Therese F. Yaeger, eds. 2000. *Appreciative Inquiry: Rethinking Human Organization Toward a Positive Theory of Change.* Champaign, IL: Stipes.

Csikszentmihalyi, Mihaly. 1996. *Creativity: Flow and the Psychology of Discovery and Invention.* New York: HarperPerennial.

———. 1993. *The Evolving Self.* New York: HarperPerennial.

———. 1990. *Flow the Psychology of Optimal Experience.* New York: HarperCollins.

Cusumano, Michael A., and Kentaro Nobeoka. 1998. *Thinking Beyond Lean: How Multi-Project Management Is Transforming Product Development at Toyota and Other Companies.* New York: Free Press.

Dalai Lama. 2003. *Estructive Emotions: How Can We Overcome Them?* Narrated by Daniel Goleman. New York: Bantam.

Daly, Herman E. 1996. *Beyond Growth: The Economics of Sustainable Development.* Boston: Beacon Press.

———, and Kenneth N. Townsend, eds. 1993. *Valuing the Earth: Economics, Ecology, Ethics.* Cambridge, MA, and London: MIT Press.

Darsø, Lotte. 2004. *Artful Creation: Learning-Tales of Arts-in-Business.* Frederiksberg, Denmark: Samfundslitteratur.

de Geus, Arie. 1997. *The Living Company.* Boston: Harvard Business School Press.

Delantey, Gerard. 1997. *Social Science: Beyond Constructivism and Realism.* Minneapolis: University of Minncsota Press.

Depraz, Natalie, Francisco J. Varela, and Pierre Vermersch. 2000. "The Gesture of Awareness, an Account of Its Structural Dynamics." In *Investigating Phenomenological Consciousness: New Methodologies and Maps.* Edited by Max Velmans. Amsterdam: Benjamin Publishers.

———, eds. 2003. *On Becoming Aware: A Pragmatics of Experiencing (Advances in Consciousness Research).* Amsterdam: Benjamin.

Dossey, Larry. 2003. *Healing Beyond the Body: Medicine and the Infinite Reach of the Mind.* Boston: Shambhala.

———. 1999. *Reinventing Medicine: Beyond Mind-Body to a New Era of Healing.* San Francisco: HarperSanFrancisco.

Dreher, Walther. 1997. *Denkspuren: Bildung von Menschen mit geistiger Behinderung— Basis einer integralen Pädagogik.* Aachen, Germany: Verlag Mainz.

Eccles, Robert G., et al. 2001. *The ValueReporting Revolution: Moving Beyond the Earnings Game.* Hoboken, NJ: John Wiley.

Eccles, Robert G., and Nitin Nohria. 1992. *Beyond the Hype: Rediscovering the Essence of Management.* Boston: Harvard Business School Press.

Edvinsson, Leif, and Michael S. Malone. 1997. *Intellectual Capital: Realizing Your Company's True Value by Finding Its Hidden Brainpower.* New York: HarperBusiness.

Eichenwald, Kurt. 2005. *Conspiracy of Fools: A True Story.* New York: Broadway Books.

Elias, Norbert. 1978, *The Civilizing Process. The History of Manners.* Translation from German by Edmund Jephcott of Über den Prozess der Zivilisation. Soziogenetische und psychogenetische Untersuchungen, Vol. 1. Oxford, Blackwell/New York: Urizen Books.

Elkington, John. 1998. *Cannibals with Forks: The Triple Bottom Line of 21st Century Business.* Gabriola, Canada: New Society.

Enriquez, Juan. 2000. *As the Future Catches You: How Genomics & Other Forces Are Changing Your Life, Work, Health & Wealth.* New York: Crown Business.

Eschenbach, Wolfram von. 1980. *Parzival.* Translated by A. T. Hatto. London: Penguin.

Fichte, Johann Gottlieb. 1994. *Introductions to the Wissenschaftslehre and Other Writings.* Tranlsated and edited by Daniel Breazeale. Indianapolis and Cambridge, U.K.: Hackett.

———, et al. 1982. *The Science of Knowledge: With the First and Second Introductions* (Texts in German Philosophy). Edited and translated by Peter Heath and John Lachs. Cambridge, U.K.: Cambridge University Press.

Fisher, Dalmar, and William R. Torbert. 1995. *Personal and Organizational Tranformations: The True Challenge of Continual Quality Improvement.* London: McGraw-Hill.

Fiumara, Gemma Corradi. 1990. *The Other Side of Language: A Philosophy of Listening.* Translated by Charles Lambert. London and New York: Routledge.

Fleck, Ludwig. 1994. *Einstehung und Entwicklung einer wissenschaftlichen Tatsache.* Frankfurt am Main: Suhrkamp.

Flores, Fernando. 1982. "Management and Communication in the Office of the Future." Ph.D. dissertation, University of California, Berkeley.

Florida, Richard. 2002. *The Rise of the Creative Class: And How It's Transforming Work, Leisure, Community and Everyday Life.* New York: Basic Books.

Foster, Richard, and Sarah Kaplan. 2001. *Creative Destruction: Why Companies That Are Built to Last Underperform the Market—and How to Successfully Transform Them.* New York: Currency.

Frick, Don M. 2004. *Robert K. Greenleaf: A Life of Servant Leadership.* San Francisco: Berrett-Koehler.

Friedman, Thomas L. 2000. *The Lexus and the Olive Tree.* New York: Anchor Books.

Fritz, Robert. 2003. *Your Life as Art*. Newfane, VT. : Newfane Press.

———. 1989. *The Path of Least Resistance: Learning to Become the Creative Force in Your Own Life*. New York: Fawcett Columbine.

Fukuyama, Francis. 1992a. *The End of History and the Last Man*. New York: Free Press.

———. 1992b. *Trust: The Social Virtues and the Creation of Prosperity*. New York: The Free Press.

Galtung, Johan. 1996. *Peace by Peaceful Means: Peace and Conflict, Development and Civilization*. London: Sage.

———. 1995 *On the Social Costs of Modernization: Social Disintegration, Atomie/Anomie and Social Development*. Research Paper. UNRISD: Geneva.

———. 1988. *Methodology and Development: Essays in Methodology*, vol. 3. Copenhagen: Ejlers.

———. 1979. *Papers on Methodology: Theory and Methods of Social Research*. Copenhagen: Ejlers.

———. 1977a. *Methodology and Ideology: Theory and Methods of Social Research*. Copenhagen: Ejlers.

———. 1977b. "Social Structure and Science Structure." In *Methodology and Ideology*. Copenhagen: Ejlers.

———, and Sohail Inayatullah. 1997. *Macrohistory and Macrohistorians: Perspectives on Individual, Social, and Civilizational Change*. Westport, CT: Praeger.

Gardner, Howard. 1995. *Leading Minds: An Anatomy of Leadership*. New York: Basic Books.

———. 1993. *Multiple Intelligences: The Theory in Practice*. New York: Basic Books.

———. 1985. *The Mind's New Science: A History of the Cognitive Revolution*. New York: Basic Books.

Gendlin, Eugene T. 1997. *A Process Model*. Chicago: University of Chicago.

———. 1981. *Focusing*. 2nd ed. New York: Bantam.

———, and Johannes Wiltschko. 2004. *Focusing in der Praxis: Eine schulenübergreifende Methode für Psychotherapie und Alltag*. 12th ed. Stuttgart: Pfeiffer bei Klett-Cotta.

Gerzon, Mark. 2003. *Leaders Beyond Borders: How to Live—and Lead—in Times of Conflict*.

Ghyczy, Tiha von, Bolko von Oetinger, and Christopher Bassford, eds. 2001. *Clausewitz on Strategy: Inspiration and Insight from a Master Strategist*. New York: John Wiley.

Giddens, Anthony. 1984. *The Constitution of Society. Outline of the Theory of*

Structuration. Cambridge: Polity Press.

Gladwell, Malcolm. 2005. *Blink: The Power of Thinking Without Thinking.* New York and Boston: Little, Brown.

———. 2000. *The Tipping Point: How Little Things Can Make a Big Difference.* New York and Boston: Little, Brown.

Glasl, Friedrich. 2002. *Konfliktmanagement: Ein Handbuch fur Führungskrafte, Beraterinnen und Berater.* 7th ed. Bern: Verlag Paul Haupt and Stuttgart: Verlag Freies Geistesleben.

———. 1999. *Confronting Conflict.* Stroud, U.K.: Hawthorn Press.

———. 1997. *The Enterprise of the Future.* Stroud, U.K..: Hawthorn Press.

Goethe, Johann Wolfgang. 1986. *Faust: Der Tragödie erster Teil.* Stuttgart: Philipp Reclam Jun.

Goffman, Erving. 1999. *The Presentation of Self in Everyday Life.* Magnolia, MA.: Peter Smith Pub., Inc.

Goleman, Daniel, Richard Boyatzis, and Annie McKee. 2002. *Primal Leadership: Realizing the Power of Emotional Intelligence.* Boston: Harvard Business School Press.

Greenleaf, Robert K. 1977. *Servant Leadership: A Journey into the Nature of Legitimate Power and Greatness.* New York and Mahwah, NJ: Paulist Press.

Gupta, Bina, ed. 2000. *The Empirical and the Transcendental: A Fusion of Horizons.* Lanham, MD: Rowman and Littlefield.

Habermas, Jürgen. 1981a. *Kleine politische Schriften.* Frankfurt am Main, Germany: Suhrkamp.

———. 1981b. *Theorie des kommunikativen Handelns erster Band.* Frankfurt am Main: Suhrkamp.

Hagel, John III, and Arthur G. Armstrong. 1997. *net.gain: Expanding Markets through Virtual Communities.* Boston: Harvard Business School Press.

Hagel, John III, and Marc Singer. 1999. "Unbundling the Corporation." *Harvard Business Review* 77, no. 2: 133–141.

Hall, Calvin S., and Gardner Lindzey. 1978. *Theories of Personality.* 3rd ed. New York: John Wiley.

Hall, David, and Roger T. Ames. 1995. *Anticipating China: Thinking Through the Narratives of Chinese and Western Culture.* Albany: State University of New York Press.

———. 1987. *Thinking Through Confucius.* Albany: State University of New York Press.

Halpern, Belle L., and Kathy Lubar. 2003. *Leadership Presence: Dramatic Techniques to Reach Out, Motivate, and Inspire.* New York: Gotham Books.

Hamel, Gary. 2000. *Leading the Revolution.* Boston: Harvard Business School Press.

———. 1996. "Strategy as Revolution." *Harvard Business Review* 74, no. 4: 69–80.

———, and Coimbatore Krishnarao Prahalad. 1994. *Competing for the Future.* Boston: Harvard Business School Press.

——— and Liisa Valikangas. 2003. "The Quest for Resilience." *Harvard Business Review* 81, no. 9: 52.

Hampden-Turner, Charles, and Alfons Trompenaars. 1993. *The Seven Cultures of Capitalism.* New York: Doubleday.

Handy, Charles. 2000. *21 Ideas for Managers: Practical Wisdom for Managing Your Company and Yourself.* San Francisco: Jossey-Bass.

———. 1998. *The Hungry Spirit.* New York: Broadway Books.

———. 1996. *Beyond Certainty: The Changing Worlds of Organizations.* Boston: Harvard Business School Press.

———. 1995a. *The Gods of Management: The Changing Work of Organizations.* New York and Oxford: Oxford University Press, 1995.

———. 1995b. *Waiting for the Mountain to Move.* London: Arrow Books.

———. 1994. *The Age of Paradox.* Boston: Harvard Business School Press.

———. 1989. *The Age of Unreason.* Boston: Harvard Business School Press.

———. 1988. *Understanding Voluntary Organizations.* London: Penguin.

Hawken, Paul. 1993. *The Ecology of Commerce: A Declaration of Sustainability.* New York: HarperBusiness.

———, Amory Lovins, and L. Hunter Lovins. 1999. *Natural Capitalism: Creating the Next Industrial Revolution.* Boston: Little, Brown.

Hawkins, David R. 2002. *Power vs. Force: The Hidden Determinants of Human Behavior.* Carlsbad, CA: Hay House.

Heidegger, Martin. 2000. *Introduction to Metaphysics.* Translated by Gregory Fried and Richard Polt. New Haven and London: Yale University Press.

———. 1997. *Unterwegs zur Sprache.* 11th ed. Stuttgart: Verlag Gunther Neske.

———. 1996. *Die Technik und die Kehre.* 9th ed. Stuttgart: Verlag Gunther Neske.

———. 1995. *Der Ursprung des Kunstwerkes.* Stuttgart: Philipp Reclam Jun.

———. 1993. *Sein und Zeit.* 17th ed. Tubingen: Max Niemeyer Verlag.

———. 1992a. *Basic Writings.* Edited by David Farrell Krell. San Francisco: HarperSanFrancisco.

———. 1992b. *Was ist Metaphysik?* 14th ed. Frankfurt am Main: Vittorio Klostermann.

———. *Über den Humanismus.* 9th ed. Frankfurt am Main: Vittorio Klostermann.

———. 1989. *Nietzsche.* 5th ed. Pfullingen: Verlag Gunther Neske.

———. 1988. *Zur Sache des Denkens.* 3rd ed. Tubingen: Max Niemeer Verlag.

———. 1986. *Vom Wesen der Wahrheit.* 6th ed. Frankfurt am Main: Vittorio Klostermann.

———. 1984. *Was heist Denken?* 14th ed. Tubingen: Max Niemeyer Verlag.

Heifetz, Ronald A. 1994. *Leadership Without Easy Answers.* Cambridge and London: Belknap.

———, and Marty Linsky. 2002. *Leadership on the Line: Staying Alive Through the Dangers of Leading.* Boston: Harvard Business School Press.

Heijden, Kee van der. 1996. *Scenarios: The Art of Strategic Conversation.* Chichester, U.K.: John Wiley.

Henderson, Rebecca M., and Kim Clark. 1994. "Managing Innovation in the Information Age." Harvard Business Review, January-February: 100-106.

———. 1990. "Architectural Innovation: The Reconfiguration of Existing Product Technologies and The Failure of Established Firms." Administrative Science Quarterly, March Vol. 35: 9-30.

Hertz, Noreena. 2002. *The Silent Takeover: Global Capitalism and the Death of Democracy.* New York: The Free Press.

Hinterhuber, Hans H., and Eric Krauthammer. 2005. *Leadership—mehr als Management.* 4th ed. Wiesbaden, Germany: Gabler Verlag.

Hippel, Eric von. 1988. *The Sources of Innovation.* New York and Oxford: Oxford University Press.

Hock, Dee W. *Birth of the Chaordic Age.* 1999. San Francisco: Berrett-Koehler.

Hosle, Vittorio. 1991. *Philosophie der ökologischen Krise.* Munich: Verlag C. H. Beck.

Huntington, Samuel P. 1996. *The Clash of Civilizations and the Remaking of World Order.* New York: Simon & Schuster.

Husserl, Edmund. 2000. *Vorlesungen zur Phänomenologie des inneren Zeitbewusstseins.* Tübingen: Max Niemeyer Verlag, 2000.

———. 1995. *Cartesianische Meditationen.* 3rd Ed. Hamburg: Felix Meiner Verlag.

———. 1993. *Arbeit an den Phänomenen: Ausgewählte Schriften.* Frankfurt am Main: Fischer Taschenbuch Verlag.

————. 1985. *Die Phänomenologische Methode: Ausgewählte Text I.* Stuttgart: Philipp Reclam Jun.

————. 1970. *Crisis of European Sciences and Transcendental Phenomenology: An Introduction to Phenomenological Philosophy.* Evanston, IL: Northwestern University Press.

International Forum on Globalization. 2002. *Alternatives to Economic Globalization: A Better World Is Possible.* San Francisco: Berrett-Koehler.

Isaacs, William. 1999. *Dialogue and the Art of Thinking Together.* New York: Doubleday.

Jaworski, Joseph. 1996. *Synchronicity: The Inner Path of Leadership.* Edited by Betty S. Flowers. San Francisco: Berrett-Koehler.

————, and Claus Otto Scharmer. 2000. *Leadership in the Digital Economy: Sensing and Actualizing Emerging Futures.* Cambridge, MA: Society for Organizational Learning, and Beverly, MA.: Generon Consulting.

Joas, Hans. 1996. *The Creativity of Action.* Translated by Jeremy Gaines and Paul Keast. Chicago: University of Chicago Press.

Johnson, Thomas H., and Anders Broms. 2000. *Profit Beyond Measure: Extraordinary Results Through Attention to Work and People.* New York: The Free Press.

Jung, Stefan, et al. 2001. *Im Dialog mit Patienten: Anatomie einer Transformation im Gesundheitswesen.* Heidelberg: Carl Auer.

Kabat-Zinn, Jon. 2005. *Coming to Our Senses: Healing Ourselves and the World Through Mindfulness.* New York: Hyperion.

————. 1994. *Wherever You Go There You Are: Mindfulness Meditation in Everyday Life.* New York: Hyperion.

Kahane, Adam. 2004. *Solving Tough Problems: An Open Way of Talking, Listening, and Creating New Realities.* San Francisco, Berrett-Koehler.

————. 2002. "Changing the World by Changing How We Talk and Listen." *Leader to Leader,* no. 26: 34–40.

Kalungu-Banda, Martin. 2006. *Leading like Madiba: Leadership Lessons from Nelson Mandela.* Cape Town: Double Story Books, a Division of Juta & Co. Ltd.

Kanter, Rosabeth Moss, John Kao, and Fred Wiersema, eds. 1997. *Innovation: Breakthrough Thinking at 3M, DuPont, GE, Pfizer, and Rubbermaid.* New York: HarperBusiness.

Kao, John. 1996. *Jamming: The Art and Discipline of Business Creativity.* New York: HarperBusiness.

Kappler, Ekkehard. 2006. Betriebswirtschaftslehre denken: Adorno für Betriebswirte

- Eine kritische Einführung zur Einführung. In Unternehmensbewertung, Rechnungslegung und Prüfung. Edited by Gunther Meeh. Sonderdruck. Hamburg: Verlag Dr. Kovac.

―――. 2004. Bild und Realität: Controllingtheorie als kritische Bildtheorie. Ein Ansatz zu einer umfassenden Controllingtheorie, die nicht umklammert. In Controlling. Theorien und Konzeptionen. Edited by Ewald Scherm and Gotthard Pietsch. München: Verlag Franz Vahlen.

―――. 2003. Theorie aus der Praxis für die Praxis - Zur Wirksamkeit strategischer Unternehmensführung. In Perspektiven der Strategischen Unternehmensführung. Theorien - Konzepte - Anwendungen. Edited by Max J. Ringlstetter, Herbert A. Henzler and Michael Mirow. Wiesbaden: Gabler Verlag.

―――. 2002. "Controlling und Ästhetik." Zeitschrift für Controlling und Management. 46 Jg., H. 6: 377.

―――. 2000. Entgrenzung. Leitfragen als zentrales Element strategischen Controllings. In Jahrbuch für Controlling und Rechnungswesen. Edited by Gerhard Seicht. Sonderdruck. LexisNexis Verlag ARD Orac.

―――. 1998. Fit für Feränderung. In FIT durch Veränderung. Edited Clemens Heidack. Festschrift für Dr. Eberhard Merz. München und Mering: Rainer Hampp Verlag.

Kappler, Ekkehard, and Thomas Knoblauch. 1997. *Innovationen-wie kommt das Neue in die Unternehmung?* Gütersloh: Verlag Bertelsmann-Stiftung.

Katzenbach, Jon R., and Douglas K. Smith. 1994. *The Wisdom of Teams: Creating the High-Performance Organization.* San Francisco: HarperBusiness.

Kaeufer Katrin, Claus Otto Scharmer, and Ursula Versteegen. 2003. "Breathing Life into a Dying System." *Reflections* 5, no. 3: 3–12.

Kaufmann, Walter, ed. 1954. *The Portable Nietzsche.* Translated by Walter Kaufmann. New York: Penguin.

Kegan, Robert. 1994. *In Over Our Heads: The Mental Demands of Modern Life.* Cambridge, MA and London: Harvard University Press.

―――. 1982. *The Evolving Self: Problem and Process in Human Development.* Cambridge, MA, and London: Harvard University Press.

―――, and Lisa Laskow Lahey. 2000. *How the Way We Talk Can Change the Way We Work.* San Francisco: Jossey-Bass.

Keller, Pierre. 1999. *Husserl and Heidegger on Human Experience.* Cambridge, U.K.: Cambridge University Press.

Kelley, Tom. 2001. *The Art of Innovation: Lessons in Creativity from IDEO, America's Leading Design Firm*. New York: Doubleday.

Kelly, Marjorie. 2001. *The Divine Right of Capital: Dethroning the Corporate Aristocracy*. San Francisco: Berrett-Koehler.

Kitaro, Nishida. 1987. *Last Writings: Nothingness and the Religious Worldview*. Honolulu: University of Hawaii Press.

Kolb, David. 1984. *Experiential Learning: Experience as the Source of Learning and Development*. Upper Saddle River, NJ: Financial Times/Prentice Hall.

Kotter, John P. 1996. *Leading Change*. Boston: Harvard Business School Press.

———, and Dan S. Cohen. 2002. *The Heart of Change: Real-Life Stories of How People Change Their Organizations*. Boston: Harvard Business School Press.

Krishnamurti, J., and David Bohm. 1985. *The Ending of Time*. San Francisco: HarperSanFrancisco.

Krogh, Georg von. 2000. *Enabling Knowledge Creation: How to Unlock the Mystery of Tacit Knowledge and Release the Power of Innovation*. Oxford: Oxford University Press.

———. 1998. "Care in Knowledge Creation." *California Management Review* 40, no. 3: 133–153.

———, and Johan Roos. 1995. *Oranizational Epistemology*. New York: St. Martin's Press.

———, Ikujiro Nonaka, and Toshihiro Nishiguchi. 2000. *Knowledge Creation: A Source of Value*. London: Macmillan.

Lauenstein, Diether. 1974. *Das Ich und die Gesellschaft: Philosophie Soziologie*. Stuttgart: Verlag Freies Geistesleben.

Lave, Jean, et al. 1991. *Situated Learning: Legitimate Peripheral Participation (Learning in Doing: Social, Cognitive & Computational Perspectives)*. Cambridge, U.K.: Cambridge University Press.

Lefort, Rosine, in collaboration with Robert Lefort. 1980. *Birth of the Other*. Translated by Marc Du Ry, Lindsay Watson, and Leonardo Rodríguez. Urbana and Chicago: University of Illinois Press.

Leonard, Dorothy. 1997. "Spark Innovation Through Empathic Design." *Harvard Business Review* 75, no. 6: 102–113.

Lewin, Kurt. 1997. *Resolving Social Conflicts & Field Theory in Social Science*. Washington, DC: American Psychological Association.

Lievegoed, Bernard C. J. 1991. *Developing Communities*. Stroud, UK: Hawthorn Press.

Lindenberg, Marc, and Coralie Bryant. 2001. *Going Global: Transforming Relief and Development NGOs*. Bloomfield, CT: Kumarian Press.

Lippitt, Lawrence L. 1998. *Preferred Futuring*. San Francisco: Berrett-Koehler.

Richard M. Locke. 2003. "The Promise and Perils of Globalization: The Case of Nike," in Management: Inventing and Delivering It's Future. Richard Schmalensee and Thomas A. Kochan, eds. Cambridge, MA, and London: MIT Press: 39-70.

Lowndes, Florin. 1997. *Die Belebung des Herzchakra: Ein Leitfaden zu den Nebenübungen Rudolf Steiners*. Stuttgart: Verlag Freies Geistesleben.

Luhmann, Niklas. 1995. *Social Systems*. Stanford, CA: Stanford University Press.

Lyotard, Jean-François. 1984. *The Postmodern Condition: A Report on Knowledge*. Translated by Geoff Bennington and Brian Massumi. Minneapolis: University of Minnesota Press.

Maanen, John Van, ed. 1998. *Qualitative Studies of Organizations*. Thousand Oaks, CA: Sage.

———. 1995. *Representation in Ethnography*. Thousand Oaks, CA: Sage.

———. 1988. *Tales of the Field: On Writing Ethnography*. Chicago and London: University of Chicago Press.

Maslow, Abraham H. 1998. *Toward a Psychology of Being*. 3rd ed. New York: John Wiley.

Maturana, Humberto R. 1999 "The Organization of the Living: A Theory of the Living Organization." *International Journal of Human-Computer Studies* 51: 149–168 August 1999.

———, and Francisco J. Varela. 1987. *The Tree of Knowledge: The Biological Roots of Human Understanding*. Boston and London: Shambhala.

McDonough, William, and Michael Braungart. 2002. *Cradle to Cradle: Remaking the Way We Make Things*. New York: North Point.

McTaggart, Lynne. 2003. *The Field: The Quest for the Secret Force of the Universe*. New York: Quill.

Mead, George Herbert. 1934. *Mind, Self, & Society from the Standpoint of a Social Behaviorist*. Edited by Charles W. Morris. Chicago and London: University of Chicago Press.

Merleau-Ponty, M. 1962. *Phenomenology of Perception*. Translated by Colin Smith. London and New York: Routledge.

Minsky, Marvin. 1988. *The Society of Mind*. New York: Simon & Schuster.

Mintzberg, Henry. 1983. *Structures in Five: Designing Effective Organizations*.

Englewood Cliffs, NJ: Prentice Hall.

Moran, Dermot, and Timothy Mooney, eds. 2002. *The Phenomenology Reader*. London: Routledge.

Morgan, Gareth. 1996. *Images of Organization*. 2nd ed. Thousand Oaks, CA: Sage.

Nagasawa, Kunihiko. 1987. *Das Ich im deutschen Idealismus und das Selbst im Zen-Buddhismus*. Munich: Alber.

Nan Huai-Chin, Master. 2004. *Diamond Sutra Explained*. Translated by Hue En (Pia Giammasi). Florham Park, NJ: Primordia.

———. 1984. *Tao & Longevity: Mind-Body Transformation*. Translated by Wen Kuan Chu. York Beach, ME: Samuel Weiser.

Naydler, Jeremy, ed. 1996. *Goethe on Science: A Selection of Goethe's Writings*. Edinburgh: Floris Books.

Nelson, Jane. 2002. *Building Partnerships: Cooperation Between the United Nations System and the Private Sector*. New York: United Nations Department of Public Information.

Neuhaus, Richard John. 1997. *The End of Democracy? The Celebrated First Things Debate with Arguments Pro and Con and "The Anatomy of a Controversy."* Dallas: Spence.

Nietzsche, Friedrich. 1999. *Thus Spoke Zarathustra*. Mineloa, New York: Dover Publications.

———. 1964. *Der Wille zur Macht*. Stuttgart: Alfred Kroner Verlag.

Nishida, Kitaro. 1990. *An Inquiry into the Good*. New Haven: Yale University Press.

Nohria, Nitin, and Sumantra Ghoshal. 1997. *The Differentiated Network: Organizing Multinational Corporations for Value Creation*. San Francisco: Jossey-Bass.

Nonaka, Ikujiro. 1994. "A Dynamic Theory of Organizational Knowledge Creation." *Organization Science* 5, no. 1: 14–37.

———. 1991. "The Knowledge Creating Company." *Harvard Business Review* 69, no. 6: 96–105.

———, and Noboru Konno. 1998. "The Concept of Ba: Building a Foundation for Knowledge Creation." *California Management Review* 50, no. 3: 40–54.

———, and Hirotaka Takeuchi. 1995. *The Knowledge-Creating Company: How Japanese Companies Create the Dynamics of Innovation*. Oxford: Oxford University Press.

———, and David Teece, eds. 2001. *Managing Industrial Knowledge: Creation, Transfer, and Utilization*. London: Sage.

————, Ryoko Toyama, and Noboru Konno. 2000. "SECI, Ba and Leadership: A Unified Model of Dynamic Knowledge Creation." *Long Range Planning* 33, no. 1.

————, Ryoko Toyama, and Claus Otto Scharmer. 2001. "Building Ba to Enhance Knowledge Creation and Innovation at Large Firms." *Dialog on Leadership.* www.dialogonleadership.org/Nonaka_et_al.html.

Normann, Richard. 2001. *Reframing Business: When the Map Changes the Landscape.* West Sussex, UK: John Wiley.

————, and Rafael Ramirez. 1998. *Designing Interactive Strategy: From Value Chain to Value Constellation.* Hoboken, NJ: John Wiley.

Northouse, Peter G. 2000. *Leadership: Theory and Practice.* 2nd ed. Thousand Oaks, CA: Sage.

Olkowski, Dorothea, and James Morley, eds. 1999. *Merleau-Ponty, Interiority and Exteriority, Psychic Life and the World.* Albany: State University of New York Press.

Olson, Mancur. 1965. *The Logic of Collective Action: Public Goods and the Theory of Groups.* Cambridge, MA.: Harvard University Press.

Orlikowski, Wanda J., JoAnne Yates, and Kazuo Okamura. 2000. "Using Technology and Constituting Structures: A Practice Lens for Studying Technology in Organizations." *Organization Science,* 11, 4: 404-428.

Orlikowski, Wanda J. . 1992. "The Duality of Technology: Rethinking the Concept of Technology in Organizations," *Organization Science,* 3, 3: 398-427.

Owen, Harrison. 1997. *Open Space Technology: A User's Guide.* San Francisco: Berrett-Koehler.

Oxfam International. 2002. *Rigged Rules and Double Standards: Trade, Globalization, and the Fight Against Poverty.* Oxford: Oxfam International.

Parkes, Graham, ed. 1990. *Heidegger and Asian Thought.* Honolulu: University of Hawaii Press.

Pearce, Joseph Chilton. 2002. *The Biology of Transcendence: A Blueprint of the Human Spirit.* Rochester, VT: Park Street Press.

Perkins, John. 2004. *Confessions of an Economic Hit Man.* San Francisco, CA: Berrett Koehler.

Perlas, Nicanor. 2003. *Shaping Globalizations: Civil Society, Cultural Power and Threefolding.* Gabriola, Canada: New Society.

Perls, Frederick S., Ralph F. Hefferline, and Paul Goodman. 2000. *Gestalttherapie: Praxis.* Translated by Wolfgang Krege and Monika Ross. 5th ed. Munich: Klett-

Cotta Deutscher Taschenbuch Verlag.

Peters, Thomas J., and Robert H. Waterman. 1982. *In Search of Excellence: Lessons from America's Best-Run Companies*. New York: HarperCollins.

Peterson, Peter G. 2004. *Running on Empty*. New York: Farrar, Straus and Giroux.

Pinchbeck, Daniel. 2006. *2012 The Return of Quetzalcoatl*. New York: Jeremy P Tarcher/Penguin.

Pine, B. Joseph, and James Gilmore. 1998. *Welcome to the Experience Economy*. Boston: Harvard Business School Press.

Pokorny, Julius. 1994. *Indogermanisches Etymologisches Wörterbuch*. 3rd ed. Tübingen and Basel: Francke Verlag.

Polanyi, Karl, 1966. *The Tacit Dimension*. New York: Doubleday.

———, 2001. *The Great Transformation*. 2nd ed. Boston: Beacon Press.

Porter, Michael E. 1998. *Competitive Strategy: Techniques for Analyzing Industries and Competitors*. Tampa: Free Press.

Portes, Alejandro. 1998. "Social Capital: Its Origins and Applications in Modern Sociology." *Annual Review of Sociology* 24:1–24.

Prahalad, Coimbatore Krishnarao. 2005. *The Fortune at the Bottom of the Pyramid: Eradicating Poverty Through Profits*. Upper Saddle River, NJ: Wharton School Publishing.

———, and Gary Hamel. 1990. "The Core Competence of the Organization." *Harvard Business Review,* May-June, 1990: 79–91.

———, and Venkatram Ramaswamy. 2000. *Co-opting Customer Competence*. Boston: Harvard Business School Press.

Pressfield, Steven. 1995. *The Legend of Bagger Vance*. New York: William Morrow and Company.

———. 2002. *The War of Art: Break Through the Blocks and Win Your Inner Creative Battles*. New York: Warner Books.

Putnam, Robert. 2000. *Bowling Alone: The Collapse & Revival of the American Community*. New York: Simon & Schuster.

———. 1995. "Bowling Alone: America's Declining Social Capital." *Journal of Democracy* 6: 65–78.

Radin, Dean. 1997. *The Conscious Universe: The Scientific Truth of Psychic Phenomena*. San Francisco: HarperEdge.

Ray, Michael. 2004. *The Highest Goal: The Secret That Sustains You in Every Moment*. San Francisco: Berrett-Koehler.

————, and Rochelle Myers. 1986. *Creativity in Business.* New York: Doubleday.

Ray, Paul H., and Sherry Ruth Anderson. 2000. *The Cultural Creatives: How 50 Million People Are Changing the World.* New York: Three Rivers Press.

Reason, Peter, and Hilary Bradbury. 2006 "Preface." In *Handbook of Action Research: Participative Inquiry and Practice,* eds. Peter Reason and Hilary Bradbury, xxiii–xxxi. London: Sage.

————, eds. 2001. *Handbook of Action Research: Participative Inquiry and Practice.* London: Sage.

Ritzer, George. 1996. *Modern Sociological Theory.* 4th ed. New York: McGraw Hill.

Risenberg, Marshall B. 2000. *Nonviolent Communication: A Language of Compassion.* Encinatas, CA: PuddleDancer Press.

Roussel, Philip A., Kamal N. Saad, and Tamara J. Erickson. 1991. *Third Generation R&D: Managing the Link to Corporate Strategy.* Boston: Harvard Business School Press.

Saxenian, Annalee. 1994. *Regional Advantage: Culture and Competition in Silicon Valley and Route 128.* Cambridge, MA, and London: Harvard University Press.

Scharmer, Claus Otto. 2001. "Self-Transcending Knowledge: Sensing and Organizing Around Emerging Opportunities." *Journal of Knowledge Management,* 5, no. 2:137–150.

————. 2000a. "Organizing Around Not-Yet-Embodied Knowledge." In *Knowledge Creation: A New Source of Value.* Edited by G. V. Krogh, I. Nonaka, and T. Nishiguchi. New York: Macmillan.

————. 2000b. "Self-Transcending Knowledge: Organizing Around Emerging Realities." *Organizational Science* 33, no. 3: 14–29.

————. 2000c. "Presencing: Learning from the Future as It Emerges." Paper presented at the Conference on Knowledge and Innovation, Helsinki, Finland, May 25–26, 2000. www.ottoscharmer.com.

————. 1996. *Reflexive Modernisierung des Kapitalismus als Revolution von Innen.* Stuttgart: M and P.

————. 1995. "Strategische Führung im Kräftedreieck Wachstum-Beschäftigung-Ökologie." *Zeitschrift für Betriebswirtschaft* 65, Number 6, S. 633–661.

————. 1991. *Ästhetik als Kategorie strategischer Führung.* Stuttgart: Urachhaus.

Scharmer, Claus Otto, K. Kaeufer, U. Versteegen. 2004. "Breathing Life into a Dying System: Recreating Healthcare from Within." In: *Reflections. The SoL Journal on Knowledge, Learning, and Change,* Volume 5, Number 3, 1-12.

————, Brian W. Arthur, Jonathan Day, Joseph Jaworski, Michael Jung, Ikujiro Nonaka, and Peter M. Senge. 2002. "Illuminating the Blind Spot: Leadership in the Context of Emerging Worlds." *Dialog on Leadership*. www.dialogonleadership.org.

———, Versteegen, Ursula, K. Käufer. 2001. "The Pentagon of Praxis." In: *Reflections: The SoL Journal on Knowledge, Learning, and Change*, Volume 2, Number 3: 36–45.

———, and Joseph Jaworski. 2000. *Leadership in the Digital Economy: Sensing and Actualizing Emerging Futures*. Cambridge, MA: Society for Organizational Learning.

———, and Peter Senge. 1996. "Infrastrukturen für lernende Organisationen." *Zeitschrift für Führung und Organisation* 1: 32–36.

Schein, Edgar. 2002. "Clinical Inquiry/Research." In *Handbook of Action Research: Participative Inquiry and Practice*, eds. Peter Reason and Hilary Bradbury, 228-237. London: Sage.

———. 1999. *The Corporate Culture Survival Guide*. San Francisco: Jossey-Bass.

———. 1998. *Process Consultation Revisited: Building the Helping Relationship*. Reading, MA: Addison-Wesley.

———. 1996. *Strategic Pragmatism: The Culture of Singapore's Economic Development Board*. Cambridge, MA, and London: MIT Press.

———. 1995. "Kurt Lewin's Change Theory in the Field and in the Classroom: Notes Toward a Model of Managed Learning." *Reflections*. www.solonline.org/res/wp/10006.html.

———. 1989. *Organizational Culture and Leadership*. San Francisco: Jossey-Bass.

———. 1988. *The Presence of the Past*. New York: Times Books.

———. 1987a. *Process Consultation* 2nd ed. Vol. I: *Its Role in Organization Development*. 2nd ed. Reading, MA: Addison-Wesley.

———. 1987b. *Process Consultation*. 2nd Edition. Volume 2: *Lessons for Managers and Consultants*. Englewood Cliffs, NJ: Prentice Hall.

———. 1987c. "The Clinical Perspective in Field Work." Newbury Park, CA: Sage Publications.

———, Peter Delisi, Paul J. Kampas, and Michael Sonduck. 2003. *DEC Is Dead, Long Live DEC: The Lasting Legacy of Digital Equipment Corporation*. San Francisco: Berrett-Koehler.

Schiller, Friedrich. 1967. *On the Aesthetic Education of Man: In a Series of Letters*. Edited and translated by Elizabeth M. Wilkinson and L. A. Willoughby. Oxford: Oxford University Press.

Schily, Konrad. 1993. *Der staatlich bewirtschaftete Geist*. Düsseldorf: Econ Verlag.

Schmundt, Wilhelm. 1982. *Erkenntnisübungen zur Dreigliederung des Sozialen Organismus: Durch Revolution der Begriffe zur Evolution der Gesellschaft.* Achberg, Germany: Achberger Verlag.

Schön, Donald. 1986. *Educating the Reflective Practitioner.* San Francisco: Jossey-Bass.

Schurmann, Reiner. 1986. *Heidegger on Being and Acting: From Principles to Anarchy.* Bloomington: Indiana University Press.

Schutz, Alfred. 1967. *The Phenomenology of the Social World.* Translated by George Walsh and Frederick Lehnert. Evanston, IL: Northwestern University Press.

Seamon, David, and Arthur Zajonc, eds. 1998. *Goethe's Way of Science: A Phenomenology of Nature.* Albany: State University of New York Press.

Sen, Amartya. 1999. *Development as Freedom.* New York: Anchor Books.

Senge, Peter. 1990. *The Fifth Discipline: The Art and Practice of the Learning Organization.* New York: Doubleday.

———, Claus Otto Scharmer, Joseph Jaworski, and Betty Sue Flowers. 2004. *Presence: Human Purpose, and the Field of the Future.* Cambridge, MA: Society for Organizational Learning.

———, et al. 1999. *The Dance of Change: The Challenges to Sustaining Momentum in Learning Organizations.* New York: Doubleday.

———. 1994. *The Fifth Discipline Fieldbook: Strategies and Tools for Building a Learning Organization.* New York: Doubleday.

Sheldrake, Rupert. 1995. *Seven Experiments That Could Change the World: A Do-It-Yourself Guide to Revolutionary Science.* New York: Riverhead Books.

Shellenberger, Michael and Nordhaus, Ted, 2004. *The Death of Environmentalism: Global Warming Politics in a Post-Environmental World.* www.thebreakthrough.org and www.evansmcdonoughcom.

Shiva, Vandana. 2000. *Stolen Harvest: The Hijacking of the Global Food Supply.* Boston: South End Press.

———. 1997. *Biopiracy: The Plunder of Nature and Knowledge.* Boston: South End Press.

———. 1993. *Monocultures of the Mind: Perspectives on Biodiversity and Biotechnology.* London and New York: Zed Books.

Sorokin, Pitirim. 1957. *Social and Cultural Dynamics: A Study of Change in Major Systems of Art, Truth, Ethics, Law and Social Relationships.* Boston: Porter Sargent.

Soros, George. 2002. *On Globalization.* New York: Public Affairs.

Spinosa, Charles, Fernando Flores, and Hubert L. Dreyfus. 1997. *Disclosing New*

Worlds: Entrepreneurship, Democratic Action, and the Cultivation of Solidarity.
Cambridge, MA: MIT Press.

Steiner, Rudolf. 1994. *How to Know Higher Worlds: A Modern Path of Initiation (Classic in Anthroposophy).* Translated by Christopher Bamford. Great Barrington, MA: Steiner.

————. 1894, 1964. *The Philosophy of Freedom.* London: The Rudolf Steiner Press.

Stiglitz, Joseph E. 2002. *Globalization and Its Discontents.* New York: W. W. Norton.

Stoltzfus, Nathan. 2001. *Resistance of the Heart: Intermarriage and the Rosenstrasse Protest in Nazi Germany.* Piscataway, NJ: Rutgers University Press.

Strebel, Paul. 1996. *Why Do Employees Resist Change?* Boston: Harvard Business School Press.

Taylor, Charles. 1989. *Sources of the Self: The Making of the Modern Identity.* Cambridge, MA: Harvard University Press.

Tichy, Noel M., and Stratford Sherman. 1994. *Control Your Destiny or Someone Else Will: Lessons in Mastering Change—the Principles that Jack Welch Is Using to Revolutionize General Electric.* New York: HarperBusiness.

Tignor, Warren W. 2005. "Dynamic Unity—Theory U and System Dynamics." In *Proceedings of the 23rd International Conference of the System Dynamics Society,* Boston, July 17–21, 2005, ed. John D. Sterman, Nelson P. Repenning, Robin S. Langer, Jennifer I. Rowe, and Joan M. Yanni. 141.

Thomas, Robert J. 1994. *What Machines Can't Do: Politics and Technology in the Industrial Enterprise.* Berkeley: University of California Press.

Tolle, Eckhart. 2003. *Stillness Speaks.* Novato, CA: New World and Vancouver: Namaste.

————. 1999. *The Power of Now.* Novato, CA: New World Library.

Torbert, Bill, et al. 2004. *Action Inquiry: The Secret of Timely and Transforming Leadership.* San Francisco: Berrett-Koehler.

Torbert, William R. 2001. "The Practice of Action Inquiry." In *Handbook of Action Research: Participative Inquiry and Practice,* eds. Peter Reason and Hilary Bradbury, 250–260. London: Sage.

————. 1991. *The Power of Balance: Transforming Self, Society, and Scientific Inquiry.* Newbury Park, CA: Sage.

Thurow, Lester. 2003. *Fortune Favors the Bold: What We Must Do to Build a New and Lasting Global Prosperity.* New York: HarperCollins.

————. *The Future of Capitalism: How Today's Economic Forces Shape Tomorrow's World.* New York: Penguin.

———. 1999. *Building Wealth: The New Rules for Individuals, Companies, and Nations in a Knowledge-Based Economy.* San Francisco: HarperBusiness.

Trompenaars, Fons. 1994. *Riding the Waves of Culture: Understanding Diversity in Global Business.* Chicago: Irwin.

Tzu, Sun. 1988. *The Art of War.* Translated by Thomas Cleary. Boston and London: Shambhala.

Ury, William. 1999. *Getting to Peace: Transforming Conflict at Home, at Work, and in the World.* New York: Viking.

Varela, Francisco J. 1999. *Ethical Know-How: Action, Wisdom, and Cognition.* Edited by Timothy Lenoir and Hans Ulrich Gumbrecht. Stanford, CA: Stanford University Press.

———, and Jonathan Shear, eds. 1999. *The View from Within: First-Person Approaches to the Study of Consciousness.* Thorverton, U.K.: Imprint Academic.

———, Evan Thompson, and Eleanor Rosch. 1991. *The Embodied Mind: Cognitive Science and Human Experience.* Cambridge, MA: MIT Press.

Vattimo, Gianni. 1992. *The Transparent Society.* Translated by David Webb. Baltimore, MD: Johns Hopkins University Press.

Velmans, Max, ed. 2000. *Investigation Phenomenal Consciousness.* Amsterdam and Philadelphia: John Benjamins.

Wallace, B. Alan. 2003. *Buddhism & Science: Breaking New Ground.* New York: Columbia University Press.

———. 2000. *The Taboo of Subjectivity: Toward a New Science of Consciousness.* Oxford and New York: Oxford University Press.

Watts, Duncan J. 2003. *Six Degrees: The Science of a Connected Age.* New York and London: W. W. Norton.

Watzlawick, Paul. 1983. *The Situation Is Hopeless but Not Serious: The Pursuit of Unhappiness.* New York and London: W. W. Norton.

Weber, Max. 1988. *Gesammelte Aufsätze zur Religionssoziologie I* (Selected Essays on the Sociology of Religion). Tübingen: J. C. G. Mohr.

Weick, Karl. 1996. "Drop Your Tools: An Allegory for Organizational Studies." *Administrative Science Quarterly* 41, no. 2: 301–313.

———. 1995. *Sensemaking in Organizations.* Thousand Oaks, CA: Sage.

———, and Kathleen M. Sutcliffe. 2001. *Managing the Unexpected: Assuring High Performance in an Age of Complexity.* San Francisco: Jossey-Bass.

Weisbord, Marvin R., and Sandra Janoff. 1995. *Future Search: An Action Guide to Finding Common Ground in Organizations and Communities*. San Francisco: Berrett-Koehler.

Weisbord, Marvin R., et al. 1995. *Discovering Common Ground: How Future Search Conferences Bring People Together to Achieve Breakthrough Innovation, Empowerment, Shared Vision, and Collaborative Action*. San Francisco: Berrett-Koehler.

Weizsacker, Ernst U. von 1994. *Earth Politics*. London: Zed Books.

Welton, Donn, ed. 1999. *The Essential Husserl: Basic Writings in Transcendental Phenomenology*. Bloomington: Indiana University Press.

Wenger, Etienne. 1998. *Communities of Practice: Learning, Meaning, and Identity*. Cambridge: Cambridge University Press.

———, Richard McDermott, and William Snyder. 2002. *Cultivating Communities of Practice*. Boston: Harvard Business School Press.

Wheatley, Margaret J. 2002. *Turning to One Another: Simple Conversations to Restore Hope to the Future*. San Francisco: Berrett-Koehler.

———. 1992. *Leadership and the New Science: Learning About Organization from an Orderly Universe*. San Francisco: Berrett-Koehler.

———, and Myron Kellner-Rogers. 1996. *A Simpler Way*. San Francisco: Berrett-Koehler.

Wheelan, Susan A., Emmy A. Pepitone, and Vicki Abt, eds. 1990. *Advances in Field Theory*. Newbury Park, CA: Sage.

Wilber, Ken. 2000a. *A Brief History of Everything*. Boston: Shambhala.

———. 2000b. *Grace and Grit: Spirituality and Healing in the Life and Death of Treya Killam Wilber*. 2nd ed. Boston: Shambhala.

———. 2000c. *Integral Psychology: Consciousness, Spirit, Psychology, Therapy*. Boston and London: Shambhala.

———. 2000d. *Sex, Ecology, Spirituality: The Spirit of Evolution*. Boston and London: Shambhala, 2000.

———. 2000e. *A Theory of Everything: An Integral Vision for Business, Politics, Science, and Spirituality*. Boston: Shambhala.

———. 1999. *The Marriage of Sense and Soul: Integrating Science and Religion*. New York: Broadway Books.

———. 1998. *The Essential Ken Wilber: An Introductory Reader*. Boston and London: Shambhala.

————. 1997. *The Eye of Spirit: An Integral Vision for a World Gone Slightly Mad.* Boston and London: Shambhala.

————, and Andrew Cohen. 2002. *Living Enlightenment: A Call for Evolution Beyond Ego.* Lenox, MA: What Is Enlightenment?

Womak, James P., and Daniel T. Jones. 1996. *Lean Thinking: Banish Waste and Create Wealth in Your Corporation.* New York: Simon & Schuster.

Womak, James P., Daniel T. Jones, and Daniel Roos. 1991. *The Machine That Changed the World: The Story of Lean Production.* New York: Perennial.

Wuthnow, Robert. 2000. *After Heaven: Spirituality in America since the 1950s.* Berkeley: University of California Press.

Yamaguchi, Ichiro. 1997. *Ki als leibhaftige Vernunft: Beitrag zur interkulturellen Phänomenologie der Leiblichkeit.* Munich: Wilhelm Fink Verlag.

Zajonc, Arthur. 1994. *Die gemeinsame Geschichte von Licht und Bewußtsein.* Translated into German by Hainer Kober. Reinbeck bei Hamburg: Rowohlt Verlag.

————. 1993. *Catching the Light.* New York: Bantam.

————, ed. 2004. *The New Physics and Cosmology: Dialogues with the Dalai Lama.* Oxford: Oxford University Press.

Zohar, Danah, and Ian Marshall. 2004. *Spiritual Capital: Wealth We Can Live By.* San Francisco: Berrett-Koehler.

Index

aborting, 248
  and T. Junge, 268
absencing, 247–48, 250
  choice to operate from social
    space of, 258
  collective, 346
  corporate, 314
  and hubris, 284–85
  and presencing, 45, 248
  shadow space of, 268
  system disabled by, 286
  and T. Junge, 267
accounting system, in Enron,
    317–18
action phase, moving to, 192
action research, 19, 55
"action turn," 16
actions
  origin of, 21, 22
  vs. perception, 29
  Rosch definition of, 478n5
  sources of, 111

and words, 437
adaptive systems, 357–59
adhocracy, 308
Adobe Systems, 32
"aesthetic," 480n11
aesthetics, 100, 463
after-action review, 294
agency, structure and, 97
"aggressive accounting," vs. fraud,
    317–18
Alexander, Christopher, 132
"all-quadrants, all-levels" (AQAL)
    approach, 102, 373
Alps, waterfalls, 165–66
altered state, 13
Alternative Nobel Prize, 198
Amber, Simone, 207, 208
analysis paralysis, 422
analytical knowledge, 167
Anderson, Harlan, 307
annihilating, and T. Junge, 268
anomie, 4, 346, 463

corporate, 314
  institutional, 319
anti-emergence, 259, 266
  vs. emergence, 269
  social space of, 247
  fundamentalism, 248–50
anti-space, dynamics between U-
    space and, 294
antinuclear protest, at Brokdorf,
    Germany, 93–94, 250–51
Apple Computer, 32–33
applied technologies (techne), 16,
    28
Archemedian point, 9–10, 463
Argyris, Chris, 30, 51, 97, 98, 104,
    275, 465
Aristotle, 30, 108, 464
  framework for causation, 368–69
  material cause, 370
  Nicomachean Ethics, 16
Armstrong, Lance, 483n18
arrogance, institutional, 317–18

About the Author

Dr. C. Otto Scharmer is a Senior Lecturer at the Massachusetts Institute of Technology and the founding chair of ELIAS (Emerging Leaders for Innovation Across Sectors), a platform that links twenty leading global institutions across the three sectors of business, government, and civil society, in order to prototype profound system innovations for a more sustainable world. He also is a visiting professor at the Center for Innovation and Knowledge Research, Helsinki School of Economics, and the founding chair of the Presencing Institute, a living lab for creating social technologies that facilitate profound innovation and systems change. Scharmer has consulted with global companies, international institutions, and cross-sector change initiatives in North America, Europe, Asia, and Africa. He has co-designed and delivered award-winning leadership programs for client organizations including DaimlerChrysler, PricewaterhouseCoopers, and Fujitsu.

He introduced the theoretical framework and practice called "presencing" in *Theory U*, in articles and in his earlier book *Presence: An Exploration of Profound Change in People, Organizations and Society* (2005), co-authored with Peter Senge, Joseph Jaworski, and Betty Sue Flowers. For more information about Scharmer and his work see www.ottoscharmer.com; and about the Presencing Institute: www.presencing.com.

About the Organizations

The Presencing Institute

The Presencing Institute focuses on developing and advancing the social technology of presencing, a set of practices and tools for collectively leading profound innovation and change. The Presencing Institute is located in Cambridge, Massachusetts. The Presencing Institute is laying the foundation for co-creating a "global action research university" that integrates science, consciousness, and profound social change. More information can be found at www.presencing.org.

The Society for Organizational Learning

SoL, The Society for Organizational Learning, is a nonprofit global membership organization that connects researchers, organizations, and consultants to create and implement knowledge for fundamental innovation and change. Founded in 1997 as an outgrowth of the MIT Center for Organizational Learning Center, the organization's members engage in a variety of forums and learning opportunities that expand their capacity for inspired performance and creating results together that could not be created alone. More information about SoL projects, resources, membership, and other publications can be found at www.solonline.org.